Bridge to Algebra

Student Text

Carnegie Learning®

THE COGNITIVE TUTOR® COMPANY

Carnegie Learning®
THE COGNITIVE TUTOR® COMPANY

Pittsburgh, PA
Phone 888.851.7094
Fax 412.690.2444

www.carnegielearning.com

Acknowledgments

We would like to thank those listed below who helped
to prepare the Cognitive Tutor® *Bridge to Algebra* Student Text:

William S. Hadley, Author
Mary Lynn Raith, Author
Kent Publishing, Inc.
Signature Design
Michele Covatto
The Carnegie Learning Development Team

ISBN-13 978-1-934800-00-3
Student Text

Printed in the United States of America
1-2005-VH
2-2006-VH
3-2006-VH
4-2007-VH
5-2007-VH
1-2008/12 HP
2-2009/4 HP

Dear Student,

You are about to begin an exciting adventure using mathematics, the language of science and technology. As you sit in front of a computer screen or video game, ride in an automobile, fly in a plane, talk on a cellular phone, or use any of the tools of modern society, realize that mathematics was critical in its invention, design, and production.

The workplace today demands that employees be technologically literate, work well in teams, and be self-starters. At Carnegie Learning, we have designed a mathematics course that uses state-of-the-art computer software with collaborative classroom activities.

As you use the Cognitive Tutor® *Bridge to Algebra* software, it actually learns about you as you learn about mathematics. As you work, you will receive "just-in-time" instruction so that you are always ready for the next problem. In the classroom, you will work with your peers to solve real-world problems. Working in groups, you will learn to use multiple representations to analyze questions and write or present your answers.

Throughout the entire process, your teacher will be a facilitator and guide in support of your learning. As a result, you will become a self-sufficient learner, moving through the software and Student Text at your own rate and discovering solutions to problems that you never thought were possible to solve.

Throughout this year, have fun while Learning by Doing!

The Cognitive Tutor® *Bridge to Algebra* Development Team

Contents

Contents

Contents

Contents

Contents

Contents

Looking Ahead to Chapter 1

Focus In Chapter 1, you will work with whole numbers and their operations. You will discover ways to find common multiples and common factors and determine whether a number is prime or composite. You will also learn how to tell whether your solution to a problem is reasonable.

Chapter Warm-up

Answer these questions to help you review skills that you will need in Chapter 1.

Find the sum or difference.

1. $27 + 94$

2. $57 - 38$

3. $83 - 68$

Find the product or quotient.

4. 8×14

5. 21×17

6. $108 \div 45$

Multiply.

7. $5 \times 5 \times 5$

8. $9 \times 9 \times 9 \times 9$

9. $3 \times 3 \times 3 \times 3 \times 3$

Read the problem scenario below.

You go to the store with $20. A notebook costs $4, a pack of pens costs $3, and a pack of pencils costs $2.

10. What is the total cost of a notebook and a pack of pens?

11. How much money do you have left after you purchase a notebook and a pack of pens?

12. Your friend goes to the same store with $25 and buys 3 notebooks. What is the total cost of 3 notebooks?

13. How much money does your friend have left after he purchases 3 notebooks?

Key Terms

© 2008 Carnegie Learning, Inc.

1

Number Sense and Algebraic Thinking

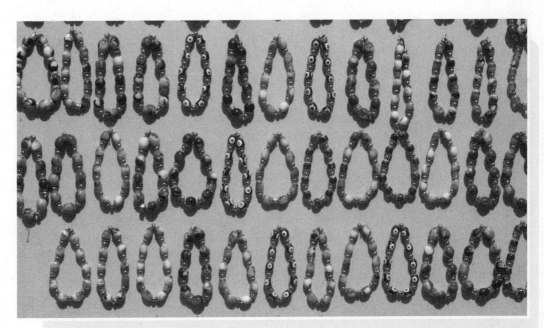

The art of attaching beads to one another to make jewelry is called beadwork. In Lesson 1.7, you will solve problems about making beaded jewelry.

Mathematical Representations

INTRODUCTION Mathematics is a human invention, developed as people encountered problems that they could not solve. For instance, when people first began to accumulate possessions, they needed to answer questions such as: How many? How many more? How many less?

People responded by developing the concepts of numbers and counting. Mathematics made a huge leap when people began using symbols to represent numbers. The first "numerals" were probably tally marks used to count weapons, livestock, or food.

As society grew more complex, people needed to answer questions such as: Who has more? How much does each person get? If there are 5 members in my family, 6 in your family, and 10 in another family, how can each person receive the same amount?

During this course, we will solve problems and work with many different representations of mathematical concepts, ideas, and processes to better understand our world. The following processes can help you solve problems.

Discuss to Understand

- Read the problem carefully.
- What is the context of the problem? Do you understand it?
- What is the question that you are being asked? Does it make sense?

Think for Yourself

- Do I need any additional information to answer the question?
- Is this problem similar to some other problem that I know?
- How can I represent the problem using a picture, a diagram, symbols, or some other representation?

Work with Your Partner

- How did you do the problem?
- Show me your representation.
- This is the way I thought about the problem—how did you think about it?
- What else do we need to solve the problem?
- Does our reasoning and our answer make sense to one another?

Work with Your Group

- Show me your representation.
- This is the way I thought about the problem—how did you think about it?
- What else do we need to solve the problem?
- Does our reasoning and our answer make sense to one another?
- How can we explain our solution to one another? To the class?

Share with the Class

- Here is our solution and how we solved it.
- We could only get this far with our solution. How can we finish?
- Could we have used a different strategy to solve the problem?

Money, Money, Who Gets the Money?
Introduction to Picture Algebra

Objectives

In this lesson, you will:
- Use picture algebra to represent a problem.
- Use the order of operations.

Key Terms

- order of operations

Throughout this course, you will be solving problems much like the problems that you encounter in real life.

Problem 1 — Building a Business Together

You and your friends Jamal and Carla decide to make some money during summer vacation by building and selling dog houses. To get the business started, Jamal contributes $25.55 and Carla contributes $34.45. You all agree that each person will earn the same amount of money after Jamal and Carla get back what they invested. During the summer, your business earns a total of $450. How much money does each person get at the end of the summer?

A. Work together as a class to complete the following tasks.

Read the problem carefully.

What is the context of the problem? Do you understand it?

What is the question that you are being asked?

B. Work by yourself to answer the following questions.

Do I need any additional information to answer the question?

Is this problem similar to some other problem that I know?

How can I represent the problem with a picture, symbols, or another representation?

You will use some of the other processes described on page 4 for Problem 1 later in the lesson. When we are solving a problem, there may be many different strategies that we can use. One useful strategy is to try to solve a simpler problem that is similar to the difficult problem. We can then use the same reasoning to solve the more difficult problem.

For example, instead of solving Problem 1, let's try to solve a simpler problem.

Problem 2 — Two Boards for a Doghouse

To build a doghouse, you and your friends cut a 12-foot board into two boards. One of the boards is 4 feet longer than the other. How long is each board?

Here is an example of when a "representation" or picture can help you to solve a problem. In the space below, draw the two boards, one underneath the other. Place one end of each board against the line. Do not worry about drawing the boards exactly to scale.

Investigate Problem 2

1. Are the boards the same length? If not, which board is longer and by how much?

2. Do you know how long any part of either board is? If so, label that part. Label the unknown parts with a question mark.

3. Can you "see" a way to solve the problem? If so, write complete sentences to explain what you need to do to solve the problem. What are the lengths of the boards?

© 2008 Carnegie Learning, Inc.

Problem 3 *Fido and Jet*

Fido and Jet are two small dogs. Fido weighs exactly 10 pounds more than Jet. Together they weigh exactly 46 pounds. How much does each dog weigh?

A. Use a representation similar to the one you used in Problem 2 to draw and label two "boards" that represent Fido's and Jet's weights.

B. Use the picture that you drew to help you solve the problem. How much does each dog weigh? Write your answer using a complete sentence.

Problem 1 Revisited

You and your friends Jamal and Carla decide to make some money during summer vacation by building and selling dog houses. To get the business started, Jamal contributes $25.55 and Carla contributes $34.45 to buy the equipment and materials. You all agree that each person will earn the same amount of money after Jamal and Carla get back what they invested. Your business earns a total of $450. How much money does each person get at the end of the summer?

A. Form a group with another partner team. Use a representation similar to the one you used in Problem 2 to draw and label three "boards" that represent the amounts of money that you, Jamal, and Carla will get at the end of the summer. Then share your picture with others in your group.

Think about how you will solve the problem and what other information you may need to solve the problem. Then have each person in the group describe how he or she thought about the problem.

Use your representation to solve the problem. Describe how you solved the problem using complete sentences.

Have each group member share his or her solution with the group. Then decide whether each member's reasoning and answer makes sense.

As a group, decide how you can explain your solution to the class. Write your explanation using complete sentences.

B. Prepare a short presentation to share with your class that describes how you solved the problem. If your group could not solve the problem, explain part of your solution, and ask the class for input as to how you can complete the problem.

Could your group have used a different strategy to solve the problem? Use complete sentences to explain why or why not.

1. Math Path: Order of Operations

When you were solving Problem 1, you may have written an **expression** such as (450 − 25.55 − 34.45) ÷ 3. To find the value of such an expression, you need to use a set of rules called the **order of operations** so that you get the same answer as everyone else in your group. In your group, read the order of operations together.

> ### Order of Operations
>
> **1.** Evaluate expressions inside grouping symbols like ( ) or [ ].
>
> **2.** Multiply and divide from left to right.
>
> **3.** Add and subtract from left to right.

2. Use the order of operations to determine whether the values of each pair of expressions are equal. The first problem was completed for you.

(4 + 2) × 5 and (111 − 21) ÷ 3

(4 + 2) × 5   (111 − 21) ÷ 3

  6 × 5   90 ÷ 3

   30   30

The expressions are equal.

17 × (5 + 1) and (13 + 21) × 3

5 + 6 × 12 and 126 ÷ 2 − 1

3. For each expression, decide where to place parentheses so that the answer is correct using the order of operations.

27 ÷ 3 + 6 + 1   6 × 15 − 12 + 3

Answer: 4   Answer: 21

Did You Know?

Variables are used to represent numbers.

1. Your friend has a guppy fish who just had babies. There are 9 baby guppies. Your friend gives several baby guppies to you. You can represent this situation as $9 - \boxed{?}$.

If your friend gives you 5 baby guppies, how many baby guppies are left? Write a complete sentence to explain how you found your answer.

Often, mathematicians use letters as placeholders when a value is not known. The letter is called a *variable*. A **variable** is a symbol used to represent a value. A **variable expression** consists of numbers, variables, and operations.

2. You manage a clothing store. The store has 9 mannequins to display outfits. Each year, you plan to purchase additional mannequins. A variable expression to represent the situation is

$$9 + m$$

where m is the number of mannequins you will purchase. Write the expression that represents the total number of mannequins if you purchase 2 mannequins. How many mannequins will you have?

Write the expression that represents the total number of mannequins if you purchase 4 mannequins. How many mannequins will you have?

3. When writing the product of a number and a variable, you do not need to use a multiplication symbol. So, the expression $5 \times y$ is the same as $5y$.

Find the value of the expression when $a = 16$.

$24 - a$ $\qquad\qquad$ $9 + a$ $\qquad\qquad$ $\dfrac{a}{4}$ $\qquad\qquad$ $3a$

4. When solving a real-life problem, you can write the important information in mathematical terms. For example, "you have 10 fewer CDs than Mary" can be written as $m - 10$, where m represents the number of CDs that Mary has. Write each phrase as a variable expression. Let n represent the number.

20 increased by a number _____

the product of 6 and a number _____

a number subtracted from 31 _____

Collection Connection
Factors and Multiples

1

Objectives

In this lesson, you will:

- List factor pairs of numbers.
- Relate factors, multiples, and divisibility.

Key Terms

- factor
- factor pair
- Commutative Property of Multiplication
- multiple
- divisible

Take Note

When you multiply two numbers to produce another number, each number that you multiply is a **factor** of the resulting number (or product). For instance, 2 is a factor of 12.

As people began to collect possessions, they needed ways to not only count them but to also group them for different reasons. Can you think of some reasons why people may want to group their possessions?

Problem 1 · Factors of 12

Your uncle has a bottle cap collection. He wants to display 12 bottle caps in each box.

A. In each box below, collect the caps into smaller groups so that there are the same number of caps in each group. Draw a circle around each group. Then record the numbers of groups and caps in the table below. Repeat this process for each box, using a different number of groups each time. The first box is already done for you.

B. Complete the third column of the table by multiplying the number of groups by the number of caps in each group.

C. A **factor pair** is two numbers that are multiplied together to produce another number. For instance, one factor pair for the number 12 is 2 × 6. Complete the table by writing the factor pair for each grouping. Record your results in the last column of the table.

Number of Groups	Number of Caps in Each Group	Number of Groups Multiplied by Number of Caps in Each Group	Product Written as Factor Pair
6	2	12	6 × 2

Investigate Problem 1

1. List all of the distinct factor pairs from your table. Is the total number of different groupings the same as the number of distinct factor pairs?

2. **Math Path: Commutative Property of Multiplication**

   In your diagram, 6 groups of 2 items looks different from 2 groups of 6 items. When you multiply the factor pairs for these groupings, though, you get the same number. This means that $6 \times 2 = 2 \times 6$.

   This is an example of a very important property of numbers, the **Commutative Property of Multiplication.** You will learn more about this property in Chapter 14. Use your factor pairs to write two other examples of the Commutative Property of Multiplication.

3. Use the factor pairs listed in your table to list all of the distinct factors of 12.

Problem 2   *Factors of 24*

Complete the table for 24 bottle caps. Use the pictures at the left if needed.

Number of Groups	Number of Caps in Each Group	Number of Groups Multiplied by Number of Caps in Each Group	Product Written as Factor Pair

Investigate Problem 2

1. List all of the distinct factors of 24.

2. In your own words, write definitions for the following terms.

   factor:

   factor pair:

3. In Problems 1 and 2, you found the distinct factors of 12 and 24 by dividing a collection of items into groups of equal size. Work together with your partner to think of another way to find the factors of a number. Then use complete sentences to write the steps for your method below.

4. Exchange the steps of your method with another pair of partners. Have them follow your directions to see if they can find the distinct factors of 30. At the same time, follow their methods to find the distinct factors of 30.

5. Use the method of your choice to find all of the distinct factors of each number listed in the table.

Number	Distinct Factors
7	
25	
31	
36	
44	
48	

Explain how you found the distinct factors of 48. Use complete sentences in your answer.

Problem 3   Getting Things Straight

A. Hot dogs are normally sold only in packages of 10. If you buy 1 package, how many hot dogs do you have?

If you buy 2 packages?

If you buy 3 packages?

If you buy 4 packages?

B. In each case, you multiply by 10 to get the total number of hot dogs. So, the total number of hot dogs is a **multiple** of what number? Write complete sentences to explain your answer.

Investigate Problem 3

1. In your own words write a definition for multiple.

multiple:

2. Find the first five multiples of each number in the table.

Number	First Five Multiples
7	
25	
31	
36	
44	
48	

3. Math Path: Factors, Multiples, Divisibility

In mathematics, there are many ways to show the relationship between a number and one of its factors. For example, we can say that:

6 is a factor of 12.
12 is a multiple of 6.
12 is divisible by 6.

Use complete sentences to explain why 12 is a multiple of 6.

Use complete sentences to explain why 12 is divisible by 6.

© 2008 Carnegie Learning, Inc.

Take Note

A number is **divisible** by another number if the quotient of the first number and the second number has a remainder of 0. So, 36 is divisible by 9 because 36 ÷ 9 = 4 with a remainder of 0.

1

1. Math Path: Common Multiple

When a multiple of one number is also a multiple of another number, the multiple is a **common multiple** of the numbers. For the numbers 10 and 12, list the first three common multiples.

Common multiples of 10 and 12:

2. What do you notice about the common multiples of 10 and 12? Use complete sentences to explain.

3. Which of these common multiples was the least number of hot dogs and buns to buy so that none were wasted?

4. Math Path: Least Common Multiple

The smallest of the common multiples is called the **least common multiple** (or LCM). For each pair of numbers, find the least common multiple and at least one other common multiple. Later in the course, we will revisit finding the LCM of larger numbers.

6 and 8   5 and 7   6 and 12

9 and 4   15 and 9   11 and 6

5. Choose the word that makes the following statement true. Then use complete sentences to explain your choice.

The LCM of two numbers is *(always, sometimes, never)* the product of the two numbers.

Do You Remember?

Rules for divisibility

1

A number is **divisible** by another number if the quotient of the first number and the second number has a remainder of 0.

Divisibility Rules

A whole number is divisible by:

2 if the number is even.	$32 \div 2 = 16$ 32 is divisible by 2.	$75 \div 2 = 37$ R 1 75 is not divisible by 2.
3 if the sum of the digits in the number is divisible by 3.	$81 \div 3 = 27$ 81 is divisible by 3.	$85 \div 3 = 28$ R 1 85 is not divisible by 3.
4 if the last two digits represent a number are divisible by 4.	$124 \div 4 = 31$ 124 is divisible by 4.	$130 \div 4 = 32$ R 2 130 is not divisible by 4.
5 if the last digit of the number is 0 or 5.	$220 \div 5 = 44$ 220 is divisible by 5.	$104 \div 5 = 20$ R 4 104 is not divisible by 5.
6 if the number is divisible by both 2 and 3.	$1842 \div 6 = 307$ 1842 is divisible by 6.	$1664 \div 6 = 277$ R 2 1664 is not divisible by 6.
8 if the last three digits represent a number are divisible by 8.	$33,112 \div 8 = 4139$ 33,112 is divisible by 8.	$17,309 \div 8 = 2163$ R 5 17,309 is not divisible by 8.
9 if the sum of the digits in the number is divisible by 9.	$963 \div 9 = 107$ 963 is divisible by 9.	$824 \div 9 = 91$ R 5 824 is not divisible by 9.
10 if the last digit of the number is 0.	$240 \div 10 = 24$ 240 is divisible by 10.	$368 \div 10 = 36$ R 8 368 is not divisible by 10.

Tell whether each number is divisible by the given number.

789

divisible by 2? _____

divisible by 3? _____

divisible by 4? _____

divisible by 6? _____

345

divisible by 2? _____

divisible by 3? _____

divisible by 5? _____

divisible by 9? _____

5614

divisible by 2? _____

divisible by 4? _____

divisible by 8? _____

divisible by 10? _____

416

divisible by 2? _____

divisible by 4? _____

divisible by 8? _____

divisible by 10? _____

8490

divisible by 2? _____

divisible by 3? _____

divisible by 6? _____

divisible by 10? _____

10,398

divisible by 2? _____

divisible by 3? _____

divisible by 4? _____

divisible by 6? _____

1.4 Kings and Mathematicians
Prime and Composite Numbers

1

Objectives

In this lesson, you will:

- Understand prime and composite numbers.
- Become familiar with the multiplicative identity.

Key Terms

- prime number
- composite number
- multiplicative identity

Problem 1   One Hundred Boxed Gifts

A king is given 100 gifts in 100 boxes by a mathematician. All of the gifts are the same size and are lined up on a long table in a single row. The mathematician tells the king that he only gets to keep the gifts if he follows the mathematician's instructions and can then answer two questions. If the king cannot answer the mathematician's questions correctly, he must give up his throne to the mathematician.

The mathematician gives the king the following instructions:

- All of the gifts are numbered from 1 to 100.

- The king cannot open the first or second gift.

- The king must open every second gift after gift Number 2 (every other gift).

- The king must then go to the next unopened gift, gift Number 3. He must not open it, but must open every third gift after gift Number 3.

- The king must go to the next unopened gift, gift Number 5. He must not open it, but must open every fifth gift after gift Number 5.

- The king must continue in this fashion until he gets to the last gift.

The mathematician asks the king to look at the number on each of the gifts that are not opened. The mathematician then asks the two important questions:

Ignoring the Number 1, in what way are all of the numbers on the unopened gifts the same and in what way are they different from the numbers on the opened gifts?

If there were more gifts, what are the next three gifts that would not have been opened?

To solve this problem, draw a diagram to represent the first 20 gifts. Then use the diagram to follow the mathematician's instructions.

1. List the numbers of the unopened gifts.

2. List the numbers of the opened gifts.

3. Answer the first of the mathematician's questions:

Ignoring the Number 1, in what way are all of the numbers on the unopened gifts the same and in what way are they different from the numbers on the opened gifts?

If you and your partner are having problems, extend your diagram to represent 30 or 40 gifts.

4. Share your answers with another pair of partners. Then work together with that team to prepare an answer to the second of the mathematician's questions:

If there were more gifts, what are the next three gifts that would not have been opened?

In the One Hundred Boxed Gifts problem, the number on each of the unopened gifts has only two factors, the number itself and 1. Numbers greater than 1 with exactly two whole number factors are called **prime numbers**. Numbers that have more than two whole number factors are called **composite numbers**. Only the number 1 has a single factor, so the number 1 is neither a prime nor a composite, which makes the number 1 very special.

Problem 2   Sieve of Eratosthenes

The One Hundred Boxed Gifts problem is very similar to a method for finding prime numbers first discovered by Greek mathematician Eratosthenes over 4000 years ago. He called it the Sieve. A sieve was a tool that was used to separate small particles from larger particles and was usually a box with a screen for a bottom so that the smaller pieces could fall through.

The Sieve of Eratosthenes screens out all of the composite numbers and leaves only the primes. Let's use it to find all of the primes up to 100. Below are the first 100 numbers written in order in an array, which is another representation!

1	2	3	4	5	6	7	8	9	10
11	12	13	14	15	16	17	18	19	20
21	22	23	24	25	26	27	28	29	30
31	32	33	34	35	36	37	38	39	40
41	42	43	44	45	46	47	48	49	50
51	52	53	54	55	56	57	58	59	60
61	62	63	64	65	66	67	68	69	70
71	72	73	74	75	76	77	78	79	80
81	82	83	84	85	86	87	88	89	90
91	92	93	94	95	96	97	98	99	100

A. Start by putting a square around the number 1 because it is neither prime nor composite.

B. Circle the number 2 and cross out all of the multiples of 2.

C. Circle the next number after 2 that is not crossed out. Then cross out its multiples that are not already crossed out.

D. Continue in this fashion until you come to the first number greater than 10 that is not crossed out. All of the remaining numbers have "been caught by the sieve" and are prime numbers.

Investigate Problem 2

1. How many of the prime numbers are even? Use complete sentences to explain your answer.

2. Is it possible that there is an even prime greater than 100? Use complete sentences to explain why or why not.

3. Explain why you need to continue crossing out numbers only until you come to the first number greater than 10 that is not crossed out. Write your answer using a complete sentence.

4. How do you know that any remaining number less than 100 must be a prime number without continuing to use the sieve process? Use complete sentences to explain your reasoning.

5. **Math Path: Multiplicative Identity**

    The number 1, besides being neither prime nor composite, is also the only number that is a factor of every number. The number 1 has the special property that when it is multiplied by any number, the product is that number. Because of this property, the number 1 is called the **multiplicative identity.**

    You have learned two properties of mathematics so far in this course. Identify the property that is shown by each example.

    21 × 15 = 15 × 21   45 × 1 = 45

© 2008 Carnegie Learning, Inc.

1.5 I Scream for Frozen Yogurt
Prime Factorization

Objectives

In this lesson, you will:

- Find the prime factorization of a number.
- Use the associative property of multiplication.

Key Terms

- prime factorization
- factor tree
- Associative Property of Multiplication

© 2008 Carnegie Learning, Inc.

Problem 1 Frozen Yogurt Containers

Your school plans to make and sell homemade frozen yogurt. They are having a contest for the container design. One of the design requirements is that the length, width, and height be whole numbers greater than 1. The container must be designed to hold about 1 gallon of frozen yogurt. One gallon of frozen yogurt takes up 210 cubic inches of space. What are the possible dimensions of the container?

A. The volume of the container must be 210 cubic inches. To find the volume of the container, multiply the container's length by its width and height:

Volume = length × width × height

Complete the table by listing three possible dimensions of the container.

Length (inches)	Width (inches)	Height (inches)	Volume (cubic inches)
			210
			210
			210

B. For each row in the table, write the volume as the product of prime numbers. Use a complete sentence to describe what you observe in each case.

Investigate Problem 1

1. Math Path: Prime Factorization

Recall that a composite number is a number that has more than two whole number factors. It turns out that every composite number can be written as the product of prime numbers. Writing a whole number as the product of prime numbers is the **prime factorization** of the number.

For example, 4 is the smallest composite number. Write 4 as the product of prime numbers.

4 = _____ × _____

2. Write each composite number as the product of primes.

6 = _____   8 = _____   9 = _____

10 = _____   12 = _____   14 = _____

Problem 2   Factor Trees

A. It may be easy to write most small numbers as products of primes. For larger numbers, it may be more difficult. Write 144 as the product of primes.

144 = _____

B. One organized representation that can help you to find the prime factorization quickly is a factor tree. A **factor tree** for 12 is shown below.

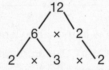

Use the steps to write a factor tree for 30. Then write the prime factorization of 30.

Begin by writing 30 at the top.

Pick any pair of whole number factors of 30 other than 1 and 30. Draw a branch from 30 to each factor.

If both of the factors are prime, then you are finished. If not, use branches to write a factor pair for any composite factors.

Continue to find factor pairs until all of the factors of 30 are prime.

Use the factor tree to write the prime factorization of 30.

30 = _____

© 2008 Carnegie Learning, Inc.

Investigate Problem 2

1. Is the factor tree in Problem 2 the only factor tree that you could write for 30? If not, find at least one more factor tree for 30.

30

_____ × _____

2. Check with your partner to see if he or she came up with the same factor trees for 30 as you. How many different factor trees are there for 30?

3. **Math Path: Associative Property of Multiplication**

   Notice that you can group the prime factors together in any order and multiply them to get the same product. For example,

   (2 × 3) × 2 = 12   and   2 × (3 × 2) = 12.

   This is an example of another important property of numbers, the **Associative Property of Multiplication.** You will learn more about this property in Chapter 14.

   Use the prime factorization of 30 to write an example of the Associative Property of Multiplication.

4. Work with your partner to construct a factor tree for each number. Then write the prime factorization of each number.

   24   81

   96

Investigate Problem 2

5. Share your factor trees with another pair of partners. For each number, are your factor trees the same as or different from the factor trees of the other pair of partners?

6. For each number, is your prime factorization the same as or different from the prime factorization of the other partner team? Use a complete sentence to answer the question.

Problem 1 Revisited

Your school plans to make and sell homemade frozen yogurt. They are having a contest for the container design. One of the design requirements is that the length, width, and height be whole numbers greater than 1. The container must be designed to hold about 1 gallon of frozen yogurt. One gallon of frozen yogurt takes up 210 cubic inches of space. What are the possible dimensions of the container?

A. Construct a factor tree for the number 210. Then write the prime factorization of 210.

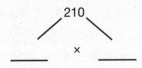

B. Use the prime factorization to list all of the possible dimensions of the container in the table below.

Length (inches)	Width (inches)	Height (inches)	Volume (cubic inches)
			210
			210
			210
			210
			210
			210

Powers That Be
Powers and Exponents

Objectives

In this lesson, you will:
- Use powers and exponents to write repeated multiplication.
- Use powers and exponents to write the prime factorization of a number.

Key Terms

- power
- base
- exponent

Problem 1 Prime Factorization

A. Use a factor tree to find the prime factorization of 64.

64

The prime factorization of 64 is _____.

B. Use a factor tree to find the prime factorization of 81.

81

The prime factorization of 81 is _____.

C. What do you notice about the prime factorizations of 64 and 81? Use a complete sentence to answer the question.

Once again, think about how mathematics was discovered. After human beings began counting their possessions, they needed to "put groups together" and "take from groups," so the operations of addition and subtraction were invented.

Much later people formed communities and began to trade goods. At this point, they needed to add the same number repeatedly. For instance, a blacksmith who made horseshoes needed to know how many shoes he would need for all of the king's 125 horses. The blacksmith could have added the number 4 repeatedly 125 times, but by multiplying 4 × 125, he saved a lot of time.

Problem 2 · Horse Sense

In the same way, suppose the blacksmith needed to shoe the horses of 4 kings. Each king had 4 bands of 4 men. Each man rode a horse (with 4 feet, of course). Each foot needed a horseshoe that took 4 nails. For the blacksmith to figure out whether he had enough nails to do the job, he could use repeated multiplication.

4 kings × 4 bands × 4 men with horses × 4 horseshoes × 4 nails

How many nails did the blacksmith need? Use a complete sentence to explain how you found this number.

Investigate Problem 2

1. Math Path: Powers

Take Note

In a power, when no exponent is written, you can assume that the exponent is 1.

$4 = 4^1$

Eventually, people devised a notation to represent repeated multiplication. This notation is called a **power**. Let's use a power to represent the number of nails that the blacksmith needs. The expression $4 \times 4 \times 4 \times 4 \times 4$ has only one factor, 4, which is repeated 5 times. You can express this expression as a power.

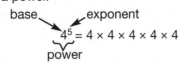

The **base** of a power is the factor and the **exponent** of the power is the number of times that the factor is repeated. The power can be read as:

4 to the fifth power
the fifth power of 4
4 raised to the fifth power

2. You can use powers to write the prime factorization of a number. For instance, the prime factorization of 64 is

$2 \times 2 \times 2 \times 2 \times 2 \times 2 = 2^6$.

Write the prime factorization of 81 using a power. How would you read this?

81 = _____

Take Note

When you write the prime factorization of a number, write the factors in increasing order. For instance,

$36 = 2^2 \times 3^2$.

3. Write the prime factorization of each number using powers. The first one is done for you.

$36 = 2 \times 2 \times 3 \times 3 = 2^2 \times 3^2$ 45 = _____

144 = _____   256 = _____

343 = _____   625 = _____

Beads and Baubles

Greatest Common Factor

Objectives

In this lesson, you will:
- Find the greatest common factor of two or more numbers.

Key Terms

- common factor
- greatest common factor (GCF)

Problem 1 Bags of Beads

Your aunt belongs to a club that makes beaded jewelry. The club wants to sell small packages of different types of beads to people who want to make their own jewelry. They plan to buy and sell three different types of beads—spacer beads, round beads, and rectangular beads. They can buy each type in bags of different quantities. The table below lists the type of bead, the quantity in each bag, and the price of a bag.

Type of Bead	Quantity per Bag	Cost per Bag
Spacer beads	40	$3.50
Round beads	72	$5.00
Rectangular beads	24	$7.50

The club members buy one bag of each type of bead. The club members want to divide the beads into packages so that each package has exactly the same number of spacer beads, round beads, and rectangular beads. They also want to make sure that they use all of the beads they buy with no beads left over.

The club members are having trouble determining the greatest number of packages they can make so that all of the beads are used and there is the same number of each type of bead in each package. Can you help?

A. Do you understand the problem? Is there anything that is unclear about the problem?

B. Think about the problem. Do you have all of the information that you need? What information do you know? How do you think you should use this information to solve the problem?

C. Talk with your partner about how each of you plans to solve the problem. Then use the plans together to find the solution.

Problem 1 *Bags of Beads*

D. When you and your partner find a solution, form a group with another partner team. In your group, try to agree on a common solution. Be sure that everyone in the group understands the solution and can explain how the solution was found.

E. Share your solution and your solution method with the entire class.

Investigate Problem 1

1. Based on your solution, how much money will the club spend on the beads that will be put into the packages? Use a complete sentence to answer the question.

2. Math Path: Greatest Common Factor

In Problem 1, you found the greatest number of packages that the club could make from three different types of beads. In other words, you were looking for the greatest number that could divide evenly into three other numbers (40, 72, and 24).

In Lessons 1.2 and 1.5, you found the factors of a number and the prime factorization of a number. We will first use these ideas to identify *common factors* of two or more numbers and then to find the *greatest common factor* of the numbers.

A **common factor** is a whole number that is a factor of two or more numbers. The **greatest common factor** (or GCF) is the greatest whole number that is a common factor of two or more numbers.

Work with your partner to complete each table. First, for each number, list the distinct factor pairs and the distinct factors. Then look at the distinct factors for both numbers to determine the common factors.

Number	Distinct Factor Pairs	Distinct Factors	Common Factors
12			
18			

Take Note

Remember, when you multiply two numbers to produce another number, each number that you multiply is a factor.

When you write a whole number as the product of prime numbers, you are writing the prime factorization of the number.

Number	Distinct Factor Pairs	Distinct Factors	Common Factors
20			
36			

Number	Distinct Factor Pairs	Distinct Factors	Common Factors
56			
70			

3. In each table in Question 2, circle the greatest common factor for each pair of numbers. What do you observe as the numbers get larger? Use a complete sentence to answer the question.

4. Find the greatest common factor of three numbers.

Number	Distinct Factor Pairs	Distinct Factors	Common Factors
24			
32			
42			

Number	Distinct Factor Pairs	Distinct Factors	Common Factors
64			
96			
128			

5. As the numbers increase, finding all of the factors and the GCF becomes more difficult and time consuming. However, there is a more efficient way to find the GCF using prime factorizations.

Let's find the prime factorizations of 64, 96, and 128, and use the results to find the GCF of the numbers.

Complete the table below by first finding the prime factorization of each number. Then list all of the common prime factors. Be sure that if a prime number is a factor of all three numbers more than once, you list it the number of times it appears. The greatest common factor is the product of the common prime factors.

Number	Prime Factorization	Common Prime Factors	Greatest Common Factor
64			
96			
128			

Was the greatest common factor the same using this method as the method that you used in Question 4?

6. Find the greatest common factor of each set of numbers by using prime factorizations.

Number	Prime Factorization	Common Prime Factors	Greatest Common Factor
54			
45			
72			

Number	Prime Factorization	Common Prime Factors	Greatest Common Factor
144			
180			
96			

Looking Back at Chapter 1

Key Terms

expression • p. 9
order of operations • p. 9
variable • p. 10
variable expression • p. 10
factor • p. 11
factor pair • p. 11
Commutative Property
  of Multiplication • p. 12
multiple • p. 14

divisible • p. 14
common multiple • p. 17
least common multiple
  • p. 17
composite number • p. 21
prime number • p. 21
multiplicative identity • p. 22
prime factorization • p. 24
factor tree • p. 24

Associative Property
  of Multiplication • p. 25
power • p. 28
base • p. 28
exponent • p. 28
common factor • p. 30
greatest common factor (GCF)
  • p. 30

Summary

Using Picture Algebra (p. 6)

You can use a picture or diagram to help you solve word problems. In your diagram, represent the known values from the problem and represent the unknown values using a question mark. Then solve the problem.

Example
Spooks and Boots are two cats. Spooks weighs exactly 9 pounds more than Boots. Together, the cats weigh 21 pounds. How much does each cat weigh?

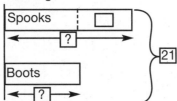

From the picture, you can see that Boots weighs 6 pounds and Spooks weighs 6 + 9, or 15 pounds.

Using the Order of Operations (p. 9)

To use the order of operations, first evaluate expressions inside grouping symbols, then multiply and divide from left to right. Finally add and subtract from left to right.

Examples
You can use the order of operations to determine whether the values of each pair of expressions are equal.

27 ÷ (4 + 9) and	(127 − 94) ÷ 3		4 × (45 − 7) and	(18 + 58) × 2
27 ÷ 9	33 ÷ 3		4 × 38	76 × 2
3	11		152	152

The expressions are not equal.   The expressions are equal.

Finding Factors (p. 11)

Example
List the distinct factors of 32.

1 × 32   2 × 16   4 × 8

The factors of 32 are 1, 2, 4, 8, 16, and 32.

Using the Commutative Property of Multiplication (p. 12)

The Commutative Property of Multiplication states that you can multiply two factors in any order. So, for any numbers a and b, then $a \times b = b \times a$.

Example   The Commutative Property of Multiplication states that the values in the expressions below are equal.

4×21 and 21×4
84   84

The expressions are equal, so $4 \times 21 = 21 \times 4$.

Finding Multiples (p. 14)

Example   List the first 5 multiples of 8.

$8 \times 1 = 8$ $8 \times 2 = 16$ $8 \times 3 = 24$ $8 \times 4 = 32$ $8 \times 5 = 40$

The first 5 multiples of 8 are 8, 16, 24, 32, and 40.

Finding Common Multiples (p. 17)

To find a common multiple of two or more numbers, list several multiples of each number. Then find the multiples the numbers have in common.

Example   The common multiples of 4 and 10 are:

Multiples of 4: 4, 8, 12, 16, **20**, 24, 28, 32, 36, **40**, 44, 48, 52, 56, **60**
Multiples of 10: 10, **20**, 30, **40**, 50, **60**

Three common multiples of 4 and 10 are 20, 40, and 60.

Finding the Least Common Multiple (p. 17)

To find the least common multiple of two or more numbers, find the smallest of the common multiples.

Example   The common multiples of 5 and 12 are:

Multiples of 5: 5, 10, 15, 20, 25, 30, 35, 40, 45, 50, 55, **60**, 65, 70, 75, 80, 85
Multiples of 12: 12, 24, 36, 48, **60**, 72, 84, 96, 108, 120

The least common multiple of 5 and 12 is 60.

Finding Prime and Composite Numbers (p. 21)

To determine whether a number is prime or composite, find the whole number factors of the number. If the only factors are 1 and the number, then the number is prime.

Examples   The only factors of 17 are 1 and 17. So, 17 is prime.

The factors of 39 are 1, 3, 13, and 39. So, 39 is composite.

Use the Multiplicative Identity (p. 22)

The multiplicative identity states that when the number 1 is multiplied by any number, the result is that number. So, for any number a, $a \times 1 = a$.

Examples   The multiplicative identity tells you that the following expressions are true.

$35 \times 1 = 35$ $1 \times 121 = 121$ $d \times 1 = d$

Writing the Prime Factorization (p. 24)

Example   To write the prime factorization of a number, use a factor tree.

The prime factorization of 45 is 3 × 3 × 5.

Using the Associative Property of Multiplication (p. 25)

The Associative Property of Multiplication states that you can group factors in any order and multiply them to get the same product. So, for any numbers *a*, *b*, and *c*, $(a \times b) \times c = a \times (b \times c)$.

Examples   The Associative Property of Multiplication states that the values of each pair of expressions are equal.

$(5 \times 31) \times 16$	and	$5 \times (31 \times 16)$	$9 \times (32 \times 17)$	and	$(9 \times 32) \times 17$
155 × 16	and	5 × 496	9 × 544	and	288 × 17
2480		2480	4896		4896

The expressions are equal.   The expressions are equal.

Writing Powers (p. 28)

To express repeated multiplication as a power, write the base raised to the number of times the base is multiplied by itself.

Example   The expression $7 \times 7 \times 7 \times 7 \times 7$ is equal to the power 7^5. You read the power as "seven raised to the fifth power."

Writing the Prime Factorization Using Powers (p. 28)

To write the prime factorization of a number using powers, find the prime factorization. Then rewrite the prime factorization using powers.

Example $54 = 2 \times 3 \times 3 \times 3 = 2 \times 3^3$

The prime factorization of 54 is 2×3^3.

Finding the Greatest Common Factor (p. 30)

To find the greatest common factor of two or more numbers, first write the prime factorization of each number. Then list the common prime factors. Be sure that if a prime number is a factor of all of the numbers more than once, you list the number the number of times it appears. The greatest common factor is the product of the common prime factors.

Example $36 = 2^2 \times 3^2$ $48 = 2^4 \times 3$ $64 = 2^6$

The common prime factors of 36, 48, and 64 are 2×2, or 2^2. So, the greatest common factor of 36, 48, and 64 is $2^2 = 4$.

Looking Ahead to Chapter 2

Focus   In Chapter 2, you will work with fractions. You will use fractions to represent portions of a whole and divide more than one whole into parts. You will also find equivalent fractions, simplify fractions, and compare and order fractions.

Chapter Warm-up

Answer these questions to help you review skills that you will need in Chapter 2.

Find the product or quotient.

1. 5×21 **2.** $124 \div 31$ **3.** $87 \div 29$

Find the least common multiple of the pair of numbers.

4. 6, 30   **5.** 9, 15   **6.** 18, 24

Find the greatest common factor of the pair of numbers.

7. 51, 27   **8.** 48, 64   **9.** 78, 90

Read the problem scenario below.

Sitara, Cecilia, and Kym have a total of 80 quarters. Sitara has 20 more quarters than Cecilia. Kym has 10 more quarters than Sitara.

10. How many quarters does Sitara have?

11. How many quarters does Cecilia have?

Key Terms

fraction ● p. 40
numerator ● p. 40
denominator ● p. 40
reasonable solution ● p. 48
equivalent fractions ● p. 54

equation ● p. 54
simplest form ● p. 58
simplest terms ● p. 58
completely simplified ● p. 58

least common denominator ●
    p. 66
less than ● p. 66
greater than ● p. 66

2

Fractions

Soccer, played with two teams of 11 players, is a popular sport in many parts of the world, particularly in Europe, Latin America, and Africa. In Lesson 2.3, you will answer questions about soccer teams in a local neighborhood sports organization.

2

Comic Strips

Dividing a Whole into Fractional Parts

Objectives

In this lesson, you will:

- Use fractions to represent parts of a whole.

Key Terms

- fraction
- numerator
- denominator

You decide to create a comic strip for your school's newspaper. To do this, you cut a strip of paper that is a little narrower than the width of a newspaper page. The strip represents one whole comic.

A. For your first comic, you want to have two frames. Your teacher will provide you with a strip of paper that represents one whole comic. Work with your partner to divide the strip into two parts of equal size by folding the strip like the one shown below. Do not measure the strip.

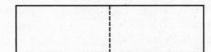 

Note: Throughout this lesson, always fold the strip as shown above so that the fold decreases the length of the longest side.

B. Write a complete sentence that describes how you divided the strip into two equal parts.

C. How can you be sure that you have two parts that are exactly the same size? Use complete sentences to explain.

1. Math Path: Fractions

We can use a fraction to represent one or more parts of a whole. A **fraction** is a number of the form $\frac{a}{b}$ where a is the **numerator** and b is the denominator. The **denominator** tells us how many equal parts the whole is divided into and the numerator tells us how many of these parts we have. The denominator of a fraction cannot be 0.

Write a fraction that represents one frame of the strip.

2. What is the denominator of the fraction from Question 1? Use complete sentences to explain what the denominator represents.

3. What is the numerator of the fraction from Question 1? Use complete sentences to explain what the numerator represents.

4. Label each part of the strip with this fraction.

Problem 2   Comic Strips with Equal Parts

A. Fold a new strip of paper. Without opening up the strip, fold the strip again. How many frames would be in your comic if you used this strip? How many equal parts do you have? Label each of the parts with the appropriate fraction.

B. Repeat the process in part (A) with a new strip of paper, but this time fold the strip a total of three times. How many frames would be in your comic if you used this strip? How many equal parts do you have? Label each of the parts with the appropriate fraction.

C. Repeat the process in part (B) with a new strip of paper, but this time fold the strip a total of four times. How many equal parts has this strip been divided into? Could you use this strip for frames of a comic? Use complete sentences to explain why or why not. Label each of the parts with the appropriate fraction.

Investigate Problem 2

1. How difficult was the process in Problem 2? Use complete sentences to describe the fractions that you can find using this process.

2. Arrange your strips in a column so that all of the left edges are lined up and the strips are ordered from the strip with the largest parts to the strip with the smallest parts. If you folded carefully, you will notice that some of the folds line up with each other. Use your fraction strips to complete each statement below.

   It takes _____ of the parts labeled as $\frac{1}{4}$ to make up one of the parts labeled as $\frac{1}{2}$.

   It takes _____ of the parts labeled as $\frac{1}{8}$ to make up two of the parts labeled as $\frac{1}{4}$.

   It takes _____ of the parts labeled as $\frac{1}{16}$ to make up three of the parts labeled as $\frac{1}{8}$.

3. Write two other sentences similar to those in Question 2 relating the parts of your fraction strips.

Problem 3   More Strips with Equal Parts

A. Divide a strip into exactly three equal parts by folding. Is this more or less difficult than dividing a strip into two equal parts? Explain your answer using complete sentences.

   Label each part of the strip with a fraction.

B. Divide another strip into three equally sized parts by folding. Then divide each of these parts into two equal parts by folding. Label each part of the strip with a fraction.

C. Take a third strip and repeat the procedure you used in part (B). Then divide each of the parts of the strip into two equal parts by folding. Label each part of the strip with an appropriate fraction.

1. You have created fraction strips for many common fractions. You can create three additional strips that are useful.

Divide a strip into exactly five equal parts by folding. Label each part of the strip with a fraction.

Divide another strip into exactly five equal parts by folding. Then divide each of these parts into two equal parts by folding. Label each part of the strip with a fraction.

Divide a third strip and repeat the procedure you used in the previous step. Then divide each of the parts of the strip into two equal parts by folding. Label each part of the strip with a fraction.

2. Arrange your strips from Question 1 in a column so that all of the left edges are lined up and the strips are ordered from the strip with the largest parts to the strip with the smallest parts. Write as many sentences as you can that relate the sizes of your fraction pieces. We will be using these fraction strips throughout this chapter and throughout the course, so be sure to keep them.

3. Circles, squares, and rectangles can also be used to represent fractions. Represent each fraction as indicated.

Use a circle to represent $\frac{3}{4}$.   Use a rectangle to represent $\frac{6}{7}$.

Use a square to represent $\frac{1}{3}$.   Use a circle to represent $\frac{5}{8}$.

© 2008 Carnegie Learning, Inc.

Use a square to represent $\frac{5}{12}$.   Use a square to represent $\frac{10}{11}$.

Use a rectangle to represent $\frac{7}{8}$.   Use a square to represent $\frac{4}{9}$.

Use a circle to represent $\frac{5}{7}$.   Use a circle to represent $\frac{11}{12}$.

4. Which fractions in Question 3 were more difficult to represent accurately? Which were easier? Use complete sentences to explain your reasoning.

2

Dividing Quesadillas
Dividing More Than One Whole into Parts

Objectives

In this lesson, you will:
- Use fractions to divide more than one whole into equally sized parts.
- Determine whether a solution is reasonable.

Key Terms

- reasonable solution

Problem 1 Quesadillas for the Class

As part of your school's international foods festival, a classmate brought quesadillas that he made for the entire class. However, he only brought 21 quesadillas for the 28 students in your class. Because your class normally works in groups of four, your teacher suggests that you give the same number of quesadillas to each group of four students. How many quesadillas should each group receive? Each group must then decide how to divide their quesadillas equally among the group members.

A. Work together as a class to complete the following tasks.

Read the problem carefully. What is a quesadilla? How many quesadillas should each group get?

B. Work by yourself to answer the following questions.

How would you divide the quesadillas equally among the group members? Use complete sentences to explain. Does each person get the same amount? How do you know?

Draw a diagram that represents the problem.

1. Explain your solution to your partner. Does your partner have the same solution? If not, do both solutions give the same answer? Do both solutions work? Choose one of the solutions to share with another partner team.

2. Form a group with another partner team. Take turns sharing the solution that you chose. Are both solutions the same? If not, do both solutions give the same answer? Do both solutions work? Choose a solution to share with the class. Use complete sentences to explain the solution that you chose.

3. Share your solution with the class. Do all of the groups have the same solution? If not, do all of the solutions give the same answer? Do all of the solutions work? Use complete sentences to explain why or why not.

Problem 2   *Analyzing Solutions*

Several students suggest ways to divide the quesadillas equally. Paula wants to have at least one piece that is one half of a quesadilla, so she starts by dividing all of the quesadillas in half.

Below are three circles that represent a group's quesadillas. Work with a partner to divide each circle into halves. Label each person's portion on the diagram.

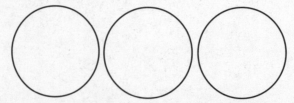

Will Paula's method work? Why or why not? If possible, explain what you need to do to make Paula's method work.
Use complete sentences.

1. Dwayne says that because each group has three quesadillas, he will divide each quesadilla into thirds. Divide each circle into thirds and label each person's portion on the diagram.

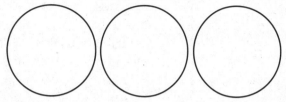

Will Dwayne's method work? Why or why not? If possible, explain what you need to do to make Dwayne's method work. Use complete sentences.

For Dwayne's method, name the different fractions and the number of each fraction that represents how much of the quesadillas each person should receive. Is this the same amount as in your group's solution? How do you know? Use complete sentences to explain.

2. Clifton wants to divide each quesadilla into eighths because he says that each person will get more pieces. Divide each circle into eighths and label each person's portion on the diagram.

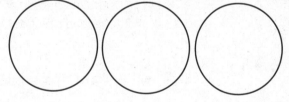

Will Clifton's method work? Why or why not? If possible, explain what you need to do to make Clifton's method work. Use complete sentences.

For Clifton's method, name the different fractions and the number of each fraction that represents how much of the quesadillas each person should receive. Is this the same amount as in your group's solution? How do you know? Use complete sentences to explain.

2

3. Juanita decides that she will first divide all of the quesadillas into any number of equal-sized pieces. Then she will give each person the same number of pieces up until the last piece or last few pieces. Then she will divide the last piece or last few pieces into four equal parts. For example, she wants to divide the quesadillas into fifths. Divide each circle into fifths and label each person's portion on the diagram.

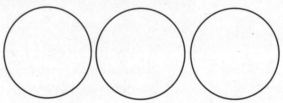

Will Juanita's method work? Why or why not? If possible, explain to your partner what you need to do to make Juanita's method work.

For Juanita's method, name the different fractions and the number of each fraction that represents how much of the quesadillas each person should receive.

4. In Lesson 2.1, you learned that a fraction is used to describe equal parts of one whole. Use complete sentences to explain what a fraction describes in this lesson.

5. **Math Path: Reasonable Solutions**

Often a solution will not make sense in the context of a problem. This means that the solution is not a **reasonable solution.**
For instance, because there are more students than quesadillas, each student should receive less than one quesadilla. So, if your solution indicated that each person should receive more than one quesadilla, you would know that you did something wrong.

Determine whether the following solution is reasonable. Use complete sentences to explain why or why not.

For the international foods festival, a teacher brings 225 biscotti for each of the 150 students in your grade. Each student receives $\frac{2}{3}$ of a biscotti.

No "I" in Team

Dividing Groups into Fractional Parts

Objectives

In this lesson, you will:

- Use fractions to represent portions of a whole.

Problem 1   Team Tally

You are a member of a local neighborhood sports organization. The organization sponsors 7 baseball teams each for boys and girls, 6 basketball teams each for boys and girls, 10 soccer teams for girls, and 6 football teams for boys.

A. Work together as a class to complete the following tasks.

Read the problem carefully. What information is known?

B. Work by yourself to answer the following questions.

How many total teams does the organization sponsor?

How many boys' teams?

How many girls' teams?

How many baseball teams?

How many basketball teams?

How many soccer teams?

How many football teams?

Draw a diagram that represents the teams.

2

Investigate Problem 1

1. What fraction of the total number of teams are girls' teams?

   What fraction are boys' teams?

   What fraction are soccer teams?

   What fraction are basketball teams?

   What fraction are football teams?

   What fraction are baseball teams?

2. What fraction of the total number of teams are not basketball teams?

   What fraction are not soccer teams?

3. Form a group with another partner team. Compare your answers to Questions 1 and 2. Are your answers the same? Take turns explaining how you got your answers and why you think they are correct.

4. As a group, write two other questions like Questions 1 and 2. Write the answers to the questions.

5. Exchange your questions with another group. Answer the questions. Then compare your answers with the other group's answers.

6. We used fractions in this problem in a slightly different way. Use complete sentences to answer each question about the fractions.

   What does the denominator of any of the fractions represent?

   What does the numerator represent?

   What is one whole?

Problem 2   *Swim Team*

Jennifer and Trevor are on the school swim team and have both won ribbons. Jennifer has 5 yellow ribbons, 8 blue ribbons, and a handful of red ribbons. Trevor has 3 blue ribbons, 4 yellow ribbons, and a handful of red ribbons.

A. The picture below shows Jennifer's yellow ribbons, which represent one fifth of her total number of ribbons. Complete the picture to show all of Jennifer's ribbons.

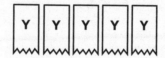

B. How many red ribbons does Jennifer have?

What fraction of her total number of ribbons are red ribbons?

What fraction of her total number of ribbons are blue ribbons?

Investigate Problem 2

1. Trevor's yellow ribbons are shown below. Draw his blue ribbons.

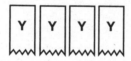

2. How many total ribbons does Trevor have if together the yellow and blue ribbons are one third of his total number of ribbons?

What fraction of his total number of ribbons are red ribbons?

3. Jennifer and Trevor put all of their ribbons together in one display.

What fraction of the ribbons are Jennifer's ribbons?

What fraction are Trevor's ribbons?

What fraction are yellow ribbons?

What fraction are blue ribbons?

What fraction are red ribbons?

2

Fair Share of Pizza
Equivalent Fractions

2

Objectives

In this lesson, you will:

- Write equivalent fractions.

Key Terms

- equivalent fractions
- equation

In this chapter, we have used fractions in many ways—to represent parts of a whole, to represent parts of more than one whole, and to represent parts of groups. One interesting thing about fractions that you may have noticed is that there can be more than one fraction that represents the same amount or quantity.

Problem 1   More Pizza?

Harriet and Bob phoned a local pizzeria to order a pizza. They wanted half of the pizza to be plain for Harriet and the other half to have pepperoni for Bob. Harriet asked the pizzeria to slice her portion in half. Bob asked to have his portion sliced into four pieces because he wanted more slices.

Even though Bob has more slices, will he get more pizza? Write a short paragraph explaining your answer. Include a diagram. You may use any representation in your explanation, including your fraction strips.

Investigate Problem 1

Use your fraction strips from Lesson 2.1 to answer the following questions.

1. Compare the fraction strip that represents $\frac{1}{2}$ to the fraction strip that represents $\frac{1}{12}$. Write complete sentences that describe what you observe.

2. Compare the fraction strip that represents $\frac{1}{8}$ to the fraction strip that represents $\frac{1}{12}$. Write complete sentences that describe what you observe.

3. How does your observation in Question 2 relate to your observation in Question 1?

4. What part of the fraction strip that represents $\frac{1}{12}$ is the same size as two parts of the fraction strip that represents $\frac{1}{8}$?

5. **Math Path: Equations and Equivalent Fractions**

   Two fractions that represent the same amount or quantity are called **equivalent fractions.** Equivalent fractions are indicated by writing an equals sign, =, between them as shown below.

   $$\frac{1}{3} = \frac{2}{6}$$

   The equals sign was developed to show the relationship between quantities that are the same but not identical. A mathematical sentence that contains an equals sign is called an **equation.** For example, in Lesson 1.2, you learned that $6 \times 2 = 2 \times 6$, where both 6×2 and 2×6 are different representations of the same quantity, but are not exactly identical.

   Write equivalent fractions for the fractions you found in Questions 1 and 2. Express your answers as equations.

6. Use the diagram below to write equivalent fractions that represent Harriet's and Bob's portions of the pizza.

_____ = _____

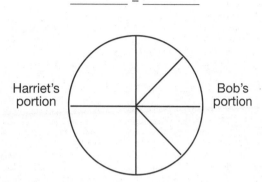

Harriet's portion

Bob's portion

2

Problem 2   Pizza Party

Harriet and Bob decide to have a pizza party. They invite all of their friends and order six pizzas. They asked the pizzeria to slice each pizza in a different way. Here's what they noticed.

$\frac{1}{2}$ of a pizza is the same amount as $\frac{6}{12}$ of a pizza, so $\frac{1}{2} = \frac{6}{12}$.

$\frac{2}{3}$ of a pizza is the same amount as $\frac{8}{12}$ of a pizza, so $\frac{2}{3} = \frac{8}{12}$.

$\frac{3}{4}$ of a pizza is the same amount as $\frac{12}{16}$ of a pizza, so $\frac{3}{4} = \frac{12}{16}$.

A. What do you notice about the numerators and denominators of the equivalent fractions? Write your ideas using complete sentences.

B. What do you need to do to both the numerator and the denominator of a fraction in order to write another fraction that is equivalent? Write your answer using a complete sentence.

Investigate Problem 2

1. Fill in the blanks so that each pair of fractions are equivalent. If possible, use your fraction strips to check your work.

$$\frac{2}{3} = \frac{\square}{6}$$ $$\frac{1}{3} = \frac{\square}{9}$$ $$\frac{2}{5} = \frac{\square}{15}$$

$$\frac{5}{6} = \frac{15}{\square}$$ $$\frac{\square}{16} = \frac{5}{8}$$ $$\frac{7}{8} = \frac{\square}{32}$$

2. Fill in the blanks so that each equality is true. If possible, use your fraction strips to check your work.

$$\frac{3}{4} = \frac{3 \times \square}{4 \times \square} = \frac{9}{12}$$ $$\frac{5}{6} = \frac{5 \times \square}{6 \times \square} = \frac{\square}{12}$$

$$\frac{5}{8} = \frac{5 \times \square}{8 \times \square} = \frac{15}{\square}$$ $$\frac{7}{40} = \frac{7 \times \square}{40 \times \square} = \frac{\square}{40}$$

3. **Math Path: Multiplicative Identity**

In Question 2, you multiplied the numerator and denominator of a fraction by the same number, such as 2. This is the same as multiplying the given fraction by a fraction with the same numerator and denominator, such as $\frac{2}{2}$. Any fraction whose numerator and denominator are the same number is equivalent to 1. For instance, the fraction $\frac{2}{2}$ is the same as 1. So, in Question 2, you were just multiplying each fraction by the number 1, the multiplicative identity. (You learned about the multiplicative identity in Lesson 1.4).

Use your fraction strips to compare the equivalent fractions $\frac{3}{4}$ and $\frac{9}{12}$. How many twelfths are the same as one fourth?

How does this help you determine what number to multiply the numerator 3 and denominator 4 by to find the equivalent fraction $\frac{9}{12}$? Use complete sentences to explain.

4. Do you think that it is always possible to find a fraction with a denominator of eight that is equivalent to a given fraction? Use complete sentences and an example to explain your answer.

2.5 When Twelfths Are Eighths
Simplifying Fractions

Objectives

In this lesson, you will:
- Write fractions in simplest form.

Key Terms

- simplest form
- simplest terms
- completely simplified

Problem 1 *Dinner Conversation*

Your aunt has made two pans of cornbread for dinner. Your younger cousins, Tobias and Henry, are having their usual argument. Tobias says that he got more of the cornbread than Henry got. Both pans of cornbread are the same size. The first pan was cut into 12 pieces and Tobias got 9 pieces. The second pan was cut into 8 pieces and Henry got 6 pieces.

A. Because you are becoming a fraction expert, you help them to settle the argument. Write a paragraph to explain who got more and why. Use your fraction strips along with any other representations that you think will be helpful.

B. Just when you think you have them convinced, in walks your other cousin, Anita, who has a third pan of cornbread that is the same size, but cut into 4 pieces. Anita took 3 of the pieces. She now joins the discussion, saying that she actually has the most because her pieces are the biggest. Write a short paragraph to explain which of the three cousins, if any, got the most cornbread.

1. In Problem 1, you were again thinking about equivalent fractions. Fill in the blanks so that each pair of fractions is equivalent. Use your fraction strips that represent $\frac{1}{4}$, $\frac{1}{8}$, and $\frac{1}{16}$.

   $$\frac{8}{16} = \frac{\square}{8} \qquad\qquad \frac{2}{8} = \frac{\square}{4} \qquad\qquad \frac{12}{16} = \frac{\square}{4}$$

2. In Question 1, the numerator and denominator of each fraction on the right of the equals sign is smaller than the numerator and the denominator of each fraction on the left of the equals sign. Are the equivalent fractions on the right smaller? Use complete sentences to explain why or why not.

3. Whenever we find an equivalent fraction whose numerator and denominator are smaller numbers than the original fraction's numerator and denominator, the new fraction is "simpler." We can say

   $\frac{1}{2}$ is simpler than $\frac{2}{4}$.

   $\frac{1}{2}$ is a simplified form of $\frac{2}{4}$.

   Notice that sometimes a simplified form can be simplified further. Which of the fractions in Question 1 can be simplified further? What is the simpler form?

4. **Math Path: Simplest Form**

   When a fraction cannot be simplified further, we say that the fraction is in **simplest form** (or in **simplest terms,** or that it is **completely simplified**). This process is sometimes called *reducing a fraction to simplest terms.*

   Fill in the blanks to write each fraction in simplest form.

   $$\frac{6}{8} = \frac{\square}{4} \qquad\qquad \frac{12}{15} = \frac{\square}{5} \qquad\qquad \frac{18}{24} = \frac{\square}{4}$$

   In each case, what did you do to the original numerator to get the new numerator? Use complete sentences to explain.

5. Fill in the blanks so that each equality is true. Use your fraction strips to verify your answers.

$$\frac{9}{12} = \frac{9 \div \square}{12 \div \square} = \frac{3}{4} \qquad \frac{10}{16} = \frac{10 \div \square}{16 \div \square} = \frac{\square}{\square} \qquad \frac{18}{24} = \frac{18 \div \square}{24 \div \square} = \frac{\square}{\square}$$

Problem 2   *Correct or Not?*

Kasha says that she simplified the following fraction completely.

$$\frac{8}{24} = \frac{8 \div 2}{24 \div 2} = \frac{4}{12}$$

A. Did Kasha simplify the fraction completely? Use complete sentences to explain your answer.

B. Determine whether each fraction is written in simplest form. If not, completely simplify the fraction.

$$\frac{18}{27} = \frac{18 \div 3}{27 \div 3} = \frac{6}{9} \qquad\qquad \frac{21}{27} = \frac{21 \div 3}{27 \div 3} = \frac{7}{9}$$

$$\frac{8}{12} = \frac{8 \div 2}{12 \div 2} = \frac{4}{6} \qquad\qquad \frac{16}{20} = \frac{16 \div 2}{20 \div 2} = \frac{8}{10}$$

C. Determine which of the following fractions are in simplest terms.

$$\frac{10}{12} \qquad \frac{9}{11} \qquad \frac{10}{25} \qquad \frac{11}{121} \qquad \frac{17}{29} \qquad \frac{44}{55}$$

D. Recall that the factors of a number are those numbers that evenly divide the number with no remainder. How can you use the factors of a number to determine when you need to simplify a fraction? Use complete sentences to explain your reasoning.

2

1. Jim simplified $\frac{24}{28}$ by first dividing both the numerator and denominator by 2 and then dividing the numerator and the denominator of the result, $\frac{12}{14}$, by 2 to get the fraction $\frac{6}{7}$.

$$\frac{24}{28} = \frac{24 \div 2}{28 \div 2} = \frac{12}{14} = \frac{12 \div 2}{14 \div 2} = \frac{6}{7}$$

Sylvia said that this was wrong. She simplified $\frac{24}{28}$ by dividing both the numerator and denominator by 4 to get the fraction $\frac{6}{7}$.

$$\frac{24}{28} = \frac{24 \div 4}{28 \div 4} = \frac{6}{7}$$

Who is correct, Sylvia or Jim? Explain your answer using complete sentences.

2. Juan said that he found another method for simplifying $\frac{24}{28}$.

He wrote the prime factorizations of the numerator and denominator and then divided out common prime factors.

$$\frac{24}{28} = \frac{\cancel{2} \times \cancel{2} \times 2 \times 3}{\cancel{2} \times \cancel{2} \times 7} = \frac{6}{7}$$

Use Juan's method to simplify each fraction.

$$\frac{12}{18} = \underline{\hspace{2cm}} = \underline{\hspace{1cm}} \qquad \frac{15}{25} = \underline{\hspace{2cm}} = \underline{\hspace{1cm}}$$

$$\frac{25}{30} = \underline{\hspace{2cm}} = \underline{\hspace{1cm}} \qquad \frac{15}{24} = \underline{\hspace{2cm}} = \underline{\hspace{1cm}}$$

$$\frac{24}{30} = \underline{\hspace{2cm}} = \underline{\hspace{1cm}} \qquad \frac{42}{56} = \underline{\hspace{2cm}} = \underline{\hspace{1cm}}$$

© 2008 Carnegie Learning, Inc.

Problem 3

Celeste's Fundamental Rule for Simplifying Fractions in One Step

Celeste looked at Juan's method and recognized that 2 × 2 is 4 and 4 is the greatest common factor (GCF) of 24 and 28. She proposed Celeste's Fundamental Rule for Simplifying Fractions in One Step. Here's the rule:

To write a fraction in simplest form in one step, divide the numerator and the denominator by their GCF.

Does Celeste's rule work? Use complete sentences to explain why or why not.

2

Investigate Problem 3

1. Use Celeste's rule to simplify each fraction.

$$\frac{24}{30} = \frac{24 \div}{30 \div} = \text{—}$$ GCF:

$$\frac{56}{72} = \frac{56 \div}{72 \div} = \text{—}$$ GCF:

$$\frac{72}{90} = \frac{72 \div}{90 \div} = \text{—}$$ GCF:

$$\frac{44}{55} = \frac{44 \div}{55 \div} = \text{—}$$ GCF:

$$\frac{36}{60} = \frac{36 \div}{60 \div} = \text{—}$$ GCF:

$$\frac{100}{150} = \frac{100 \div}{150 \div} = \text{—}$$ GCF:

2. In this lesson, you have found several methods for simplifying fractions completely. Explain how you know when a fraction is completely simplified. Use complete sentences.

2

When Bigger Means Smaller
Comparing and Ordering Fractions

Objectives

In this lesson, you will:

- Compare and order fractions.

Key Terms

- least common denominator
- less than
- greater than

2

Problem 1   *Something's Fishy*

Your friends Tasha and Courtney are twins. They each have identical tropical fish tanks in their room, except that the number of fish in each tank is different. Tasha has 9 tetras and 5 of them are blue. Courtney has 9 tetras and 4 of them are blue.

A. Tasha and Courtney are arguing how someone knows when one fraction is greater than another.

Tasha says that the sizes of the numbers in the numerator and denominator are not important, but rather it is the quantity that the fraction represents that is important.

Courtney says that the size of the numerator tells you how big the fraction is. Who is correct? How can you explain to both of them how you know whether one fraction is greater than another? Use the fraction of blue fish in each of their fish tanks in your explanation.

B. Work with your partner to decide which fraction in each pair is greater. Circle the greater fraction.

$\dfrac{5}{8}$ and $\dfrac{7}{8}$ $\dfrac{5}{12}$ and $\dfrac{7}{12}$ $\dfrac{5}{8}$ and $\dfrac{1}{2}$ $\dfrac{5}{6}$ and $\dfrac{11}{12}$

Write complete sentences to explain how you knew which of the fractions was greater in each pair.

1. We can use our knowledge of common fractions like $\frac{1}{2}$, $\frac{1}{3}$, $\frac{2}{3}$, $\frac{1}{4}$, and $\frac{3}{4}$ to help us compare fractions. For example, to compare the fractions $\frac{5}{8}$ and $\frac{11}{12}$ you know that $\frac{5}{8}$ is close to $\frac{4}{8}$, which equals $\frac{1}{2}$, and $\frac{11}{12}$ is close to 1. Because $\frac{1}{2}$ is less than 1, you can estimate that $\frac{5}{8}$ is less than $\frac{11}{12}$.

   Use this method to compare the following fraction pairs. Circle the greater fraction. Write complete sentences to explain how you knew which of the fractions was greater in each pair.

   $\frac{5}{12}$ and $\frac{10}{11}$

   $\frac{5}{6}$ and $\frac{7}{16}$

   $\frac{7}{24}$ and $\frac{1}{6}$

   $\frac{11}{15}$ and $\frac{17}{20}$

2. The method in Question 1 works pretty well for familiar fractions with relatively small denominators. Study the following fractions, and try to circle the greater fraction in each pair.

   $\frac{5}{24}$ and $\frac{7}{30}$ $\frac{7}{20}$ and $\frac{11}{30}$ $\frac{11}{25}$ and $\frac{17}{32}$ $\frac{13}{18}$ and $\frac{17}{24}$

3. As you can see, using the method in Question 1 becomes more difficult when the fractions have larger denominators, so we need to find a method that works for all fractions. Begin by comparing fractions using your fraction strips. Write all of the fractions that can be represented using the strips that represent $\frac{1}{4}$ and $\frac{1}{8}$.

   Then order the fractions from greatest to smallest. Why was this easy to do? Use complete sentences to explain.

Investigate Problem 1

4. List all of the fractions with denominators of 9 and 12 in order without using your fraction strips. Then check your answer using the fraction strips.

Why was this more difficult than ordering the fractions in Question 3? Use complete sentences to explain.

Problem 2 · A Better Way

A. Use the circles below to compare the fractions $\frac{3}{4}$ and $\frac{5}{6}$.

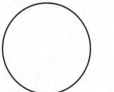

Write complete sentences to explain how you compared the fractions.

B. Here is a much more efficient method for comparing fractions. Take out your fraction strips for $\frac{1}{4}$, $\frac{1}{6}$, and $\frac{1}{12}$. Line up the strips so that the strip for $\frac{1}{12}$ is between the other two strips. How many twelfths are there in $\frac{3}{4}$? How many twelfths are there in $\frac{5}{6}$?

Investigate Problem 2

1. Knowing how many twelfths there are in each fraction makes it easy to compare $\frac{3}{4}$ and $\frac{5}{6}$. Recall from Lesson 1.3 that 12 is a common multiple of both 4 and 6. In fact, 12 is the least common multiple (LCM) of 4 and 6. Use complete sentences to explain why.

2. Math Path: Least Common Denominator

When we are working with fractions, you can use the LCM of the denominators to help you compare fractions. The LCM of two or more denominators is called the **least common denominator.** For example, 12 is the LCD of $\frac{3}{4}$ and $\frac{5}{6}$ because 12 is the LCM of 4 and 6. You can compare the fractions by writing fractions equivalent to $\frac{3}{4}$ and $\frac{5}{6}$ such that their denominators are 12.

$$\frac{3}{4} = \frac{3 \times 3}{4 \times 3} = \frac{9}{12} \qquad\qquad \frac{5}{6} = \frac{5 \times 2}{6 \times 2} = \frac{10}{12}$$

Now it is easy to see that $\frac{9}{12}$ is less than $\frac{10}{12}$ because we are comparing parts of the whole that is divided into the same number of parts, twelfths. So, you know that $\frac{3}{4}$ is less than $\frac{5}{6}$.

Find the LCD of fractions. Then use the LCD to rewrite each fraction. Circle the original fraction that is greater.

$$\frac{7}{8}, \frac{5}{6} \qquad \frac{7}{8} = \frac{7 \times}{8 \times} = \frac{}{} \qquad \frac{5}{6} = \frac{5 \times}{6 \times} = \frac{}{}$$

$$\frac{7}{9}, \frac{5}{6} \qquad \frac{7}{9} = \frac{7 \times}{9 \times} = \frac{}{} \qquad \frac{5}{6} = \frac{5 \times}{6 \times} = \frac{}{}$$

$$\frac{1}{6}, \frac{2}{15} \qquad \frac{1}{6} = \frac{1 \times}{6 \times} = \frac{}{} \qquad \frac{2}{15} = \frac{2 \times}{15 \times} = \frac{}{}$$

$$\frac{5}{8}, \frac{2}{3} \qquad \frac{5}{8} = \frac{5 \times}{8 \times} = \frac{}{} \qquad \frac{2}{3} = \frac{2 \times}{3 \times} = \frac{}{}$$

$$\frac{7}{20}, \frac{11}{30} \qquad \frac{7}{20} = \frac{7 \times}{20 \times} = \frac{}{} \qquad \frac{11}{30} = \frac{11 \times}{30 \times} = \frac{}{}$$

3. You can use the symbols **< (less than)** and **> (greater than)** to write a statement that compares two numbers. For example, you can say that $\frac{3}{4}$ is smaller than $\frac{5}{6}$ by writing $\frac{3}{4} < \frac{5}{6}$. Write a statement using < or > that compares each fraction pair in Question 2.

Looking Back at Chapter 2

Key Terms

fraction ⚬ p. 40
numerator ⚬ p. 40
denominator ⚬ p. 40
reasonable solution ⚬ p. 48
equivalent fractions ⚬ p. 54

equation ⚬ p. 54
simplest form ⚬ p. 58
simplest terms ⚬ p. 58
completely simplified ⚬ p. 58

least common denominator ⚬
  p. 66
less than ⚬ p. 66
greater than ⚬ p. 66

Summary

Writing Fractions (p. 40)

To write a fraction from a model, find the total number of parts. This number is the denominator. Then find the number of shaded parts. This number is the numerator.

Examples

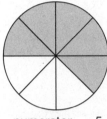

$$\frac{\text{numerator}}{\text{denominator}} = \frac{5}{8}$$

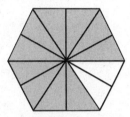

$$\frac{\text{numerator}}{\text{denominator}} = \frac{10}{12}$$

Using a Model to Represent Fractions (p. 42)

To use a circle to represent the fraction $\frac{a}{b}$, first divide the circle into b equal sections.

Then shade a sections of the circle.

Example   To use a circle to represent $\frac{3}{8}$, first divide the circle into 8 equal sections.

Then shade 3 of the sections.

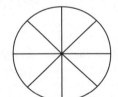  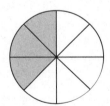

Dividing More Than One Whole into Parts (p. 45)

To divide more than one whole into n equal parts, first draw a diagram that represents all of the wholes. Then, divide each whole into n equal parts.

Example   To divide 4 pans of quiche for 5 family members, draw a diagram of the 4 pans of quiche. Then, divide each quiche into 5 equal parts. Each family member gets $\frac{4}{5}$ pan of quiche.

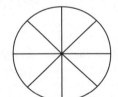

Determining Whether an Answer is Reasonable (p. 48)

To determine if an answer is a reasonable solution to a problem, think about the answer in the context of the problem.

Example

Dara is working in a computer lab. The lab has 50 computers and 36 keyboards. Dara decides that each computer gets $\frac{18}{25}$ keyboard.

The solution is *not* reasonable because each computer must have 1 whole keyboard to function properly. It doesn't make sense to use a part of a keyboard with a computer.

Dividing Groups into Fractional Parts (p. 49)

To find the fraction of items that you have out of a group of items, first find the number of items you have out of the group. This number is the numerator. Then find the total number of items in the group. This number is the denominator.

Example

A flower garden has 7 daisies, 12 violets, and 9 carnations. First draw a diagram of the situation.

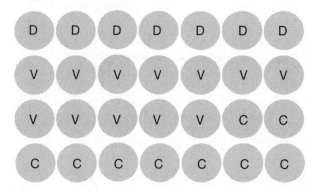

To write the fraction of the total flowers that are carnations, write the number of carnations as the numerator and the total number of flowers as the denominator. Carnations make up $\frac{9}{28}$ of the garden. To write the number of violets as a fraction of the total number of flowers, write the number of violets as the numerator and the total number of flowers as the denominator: $\frac{12}{28}$.

To write the number of daisies as a fraction of the total number of flowers, write the number of daisies as the numerator and the total number of flowers as the denominator: $\frac{7}{28}$.

Writing Equivalent Fractions (p. 54)

To write a fraction that is equivalent to a given fraction, multiply the numerator and denominator by the same number (that is, multiply the given fraction by the multiplicative identity, 1).

Examples

$$\frac{5}{7} = \frac{5 \times 4}{7 \times 4} = \frac{20}{28} \qquad \frac{4}{9} = \frac{4 \times 7}{9 \times 7} = \frac{28}{63} \qquad \frac{16}{21} = \frac{16 \times 5}{21 \times 5} = \frac{80}{105}$$

Writing Fractions in Simplest Form (p. 58)

To completely simplify a fraction, divide the numerator and the denominator by their GCF.

Examples

$$\frac{54}{171} = \frac{54 \div 9}{171 \div 9} = \frac{6}{19} \qquad\qquad \frac{112}{132} = \frac{112 \div 4}{132 \div 4} = \frac{28}{33}$$

$$\frac{96}{384} = \frac{96 \div 96}{384 \div 96} = \frac{1}{4} \qquad\qquad \frac{350}{1050} = \frac{350 \div 350}{1050 \div 350} = \frac{1}{3}$$

Comparing Fractions (p. 66)

To compare two fractions, use the least common denominator (LCD) to rewrite the fractions so that they have the same denominator. Then use <, >, or = to write a statement that compares the fractions.

Examples

$\dfrac{5}{6}$ and $\dfrac{4}{7}$ $\qquad$ $\dfrac{7}{8}$ and $\dfrac{11}{12}$ $\qquad$ $\dfrac{1}{9}$ and $\dfrac{2}{5}$

LCD: 42 $\qquad\qquad$ LCD: 24 $\qquad\qquad$ LCD: 45

$$\frac{5 \times 7}{6 \times 7} = \frac{35}{42} \qquad \frac{7 \times 3}{8 \times 3} = \frac{21}{24} \qquad \frac{1 \times 5}{9 \times 5} = \frac{5}{45}$$

$$\frac{4 \times 6}{7 \times 6} = \frac{24}{42} \qquad \frac{11 \times 2}{12 \times 2} = \frac{22}{24} \qquad \frac{2 \times 9}{5 \times 9} = \frac{18}{45}$$

$$\frac{5}{6} > \frac{4}{7} \qquad\qquad \frac{7}{8} < \frac{11}{12} \qquad\qquad \frac{1}{9} < \frac{2}{5}$$

Ordering Fractions (p. 66)

To order fractions, use the least common denominator (LCD) to rewrite the fractions so that they have the same denominator. Then write the fractions in order from least to greatest.

Example

The LCD of $\dfrac{2}{3}, \dfrac{5}{6}, \dfrac{7}{8},$ and $\dfrac{5}{12}$ is 24.

$$\frac{2}{3} = \frac{2 \times 8}{3 \times 8} = \frac{16}{24} \qquad \frac{5}{6} = \frac{5 \times 4}{6 \times 4} = \frac{20}{24} \qquad \frac{7}{8} = \frac{7 \times 3}{8 \times 3} = \frac{21}{24} \qquad \frac{5}{12} = \frac{5 \times 2}{12 \times 2} = \frac{10}{24}$$

The fractions in order from least to greatest are $\dfrac{5}{12}, \dfrac{2}{3}, \dfrac{5}{6},$ and $\dfrac{7}{8}$.

Looking Ahead to Chapter 3

Focus

In Chapter 3, you will work with fractions and mixed numbers. You will add, subtract, multiply, and divide fractions and mixed numbers. You will write fractions as mixed numbers and mixed numbers as fractions. You will also learn to work with measurements in customary units and convert measurements.

Chapter Warm-up

Answer these questions to help you review skills that you will need in Chapter 3.

Perform the indicated operation.

1. $138 + 587$

2. $964 - 26$

3. 14×52

4. 39×23

5. $1020 \div 68$

6. $2108 \div 31$

Write a fraction that is equivalent to the given fraction.

7. $\dfrac{5}{9}$

8. $\dfrac{17}{21}$

9. $\dfrac{25}{56}$

Write the fraction in simplest form.

10. $\dfrac{18}{27}$

11. $\dfrac{24}{64}$

12. $\dfrac{36}{108}$

Read the problem scenario below.

You ride a bicycle with tires that are 26 inches in diameter. You pedal at a rate of 50 revolutions per minute. You can travel about 340 feet in one minute.

13. Which units are used to measure distance?

14. Which units are used to measure time?

Key Terms

like fractions ● p. 75

unlike fractions ● p. 75

least common denominator ● p. 78

improper fractions ● p. 82

mixed number ● p. 82

U.S. customary system ● p. 85

metric system ● p. 85

remainder ● p. 89

multiplicative identity ● p. 91

multiplicative inverse ● p. 91

reciprocal ● p. 91

customary units of measure ● p. 101

length ● p. 101

inch ● p. 101

foot ● p. 101

yard ● p. 101

mile ● p. 101

capacity ● p. 101

fluid ounce ● p. 101

cup ● p. 101

pint ● p. 101

quart ● p. 101

gallon ● p. 101

weight ● p. 101

ounce ● p. 101

pound ● p. 101

ton ● p. 101

3

Operations with Fractions and Mixed Numbers

People in the U.S. eat an average of 4.5 pounds of strawberries each year. In Lesson 3.5, you will divide quarts of berries among people in order to learn about fraction division.

3

Who Gets What?

Adding and Subtracting Fractions with Like Denominators

Objectives

In this lesson, you will:
- Add and subtract like fractions.

Key Terms

- like fractions
- unlike fractions

Problem 1   Understanding Inheritance

After humankind began dividing wholes into parts, they had two problems:

How much do two or more people have altogether?

How much more does one person have than another?

For example, when a person dies, his or her possessions are divided among his or her children. The part that each child receives is called an inheritance.

A. In a family with two children, the oldest child receives two fifths of an inheritance and the youngest child receives one fifth. What fraction of the total inheritance do they receive altogether? Use your fraction strips to model the problem and find the answer.

B. Suppose that the oldest child receives three eighths of an inheritance and the youngest child receives two eighths. What fraction of the total inheritance do they receive altogether?

C. Suppose that four children in a family each receive $\frac{2}{9}$ of an inheritance. What fraction of the total inheritance do they receive altogether?

D. In parts (A), (B), and (C), you were adding fractions. Write your answer to each fraction addition problem below.

$$\frac{2}{5} + \frac{1}{5} = \qquad \frac{3}{8} + \frac{2}{8} = \qquad \frac{2}{9} + \frac{2}{9} + \frac{2}{9} + \frac{2}{9} =$$

E. Study each problem and answer. Then write complete sentences that explain how you can find the answer to a fraction addition problem without using fraction strips.

F. In each problem, what do you notice about the denominators of the addends and the denominator of the sum? Explain what you notice using complete sentences.

Take Note

Remember, when you add two numbers to produce another number, each number that you add is an *addend*.

1. Suppose that a child receives $\frac{4}{5}$ of an inheritance and a nephew receives $\frac{1}{5}$ of the inheritance. Use fraction subtraction to find the difference in the fractions of the inheritance that the child and the nephew receive. You may want to use your fraction strips to model the problem.

2. In California, if a person who has a spouse and four children dies with no will, then the spouse receives $\frac{4}{12}$ of the inheritance and each child receives $\frac{2}{12}$. Find the difference in the fractions of the inheritance that the spouse receives and one child receives. Simplify your answer, if possible.

3. In Massachusetts, if a person who has a spouse and three children dies with no will, then the spouse receives $\frac{3}{6}$ of the inheritance and each child receives $\frac{1}{6}$. Find the difference in the fraction of the inheritance that the spouse receives and one child receives. Simplify your answer, if possible.

4. In Questions 1, 2, and 3, you were subtracting fractions. For each question, write a fraction subtraction problem. Then find each difference.

5. Study each problem and answer. Then write complete sentences that explain how you can find the answer to a fraction subtraction problem without using fraction strips.

6. In each problem, what do you notice about the denominators of the fractions? Explain what you notice using complete sentences.

7. Math Path: Like and Unlike Fractions

Fractions that have the same denominator are called **like fractions.** Fractions that have different denominators are called **unlike fractions.** Which kind of fractions have we been adding and subtracting so far in this lesson? Work with your partner to write a rule for adding like fractions. Then write a rule for subtracting like fractions.

Rule for adding like fractions:

Rule for subtracting like fractions:

3

8. Use the rules that you wrote in Question 7 to find each sum and/or difference. Simplify your answer, if possible.

$$\frac{2}{5} + \frac{2}{5} = \qquad \frac{2}{7} + \frac{3}{7} = \qquad \frac{1}{8} + \frac{1}{8} =$$

$$\frac{6}{7} - \frac{3}{7} = \qquad \frac{1}{10} + \frac{3}{10} = \qquad \frac{8}{9} - \frac{2}{9} =$$

$$\frac{2}{7} + \frac{2}{7} + \frac{2}{7} = \qquad \frac{1}{6} + \frac{1}{6} + \frac{1}{6} =$$

$$\frac{1}{10} + \frac{3}{10} + \frac{3}{10} + \frac{1}{10} = \qquad \frac{5}{8} + \frac{1}{8} + \frac{1}{8} - \frac{3}{8} =$$

$$\frac{1}{12} + \frac{1}{12} + \frac{5}{12} = \qquad \frac{1}{16} + \frac{7}{16} - \frac{5}{16} =$$

© 2008 Carnegie Learning, Inc.

Take Note

Remember that the order of operations tells you to add and subtract real numbers from left to right.

3

Old-Fashioned Goodies

Adding and Subtracting Fractions with Unlike Denominators

Objectives

In this lesson, you will:

● Add and subtract unlike fractions.

Key Terms

● least common denominator

Problem 1   Candy Store

Your aunt is opening a store that sells old-fashioned goodies. She wants to offer molasses candy, hardtack candy, and popcorn balls. She has a recipe for popcorn balls that uses $\frac{1}{3}$ cup of corn syrup and a recipe that uses $\frac{1}{2}$ cup of corn syrup. If she wants to make one batch of each recipe, how much corn syrup does she need altogether?

A. Work with your partner and use your fraction strips to model the problem. Can you find an exact answer using just your $\frac{1}{2}$ and $\frac{1}{3}$ fraction strips? Use complete sentences to explain your answer.

B. Try using other fraction strips to find the answer. Were you able to find an exact answer? Use complete sentences to explain why or why not.

C. Form a group with another partner team. Take turns sharing how you solved the problem.

D. Which fraction strip helped you solve the problem? Is there only one fraction strip that will work? Use complete sentences to explain.

E. Use the fraction strip from part (D) to find an equivalent fraction for $\frac{1}{2}$. Then use this fraction strip to find an equivalent fraction for $\frac{1}{3}$. Now use your rule from Lesson 3.1 to add these two like fractions. Is your answer the same as your answer from Part (B)?

Investigate Problem 1

Work in your group and use your fraction strips to solve each problem.

1. Hardtack candy is an old-fashioned type of candy that uses flavoring oils like peppermint or cinnamon. Suppose you have two recipes for a batch of hardtack candy. One recipe calls for a dram (or $\frac{1}{4}$ tablespoon) of flavoring oil and another recipe uses a teaspoon (or $\frac{1}{3}$ tablespoon) of flavoring oil. How much total flavoring oil do you need to make one batch of both recipes? Use a complete sentence to write your answer.

2. A recipe for maple candy uses $\frac{3}{8}$ cup of brown sugar and a recipe for molasses candy uses $\frac{1}{2}$ cup of brown sugar. How much total brown sugar do you need to make one batch of both kinds of candy? Use a complete sentence to write your answer.

3. In your group, discuss how you solved these problems. For each problem, identify which fraction strips you used and explain your choices.

4. In your group, write a rule for adding unlike fractions.

   Rule for adding unlike fractions:

5. **Math Path: Least Common Denominator**

   You have seen that adding unlike fractions is different from adding like fractions. With like fractions, you can add the numerators to find your answer because the wholes are divided into the same number of parts. When you add unlike fractions, you cannot just add the numerators because the wholes are divided into different numbers of parts. So, you must first write the fractions as equivalent fractions that have the same number of parts, or denominator. It is most efficient to use the **least common denominator** (LCD), although any common denominator will work. Why is it more efficient to use the LCD? Use complete sentences to explain.

© 2008 Carnegie Learning, Inc.

6. Often it is easier to write fraction addition problems vertically. Let's do the fraction addition problems on the previous pages using this method. Start by finding the LCD. Why? Next, write equivalent fractions that have the LCD as their denominators. Finally, add the resulting fractions.

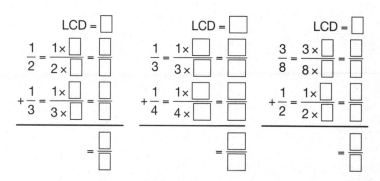

7. When we subtract unlike fractions, we follow a similar procedure. If a child got $\frac{1}{2}$ of an inheritance but gave away $\frac{1}{3}$ of it, how much would he have left? Use your fraction strips to model this problem. Do we have the same type of dilemma that we had when we added $\frac{1}{2}$ and $\frac{1}{3}$? Use an additional fraction strip to solve the problem. Which fraction strip did you use? Why? Use the space below to write the steps you need to follow to subtract unlike fractions.

8. Suppose that Erica had $\frac{7}{8}$ of a pizza and gave your little brother Manuel $\frac{1}{4}$. How much does Erica have left? Do this problem numerically below and write an explanation of what you are doing and why so that Erica can explain it to Manuel.

$$LCD = \square$$

$$\frac{7}{8} = \frac{7 \times \square}{8 \times \square} = \frac{\square}{\square}$$

$$-\frac{1}{4} = \frac{1 \times \square}{4 \times \square} = \frac{\square}{\square}$$

$$= \frac{\square}{\square}$$

9. Find each difference numerically. Simplify your answer, if possible.

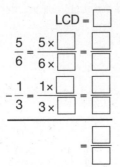
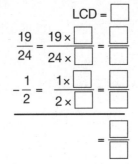

$$\frac{5}{6} - \frac{1}{3} =$$

$$\frac{19}{24} - \frac{1}{2} =$$

LCD = ☐

$$\frac{5}{6} = \frac{5 \times \square}{6 \times \square} = \frac{\square}{\square}$$

$$-\frac{1}{3} = \frac{1 \times \square}{3 \times \square} = \frac{\square}{\square}$$

$$= \frac{\square}{\square}$$

LCD = ☐

$$\frac{19}{24} = \frac{19 \times \square}{24 \times \square} = \frac{\square}{\square}$$

$$-\frac{1}{2} = \frac{1 \times \square}{2 \times \square} = \frac{\square}{\square}$$

$$= \frac{\square}{\square}$$

10. Find each sum or difference.

$$\frac{11}{12} - \frac{2}{3} =$$

$$\frac{1}{12} + \frac{1}{4} =$$

$$\frac{11}{18} + \frac{1}{3} =$$

$$\frac{13}{15} - \frac{2}{3} =$$

$$\frac{1}{6} + \frac{2}{5} =$$

$$\frac{3}{10} + \frac{2}{5} =$$

$$\frac{5}{16} + \frac{1}{4} =$$

$$\frac{17}{18} - \frac{2}{3} =$$

$$\frac{3}{4} + \frac{1}{8} + \frac{1}{8} =$$

3.3 Fun and Games
Improper Fractions and Mixed Numbers

Objectives

In this lesson, you will:
- Write improper fractions as mixed numbers.
- Write mixed numbers as improper fractions.

Key Terms
- improper fraction
- mixed number

Problem 1   Making a Spinner

You and your friend have created your own board game. Now you need to make a circular spinner for the game. You want the spinner to have two colors, red and blue. You divide the spinner into 5 equal parts and paint $\frac{3}{5}$ of the spinner red and $\frac{2}{5}$ of the spinner blue.

A. In the game, Player 1 moves a red game piece 1 space if the spinner lands on red. Otherwise, Player 1 does not move the game piece. In a similar way, Player 2 moves a blue game piece 1 space if the spinner lands on blue. Otherwise, Player 2 does not move the game piece. Is the spinner fair? Use complete sentences to explain why or why not.

B. Write the fraction addition problem that represents the total part of the spinner that is painted.

C. What do you know about a fraction whose numerator and denominator are equal? Explain your answer using complete sentences.

D. What if you wanted to paint the spinner so that $\frac{3}{5}$ of the spinner was red and $\frac{3}{5}$ of the spinner was blue? Is this possible? Use complete sentences to explain.

1. Write the fraction addition problem that represents the situation in Part (D) of Problem 1 and find the answer.

2. Is your answer to Question 1 less than, equal to, or greater than 1? How do you know? Use complete sentences to explain.

3. What can you conclude about a fraction whose numerator is greater than its denominator? Write your answer using a complete sentence.

4. Math Path: Improper Fractions

A fraction whose numerator is greater than its denominator is called an **improper fraction.** Usually we do not write an answer as an improper fraction. Instead, we simplify the answer by writing the improper fraction as a **mixed number.** A mixed number is a number that is the sum of a whole number and a fraction. For instance, you can write your answer to Question 1 as the sum of a whole number and a fraction. Because you know that $\frac{5}{5}$ is equal to one whole, you can write $\frac{6}{5}$ as $\frac{5}{5} + \frac{1}{5}$, or 1 whole and $\frac{1}{5}$ which is the mixed number $1\frac{1}{5}$.

Write each improper fraction as a mixed number.

$\frac{7}{4} =$ $\qquad$ $\frac{9}{8} =$ $\qquad$ $\frac{12}{5} =$ $\qquad$ $\frac{9}{4} =$

$\frac{16}{9} =$ $\qquad$ $\frac{11}{4} =$ $\qquad$ $\frac{14}{3} =$ $\qquad$ $\frac{25}{6} =$

5. Find the sum. Simplify your answer, if possible.

$\frac{3}{4} + \frac{3}{4} =$ $\qquad\qquad$ $\frac{7}{8} + \frac{5}{8} =$

$\frac{5}{6} + \frac{1}{6} =$

$\frac{1}{4} + \frac{5}{6} =$ $\qquad\qquad$ $\frac{3}{4} + \frac{1}{3} =$ $\qquad\qquad$ $\frac{5}{8} + \frac{2}{3} =$

3

Take Note

Remember when you learned long division? When you divided and got a remainder, you were told to write the remainder over the divisor. For example, when you divided 27 by 5, you were really just writing the improper fraction $\frac{27}{5}$ as $5\frac{2}{5}$.

$$5\frac{2}{5}$$
$$5\overline{)27}$$
$$\underline{25}$$
$$2$$

Problem 2

You are making jump ropes for your cousins. You need $1\frac{1}{4}$ yards of rope for your older cousin Teesha's jump rope and $\frac{3}{4}$ yard of rope for your younger cousin Samantha's jump rope. How much more rope do you need for Teesha's jump rope?

A. Write the subtraction problem that represents this situation.

B. To subtract $\frac{3}{4}$ from $1\frac{1}{4}$, you cannot subtract the numerator 3 from the numerator 1, so you need to regroup $1\frac{1}{4}$ as $\frac{4}{4}$ and $\frac{1}{4}$. Fill in the blanks to regroup, then subtract.

$$1\frac{1}{4} - \frac{3}{4} = \left(\frac{4}{4} + \frac{1}{4}\right) - \frac{3}{4} = \frac{\square}{4} - \frac{3}{4} = \frac{\square}{4} = \frac{\square}{\square}$$

Take Note

Regrouping a mixed number to subtract is similar to regrouping to subtract whole numbers. For instance, to subtract 19 from 23, you need to regroup 23 as 1 ten and 13 ones so that you can subtract 9 from 13.

$$\begin{array}{r} {\scriptstyle 1\ 13} \\ \cancel{2}\ \cancel{3} \\ -1\ 9 \\ \hline 4 \end{array}$$

Investigate Problem 2

1. To write a mixed number as an improper fraction, we need to write the whole number as an equivalent number of fractional parts and then add the like fractions. Fill in the blanks to write $2\frac{1}{5}$ as an improper fraction.

$$2\frac{1}{5} = 2 + \frac{1}{5} = \frac{\square}{5} + \frac{1}{5} = \frac{\square}{5}$$

2. Write each mixed number as an improper fraction.

$3\frac{1}{4} =$ $1\frac{3}{8} =$ $2\frac{1}{7} =$

$1\frac{5}{6} =$ $5\frac{1}{3} =$ $3\frac{1}{9} =$

3. Find each difference.

$1\frac{3}{8} - \frac{5}{8} =$ $1\frac{3}{5} - \frac{4}{5} =$ $1\frac{1}{8} - \frac{3}{4} =$

$1\frac{1}{3} - \frac{5}{6} =$ $1\frac{3}{7} - \frac{5}{7} =$ $1\frac{2}{9} - \frac{2}{3} =$

3

3

Parts of Parts
Multiplying Fractions

Objectives

In this lesson, you will:
- Multiply fractions.

Key Terms

- U.S. customary system
- metric system

When humankind began to group together in societies, the concept of ownership and inheritance became very important. Eventually as the population increased, there was a need to extend this ownership to plots of land.

Problem 1   The First Gardens

A. A rectangle was likely one of the first shapes that humans used to designate plots of land. They measured the plots by walking and measuring the distance with the number of steps (or paces) they had to take. You probably remember that the area of a rectangle can be found by multiplying its length by its width.
In the plot below, the length is 5 paces and the width is 3 paces. What is the area of the plot?

5 paces

3 paces

B. What are the units for the area of the plot? Use complete sentences to explain your choice.

C. The problem that eventually occurred was that different people have different paces. Why would this be a problem? Write your answer using a complete sentence.

D. Eventually people developed whole systems of measurement to ensure consistency. The two measurement systems that are used today are the **United States customary system** and the **metric system.** Write as many units as you know in the U.S. customary system and in the metric system.

U.S. customary system:

Metric system:

You will learn more about each of these systems in this chapter and in Chapter 4.

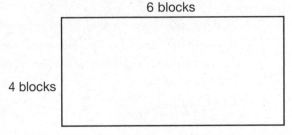

Investigate Problem 1

1. A group of students at your school decides to turn a plot of land in the city into a community garden. Find the area of the plot of land below. Be sure to include the units in your answer.

6 blocks

4 blocks

2. As part of the group, your job is to divide each square block into garden plots. How do you find the area of a part of a block? Suppose you need to find the area of a plot that has a length of $\frac{1}{2}$ of a block and a width of $\frac{1}{3}$ of a block. Use the diagram below to determine the number of parts that one square block can be divided into in this way.

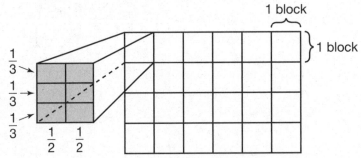

1 block

1 block

$\frac{1}{3}$
$\frac{1}{3}$
$\frac{1}{3}$

$\frac{1}{2}$ $\frac{1}{2}$

3. What does each of these parts represent? What is the area of a part? Use complete sentences to answer each question.

4. Represent this problem as a fraction multiplication problem. Then find the product.

5. What is the area of a plot that is $\frac{2}{3}$ block long and $\frac{1}{2}$ block wide?

Use the square to draw a diagram that represents this problem.

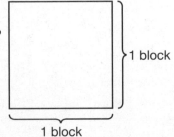

1 block

1 block

© 2008 Carnegie Learning, Inc.

6. The situation in Question 5 can be written as the product of two fractions. Write an expression that represents this situation in Question 5.

7. What is the area of a plot that is $\frac{2}{3}$ mile wide and $\frac{3}{4}$ mile long?

Use the diagram below. Explain how you found your answer. Then write and evaluate the expression that represents this situation. Simplify your answer, if possible.

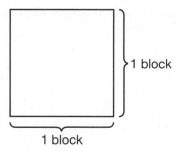

1 block

1 block

8. Form a group with another partner team. Review the products of fractions that you wrote. Then work with your group to determine a procedure for finding the answers without using a diagram. Explain your procedure using complete sentences.

3

9. Each group should take turns sharing their procedure with the entire class. Does everyone agree with your group's procedure?

10. Use your procedure to multiply each fraction. Write each answer in simplest form.

$$\frac{2}{3} \times \frac{2}{5} =$$

$$\frac{3}{8} \times \frac{5}{7} =$$

$$\frac{3}{4} \times \frac{5}{6} =$$

$$\frac{4}{5} \times \frac{5}{8} =$$

11. Examine the methods used below to multiply and simplify $\frac{3}{8} \times \frac{4}{9}$.

$$\frac{3}{8} \times \frac{4}{9} = \frac{12}{72} = \frac{12 \div 12}{72 \div 12} = \frac{1}{6}$$

$$\frac{3}{8} \times \frac{4}{9} = \frac{12}{72} = \frac{\overset{1}{\cancel{12}} \times 1}{\underset{1}{\cancel{12}} \times 6} = \frac{1}{6}$$

$$\frac{3}{8} \times \frac{4}{9} = \frac{\overset{1}{\cancel{3}} \times \overset{1}{\cancel{2}} \times \overset{1}{\cancel{2}}}{\underset{1}{\cancel{2}} \times \underset{1}{\cancel{2}} \times 2 \times \underset{1}{\cancel{3}} \times 3} = \frac{1}{6}$$

$$\frac{\overset{1}{\cancel{3}}}{\underset{2}{\cancel{8}}} \times \frac{\overset{1}{\cancel{4}}}{\underset{3}{\cancel{9}}} = \frac{1}{6}$$

$$\frac{3}{8} \times \frac{4}{9} = \frac{\overset{1}{\cancel{12}}}{\underset{6}{\cancel{72}}} = \frac{1}{6}$$

$$\frac{3}{8} \times \frac{4}{9} = \frac{\overset{4}{\cancel{12}}}{\underset{24}{\cancel{72}}} = \frac{\overset{1}{\cancel{4}}}{\underset{6}{\cancel{24}}} = \frac{1}{6}$$

Discuss each of the methods with your group. Do all methods produce the same answer?

How are the methods alike? How are the methods different? Use complete sentences to answer each question.

Are all of the methods correct? Use complete sentences to explain your answer.

What conclusions can you make about the procedure for multiplying fractions?

3.5 Parts in a Part
Dividing Fractions

Objectives

In this lesson, you will:
- Divide fractions.

Key Terms
- remainder
- multiplicative identity
- multiplicative inverse
- reciprocal

Take Note

Recall that the **remainder** is the whole number left over in a division problem if the divisor does not divide the dividend evenly. For example, when 17 is divided by 3, the remainder is 2.

$$\begin{array}{r} 5 \\ 3\overline{)17} \\ \underline{15} \\ 2 \end{array}$$

Problem 1   Dividing Berries

Suppose that you want to solve the division problem $\frac{3}{4} \div \frac{1}{3}$. Let's first review what we know about division.

A. Remember that one way to think about division is to think of it as repeated subtraction. For example, to solve the division problem $12 \div 3$, ask yourself, "How many times can I take a group of 3 quarts of berries away from a group of 12 quarts of berries?" Draw a diagram to explain your answer.

B. Another way to think about the division problem $12 \div 3$ is to think of dividing 12 quarts of berries evenly among 3 people. This strategy works pretty well when the number you are dividing by is a factor of the dividend, but what happens when we need to divide 13 quarts of berries evenly among 3 people? How much does each person receive? Explain to your partner how you found your answer.

C. You may remember that when you first learned about division, you divided 13 by 4 and wrote the answer as 3 with a remainder of 1. Later you were probably told to express the amount left over as a fraction by writing the remainder over the divisor. Does it make sense to you now why you wrote the amount left over as a fraction? Explain this to your partner, and listen to his or her explanation. Do the two of you agree? Explain why or why not using complete sentences.

3

1. Before we evaluate the fraction division problem $\frac{3}{4} \div \frac{1}{3}$, consider $\frac{3}{4} \div \frac{1}{2}$. Another way to think of this problem is to ask, "How many $\frac{1}{2}$s are there in $\frac{3}{4}$? Use your fraction strips and your knowledge of subtracting fractions to determine how many times you can subtract $\frac{1}{2}$ from $\frac{3}{4}$. How much will be left over? This is the remainder. Use complete sentences in your answers.

2. Consider $\frac{2}{4} \div \frac{1}{2}$. Use your fraction strips to determine the number of $\frac{1}{2}$s that there are in $\frac{2}{4}$. How much is left over? Use a complete sentence to answer the question.

3. In both Questions 1 and 2, the whole number parts in the answer are the same, but with $\frac{3}{4} \div \frac{1}{2}$ we have a remainder.

   If we were working with whole numbers, we would simply write the amount left over as a fraction with the remainder as the numerator and the divisor as the denominator. In Question 1, the remainder is a fraction and the divisor is also a fraction. Write the amount left over as a fraction divided by a fraction.

   Amount left over: $\dfrac{\dfrac{\Box}{\Box} \leftarrow \text{Remainder}}{\dfrac{\Box}{\Box} \leftarrow \text{Denominator}}$

4. According to the definition of a fraction, the question we want to answer is "What part of the denominator is represented by the numerator?" Write both the numerator and denominator as like fractions. Can you answer the question now? Work with your partner to determine the final answer to the following fraction division problem. Then share how you found your answer with another partner team.

   $$\frac{3}{4} \div \frac{1}{2} =$$

5. Now let's evaluate our original expression, $\dfrac{3}{4} \div \dfrac{1}{3}$. How many $\dfrac{1}{3}$s are there in $\dfrac{3}{4}$? What amount is left over? What part of $\dfrac{1}{3}$ is this? Use complete sentences to explain how you know.

6. Math Path: Dividing Fractions

Using either fraction strips or like denominators to divide fractions will become difficult as we work with fractions with larger denominators. There is a more efficient and easier method for dividing fractions. This method works because of some special properties that we discovered earlier:

Division by 1: Whenever we divide any number by 1, the answer is always the number itself.

$a \div 1 = a$

Multiplicative identity: The product of any number and 1 is the number. So, the **multiplicative identity** is the number 1.

$a \times 1 = a$

Fractions equal to 1: Any fraction whose nonzero numerator and nonzero denominator are the same is equal to 1.

$\dfrac{a}{a} = 1$

Multiplicative inverse: The product of any nonzero number and its multiplicative inverse is 1. The **multiplicative inverse** of a number is also known as the **reciprocal** of the number.

$\dfrac{a}{b} \times \dfrac{b}{a} = 1$

Examine the division of fractions shown below.

$$\dfrac{3}{4} \div \dfrac{1}{2} = \dfrac{\frac{3}{4}}{\frac{1}{2}} = \dfrac{\frac{3}{4}}{\frac{1}{2}} \times \dfrac{\frac{2}{1}}{\frac{2}{1}} = \dfrac{\frac{3 \times 2}{4 \times 1}}{\frac{1 \times 2}{2 \times 1}} = \dfrac{\frac{6}{4}}{1} = \dfrac{^3\cancel{6}}{_2\cancel{4}} = \dfrac{3}{2} = 1\dfrac{1}{2}$$

Fractions equal to 1: $\dfrac{\frac{2}{1}}{\frac{2}{1}}$ Multiplicative identity: $\dfrac{3}{4} \times \dfrac{\frac{2}{1}}{\frac{1}{2}}$

Multiplicative inverse: $\dfrac{1 \times 2}{2 \times 1}$ Division by 1: $\dfrac{\frac{6}{4}}{1}$

Circle each property listed above in the fraction division problem.

7. Compare the division of fractions in Question 6 with the following.

$$\frac{3}{4} \div \frac{1}{2} = \frac{3}{4} \times \frac{2}{1} = \frac{\overset{3}{\cancel{6}}}{\underset{2}{\cancel{4}}} = \frac{3}{2} = 1\frac{1}{2}$$

Is the method used above the same as the method used in Question 6? How do you know? Which steps have been removed? Use complete sentences to write your answers.

8. Use the method demonstrated in Question 7 to evaluate the expression $\frac{3}{4} \div \frac{1}{3}$.

$$\frac{3}{4} \div \frac{1}{3} =$$

9. Use the method in Question 7 to find each quotient.

$$\frac{3}{8} \div \frac{3}{4} =$$

$$\frac{5}{6} \div \frac{2}{3} =$$

$$\frac{7}{8} \div \frac{3}{4} =$$

$$\frac{11}{12} \div \frac{1}{3} =$$

$$\frac{9}{10} \div \frac{2}{5} =$$

3.6 All That Glitters
Adding and Subtracting Mixed Numbers

Objectives

In this lesson, you will:
- Add and subtract mixed numbers.

Key Terms

- mixed number

In Lesson 3.3, we said that a *mixed number* has a whole number part and a fractional part. Because we know how to add, subtract, multiply, and divide fractions, we can now solve problems involving operations with mixed numbers.

Problem 1   Gold Ingots

Suppose that you are a treasure hunter searching a Spanish shipwreck from the 1600s and you find gold bars, called ingots. The treasure consists of whole gold ingots, one-half ingots, and one-third ingots. If you find $3\frac{1}{3}$ gold ingots on the first day and $1\frac{1}{3}$ gold ingots on the second day, what is the total number of ingots that you have?

A. Represent this problem by drawing a diagram below of the amount you found on the first day and the second day.

B. How many full bars do you have? What fractional part of a bar do you have? Use a complete sentence to write your answer.

C. Write your total as a single mixed number. Then use complete sentences to explain how you can find this total without drawing a picture.

1. Use the method you described in part (C) to find each sum.

$2\dfrac{1}{3} + 3\dfrac{1}{3} =$ $\qquad$ $1\dfrac{2}{5} + 4\dfrac{2}{5} =$ $\qquad$ $5\dfrac{3}{8} + 4\dfrac{1}{4} =$

$3\dfrac{1}{3} + 3\dfrac{1}{6} =$ $\qquad$ $4\dfrac{1}{3} + 3\dfrac{2}{3} =$ $\qquad$ $5\dfrac{4}{7} + 2\dfrac{3}{7} =$

2. If you find $2\dfrac{3}{5}$ gold ingots and then find an additional $3\dfrac{3}{5}$ ingots, how many ingots do you have altogether? Draw a diagram that represents the problem. Use your diagram to answer Question 3.

3. How many full bars do you have? What fractional part of a bar do you have? Write your answer using a complete sentence.

4. Write your total as a single mixed number. Then use complete sentences to explain how you can get this answer without drawing a picture.

5. Use the method you described in Question 4 to find each sum.

$3\dfrac{2}{3} + 2\dfrac{2}{3} =$ $\qquad$ $2\dfrac{4}{5} + 2\dfrac{4}{5} =$ $\qquad$ $3\dfrac{7}{8} + 5\dfrac{1}{4} =$

$5\dfrac{2}{3} + 6\dfrac{5}{6} =$ $\qquad$ $9\dfrac{2}{3} + 3\dfrac{5}{9} =$ $\qquad$ $7\dfrac{5}{5} + \dfrac{4}{9} =$

6. What if you found $3\frac{2}{3}$ ingots and gave your friend $1\frac{1}{3}$ of them?

Draw a diagram that represents the problem. Use your diagram to answer Question 7.

7. How many full bars do you have? What fractional part of a bar do you have? Write your answer using a complete sentence.

8. Write your total as a single mixed number. Then use complete sentences to explain how you can get this answer without drawing a picture.

9. Use the method you described in Question 8 to find each difference.

$3\frac{2}{3} - 1\frac{1}{3} =$ $5\frac{4}{5} - 2\frac{3}{5} =$ $5\frac{7}{8} - 2\frac{3}{8} =$

$6\frac{2}{3} - 5\frac{1}{6} =$ $3\frac{2}{5} - 3\frac{3}{10} =$ $7\frac{4}{5} - \frac{2}{3} =$

10. What if you found $3\frac{1}{3}$ ingots and gave your friend $1\frac{2}{3}$ of them?

Draw a diagram that represents the problem. Use your diagram to answer Question 11.

11. How many full bars do you have? What fractional part of a bar do you have? Write your answer using a complete sentence.

12. Write your total as a single mixed number. What additional step do you need to include when performing the subtraction? Use complete sentences to explain how you can get this answer without drawing a picture.

13. Use the method you described in Question 12 to find each difference.

$4\frac{1}{3} - 2\frac{2}{3} =$ $4\frac{2}{5} - 3\frac{3}{5} =$

$4\frac{1}{8} - \frac{3}{8} =$ $4\frac{1}{3} - 1\frac{5}{6} =$

$9\frac{1}{5} - 2\frac{9}{10} =$ $8\frac{1}{5} - 4\frac{2}{3} =$

$6\frac{7}{12} - 3\frac{7}{8} =$ $5\frac{1}{6} - 1\frac{5}{9} =$

Project Display
Multiplying and Dividing Mixed Numbers

Objectives

In this lesson, you will:
- Multiply and divide mixed numbers.

Key Terms

- reciprocal

You may remember that when we multiplied two fractions in Lesson 3.4, we used an area model to find the product. We can also use an area model to find the product of two mixed numbers.

Problem 1   Model of Your School

For a project, you are making a scale model of your school from foam board. You mark a rectangle on the board so that the rectangle's length is $1\frac{1}{2}$ feet and its width is $1\frac{1}{3}$ feet, as shown in the diagram.

The area of the rectangular piece of board is the product of the rectangle's length and width, or $1\frac{1}{2} \times 1\frac{1}{3}$ feet.

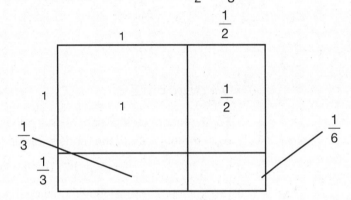

A. We can add the areas of the parts to find the total area. Fill in the blanks to find the total area.

$$1 + \frac{1}{3} + \frac{1}{2} + \frac{1}{6} = 1 + \frac{\square}{6} + \frac{\square}{6} + \frac{1}{6} = 1 + \frac{\square}{6} = \square$$

B. We can also write the mixed numbers $1\frac{1}{2}$ and $1\frac{1}{3}$ as improper fractions and then multiply. Fill in the blanks to find the area.

$$1\frac{1}{2} \times 1\frac{1}{3} = \frac{\square}{2} \times \frac{\square}{3} = \frac{\square}{\square} = \frac{2}{1} = 2$$

It is more efficient to multiply mixed numbers by first writing them as improper fractions and then using the procedure for multiplying fractions.

Investigate Problem 1

1. Find each product.

$2\dfrac{2}{3} \times 1\dfrac{1}{3} =$ $\qquad$ $2\dfrac{1}{2} \times 3\dfrac{1}{5} =$

$2\dfrac{1}{4} \times 4\dfrac{2}{3} =$ $\qquad$ $4\dfrac{1}{5} \times 2\dfrac{1}{7} =$

$1\dfrac{2}{5} \times 2\dfrac{3}{4} =$ $\qquad$ $3\dfrac{3}{8} \times 2\dfrac{2}{3} =$

$4\dfrac{1}{6} \times \dfrac{1}{2} =$ $\qquad$ $1\dfrac{5}{6} \times \dfrac{1}{2} =$

$2\dfrac{5}{8} \times 4 =$ $\qquad$ $3 \times 2\dfrac{3}{4} =$

Problem 2 · Making Model Desks

For the model of your school, you need to make a teacher's desk for each room. You cut the models for the tops of the desks out of balsa wood that is $1\dfrac{1}{4}$ inches wide. The length of the piece of balsa wood is $4\dfrac{1}{2}$ inches. How many model desk tops can you cut if you want each model to be $\dfrac{3}{4}$ inch by $1\dfrac{1}{4}$ inches?

A. Use your ruler to divide the wood to find the number of model desk tops that you can make.

$1\dfrac{1}{4}$ in.

$4\dfrac{1}{2}$ in.

B. This situation can be written as the quotient of two mixed numbers. Write and evaluate an expression that represents this situation.

© 2008 Carnegie Learning, Inc.

Investigate Problem 2

1. Math Path: Reciprocal

Recall from Lesson 3.5 that dividing by a fraction is the same as multiplying by the multiplicative inverse, or *reciprocal,* of the fraction. We can also divide mixed numbers by first writing them as improper fractions and then multiplying by the reciprocal. Fill in the blanks to find the product.

$$1\frac{2}{3} \div 1\frac{1}{2} = \frac{\square}{3} \div \frac{\square}{2} = \frac{5}{3} \times \frac{2}{3} = \frac{\square}{\square} = 1\frac{1}{9}$$

2. Find each quotient.

$$2\frac{1}{2} \div 3\frac{1}{3} =$$

$$2\frac{3}{4} \div 4\frac{2}{3} =$$

$$4\frac{1}{4} \div 2\frac{2}{3} =$$

$$3\frac{4}{5} \div 2\frac{3}{8} =$$

$$4\frac{3}{5} \div 1\frac{3}{7} =$$

$$4\frac{2}{3} \div 3\frac{4}{5} =$$

3. Find each quotient. Then check whether your answer is reasonable by rounding each mixed number to the nearest whole number and then dividing the whole numbers.

$$7\frac{2}{3} \div 1\frac{2}{3} =$$

$$6\frac{2}{9} \div 2\frac{7}{9} =$$

$$3\frac{1}{12} \div 1\frac{1}{6} =$$

$$8\frac{1}{8} \div 2\frac{1}{4} =$$

$$5\frac{3}{4} \div 2\frac{2}{3} =$$

$$4\frac{1}{5} \div 1\frac{5}{6} =$$

3

Carpenter, Baker, Mechanic, Chef
Working with Customary Units

Objectives

In this lesson, you will:

- Convert between customary units of measure.

Key Terms

- customary units of measure
- length: inch, foot, yard, mile
- capacity: fluid ounce, cup, pint, quart, gallon
- weight: ounce, pound, ton

After humankind began to own land and possessions, they needed to have a way to measure them.

Problem 1   Measure Up

At first people used body parts as measures. For instance, the length of a person's foot became the unit "one foot." The width of a person's thumb became the unit "one inch." The distance from a person's elbow to the tip of his or her finger became the unit "one cubit."

A. Turn to your partner and compare each of these "units of measure." What do you notice? Use complete sentences to describe your observations.

B. Obviously, there was a problem. People solved the problem by establishing standard units of measure that we use today, such as:

- inch, foot, yard, and mile to measure distance
- ounce, pound, and ton to measure weight
- fluid ounce, cup, pint, quart, and gallon to measure capacity

Work with your partner to complete the table that shows how the units are related.

U.S. Customary Units of Measure		
Length	**Weight**	**Capacity**
1 foot =_____inches	1 pound = ____ounces	1 cup = 8 fluid ounces
1 yard =_____feet	1 ton = _____pounds	1 pint = _____cups
1 yard = 36 inches		1 quart = _____pints
1 mile = _____feet		1 gallon = _____quarts
1 mile = 1760 yards		

1. Math Path: U.S. Customary System of Measure

Even when units were standardized, different countries often had different standard units of measure. The units shown in the table in part (B) are part of the U.S. customary system of measure.

One problem with the U.S. customary system is that the smallest unit of measure may not be small enough. For instance, how long is an object if its length is less than one inch? The U.S. customary system relies on fractional parts of measures. In fact, an inch on a ruler is divided into several different fractional parts. Below is an inch on a ruler that has been magnified. Label the fraction of an inch that each mark represents between 0 inch and 1 inch.

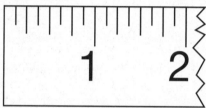

2. Use a ruler to measure each line segment. Be sure to include units in your answer.

Length = _____

_____

Length = _____

_____

Length = _____

_____

Length = _____

_____

Length = _____

_____

Length = _____

_____

A carpenter is building a house and needs to cut a 12-foot long board into pieces with the following lengths:

- Three pieces that are each $8\frac{3}{4}$ inches

- Four pieces that are each $6\frac{7}{8}$ inches

- Five pieces that are each $11\frac{5}{16}$ inches

Can she cut all of these pieces from the 12-foot board? If she can, what is the length of the board that she has left over? If she cannot, which pieces can she cut so that she wastes the least amount of material? Use complete sentences to explain your reasoning. Be prepared to share your solution with the class.

3

Problem 2B *Baker*

A baker wants to make the very best bread, and he must add just the right amount of yeast by weight. He wants to make the following:

- Four batches that each use $2\frac{3}{4}$ ounces of yeast

- Ten batches that each use $4\frac{2}{3}$ ounces of yeast

- Eight batches that each use $4\frac{1}{2}$ ounces of yeast

If he can only buy yeast by the pound, will one pound be enough? Exactly how much yeast will he need? If yeast sells for $3.98 per pound, how much money will the baker spend on yeast? Will he have any yeast left over? If so, how much will he have? Use complete sentences to explain your reasoning. Be prepared to share your solution with the class.

Problem 2C *Mechanic*

A mechanic owns a garage. The floor of the garage cannot hold more than 24,000 pounds of weight. In the garage, the mechanic has:

- Two cars that each weigh $1\frac{6}{10}$ tons

- Three trucks that each weigh $2\frac{7}{20}$ tons

- Eight motors that each weigh $\frac{1}{8}$ ton

Has the mechanic exceeded the floor's weight limit? If so, by how many tons is he over the limit? If not, how many more $\frac{1}{8}$-ton engines could he have in the garage? Use complete sentences to explain your reasoning. Be prepared to share your solution with the class.

Problem 2D *Chef*

A chef needs to make several large batches of different kinds of cookies. He has the following cookies to make:

- Five batches that each require $\frac{3}{4}$ cup of vanilla extract

- Six batches that each require $\frac{2}{3}$ cup of vanilla extract

- Eight batches that each require $\frac{1}{4}$ cup of vanilla extract

How much vanilla extract will he need to buy? If he can only buy it by the quart, will one quart be enough? If not, how many quarts will he need? Use complete sentences to explain your reasoning. Be prepared to share your solution with the class.

Looking Back at Chapter 3

Key Terms

like fractions   p. 75

unlike fractions   p. 75

least common denominator   p. 78

improper fractions   p. 82

mixed number   p. 82

U.S. customary system   p. 85

metric system   p. 85

remainder   p. 89

multiplicative identity   p. 91

multiplicative inverse   p. 91

reciprocal   p. 91

customary units of measure   p. 101

length   p. 101

inch   p. 101

foot   p. 101

yard   p. 101

mile   p. 101

capacity   p. 101

fluid ounce   p. 101

cup   p. 101

pint   p. 101

quart   p. 101

gallon   p. 101

weight   p. 101

ounce   p. 101

pound   p. 101

ton   p. 101

Summary

Adding Fractions with Like Denominators (p. 75)

To add fractions with like denominators, first add the numerators, then write a fraction using the sum of the numerators and the like denominator. Finally, simplify if possible.

Examples

$$\frac{1}{9}+\frac{4}{9}=\frac{1+4}{9}=\frac{5}{9}$$

$$\frac{1}{12}+\frac{3}{12}+\frac{5}{12}=\frac{1+3+5}{12}=\frac{9}{12}=\frac{3}{4}$$

Subtracting Fractions with Like Denominators (p. 75)

To subtract two fractions with like denominators, first subtract the numerators, then write a fraction using the difference of the numerators and the like denominator. Finally, simplify if possible.

Examples

$$\frac{7}{8}-\frac{2}{8}=\frac{7-2}{8}=\frac{5}{8}$$

$$\frac{11}{12}-\frac{8}{12}=\frac{11-8}{12}=\frac{3}{12}=\frac{1}{4}$$

Adding Fractions with Unlike Denominators (p. 78)

To add two fractions with unlike denominators, first find the least common denominator (LCD), then write equivalent fractions using the LCD. Next, add the resulting fractions. Finally, simplify if possible.

Examples

$$\frac{1}{4}+\frac{1}{6}=?$$

LCD: <u>12</u>

$$\frac{1}{4}=\frac{1\times3}{4\times3}=\frac{3}{12}$$

$$+\frac{1}{6}=\frac{1\times2}{6\times2}=\frac{2}{12}$$

$$=\frac{5}{12}$$

$$\frac{1}{9}+\frac{5}{12}=?$$

LCD: <u>36</u>

$$\frac{1}{9}=\frac{1\times4}{9\times4}=\frac{4}{36}$$

$$+\frac{5}{12}=\frac{5\times3}{12\times3}=\frac{15}{36}$$

$$=\frac{19}{36}$$

Subtracting Fractions with Unlike Denominators (p. 78)

To subtract two fractions with unlike denominators, first find the least common denominator (LCD), then write equivalent fractions using the LCD. Next, subtract the resulting fractions. Finally, simplify if possible.

Examples

$$\frac{11}{15} - \frac{2}{3} = ?$$

LCD: 15

$$\frac{11}{15} = \frac{11 \times 1}{15 \times 1} = \frac{11}{15}$$
$$-\frac{2}{3} = \frac{2 \times 5}{3 \times 5} = \frac{10}{15}$$
$$= \frac{1}{15}$$

$$\frac{8}{9} - \frac{1}{12} = ?$$

LCD: 36

$$\frac{8}{9} = \frac{8 \times 4}{9 \times 4} = \frac{32}{36}$$
$$-\frac{1}{12} = \frac{1 \times 3}{12 \times 3} = \frac{3}{36}$$
$$= \frac{29}{36}$$

Writing Improper Fractions as Mixed Numbers (p. 82)

To write an improper fraction as a mixed number, use long division.

Examples

$$\frac{28}{5} : \quad 5\overline{)28} \;\; \begin{array}{r} 5 \\ \underline{25} \\ 3 \end{array}$$

So, $\frac{28}{5} = 5\frac{3}{5}$.

$$\frac{37}{6} : \quad 6\overline{)37} \;\; \begin{array}{r} 6 \\ \underline{36} \\ 1 \end{array}$$

So, $\frac{37}{6} = 6\frac{1}{6}$.

Writing Mixed Numbers as Improper Fractions (p. 83)

To write a mixed number as an improper fraction, write the whole number as an equivalent fraction whose denominator is the same as the fractional part of the mixed number, then add the like fractions.

Examples

$$3\frac{3}{8} = 3 + \frac{3}{8} = \frac{24}{8} + \frac{3}{8} = \frac{27}{8}$$

So, $3\frac{3}{8} = \frac{27}{8}$.

$$7\frac{4}{9} = 7 + \frac{4}{9} = \frac{63}{9} + \frac{4}{9} = \frac{67}{9}$$

So, $7\frac{4}{9} = \frac{67}{9}$.

Multiplying Fractions (p. 86)

To multiply two fractions, first multiply the numerators, then multiply the denominators. Finally, simplify if possible.

Examples

$$\frac{3}{7} \times \frac{5}{6} = \frac{3 \times 5}{7 \times 6} = \frac{15}{42} = \frac{5}{14}$$

$$\frac{11}{15} \times \frac{5}{9} = \frac{11 \times 5}{15 \times 9} = \frac{55}{135} = \frac{11}{27}$$

Dividing Fractions (p. 92)

To divide two fractions, first find the reciprocal of the divisor, then multiply the dividend by the reciprocal of the divisor. Finally, simplify if possible.

Examples

$$\frac{5}{6} \div \frac{3}{4} = \frac{5}{6} \times \frac{4}{3} = \frac{20}{18} = \frac{10}{9} = 1\frac{1}{9}$$

$$\frac{7}{8} \div \frac{2}{5} = \frac{7}{8} \times \frac{5}{2} = \frac{35}{16} = 2\frac{3}{16}$$

3

Adding Mixed Numbers (p. 94)

To add two mixed numbers, first write the fractional parts using the LCD, then add the fractional parts. Next, add the whole number parts. Finally, simplify if possible.

Examples

$$2\frac{1}{4} = 2\frac{2}{8}$$
$$+ 1\frac{3}{8} = 1\frac{3}{8}$$
$$= 3\frac{5}{8}$$

$$4\frac{5}{6} = 4\frac{15}{18}$$
$$+ 2\frac{1}{9} = 2\frac{2}{18}$$
$$= 6\frac{17}{18}$$

$$7\frac{2}{3} = 7\frac{20}{30}$$
$$+ 3\frac{9}{10} = 3\frac{27}{30}$$
$$= 10\frac{47}{30} = 11\frac{17}{30}$$

Subtracting Mixed Numbers (p. 95)

To subtract two mixed numbers, first rewrite the fractional parts using the LCD. Then regroup the fractional parts if necessary and subtract the fractional parts. Next, subtract the whole number parts. Finally, simplify if possible.

Examples

$$7\frac{8}{11} = 7\frac{16}{22}$$
$$- 2\frac{1}{2} = 2\frac{11}{22}$$
$$= 5\frac{5}{22}$$

$$12\frac{5}{8} = 12\frac{5}{8} = 11\frac{13}{8}$$
$$- 7\frac{3}{4} = 7\frac{6}{8} = 7\frac{6}{8}$$
$$= 4\frac{7}{8}$$

Multiplying Mixed Numbers (p. 97)

To multiply two mixed numbers, first write each mixed number as an improper fraction, then multiply the improper fractions. Finally, simplify if possible.

Examples

$$2\frac{6}{7} \times 3\frac{1}{4} = \frac{20}{7} \times \frac{13}{4} = \frac{260}{28} = \frac{65}{7} = 9\frac{2}{7}$$

Dividing Mixed Numbers (p. 99)

To divide two mixed numbers, first write each mixed number as an improper fraction. Then, multiply by the reciprocal. Finally, simplify if possible.

Examples

$$5\frac{3}{8} \div 3\frac{1}{4} = \frac{43}{8} \div \frac{13}{4} = \frac{43}{\underset{2}{8}} \times \frac{\overset{1}{4}}{13} = \frac{43}{26} = 1\frac{17}{26}$$

Converting Between Customary Units of Measure (p. 101)

To convert between customary units of measure, you need to know the values for common customary units, as shown in Lesson 3.8.

Example

You are making 6 bracelets. Each bracelet uses $6\frac{1}{2}$ inches of string.

How many feet of string will you use for all 6 bracelets?

$$6 \times 6\frac{1}{2} = \frac{6}{1} \times \frac{13}{2} = \frac{78}{2} = 39;\ 39 \text{ in.} \times \frac{1\text{ ft}}{12\text{ in.}} = \frac{39}{1} \text{ in.} \times \frac{1\text{ ft}}{12\text{ in.}} = \frac{39}{12} \text{ ft} = 3\frac{1}{4} \text{ ft}$$

You will use $3\frac{1}{4}$ feet of string.

3

Looking Ahead to Chapter 4

Focus   In Chapter 4, you will work with decimals. You will write decimals in different forms. You will compare, order, and round decimals. You will add, subtract, multiply, and divide decimals. You will also learn to work with measurements in metric units and convert measurements.

Chapter Warm-up

Answer these questions to help you review skills that you will need in Chapter 4.

Perform the indicated operation.

1. 1047 + 398
2. 15,743 − 207
3. 49 × 56
4. 931 × 574
5. 3822 ÷ 42
6. 5355 ÷ 63

Find the sum or difference of the mixed numbers.

7. $9\frac{8}{11} + 3\frac{7}{8}$
8. $11\frac{2}{3} + 14\frac{5}{18}$
9. $16\frac{1}{2} - 4\frac{5}{6}$

Complete the statement.

10. 25 lb = _____ oz
11. 4 gallons = _____ cups
12. 8 inches = _____ foot

Read the problem scenario below.

You are a statistician for your school's track team. The table shows the finishing times in minutes for a 200-meter race.

Runner	Time (minutes)	Runner	Time (minutes)	Runner	Time (minutes)
Jack	$\frac{5}{6}$	Gary	$\frac{7}{12}$	Ivan	$\frac{8}{18}$
Allison	$\frac{11}{18}$	Janessa	$\frac{1}{3}$	Claudia	$\frac{1}{2}$

13. Order the times from least to greatest.

14. Which team member finished third?

Key Terms

decimal   p. 113

place-value chart   p. 116

standard form   p. 116

expanded form   p. 117

round a decimal   p. 122

base-ten pieces   p. 125

product   p. 127

quotient   p. 131

dividend   p. 131

divisor   p. 132

metric system   p. 133

meter   p. 134

gram   p. 134

liter   p. 134

4

Decimals

Dogs range in height from just a few inches to nearly three feet.
In Lesson 4.3, you will compare the heights of different breeds of dogs
using decimals.

4

Cents Sense

Decimals as Special Fractions

Objectives

In this lesson, you will:
- Write decimals as special fractions.

Key Terms

- decimal

As societies formed and people began to barter, trade, and sell goods, the need for money arose. Early forms of money included shells, beads, and precious stones. As commerce expanded, people needed a more precise system. Initially, people used different weights of precious metals such as gold and silver, but this was cumbersome and not accurate. Eventually, systems using standard coins and paper currency developed. These systems were almost always based on decimals or multiples of 10.

Problem 1   U.S. Monetary System

A. In the United States, our monetary system is based on multiples of 10. Complete each statement.

_____ pennies = 1 dime   _____ dimes = 1 dollar

_____ pennies = 1 dollar

B. The U.S. monetary system also uses coins that are not multiples of 10. Complete each statement.

_____ pennies = 1 nickel   _____ nickels = 1 quarter

_____ dimes = 1 half-dollar   _____ quarters = 1 dollar

_____ half-dollars = 1 dollar   _____ nickels = 1 half-dollar

_____ quarters = 1 half-dollar   _____ nickels = 1 dime

In almost every case, each number you wrote was either 10 or a factor of 10. What are the exceptions to this?

C. Write the numbers of dollars, dimes, and pennies there are in each amount of money. Start by writing the greatest number of dollars in the amount, then the greatest number of dimes in the amount that remains, and then the number of pennies.

$4.25 = _____ dollars + _____ dimes + _____ pennies

$5.69 = _____ dollars + _____ dimes + _____ pennies

Two dollars and five cents = _____ dollars + _____ dimes
                                          + _____ pennies

$6.73 = _____ dollars + _____ dimes + _____ pennies

Four dollars and thirty-four cents = _____ dollars + _____ dimes
                                                  + _____ pennies

Investigate Problem 1

1. What do you notice about the amount of money and the number of dollars, dimes, and pennies in Part (C) of Problem 1? Use a complete sentence in your answer.

Take Note

The word "cent" comes from the same root as the word "century" which means 100 years.

2. Complete each statement.

   1 penny = _____ dime   1 dime = _____ dollar

   1 penny = _____ dollar   1 penny = _____ nickel

   1 nickel = _____ quarter   1 dime = _____ half-dollar

   1 quarter = _____ dollar   1 half-dollar = _____ dollar

   1 penny = _____ quarter   1 quarter = _____ half-dollar

   1 nickel = _____ dime

3. What do you notice about all of the relationships in Question 2? Use a complete sentence in your answer.

4. Let's take a look at how we can write values of money using fractions. First, complete each statement.

   $2.35 = _____ dollars + _____ dimes + _____ pennies

   $3.67 = _____ dollars + _____ dimes + _____ pennies

   $5.89 = _____ dollars + _____ dimes + _____ pennies

   Rewrite each digit below as a part of a dollar. Use the relationships between dimes and dollars and between pennies and dollars that you found in Question 2.

   $2.35 = _____ dollars + (3 _____ of a dollar) + (5 _____ of a dollar)

   $3.67 = _____ dollars + (6 _____ of a dollar) + (7 _____ of a dollar)

   $5.89 = _____ dollars + (8 _____ of a dollar) + (9 _____ of a dollar)

5. What do you notice about the fractions you used above? Use a complete sentence in your answer.

6. The fractions in Question 4 are special fractions with denominators that are multiples of what number?

7. Math Path: Decimals

A **decimal** is a number that is written using a system based on multiples of 10. This system is called the *base-ten place-value system.* You will learn more about this system in the next lesson. Each position of a digit in a decimal is 10 times the value of the position to its right. Let's take a look at two ways that we can write decimals. Complete each statement. The first statement is completed for you.

45.123 = 4 tens + 5 ones + 1 tenth + 2 hundredths + 3 thousandths

$45.123 = $ ____ 10s + ____ 1s + ____ $\frac{1}{10}$s + ____ $\frac{1}{100}$s + ____ $\frac{1}{1000}$s

343.43 = ____ hundreds + ____ tens + ____ ones + ____ tenths
+ ____ hundredths

$343.43 = $ ____ 100s + ____ 10s + ____ 1s + ____ $\frac{1}{10}$s + ____ $\frac{1}{100}$s

8. Use the results of Question 7 to explain why decimals are just special fractions. Use complete sentences in your answer.

Problem 2   *Bolivar and Yen*

People in Venezuela use a coin called a bolivar. People in Japan use a coin called a yen.

A. On a particular day, $.05 U.S. is equal to 107.365 bolivares. Complete each statement.

107.365 bolivares = ____ whole bolivar + (3 ____ of a bolivar)

+ (6 ____ of a bolivar) + (5 ____ of a bolivar)

332.095 bolivares = ____ hundreds + ____ tens + ____ ones
+ ____ tenths + ____ hundredths + ____ thousandths

332.095 bolivares = ____ 100s + ____ 10s + ____ 1s + ____ $\frac{1}{10}$s
+ ____ $\frac{1}{100}$s + ____ $\frac{1}{1000}$s

B. On a particular day, $5.00 U.S. is equal to 529.635 yen. Complete each statement.

529.635 yen = ____ whole yen + (6 ____ of a yen)

+ (3 ____ of a yen) + (5 ____ of a yen)

529.635 yen = ____ hundreds + ____ tens + ____ ones
+ ____ tenths + ____ hundredths + ____ thousandths

529.635 yen = ____ 100s + ____ 10s + ____ 1s + ____ $\frac{1}{10}$s
+ ____ $\frac{1}{100}$s + ____ $\frac{1}{1000}$s

4

What's In a Place?
Place Value and Expanded Form

Objectives

In this lesson, you will:
- Represent decimals using a place-value chart.
- Write decimals in word form.
- Use expanded form to write decimals.

Key Terms

- place-value chart
- standard form
- expanded form

Problem 1   Softball Stats

In softball, a batting average (AVG) is the number of hits divided by the number of times that a player bats. The home run ratio (HRR) is the number of times that a player bats divided by the number of home runs the player scores. The earned run average (ERA) is a measure of how many runs a pitcher allows.

The table shows the statistics for the top three players on your team.

Player	AVG	HRR	ERA
Sam	0.378	16.5	---
Keesha	---	---	1.89
Jamal	0.294	25.0	---

A. From Lesson 4.1, you know that decimals are special fractions whose digits have values based on their positions. Complete each statement.

$0.378 = $ ____ 10s + ____ 1s + ____ $\frac{1}{10}$s + ____ $\frac{1}{100}$s + ____ $\frac{1}{1000}$s

$16.5 = $ ____ ten + ____ ones + ____ tenths + ____ hundredths + ____ thousandths

$1.89 = $ ____ 10s + ____ 1s + ____ $\frac{1}{10}$s + ____ $\frac{1}{100}$s + ____ $\frac{1}{1000}$s

$0.294 = $ ____ tens + ____ ones + ____ tenths + ____ hundredths + ____ thousandths

$25.0 = $ ____ 10s + ____ 1s + ____ $\frac{1}{10}$s + ____ $\frac{1}{100}$s + ____ $\frac{1}{1000}$s

B. In each decimal above, what determines the value of each digit? Use complete sentences to explain.

C. Which statistic uses decimals with digits only to the tenths place?

Which statistic uses decimals with digits only to the tenths and hundredths places?

Which statistic uses decimals with digits to the thousandths place?

4

1. There are actually two things that determine the value of a digit in a decimal. One of them is the numeral or digit. What is the other thing that determines the value of a digit? Write your answer using a complete sentence.

2. **Math Path: Place Value**

   The chart below is a **place-value chart.** The decimal 453.269 is written in **standard form.** Complete the chart by writing the appropriate place value of each digit in the decimal in words in the first row. Then write the place value as a number or fraction in the second row.

Place-Value Chart						
Value in Words	hundreds			.			
Value as a Number or Fraction				$\frac{1}{10}$		
	4	5	3	.	2	6	9

3. For each number, identify the place value of the given digit.

   12,409.53

   What is the place value of 1?   What is the place value of 4?

   What is the place value of 3?   What is the place value of 0?

   34.5802

   What is the place value of 5?   What is the place value of 0?

   What is the place value of 3?   What is the place value of 2?

4. Each decimal is written in word form. Use your knowledge of place value to write the decimal as a number.

   Three hundred sixty-five and thirty-four hundredths =

   Eight thousand nine hundred seventy-one and twenty-one hundredths =

   Four hundred and six thousandths (Be careful here!) =

5. Write each decimal in word form.

   12.3 =

   360.23 =

   457.912 =

© 2008 Carnegie Learning, Inc.

4

Take Note

Remember that when you write a number in word form, the "and" represents a decimal point. For instance, to write 425 in word form, you write four hundred twenty-five, *not* four hundred *and* twenty-five.

Problem 2 *It's Official*

An official softball, according to the International Softball Federation, has a circumference (distance around) between 11.875 inches and 12.125 inches.

Sometimes it is necessary to write decimals in **expanded form.** In expanded form, a decimal is written as a sum of products. Each product has a power of 10 or a power of 0.1 as a factor.

We already wrote decimals in a similar form using fractions. First complete the following statement.

$$11.875 = \underline{\quad} 10s + \underline{\quad} 1s + \underline{\quad} \frac{1}{10}s + \underline{\quad} \frac{1}{100}s + \underline{\quad} \frac{1}{1000}s$$

Now write the decimal as a sum of products.

$$11.875 = (\underline{\quad} \times 10) + (\underline{\quad} \times 1) + \left(\underline{\quad} \times \frac{1}{10}\right) + \left(\underline{\quad} \times \frac{1}{100}\right) + \left(\underline{\quad} \times \frac{1}{1000}\right)$$

Finally, write the decimal in expanded form.

$$11.875 = (\underline{\quad} \times 10) + (\underline{\quad} \times 1) + (\underline{\quad} \times 0.1) + (\underline{\quad} \times 0.01) + (\underline{\quad} \times 0.001)$$

Investigate Problem 2

Take Note

Whenever you write a decimal in expanded form and one of the digits is 0, you do not need to include the expanded form for 0.

1. Write each decimal in expanded form.

   45.3 =

   709.65 =

   999.902 =

2. Each decimal is written as a sum of products. Write each decimal in expanded form, in standard form, and in word form.

$$(3 \times 10) + (6 \times 1) + \left(9 \times \frac{1}{10}\right) + \left(7 \times \frac{1}{100}\right) + \left(4 \times \frac{1}{1000}\right)$$

   Expanded form:

   Standard form:

   Word form:

$$(6 \times 10) + \left(9 \times \frac{1}{10}\right) + \left(3 \times \frac{1}{100}\right) + \left(4 \times \frac{1}{1000}\right) + \left(2 \times \frac{1}{10,000}\right)$$

   Expanded form:

   Standard form:

   Word form:

4

4

My Dog Is Bigger Than Your Dog
Decimals as Fractions: Comparing and Rounding Decimals

Objectives

In this lesson, you will:
- Write decimals as fractions.
- Compare and order decimals.
- Round decimals.

Key Terms
- round a decimal

Once we can read decimals and write them in expanded form, we also need to convert them to fractions or mixed numbers to compare them.

Problem 1 Dog Heights

You and your friends belong to a kennel club. At the club meeting, you decide to measure your dogs. A dog's height is measured to the highest point on the dog's back between its shoulder blades. The table shows the heights of the dogs.

	Dog Breed	Height
Eddie	cocker spaniel	13.25 inches
Harold	beagle	12.625 inches
Lakeisha	Jack Russell terrier	12.50 inches
Yung	sheltie	13.375 inches

A. Work with your partner to write the decimal height of the cocker spaniel as a mixed number. First write the decimal in expanded form.

$$13.25 = (1 \times 10) + (3 \times 1) + \left(2 \times \frac{1}{10}\right) + \left(5 \times \frac{1}{100}\right) = 13 + \frac{2}{10} + \frac{5}{100}$$

B. Next, find the LCD of the fractions. Then rewrite the fractions and add.

$$13 + \frac{2}{10} + \frac{5}{100} = 13 + \frac{20}{100} + \frac{5}{100} = 13\frac{25}{100}$$

C. Write the height of the beagle in expanded form. Then write the fractions with like denominators and add.

$$12.625 = \left(\square \times 10\right) + \left(\square \times 1\right) + \left(\square \times \frac{1}{10}\right) + \left(\square \times \frac{1}{100}\right) + \left(\square \times \frac{1}{1000}\right)$$

$$= \square + \frac{\square}{10} + \frac{\square}{100} + \frac{\square}{1000}$$

$$= \square + \frac{\square}{1000} + \frac{\square}{1000} + \frac{\square}{1000}$$

$$= \square + \frac{\square}{1000}$$

4

Take Note

To write a proper fraction with a denominator that is a power of 10 as a decimal, write the digits in the numerator and place the decimal point to the left of the digits. For example,

$\dfrac{425}{1000} = 0.425.$

1. Write each decimal as a mixed number.

$32.402 = (\boxed{} \times 10) + (\boxed{} \times 1) + \left(\boxed{} \times \dfrac{1}{10}\right) + \left(\boxed{} \times \dfrac{1}{100}\right) + \left(\boxed{} \times \dfrac{1}{1000}\right)$

$= \boxed{} + \dfrac{\boxed{}}{10} + \dfrac{\boxed{}}{100} + \dfrac{\boxed{}}{1000}$

$= \boxed{} + \dfrac{\boxed{}}{1000} + \dfrac{\boxed{}}{1000}$

$= \boxed{} + \dfrac{\boxed{}}{1000}$

29.08 =

=

=

12.0045 =

=

=

=

=

100.405 =

=

=

=

=

Problem 2 *Top Dog*

Form a group with another partner team to discuss how you can compare the heights of the dogs to determine which is the tallest dog.

A. Harold says that you can always tell which of two decimals is greater by which number has the most digits. Is Harold correct? Use complete sentences to explain why or why not.

B. Eddie says that you can tell by looking at the last digit of each decimal. If the last digit is greater, then the decimal is greater. Is Eddie correct? Use complete sentences to explain why or why not.

C. Lakeisha says that neither Harold nor Eddie is correct. In fact, she says that you need to look at the place value of the right-most digit first. If these digits in each decimal have the same value, then you keep comparing the place value of each digit from right to left until the place value of one is greater than the other. She says that only then will you know which decimal is greater. Is Lakeisha correct? Use complete sentences to explain why or why not.

D. Finally, Yung says that you can write both of the decimals as mixed numbers or fractions and then decide which is greater. Is Yung correct? Use complete sentences to explain why or why not.

E. Do you have your own way to tell when one decimal is greater than another? Discuss this with your group. Then use your method to determine which dog is the tallest. Write your answer using complete sentences.

4

Investigate Problem 2

1. Sometimes you need to round whole numbers. Similarly, you sometimes need to round decimals. Round each whole number.

   567 rounded to the nearest ten =
   743 rounded to the nearest hundred =
   5432 rounded to the nearest thousand =

   In each case, how did you determine your answer? Use a complete sentence to explain.

2. Round each whole number.

   745 rounded to the nearest ten =
   850 rounded to the nearest hundred =

   In each case, how did you determine your answer? Were these whole numbers more difficult to round than those in Question 1? Use complete sentences to explain.

3. What rule did you use to round the whole numbers in Question 2?

4. **Math Path: Rounding Decimals**

   You can use a similar rule to round decimals.

   ### Rounding Decimals

   To **round a decimal** to a given place value, look at the digit to the right of the place where you want to round the decimal.

   - If the digit is 4 or less, round down.
   - If the digit is 5 or greater, round up.

5. Round each decimal to the given place value in the table.

Number	Rounded to the nearest ten	Rounded to the nearest one	Rounded to the nearest tenth	Rounded to the nearest hundredth	Rounded to the nearest thousandth
23.1768					
45.3455					
125.3578					
435.9008					
236.0895					

© 2008 Carnegie Learning, Inc.

Making Change and Changing Hours
Adding and Subtracting Decimals

Objectives

In this lesson, you will:
- Add and subtract decimals.
- Represent decimals using base-ten pieces.

Key Terms
- base-ten pieces

Problem 1   Making Change

Jenny works in her family's small convenience store. Her job is to take money and make change. She finds the total cost and then determines the correct change. Last week, a customer bought three items: one item that cost $2.34, a second item that cost $0.98, and a third item that cost three dollars and nine cents.

A. Help Jenny by finding the total cost of all three items. Show your work below.

B. The customer gave Jenny a ten dollar bill. How much change did Jenny give the customer? Show your work below.

C. Compare your work and your answers to Parts (A) and (B) with your partner.

D. Tom, Jenny's younger brother, added the three items as shown below.

$$
\begin{array}{r}
\$2.34 \\
\$.98 \\
+ \ \$3.90 \\
\hline
\$16.04
\end{array}
$$

Does Tom's answer agree with your answer? Use complete sentences to explain why or why not.

1. With your partner, decide what Tom needs to learn in order to add and subtract money correctly. Write your answer using a complete sentence.

2. Form a group with another partner team. With your group, write the rule(s) that must be followed in order to correctly add or subtract money.

3. Let's take a look at the rules for adding and subtracting decimals. These rules are similar to the rules for adding and subtracting money. Suppose we want to add 4.05 and 12.341. What is one important step that we must do in order to get the correct answer? Use a complete sentence to answer the question.

4. Recall that decimals are special fractions. We can add the decimals by first writing them as mixed numbers. This will help us to understand how the rules for adding decimals were developed. Complete the statement to rewrite 12.341. The decimal 4.05 is already rewritten for you.

$$4.05 = (4 \times 1) + \left(0 \times \frac{1}{10}\right) + \left(5 \times \frac{1}{100}\right) = 4 + \frac{0}{100} + \frac{5}{100} = 4\frac{5}{100}$$

$$12.341 = 12 + \frac{\square}{10} + \frac{\square}{100} + \frac{\square}{1000} = 12 + \frac{\square}{1000} + \frac{\square}{1000} + \frac{\square}{1000} = 12\frac{341}{1000}$$

5. Now the addition problem is a mixed number addition problem. Complete the problem by writing the fractional parts with the LCD. Then find the sum of the mixed numbers. Finally, write the sum as a decimal.

$$4\frac{5}{100} = 4\frac{\square}{\square}$$

$$+12\frac{341}{1000} = 12\frac{\square}{\square}$$

$$= \square\frac{\square}{\square} = \square$$

6. Use what you learned in Question 5 to complete the decimal subtraction problem.

4.5 – 2.34 =

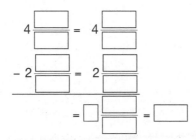

7. Work with your group to explain why we have the rule about decimal points for adding and subtracting decimals. Use the results of Questions 5 and 6. Explain your reasoning to each other. Then write your explanation using complete sentences.

8. Find each sum or difference. Be sure to properly apply the rule for decimals.

23.05 + 2.301 =   400.1 + 6.202 =

45.23 – 9.08 =   1.0003 – 0.9 =

203.901 – 2.0451 =   54.2 + 45.09 + 6.09 =

9. Math Path: Base-Ten Pieces

We can represent decimals using **base-ten pieces.**

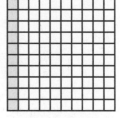   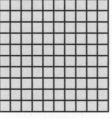   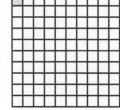

1 one-piece   1 tenth-piece   1 hundredth-piece

What decimal do the base-ten pieces below represent?

    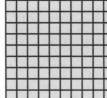   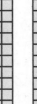

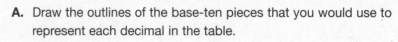

Because of a special sale, Jenny increased the number of hours that she worked each day during a particular week. She kept track of the hours in a table.

A. Draw the outlines of the base-ten pieces that you would use to represent each decimal in the table.

1.75

1.5

2.15

Day	Number of Hours
Monday	1.75
Wednesday	1.5
Thursday	2.15

B. Work with your partner to determine how you can use the base-ten pieces to find the total number of hours that Jenny worked during the week. Draw the outlines of the base-ten pieces that you would use to represent the sum.

1.75 + 1.5 + 2.15 =

4

Investigate Problem 2

1. Draw the outlines of the base-ten pieces to represent each decimal and the sum.

2.09 + 0.93 =

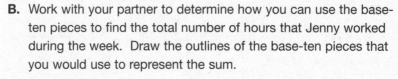

4.5 Rules Make the World Go Round
Multiplying Decimals

Objectives

In this lesson, you will:
- Multiply decimals.

Key Terms

- product

Take Note

Remember that the result of multiplying two decimals is the *product* of the two decimals.

Problem 1   The Planets

You are making a scale model of the planets for science class. If you make the Sun out of a ball that is 30 inches in diameter, you can make the planets to scale using the diameters in the table.

A. If you changed your mind and wanted to use a ball with a 42-inch diameter for the Sun, you would need to multiply each diameter in the table by 1.4. To find the diameter for Saturn, you need to multiply 2.6×1.4.

Planet	Diameter
Mercury	0.103
Venus	0.26
Earth	0.276
Mars	0.147
Jupiter	3.09
Saturn	2.6
Uranus	1.1
Neptune	1.07

You asked four of your friends to help. When you did, you got the four different answers below.

36.4   3.64   0.364   3.6

Which answer is correct? Use complete sentences to explain how you know.

B. Let's examine this problem by representing the decimals using improper fractions. By doing this, we may gain some insight into the rule for multiplying decimals. Work with your partner to complete the steps below.

*When you multiply decimals, the number of decimal places in the **product** is equal to the sum of the number of decimal places in the factors.*

- Write the decimals as mixed numbers.
- Then write the mixed numbers as improper fractions.
- Perform the multiplication.
- Write the answer as a mixed number.
- Write the mixed number as a decimal.

$$2.6 = 2 + \frac{\Box}{10} = \frac{\Box}{10} + \frac{\Box}{10} = \frac{\Box}{10} \qquad 1.4 = 1 + \frac{\Box}{10} = \frac{\Box}{10} + \frac{\Box}{10} = \frac{\Box}{10}$$

$$\frac{\Box}{10} \times \frac{\Box}{10} = \frac{\Box}{\Box} = \Box\frac{\Box}{\Box} = \Box$$

4

1. Discuss the result you got in Part (B) with your partner to see if your answer "explains" the rule for multiplying decimals.

2. To be sure that you understand the reasons behind the rule, multiply the decimals.

   $2.5 \times 1.001 =$

   $2.5 = 2\dfrac{\boxed{}}{10} = \dfrac{\boxed{}}{\boxed{}}$ $1.001 = 1\dfrac{\boxed{}}{\boxed{}} = \dfrac{\boxed{}}{\boxed{}}$

   $\dfrac{\boxed{}}{\boxed{}} \times \dfrac{\boxed{}}{\boxed{}} = \dfrac{\boxed{}}{\boxed{}} = \boxed{}\,\dfrac{\boxed{}}{\boxed{}} = \boxed{}$

3. Does your answer to Question 2 support your conclusion in Question 1? Use complete sentences to explain why or why not.

4. Find each product.

   $2.34 \times 2.5 =$ $400.1 \times 1.01 =$ $2.001 \times 3.4 =$

   $6.45 \times 3.1 =$ $0.001 \times .03 =$ $4.004 \times 0.002 =$

Problem 1 Revisited   The Planets

A. Because you want to use a ball with a 42-inch diameter instead of a ball with a 30-inch diameter for the Sun, you need to multiply each diameter in the table by 1.4. The new diameter for Saturn is done for you. Complete the table.

B. Suppose that you wanted to use a ball with a 20-inch diameter instead of a 30-inch diameter for the Sun. Would the decimal that you multiply each diameter by be less than or greater than 1? Use complete sentences to explain.

Planet	Diameter (Sun is 30 in.)	New Diameter (Sun is 42 in.)
Mercury	0.103	
Venus	0.26	
Earth	0.276	
Mars	0.147	
Jupiter	3.09	
Saturn	2.6	3.64
Uranus	1.1	
Neptune	1.07	

4.6

The Better Buy
Dividing Decimals

Objectives

In this lesson, you will:

- Divide decimals by whole numbers.
- Divide decimals by decimals.

Key Terms

- dividend
- divisor
- quotient

Problem 1 · Unit Prices

You want to buy a special gift for your cousin, whose favorite hobby is knitting. You find a web site that sells handspun yarn. You can buy 2.4 ounces of llama yarn for $10.08 or 3.6 ounces of mohair yarn for $20.16. Which type of yarn is the most economical buy?

A. To determine the most economical buy, work with your partner to solve $10.08 \div 2.4$.

Complete the process below by first rewriting the decimals as mixed numbers. Then rewrite the mixed numbers as improper fractions and divide.

$$10.08 = 10\frac{8}{100} = \frac{1008}{100} \qquad 2.4 = 2\frac{\square}{\square} = \frac{\square}{\square}$$

$$\frac{1008}{100} \div \frac{\square}{\square} = \frac{1008}{100} \times \frac{\square}{\square} = \frac{\square}{\square} = \frac{\square}{\square} = \square\frac{\square}{\square} = \square\frac{\square}{\square}$$

B. The result of Part (A) is a mixed number. Write the mixed number as a decimal.

$$10.08 \div 2.4 = \boxed{}$$

C. Use the method from Part (A) to divide 20.16 by 3.6.

$$20.16 = 20\frac{\square}{\square} = \frac{\square}{\square} \qquad 3.6 = 3\frac{6}{10} = \frac{36}{10}$$

$$\frac{\square}{\square} \div \frac{36}{10} = \frac{\square}{\square} \times \frac{\square}{\square} = \frac{\square}{\square} = \frac{\square}{\square} = \square\frac{\square}{\square} = \square$$

D. Based on your results from Parts (B) and (C), which type of yarn is the most economical buy? Use complete sentences to explain your answer.

4

Investigate Problem 1

1. To find a method for dividing decimals that is not complicated, we need to look in a different direction. Complete the whole number division problems.

$$13\overline{)273} \qquad\qquad\qquad 12\overline{)2802}$$

2. In the expression $12\overline{)2802}$, you get a remainder. You can write the remainder as a fraction, and then write the fraction as a decimal by writing it with a denominator that is a power of 10: 10, 100, 1000, and so on. Let's look at how to write the fraction $\frac{3}{4}$ as a decimal. Remember that when you first learned to divide whole numbers, such as $8 \div 2$, you divided 8 into 2 equal groups. In the same way, you can think of the fraction $\frac{3}{4}$ as $3 \div 4$, or 3 divided into 4 equal groups. You know that $3 = \frac{30}{10}$. If you divide 30 tenths into 4 equal groups, how many tenths will be in each group? What is left over? Use the base-ten pieces to help you.

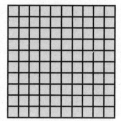 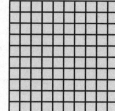 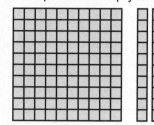

So, 3 is 4 groups of $\frac{7}{10}$ with $\frac{2}{10}$ as a remainder. You know that $\frac{2}{10} = \frac{20}{100}$. If you divide 20 hundredths into 4 equal groups, how many hundredths will be in each group? What is left over?

So, $\frac{2}{10}$ is 4 groups of $\frac{5}{100}$. Complete the statement to write $\frac{3}{4}$ as a decimal.

Four equal groups of 3 is $\dfrac{\boxed{}}{10} + \dfrac{\boxed{}}{100} = \dfrac{75}{100} = \boxed{}$.

© 2008 Carnegie Learning, Inc.

3. There is a much less complicated process that uses what we know about whole number division. To find the **quotient** $4\overline{)3}$, first add a decimal point and a zero to the right of the **dividend** (see Step 1). When you do this, you are really rewriting the 3 as $\frac{30}{10}$. When you divide, you write $\frac{7}{10}$ as a decimal in the quotient (see Step 2). But after subtracting, you still have $\frac{2}{10}$ left over, which you can write as $\frac{20}{100}$ by adding an additional zero in the dividend (see Step 3). Divide again. Because there is no remainder, the problem is complete (see Step 4).

Step 1:
$$4\overline{)3.\square}$$

Step 2:
$$\begin{array}{r} 0.\square \\ 4\overline{)3.0} \\ 2\,8 \\ \hline 2 \end{array}$$

Step 3:
$$\begin{array}{r} 0.7 \\ 4\overline{)3.00} \\ 2\,8 \\ \hline 2\square \end{array}$$

Step 4:
$$\begin{array}{r} 0.75 \\ 4\overline{)3.00} \\ 2\,8 \\ \hline 20 \\ 20 \\ \hline 0 \end{array}$$

4. Use Steps 1–4 to write $\frac{7}{8}$ as a decimal.

5. The method used in Question 3 works any time you want to divide a whole number or decimal by a whole number. Find each quotient.

$$8\overline{)75} \qquad 23\overline{)983} \qquad 16\overline{)99.2}$$

$$45\overline{)10.35} \qquad 60\overline{)24.6} \qquad 25\overline{)7.4}$$

Take Note

To summarize, when you divide a decimal by a whole number, divide as you would with whole numbers. The decimal point in the quotient should line up with the decimal point in the dividend.

4

When we want to divide by a decimal, we need to write the expression as an equivalent expression in which the **divisor** is a whole number. If we do this, we can use the method in Question 3. To find the quotient 8.66 ÷ 2.4, we first write the division as a fraction.

Because $8.66 = \dfrac{866}{100}$ and $2.4 = \dfrac{24}{10}$, we can write 8.66 ÷ 2.4 as

$\dfrac{866}{100} \div \dfrac{24}{10} = \dfrac{\frac{866}{100}}{\frac{24}{10}}$. Remember that you can multiply any

number by the multiplicative identity 1 and not change the

value. So, multiply the fraction by $\dfrac{10}{10} = 1$. What is the numerator

of the fraction as a decimal?

$$\dfrac{\frac{866}{\cancel{100}}^{10}}{\frac{24}{\cancel{10}}} \times \dfrac{\cancel{10}}{\cancel{10}} = \dfrac{\frac{866}{10}}{24} = \dfrac{\boxed{}}{24}$$

This type of multiplication is what we need to do when we are dividing by a decimal. After multiplying to get a whole number, we can divide using the method in Question 3. Complete the division.

$$24\overline{)86.6}$$

6. Work with your partner to write a rule that summarizes what you do when dividing a decimal by a decimal. Then use the rule to find the quotients.

$13.78 \div 5.3 =$ $\qquad$ $5.69\overline{)41.537}$

4·7 Bonjour!
Working with Metric Units

Objectives

In this lesson, you will:
- Use metric units to measure length, mass, and capacity.
- Choose the appropriate unit of measure.

Key Terms

- metric system
- meter
- gram
- liter

The customary system can be difficult and time-consuming to use because it depends on fractions. About 400 years ago, scientists proposed a measurement system based on decimals. France was the first nation to officially adopt this system, called the **metric system.** This system has become the basis for the International System of Units that is currently used in many countries.

Problem 1   Measurement in France

For a project, everyone in your class chooses a pen pal. Your pen pal is from France. As you exchange letters, you notice that she uses centimeters and meters when she describes the length of something. She uses grams and kilograms when she writes about the mass of something. She uses liters and milliliters to discuss the capacity of something.

You wonder how these measurements compare to those used in the United States. She sends you the following information:

A meter is the length of a yardstick plus the length of a piece of chalk.

A centimeter is about the width of the tip of your pinky finger.

A gram is the mass of a large thumbtack. A nickel weighs 5 grams.

A kilogram is about the mass of a large book.

A liter is about the capacity of a large bottle of water.

A milliliter is about the capacity of an eyedropper.

A. Your pen pal writes that she has a "chien" that has a mass of 9.5 kilograms. Is she talking about a car or a dog? Use complete sentences to explain your answer.

It must be her dog that weighs 9.5 kg. A car would weigh more than nine times that of a large book.

B. Your pen pal writes that her "éscritoire" at school is 0.65 meters wide. Is she talking about a desk or a book? Use complete sentences to explain your answer.

It must be her desk that is 0.65 m wide. A book that size would be way too wide!

1. Math Path: The Metric System

One advantage of the metric system is the way in which units are named. The naming convention is built on six main prefixes.

kilo-	which means 1000	deci-	which means $\frac{1}{10}$
hecto-	which means 100	centi-	which means $\frac{1}{100}$
deka-	which means 10	milli-	which means $\frac{1}{1000}$

By putting each prefix together with a root word for a base unit of length, mass, or capacity, you have all of the units of the metric system.

The **meter** is the metric base unit of length.

The **gram** is the metric base unit of mass.

The **liter** is the metric base unit of capacity.

For example, a *kilometer* is 1000 meters, and a *milliliter* is $\frac{1}{1000}$ of a liter. Work with your partner to write each unit of measure and its meaning in the table below.

kilo-	hecto-	deka-	unit	deci-	centi-	milli-
kilometer 1000 meters			meter 1 meter			
			liter 1 liter			
			gram 1 gram			

4

Take Note

Abbreviations for commonly-used metric units are listed:

kilometer: km

centimeter: cm

meter: m

liter: l

milliliter: mL

kilogram: kg

gram: g

2. Because this system is based on powers of 10, making conversions is straightforward. Complete each conversion.

$5.4 \text{ kilograms} \times \dfrac{\boxed{} \text{ grams}}{1 \text{ kilogram}} = \boxed{} \text{ grams}$

$235 \text{ milliliters} \times \dfrac{1 \text{ liter}}{\boxed{} \text{ milliliters}} = \boxed{} \text{ liter}$

$37.8 \text{ dekameters} \times \dfrac{1 \text{ kilometer}}{\boxed{} \text{ dekameters}} = \boxed{} \text{ kilometer}$

3. Complete each row of the table by converting the given measures to all of the other units in the row.

kilo-	hecto-	deka-	unit	deci-	centi-	milli-
1 kilometer	10 hectometers		1000 meters			
			$\frac{1}{10}$ liter	1 deciliter		
					$\frac{1}{10}$ centimeter	1 millimeter

4. Because conversions in the metric system are based on powers of 10, we can convert by multiplying or dividing by powers of 10. We also know that when we multiply by 10, the answer can be found by adding a zero to the right of a whole number or by moving the decimal one place to the right.

What are the rules for multiplying a decimal and a whole number by 100? Use complete sentences in your answer.

What are the rules for multiplying a decimal and a whole number by 1000? Use complete sentences in your answer.

What are the rules for multiplying a decimal and a whole number by any other multiple of 10? Use complete sentences in your answer.

What are the rules for dividing a decimal and a whole number by 10? Use complete sentences in your answer.

What are the rules for dividing a decimal and a whole number by 100? Use complete sentences in your answer.

What are the rules for dividing a decimal and a whole number by 1000? Use complete sentences in your answer.

What are the rules for dividing a decimal and a whole number by any other power of 10? Use complete sentences in your answer.

4

5. The rules from Question 4 allow you to easily convert measurements. For example, to convert kilometers to meters, you *multiply* the number of kilometers by 1000. To convert centimeters to meters, you *divide* the number of centimeters by 10.

Use the rules from Question 4 to convert each measurement.

10 hectometers = _____ decimeters

2 kilograms = _____ grams

25 millimeters = _____ meter

34.5 centimeters = _____ dekameter

23 decigrams _____ dekagram

2.34 meters = _____ centimeters

6. Conversions between the U.S. customary system and the metric system are not as easy as converting within the metric system. Here are some ways to think about how the two systems are related.

A meter is a little longer than a yard.

A liter is a little more than a quart.

A kilogram is a little heavier than 2 pounds.

For each of the objects in the table, select the most appropriate metric unit and customary unit to use to measure them.

Item	Metric Unit	Customary Unit
height of a tree		
mass of a pin		
volume of water in a tub		
length of your classroom		
width of this page		
mass of a person		
volume of liquid in a cup		

7. Use what you have learned about metric units to write a paragraph to your pen pal. In the paragraph, describe the length of an object, the mass of a second object, and the capacity of a third object using metric units.

Paragraphs will vary but should include a customary measure of each: length, mass, and capacity.

© 2008 Carnegie Learning, Inc.

4

Looking Back at Chapter 4

Key Terms

decimal • p. 113
place-value chart • p. 116
standard form • p. 116
expanded form • p. 117
round a decimal • p. 122

base-ten pieces • p. 125
product • p. 127
quotient • p. 131
dividend • p. 131
divisor • p. 132

metric system • p. 133
meter • p. 134
gram • p. 134
liter • p. 134

Summary

Writing Decimals as Special Fractions (p. 113)

In a decimal, each position of a digit is 10 times the value of the position to its right.

Examples
26.356 = $\underline{2}$ tens + $\underline{6}$ ones + $\underline{3}$ tenths + $\underline{5}$ hundredths + $\underline{6}$ thousandths

26.356 = $\underline{2}$ 10s + $\underline{6}$ 1s + $\underline{3}$ $\frac{1}{10}$s + $\underline{5}$ $\frac{1}{100}$s + $\underline{6}$ $\frac{1}{1000}$s

532.48 = $\underline{5}$ hundreds + $\underline{3}$ tens + $\underline{2}$ ones + $\underline{4}$ tenths + $\underline{8}$ hundredths

532.48 = $\underline{5}$ 100s + $\underline{3}$ 10s + $\underline{2}$ 1s + $\underline{4}$ $\frac{1}{10}$s + $\underline{8}$ $\frac{1}{100}$s

Writing Decimals in Word Form as Numbers (p. 116)

To write a decimal in word form as a number, use your knowledge of place value. Remember that the word "and" represents the decimal point.

Examples
Seventy-three and sixteen hundredths = $\underline{73.16}$

Four hundred fifty-six and three hundred twenty-one thousandths = $\underline{456.321}$

Five hundred and nine hundredths = $\underline{500.09}$

Writing Decimals in Word Form (p. 116)

When writing a decimal in word form, remember to write only the decimal point as the word "and."

Examples
18.145 = Eighteen and one hundred forty-five thousandths

207.98 = Two hundred seven and ninety-eight hundredths

1001.007 = One thousand one and seven thousandths

Writing Decimals in Expanded Form (p. 117)

To write a decimal in expanded form, write the decimal as a sum of products using fractions and then write the decimal in expanded form.

Examples

$$57.12 = (5 \times 10) + (7 \times 1) + \left(1 \times \frac{1}{10}\right) + \left(2 \times \frac{1}{100}\right)$$

$$57.12 = (5 \times 10) + (7 \times 1) + (1 \times 0.1) + (2 \times 0.01)$$

$$31.054 = (3 \times 10) + (1 \times 1) + \left(5 \times \frac{1}{100}\right) + \left(4 \times \frac{1}{1000}\right)$$

$$31.054 = (3 \times 10) + (1 \times 1) + (5 \times 0.01) + (4 \times 0.001)$$

Writing Decimals in Standard Form (p. 117)

To write a decimal in standard form, find the sum of the products.

Examples

$$(7 \times 10) + (3 \times 1) + (8 \times 0.1) + (5 \times 0.01) + (6 \times 0.001)$$

Standard form: 73.856

$$(8 \times 100) + (1 \times 1) + (2 \times 0.1) + (4 \times 0.01) + (9 \times 0.001)$$

Standard form: 801.249

Writing Decimals as Mixed Numbers (p. 119)

To write a decimal as a mixed number, first write the decimal as a sum of products using fractions. Then write the whole number part. Finally, write the fractions with like denominators and add.

Example

$$927.415 = (\underline{9} \times 100) + (\underline{2} \times 10) + (\underline{7} \times 1) + \left(\underline{4} \times \frac{1}{10}\right) + \left(\underline{1} \times \frac{1}{100}\right) + \left(\underline{5} \times \frac{1}{1000}\right)$$

$$= \underline{927} + \frac{4}{10} + \frac{1}{100} + \frac{5}{1000}$$

$$= \underline{927} + \frac{400}{1000} + \frac{10}{1000} + \frac{5}{1000}$$

$$= \underline{927} \frac{415}{1000}$$

Comparing and Ordering Decimals (p. 121)

To compare decimals, compare the digits in corresponding place values from left to right. If the digits in a place value are the same, keep comparing the digits in corresponding place values from left to right until the digit in the place value of one decimal is greater than the digit in the same place value of the other decimal.

Example

714.563   714.539   714.529   714.599

The digits in the hundreds, tens, ones, and tenths places are identical. The digits in the hundredths place are different. So, the numbers from least to greatest are 714.529, 714.539, 714.563, and 714.599.

Rounding Decimals (p. 122)

To round a decimal, look at the digit to the right of the place where you want to round the decimal. If the digit is 4 or less, round down. If the digit is 5 or greater, round up.

Examples

Number	Rounded to the Nearest Ten	Rounded to the Nearest One	Rounded to the Nearest Tenth	Rounded to the Nearest Hundredth	Rounded to the Nearest Thousandth
64.2367	60	64	64.2	64.24	64.237
358.7491	360	359	358.7	358.75	358.749
981.0172	980	981	981.0	981.02	981.017

Adding and Subtracting Decimals (p. 123)

To add or subtract decimals, arrange the numbers vertically so that the decimal points line up. Then add or subtract as you would with whole numbers.

Examples

$$\begin{array}{r} 3.056 \\ + \ 2.14 \\ \hline 5.196 \end{array} \qquad \begin{array}{r} 15.7 \\ - \ 8.32 \\ \hline 7.38 \end{array} \qquad \begin{array}{r} 2.052 \\ 6.743 \\ + \ 1.859 \\ \hline 10.654 \end{array} \qquad \begin{array}{r} 10.619 \\ 3.047 \\ + \ 7.681 \\ \hline 21.347 \end{array}$$

Multiplying Decimals (p. 127)

When multiplying decimals, the total number of decimal places in the product is equal to the sum of the numbers of decimal places in the factors.

Examples $3.004 \times 4.9 = 14.7196$

$$\begin{array}{r} 3.004 \\ \times \quad 4.9 \\ \hline 2\ 7036 \\ 12\ 0160 \\ \hline 14.7196 \end{array}$$

The factors have a total of 4 decimal places, so the product has 4 decimal places.

Dividing Decimals by Whole Numbers (p. 131)

To divide a decimal by a whole number, use long division. As necessary, add a decimal point and zeros after the dividend.

Examples

$$\begin{array}{r} 0.16 \\ 49\overline{)7.84} \\ \underline{49} \\ 294 \\ \underline{294} \\ 0 \end{array} \qquad \begin{array}{r} 0.35 \\ 32\overline{)11.20} \\ \underline{96} \\ 160 \\ \underline{160} \\ 0 \end{array}$$

Dividing Decimals by Decimals (p. 132)

To divide a decimal by a decimal, first multiply the divisor and dividend by an appropriate multiple of 10, then use long division.

Examples

$$4.56\overline{)14.82} \rightarrow 456\overline{)1482.00}$$

```
           3.25
    456)1482.00
        1368
         114 0
          91 2
          22 80
          22 80
              0
```

Multiply the divisor and dividend by 100.

Converting Measurements in Larger Metric Units to Smaller Metric Units (p. 134)

To convert a measurement in a larger metric unit to a smaller metric unit, multiply by an appropriate multiple of 10.

Examples

$$54 \text{ kilometers} = 54 \text{ kilometers} \times \frac{100,000 \text{ centimeters}}{1 \text{ kilometer}} = 5,400,000 \text{ centimeters}$$

$$7.2 \text{ hectograms} = 7.2 \text{ hectograms} \times \frac{100 \text{ grams}}{1 \text{ hectogram}} = 720 \text{ grams}$$

Converting Measurements in Smaller Metric Units to Larger Metric Units (p. 134)

To convert a measurement in a smaller metric unit to a larger metric unit, divide by an appropriate multiple of 10.

Examples

$$8245.3 \text{ millimeters} = 8245.3 \text{ millimeters} \times \frac{1 \text{ hectometers}}{100,000 \text{ millimeter}} = 0.082453 \text{ hectometers}$$

$$782.54 \text{ centigrams} = 782.54 \text{ centigrams} \times \frac{1 \text{ dekagram}}{1000 \text{ centigrams}} = 0.78254 \text{ dekagrams}$$

Choosing an Appropriate Unit of Measure (p. 136)

Example

To choose an appropriate unit of measure, use the real-life examples from Lesson 4.7 (p. 136) to approximate the measure.

Item	Metric Unit	Customary Unit
height of a tree	meter	foot or yard
mass of a pin	milligram	ounce
volume of liquid in a cup	dl or cl	cup or oz

Looking Ahead to Chapter 5

Focus   In Chapter 5, you will work with ratios, rates, and proportions. You will write ratios, rates, unit rates, and proportions. You will compare ratios, compare rates, and solve proportions.

Chapter Warm-up

Answer these questions to help you review skills that you will need in Chapter 5.

Write a fraction that is equivalent to the given fraction.

1. $\dfrac{3}{8}$

2. $\dfrac{16}{24}$

3. $\dfrac{27}{36}$

4. $\dfrac{15}{22}$

5. $\dfrac{9}{11}$

6. $\dfrac{5}{12}$

Fill in the blank with the correct number.

7. $\underline{\ ?\ } + 3 = 28$

8. $5 \times \underline{\ ?\ } = 35$

9. $\dfrac{?}{9} = 7$

Read the problem scenario below.

Sofia, Marian, Brianna, and Cassandra are comparing the number of dance CDs each person has in her CD collection. Three-fifths of Sofia's CD collection are dance CDs. Five-sixths of Marian's CD collection are dance CDs. Brianna's dance CDs make up $\dfrac{2}{9}$ of her CD collection. Cassandra's dance CDs make up $\dfrac{1}{3}$ of her CD collection.

10. Order the fractions from least to greatest.

11. Who has the greatest fraction of dance CDs in her collection?

12. Who has the least fraction of dance CDs in her collection?

Key Terms

ratio • p. 145
rate • p. 150
proportion • p. 150

means • p. 151
extremes • p. 151

unit rate • p. 156
variable • p. 160

5

Ratio and Proportion

A fluorescent light bulb is approximately four times more efficient than an incandescent light bulb. In Lesson 5.3, you will determine the number of watts of energy saved by switching to fluorescent light bulbs.

5

5

5.1 Heard It and Read It
Ratios and Fractions

Objectives

In this lesson, you will:
- Write ratios as fractions.
- Compare ratios.

Key Terms
- ratio

Problem 1   Overheard in the Hall

On a typical morning before classes begin, you overhear the following comments.

Miss Brunner: Four out of five students passed the test!

Jamul: At the game last night, he made 3 out of every 5 free throws.

Mr. Ellis: For every 8 classes you will have 10 assignments.

Principal Spencer: Eight of ten students are from the city.

Tina: I spend 5 minutes playing scales for every 15 minutes of piano practice.

Janitor Johnson: Three-fourths of the cars in the parking lot are red.

Lee: She scores a goal for every two soccer games that she plays.

In each of these comments, someone is comparing two different numbers. In mathematics, we often use a ratio to make a comparison. A **ratio** is a comparison of two numbers using division. We can write a ratio as a fraction or using a colon. For instance, you can write, "On average in the school store, 3 out of 5 pens are blue" in two ways.

As a fraction: $\dfrac{3 \text{ blue pens}}{5 \text{ pens}}$

Using a colon: 3 blue pens : 5 pens

When you use a colon, you read the colon as the word *to*.
For instance, the statement "3 blue pens : 5 pens" is read as "3 blue pens to 5 pens." You can see that it is important to include the quantity names in order to be clear about exactly what is being compared.

Write the following comment in two ways.

"I have 7 CDs in my locker and 5 of them are dance music."

As a fraction:

Using a colon:

1. Work with your partner to write each phase that you overheard in the hall as a ratio in two ways.

   Miss Brunner: Four out of five students passed the test!

   As a fraction: $\dfrac{\text{4 students who passed the test}}{\boxed{}}$

   Using a colon: 4 students who passed the test :

   _____

   Jamul: At the game last night, he made 3 out of every 5 free throws.

   As a fraction:

   Using a colon:

   Mr. Ellis: For every 8 classes you will have 10 assignments.

   As a fraction:

   Using a colon:

   Principal Spencer: Eight of ten students are from the city.

   As a fraction:

   Using a colon:

   Tina: I spend 5 minutes playing scales for every 15 minutes of piano practice.

   As a fraction:

   Using a colon:

   Janitor Johnson: Three fourths of the cars in the parking lot are red.

   As a fraction:

   Using a colon:

   Lee: She scores a goal for every two soccer games that she plays.

   As a fraction:

   Using a colon:

Problem 2 *Ratios in the News*

In the school newspaper, you read the following paragraph of a story:

So far in the baseball season, James has gotten 5 hits out of every 6 times that he was up to bat. Mannie has gotten 10 hits out of every 12 times that he was up to bat.

A. James says that he does better than Mannie, but Mannie disagrees and says that he does better. Write each statement in the story as a ratio, including the quantity names. Then use complete sentences to explain whether you agree with James or Mannie and why.

B. When are different ratios equivalent? Use a complete sentence in your answer.

C. Suppose that you are writing for the sports column of the school paper. Write two sentences for the column with information that could be written as two equivalent ratios.

D. Because ratios can be written as fractions, sometimes people try to add and subtract them just like fractions. Suppose that Janitor Johnson observed the following.

3 out of every 4 cars are red.

1 out of every 4 drivers is a man.

Write these two statements as ratios. Be sure to include the quantity names.

E. Herman says that you can just add these ratios to get 1, but Kendra says that you can't add them because the quantities are not the same. Do you agree with Herman, Kendra, or neither person? Use complete sentences to explain.

1. In the newspaper club, there are 20 boys and 30 girls.

   Write the ratio of the number of boys to the number of girls.

   Write the ratio of the number of boys to the total number of club members.

   Write the ratio of the number of girls to the total number of club members. Is this ratio greater than or less than the ratio of the number of boys to the total number of club members?

   Write the ratio of the total number of club members to the number of girls.

   Write the ratio of the total number of club members to the number of boys.

   Write the ratio of the number of girls to the number of boys. Is this ratio greater than or less than the ratio of the number of boys to the number of girls?

2. For each statement below, write at least three different ratios. Be sure to include the quantity names. If possible, simplify the ratio by writing it as a fraction in simplest form. Then order the ratios that you wrote from least to greatest.

   Five teachers out of every ten male teachers are over six feet tall.

   At the high school, there are 300 male students and 400 female students.

   I got 45 questions correct on a 60-question test.

5

Equal or Not, That Is the Question
Writing and Solving Proportions

Objectives

In this lesson, you will:
- Write proportions.
- Solve proportions using equivalent ratios and rates.
- Find the means and extremes of a proportion.

Key Terms

- rate
- proportion
- means
- extremes

Problem 1   Scholastic Quiz

As team members of your school's Scholastic Quiz, students must answer academic questions. Henry answered 5 out of 6 questions correctly, Janine answered 10 out of 12 questions correctly, and Kenton answered 9 out of 10 questions correctly. For the final question, you as the captain need to decide who should answer based on past performance.

A. Write each team member's performance as a ratio.

B. Use the ratios to decide who should answer the question. Explain your reasoning using complete sentences.

C. If your first choice is unavailable, who should be your second choice? Use complete sentences to explain.

D. Compare your answer to Part (C) with your partner. Do you and your partner agree? If you do agree, could another team member possibly be your second choice? Use complete sentences to explain why or why not.

5

1. In the Lightning Round of the Scholastic Quiz, one member of the team is chosen to answer as many questions as possible in ten minutes. The table shows the performance of the team members during practice.

Team Member	Number of Questions Answered Correctly in a Time Period
Henry	3 questions correctly in 5 minutes
Janine	12 questions correctly in 20 minutes
Kenton	1 question correctly in 2 minutes

Each quantity in the table is a **rate,** a ratio of two quantities that are measured in different units. In this case the units are "number of questions" and "minutes."

Write the rate for each team member. Then find another rate that is equal to this rate.

Henry: $\dfrac{\boxed{}\text{ correct questions}}{\boxed{}\text{ minutes}}$ $\dfrac{\boxed{}\text{ correct questions}}{10\text{ minutes}}$

Janine: $\dfrac{\boxed{}\text{ correct questions}}{\boxed{}\text{ minutes}}$ $\dfrac{\boxed{}\text{ correct questions}}{10\text{ minutes}}$

Kenton: $\dfrac{\boxed{}\text{ correct question}}{\boxed{}\text{ minutes}}$ $\dfrac{\boxed{}\text{ correct questions}}{10\text{ minutes}}$

2. **Math Path: Proportions**

When two ratios or rates are equal, we can write them as a proportion. A **proportion** is an equation that states that two ratios or rates are equivalent, or equal. You write a proportion by placing an equals sign between two equivalent ratios or rates or by using a double colon in place of the equals sign.

$$\frac{8 \text{ correct questions}}{4 \text{ minutes}} = \frac{2 \text{ correct questions}}{1 \text{ minute}}$$

8 correct questions : 4 minutes :: 2 correct questions : 1 minute

Write a proportion for each of the team members in Question 1.

Henry:

Janine:

Kenton:

© 2008 Carnegie Learning, Inc.

Take Note

You can read the proportion at the right in two ways:

"Eight correct questions in four minutes is the same as two correct questions in one minute."

"Eight correct questions is to four minutes as two correct questions is to one minute."

Problem 2   Essay Questions

For the last part of the Scholastic Quiz, the team members must answer different essay questions worth different numbers of points. You are competing with another team who has received 30 points out of a possible 36 points. Your team has answered three essay questions that are worth a total of 18 points. You need to determine the number of points that your team must receive in order to tie the first team.

When you do not know a quantity in one of the ratios, you can use a question mark to represent what is not known. In the proportion below, a question mark represents the number of points that you must receive in order to tie the other team.

$$\frac{30 \text{ points}}{36 \text{ possible points}} = \frac{? \text{ points}}{18 \text{ possible points}}$$

When you find the unknown quantity in the proportion above, you are solving the proportion. What number of points will make the proportion true? Determine the number of points by finding an equivalent ratio.

$$\frac{30 \text{ points}}{36 \text{ possible points}} = \frac{\boxed{} \text{ points}}{18 \text{ possible points}}$$

Investigate Problem 2

1. For each proportion, find an equivalent ratio to determine the unknown quantity.

$$\frac{12 \text{ cans of dog food}}{7 \text{ days}} = \frac{\boxed{} \text{ cans of dog food}}{21 \text{ days}} \qquad \frac{7 \text{ lawns}}{14 \text{ days}} = \frac{\boxed{} \text{ lawns}}{6 \text{ days}}$$

2. **Math Path: Means and Extremes**

   When we write a proportion such as 7 lawns : 14 days :: 3 lawns : 6 days, the two quantities in the middle are called the **means** and the two quantities at the beginning and the end of the proportion are called the **extremes.** For this proportion, what are the means?

   For this proportion, what are the extremes?

   What is the result if we find the product of the means? Use a complete sentence in your answer.

   What is the result if we find the product of the extremes? Use a complete sentence in your answer.

5

3. In the following proportion, what are the means? What are the extremes?

$$\frac{2 \text{ red marbles}}{5 \text{ blue marbles}} = \frac{8 \text{ red marbles}}{20 \text{ blue marbles}}$$

What is the product of the means?

What is the product of the extremes?

4. Decide whether the following proportion is correct.

3 misses : 8 hits :: 9 misses : 20 hits

What is the product of the means?

What is the product of the extremes?

How can you determine if a proportion is correct? Use complete sentences to explain your reasoning.

5. In each proportion, find the missing quantity in two ways. First, use equivalent ratios. Then use what you learned about means and extremes. Write complete sentences to explain how you used each method to find the missing quantity.

$$\frac{10 \text{ quarts}}{3 \text{ pounds}} = \frac{\boxed{}}{21 \text{ pounds}}$$

5 miles : 2 gallons of gas :: 20 miles : $\boxed{}$

3 hours : 54 copies :: [   ] : 216 copies

$$\frac{10 \text{ cars}}{\$45,000} = \frac{100 \text{ cars}}{\boxed{}}$$

16 trees : 6 lots :: [   ] : 36 lots

$$\frac{21 \text{ beaches}}{50 \text{ people}} = \frac{\boxed{}}{1000 \text{ people}}$$

$$\frac{14}{18} = \frac{21}{\boxed{}}$$

9 : 20 :: 81: [   ]

5

The Survey Says
Using Ratios and Rates

Objectives

In this lesson, you will:

- Find unit rates.
- Write and solve proportions.

Key Terms

- unit rate

Problem 1   Smart Consumer Survey

A. The economics club in your school is conducting a survey about being a smart consumer. There are 5 girls for every 4 boys who complete the survey. Write all of the different ratios involving the survey respondents that you can. Be sure to include the quantity names.

B. Compare the ratios that you wrote with those that your partner wrote. Write the ones that either of you are missing.

C. Suppose that your school has a total of 90 students who completed the survey. How many of the students who completed the survey are boys? How many of the students who completed the survey are girls? Use complete sentences to explain how you got your answers.

D. Write as many ratios using the information in Part (C) as you can.

E. Suppose that your school has a total of 450 students who completed the survey. How many of the students who completed the survey are boys? How many of the students who completed the survey are girls?

5

Investigate Problem 1

1. Math Path: Unit Rate

A **unit rate** is a rate that has a denominator of 1 unit. Write each of the rates as a unit rate.

$$\frac{340 \text{ miles}}{10 \text{ gallons}} = \frac{(340 \div 10) \text{ miles}}{(10 \div 10) \text{ gallons}} = \frac{\boxed{}}{1 \text{ gallon}}$$

$$\frac{\$240}{20 \text{ pounds}} = \frac{\$(240 \div 20)}{(20 \div 20) \text{ pounds}} = \frac{\boxed{}}{1 \text{ pound}}$$

Problem 2A   Smart Energy Consumption

The smart consumer survey states that for every 100 watts of power that a regular light bulb uses, a compact fluorescent bulb uses 32 watts. The average student who answers the survey has 10 regular light bulbs in his or her home. How many watts of power would each student use on average if he or she switched to compact fluorescent bulbs? How many watts of power would each student save on average by switching to compact fluorescent bulbs? Use proportions to help you solve this problem. Use complete sentences to explain your reasoning. Be prepared to share your solution with the class.

Problem 2B   Smart Driving

The smart consumer survey states that a hybrid car gets 1200 miles for every 20 gallons of gasoline used. If the average student who answers the survey drove a hybrid car 300 miles on vacation in the summer, how many gallons of gas would he or she use? If a hybrid car used 30 gallons of gasoline, how far could a student drive on vacation? Use proportions to help you solve this problem. Use complete sentences to explain your reasoning. Be prepared to share your solution with the class.

Problem 2C

The smart consumer survey asks students to name the better buy—a 14-ounce box of corn flakes that costs $2.52 or a 20-ounce box that costs $3.00. What would the price of the 14-ounce box need to be in order for the 14-ounce box to have the same unit price as the 20-ounce box? If a box had the same unit price as the 14-ounce box and cost $4.50, how many ounces would be in the box? Use proportions to help you solve this problem. Use complete sentences to explain your reasoning. Be prepared to share your solution with the class.

Problem 2D Smart Working

The smart consumer survey asks students to decide which pays a higher hourly wage—a job that pays $130 per week for 20 hours of work or a job that pays $28 per day for 4 hours of work. What would the payment per hour need to be in order for the weekly wage to be the same as the daily wage? If a full-time job paid the same wage as the 20-hour per week job, and the worker received $260, how many hours would the worker be working? Use proportions to help you solve this problem. Use complete sentences to explain your reasoning. Be prepared to share your solution with the class.

5

5

Who's Got Game?

Using Proportions to Solve Problems

Objectives

In this lesson, you will:

- Solve problems using proportions.

Key Terms

- variable

Problem 1   Video Games

A company designs and produces video games. For every 8 games that the company designs, only 3 on average become great sellers. If they design 48 games, how many of these would the company expect to become great sellers?

A. Write a proportion to help you find the answer.

B. With your partner, compare the steps that you used to solve the proportion and find the answer. List all of the steps in your method below.

C. Check that your method will work for any proportion by finding the number of games that the company needs to design in order to have 21 great sellers.

D. In Lesson 3.8, we learned about the customary system of measurement and in Lesson 4.7, we learned about the metric system of measurement. Sometimes we must convert from one measurement system to the other. Suppose that you need to ship video games from the United States to Canada. You can use the fact that 1 kilogram is about 2.2 pounds. Write this relationship as a rate.

E. Suppose that you need to ship a box of video games that weighs 22 pounds. Use the rate you wrote in Part (D) to write a proportion to find the number of kilograms that there are in 22 pounds. Use your method from Part (B) to solve the proportion.

1. Math Path: Solving Proportions with Variables

Because the proportion that you wrote in Part (E) includes a decimal quantity, we need to find an efficient method for solving proportions such as this one. When we solve a proportion, we are finding a missing, or unknown, quantity. We can use a symbol to represent the quantity. Because an unknown quantity's value is different, or varies, from problem to problem, the symbol is called a **variable.** It is convenient to use a letter to represent a variable.

Suppose we have 66 pounds that we need to convert to kilograms. We can set up the following proportion to find the number of kilograms in 66 pounds.

$$\frac{1 \text{ kilogram}}{2.2 \text{ pounds}} = \frac{x \text{ kilograms}}{66 \text{ pounds}}$$

Because we know that the product of the means equals the product of the extremes, we can write:

66 kilogram-pounds = $(x \cdot 2.2)$ kilogram-pounds

In order to solve the proportion, we need to find the number that we can multiply by 2.2 to get 66 as a product. We can use mental math to find the number. We can also find this number by dividing both sides of the equation by 2.2 kilogram-pounds.

$$\frac{66 \text{ kilogram-pounds}}{2.2 \text{ kilogram-pounds}} = \frac{(x \cdot 2.2) \text{ kilogram-pounds}}{2.2 \text{ kilogram-pounds}}$$

When you do this, numbers and units divide out to get:

$$\frac{66 \ \cancel{\text{kilogram-pounds}}}{2.2 \ \cancel{\text{kilogram-pounds}}} = \frac{(x \cdot \cancel{2.2}) \ \cancel{\text{kilogram-pounds}}}{\cancel{2.2} \ \cancel{\text{kilogram-pounds}}}$$

$$\frac{66}{2.2} = x$$

When we find the quotient, we have solved the proportion. So, $x = 30$ and 66 pounds is equivalent to 30 kilograms.

2. We can use this process to solve any proportion. Solve each proportion. Be sure to show all of your work.

$$\frac{2 \text{ gallons}}{9 \text{ miles}} = \frac{x \text{ gallons}}{36 \text{ miles}}$$

$$\frac{2 \text{ trees}}{48 \text{ oranges}} = \frac{x \text{ trees}}{24 \text{ oranges}}$$

5

Investigate Problem 1

$$\frac{8 \text{ games}}{3 \text{ great sellers}} = \frac{172 \text{ games}}{x \text{ great sellers}}$$

$$\frac{4 \text{ defective light bulbs}}{500 \text{ light bulbs}} = \frac{42 \text{ defective light bulbs}}{x \text{ light bulbs}}$$

There are many practical and useful problems that can be solved by setting up ratios and proportions. Form a group with another partner team to solve the following problem using proportions. Be sure to show all of your work.

Problem 2 Video Game Inventory

A store that sells video games looked back at their sales over the last year in order to decide which games to order for next year. The table shows a summary of last year's sales.

Game	X	Y	Z	W
Number Sold	120	80	50	150

A. How many total games were sold last year?

B. If the store wants to order a total of 1000 games this year, how many of each game should the store order?

C. If the store wants to order a total of 240 games this year, how many of each game should the store order?

5

Looking Back at Chapter 5

Key Terms

ratio ● p. 145
rate ● p. 150
proportion ● p. 150

means ● p. 151
extremes ● p. 151

unit rate ● p. 156
variable ● p. 160

Summary

Writing Ratios as Fractions and Using Colons (p. 145)

To write the ratio of one quantity to another quantity as a fraction, write the first quantity with its units in the numerator and write the second quantity with its units in the denominator. To write the ratio of one quantity to another quantity using colons, write the first quantity with its units, then write a colon and the second quantity with its units.

Examples
There are 8 girls and 9 boys in the school drama club. The ratio of boys to girls is 8 girls to 9 boys.

Ratio as a fraction: $\dfrac{8 \text{ girls}}{9 \text{ boys}}$

Ratio using a colon: 8 girls : 9 boys

You have 5 red marbles, 4 blue marbles, and 3 yellow marbles in a bag. The ratio of red and yellow marbles to the total number of marbles in the bag is 8 red and yellow marbles to 12 marbles.

Ratio as a fraction: $\dfrac{8 \text{ red and yellow marbles}}{12 \text{ marbles}}$

Ratio using a colon: 8 red and yellow marbles : 12 marbles

Comparing Ratios (p. 148)

To compare ratios, first write the ratios as fractions, then compare the fractions.

Example
In the parking lot, there are 20 blue cars and 40 red cars.

The ratio of the number of blue cars to the number of red cars is $\dfrac{20 \text{ blue cars}}{40 \text{ red cars}} = \dfrac{1 \text{ blue car}}{2 \text{ red cars}}$.

The ratio of the number of blue cars to the total number of cars is $\dfrac{20 \text{ blue cars}}{60 \text{ total cars}} = \dfrac{1 \text{ blue car}}{3 \text{ total cars}}$.

The ratio of the number of red cars to the total number of cars is $\dfrac{40 \text{ red cars}}{60 \text{ total cars}} = \dfrac{2 \text{ red cars}}{3 \text{ total cars}}$.

The ratio of the number of red cars to the number of blue cars is $\dfrac{40 \text{ red cars}}{20 \text{ blue cars}} = \dfrac{2 \text{ red cars}}{1 \text{ blue car}}$.

The ratios in order from least to greatest are $\dfrac{1 \text{ blue car}}{3 \text{ total cars}}$, $\dfrac{1 \text{ blue car}}{2 \text{ red cars}}$, $\dfrac{2 \text{ red cars}}{3 \text{ total cars}}$, and $\dfrac{2 \text{ red cars}}{1 \text{ blue car}}$.

© 2008 Carnegie Learning, Inc.

Writing Proportions (p. 150)

To write a proportion, place an equals sign between two equivalent ratios or rates, or use a double colon instead of an equals sign when you are using a colon to write the ratios or rates.

Example   The following statements represent the same proportion.

225 miles in 5 hours is the same as 45 miles in 1 hour.

$$\frac{225 \text{ miles}}{5 \text{ hours}} = \frac{45 \text{ miles}}{1 \text{ hour}} \qquad\qquad 225 \text{ miles} : 5 \text{ hours} :: 45 \text{ miles} : 1 \text{ hour}$$

Writing Equivalent Ratios and Rates (p. 150)

To write a ratio or rate that is equivalent to a given ratio or rate, first write the ratio or rate as a fraction. Then write an equivalent fraction using the same units.

Example

$$\frac{8 \text{ gallons}}{2 \text{ minutes}} = \frac{(8 \div 2) \text{ gallons}}{(2 \div 2) \text{ minutes}} = \frac{4 \text{ gallons}}{1 \text{ minute}}$$

$$\frac{8 \text{ gallons}}{2 \text{ minutes}} = \frac{(8 \cdot 30) \text{ gallons}}{(2 \cdot 30) \text{ minutes}} = \frac{240 \text{ gallons}}{60 \text{ minutes}}$$

Using Equivalent Ratios and Rates to Solve Proportions (p. 151)

To solve a proportion, use equivalent ratios or rates to complete the proportion.

Example

$$\frac{17.5 \text{ women's teams}}{16 \text{ men's teams}} = \frac{? \text{ women's teams}}{32 \text{ men's teams}}$$

$$\frac{17.5 \text{ women's teams}}{16 \text{ men's teams}} = \frac{35 \text{ women's teams}}{32 \text{ men's teams}}$$

Using Means and Extremes to Solve Proportions (p. 151)

To solve a proportion, first identify the means and extremes. Then set the product of the means equal to the product of the extremes and solve for the missing quantity.

Example   1200 people : 5 buildings :: __?__ people : 14 buildings

The means are 5 buildings and __?__ people. The extremes are 1200 people and 14 buildings.

$5 \times \boxed{?} = 1200 \times 14$

$5 \times \boxed{?} = 16{,}800$

$\boxed{?} = 3360$

So, the proportion is 1200 people : 5 buildings :: 3360 people : 14 buildings.

Finding Unit Rates (p. 156)

To find a unit rate for a given rate, write an equivalent rate with a denominator of 1 unit.

Examples

$$\frac{\$3.45}{3 \text{ pounds}} = \frac{\$(3.45 \div 3)}{(3 \div 3) \text{ pounds}} = \frac{\$1.15}{1 \text{ pound}}$$

$$\frac{90 \text{ miles}}{120 \text{ minutes}} = \frac{(90 \div 120) \text{ miles}}{(120 \div 120) \text{ minutes}} = \frac{0.75 \text{ mile}}{1 \text{ minute}}$$

5

Using Unit Rates to Make a Comparison (p. 156)

You can use unit rates to compare rates. To compare two rates, write the unit rates for each rate and then compare the unit rates.

Example

A grocery deli charges $4.59 for 1.5 pounds of maple ham. The deli charges $5.25 for 1.75 pounds of bologna.

maple ham:

$$\frac{\$4.59}{1.5 \text{ pounds}} = \frac{\$3.06}{1 \text{ pound}}$$

bologna:

$$\frac{\$5.25}{1.75 \text{ pounds}} = \frac{\$3.00}{1 \text{ pound}}$$

The maple ham is $3.06 per pound and the bologna is $3.00 per pound. So, the bologna is the better buy.

Using a Proportion to Solve a Problem (p. 159)

You can often use a proportion to solve a problem that involves rates or ratios. To solve a problem using a proportion, first write any rates or ratios from the given information. Then, when appropriate, set the ratios or rates equal to each other and solve for the missing quantity.

Example

You are making fruit punch for a party. According to the fruit punch recipe, you need 12 ounces of orange juice for every 360 ounces of fruit punch. You have 16 ounces of orange juice. How many ounces of fruit punch can you make?

$$\frac{12 \text{ ounces orange juice}}{360 \text{ ounces fruit punch}} = \frac{16 \text{ ounces orange juice}}{? \text{ ounces fruit punch}}$$

Because $\frac{12}{360} = \frac{1}{30} = \frac{16}{480}$,

$$\frac{12 \text{ ounces orange juice}}{360 \text{ ounces fruit punch}} = \frac{16 \text{ ounces orange juice}}{480 \text{ ounces fruit punch}}$$

So, you can make 480 ounces of fruit punch with 16 ounces of orange juice.

Solving Proportions with Variables (p. 160)

To solve a proportion with variables, first set up the proportion. Then set the product of the means equal to the product of the extremes. Next, use mental math or divide both sides of the equation by the number that is in the product with the variable.

Examples

$$\frac{3 \text{ trees}}{52 \text{ apples}} = \frac{x \text{ trees}}{780 \text{ apples}}$$

$$3 \cdot 780 = 52 \cdot x$$

$$2340 = 52x$$

$$\frac{2340}{52} = \frac{52x}{52}$$

$$45 = x$$

$$\frac{7 \text{ defective headphones}}{480 \text{ headphones}} = \frac{x \text{ defective headphones}}{2400 \text{ headphones}}$$

$$7 \cdot 2400 = 480 \cdot x$$

$$16,800 = 480x$$

$$\frac{16,800}{480} = \frac{480x}{480}$$

$$35 = x$$

5

Looking Ahead to Chapter 6

Focus   In Chapter 6, you will work with percents. You will write decimals and fractions as percents and write percents as decimals and fractions. You will work with benchmark percents and proportions. You will also learn how to find percent increase and percent decrease.

Chapter Warm-up

Answer these questions to help you review skills that you will need in Chapter 6.

Write each ratio as a fraction.

There are 15 marbles in a jar. Nine of the marbles are red and six of the marbles are blue.

1. Write the ratio of the number of red marbles to the total number of marbles.

2. Write the ratio of the number of blue marbles to the total number of marbles.

Write each decimal as a fraction.

3. 45.72

4. 185.963

For each proportion, determine the unknown quantity.

5. $\dfrac{4 \text{ games}}{6 \text{ days}} = \dfrac{? \text{ games}}{12 \text{ days}}$

6. $\dfrac{2 \text{ pencils}}{5 \text{ pens}} = \dfrac{? \text{ pencils}}{50 \text{ pens}}$

7. $\dfrac{9 \text{ cats}}{12 \text{ dogs}} = \dfrac{? \text{ cats}}{20 \text{ dogs}}$

Read the problem scenario below.

Daniel finished 11 homework problems in 4 hours.

8. Write the rate at which Daniel completes the problems.

9. How many homework problems would Daniel finish in 8 hours?

© 2008 Carnegie Learning, Inc.

Key Terms

6

Percents

Zoology is a branch of biology which involves the study of animals. In Lesson 6.2, you will solve problems like those that a zoologist would solve, such as finding the mass of the brains of different animals.

6

6.1

One in a Hundred

Percents

Objectives

In this lesson, you will:

- Write percents as decimals and fractions.
- Write decimals and fractions as percents.

Key Terms

- percent

Take Note

The symbol for percent, %, was created from the number 100 by slanting the 1 and using the two zeroes to signify a fraction.

Take Note

When a percent is less than 100%, the decimal representation is less than 1. When a percent is greater than 100%, the decimal representation is greater than 1.

Human beings developed fractions to deal with parts of wholes, decimals to make computations easier, and ratios and proportions to solve problems. However, they needed a way to think about proportional parts that was consistent and efficient. So, the concept of *percent* was born.

Problem 1

You are volunteering at your local public library. The librarian wants to order some new children's books, and asks you to do some research. You find a recent survey titled *Teachers' Top 100 Books*. Eight of the books are by Dr. Seuss.

A. The librarian wants to know the *percent* of the books that are by Dr. Seuss. You know that the word percent means "per cent" or "per hundred." You determine that the ratio of Dr. Seuss' books to the total number of books is 8 to 100. A **percent** is a ratio whose denominator is 100. For example, 8% or 8 per hundred can be written as $\frac{8}{100}$, which simplifies to $\frac{2}{25}$.

Work with your partner to write each percent as a fraction.

10%   75%   30%

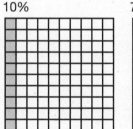 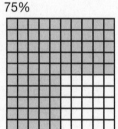 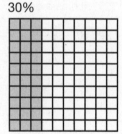

B. Because percent is per hundred, we can write a percent as a decimal by first writing the percent as a fraction with a denominator of 100 and then writing the fraction as a decimal. For example, $12\% = \frac{12}{100} = 0.12$. Write each percent as a decimal.

45%   92%   11%

6%   70%   100%

© 2008 Carnegie Learning, Inc.

6

1. We can also write decimals as percents by writing the decimal as a fraction with a denominator of 100 and then writing the fraction as a percent. For example, $0.15 = \frac{15}{100} = 15\%$. Write each decimal as a percent.

   0.34   0.50   0.65

   0.08   0.1   1.0

2. Writing fractions as percents is slightly more complicated. We can write the fraction with a denominator of 100.
   $$\frac{1}{4} = \frac{25}{100} = 25\%$$
   We can also write the fraction as a decimal and then as a percent.

   $\frac{7}{20}$ $20\overline{)7.00}$ 0.35 $0.35 = 35\%$

   Work with your partner to write each fraction as a percent using either method.
   $\frac{4}{5}$ $\frac{11}{20}$ $\frac{21}{25}$

   $\frac{1}{8}$ $\frac{13}{40}$ $\frac{1}{3}$

Take Note

Percents can be decimal numbers, like 20.5%, as well as whole numbers. As a fraction, the percent 20.5% is $\frac{20.5}{100}$ and as a decimal, the percent is 0.205.

3. What was different about writing $\frac{1}{3}$ as a percent? Use a complete sentence to explain.

4. Because 3 does not divide evenly into 1, we usually write the remainder as a fraction. So, $\frac{1}{3}$ is usually written as $33\frac{1}{3}\%$. Write each fraction as a percent.
   $\frac{5}{6}$ $\frac{5}{12}$ $\frac{7}{15}$

   $\frac{5}{9}$ $\frac{3}{7}$ $\frac{3}{11}$

© 2008 Carnegie Learning, Inc.

Problem 2 *Library Survey Results*

A. The librarian asks you to analyze the results of her survey of 100 library users. The survey results are shown below. Help the librarian analyze the data by completing the table.

Improvement	Fraction	Decimal	Percent
60 out of 100 requested more books	$\frac{3}{5}$	0.6	60%
30 out of 100 requested more computers for public use	$\frac{3}{10}$		
35 out of 100 requested more up-to-date fiction books		0.35	
47 out of 100 requested a larger building			47%
56 out of 100 requested more up-to-date nonfiction books		0.56	
55 out of 100 requested that the library be open more hours			55%
48 out of 100 requested more books on tape	$\frac{12}{25}$		
5 out of 100 requested more movie titles	$\frac{1}{20}$		
3 out of 100 requested additional branches of the library be opened		0.03	
100 out of 100 requested more CD titles			100%

B. Form a group with another partner team. Compare your answers in the table. Be sure that if you have any answers on which you do not agree, you work together to find out why.

6

6

6.2 Brain Waves

Making Sense of Percents

Objectives

In this lesson, you will:

- Use benchmark percents of 1% and 10% to find the percent of a number.

Key Terms

- benchmark percent

Now that we know that percent means per hundred, let's see what this tells us about the percent of a particular number.

Problem 1 Chimpanzees

For science class you are writing a report about the amount of water in the brains of different animals. You learn that the average mass of a chimpanzee's brain is about 400 grams. You know that 78% of the chimpanzee's brain is water. You want to find the mass of the water in the chimpanzee's brain.

A. To find the mass of water, you are really finding 78% of 400 grams. First, let's find some common percents of 400.

What is 1% or $\frac{1}{100}$ of 400?

What is 10% of 400?

What is 100% of 400?

What is 200% of 400?

Use complete sentences to explain how you found the answers.

B. Because you know 1% of 400, you can find some other percents of 400.

What is 35% of 400?

What is 60% of 400?

What is 66% of 400?

What is 78% of 400?

Use complete sentences to explain how you found the answers.

1. Math Path: Benchmark Percents

A **benchmark percent** is a percent that is commonly used, such as 1% or 10%. You can use benchmark percents to find the percent of any number.

What is 1% or $\frac{1}{100}$ of 120?

What is 10% of 120?

What is 100% of 120?

What is 200% of 120?

2. Use the answer that you found for 1% of 120 to find some other percents of 120.

What is 45% of 120?

What is 70% of 120?

What is 13% of 120?

What is 85% of 120?

Use complete sentences to explain how you found these answers.

3. Use benchmark percents to find each percent of 65.

What is 1% or $\frac{1}{100}$ of 65?

What is 10% of 65?

What is 100% of 65?

What is 200% of 65?

4. Use the answer that you found for 1% of 65 to find some other percents of 65.

What is 12% of 65?

What is 50% of 65?

What is 73% of 65?

What is 55% of 65?

Use complete sentences to explain how you found these answers.

6

Finding 1% of a number allows us to find any percent of the number by just multiplying the number representing the percent by 1% of the number. This method works best when we need to find multiple percents of the same number.

Problem 2   *Comparing Brains*

In your report, you want to compare the weight of a chimpanzee's brain with the weights of the brains of other mammals.

A. In some cases, a chimpanzee's brain weight is more than that of other mammals. Complete the table by finding the average weight of each mammal's brain. In this case, suppose that a chimpanzee's brain weighs 400 grams.

Animal	Lion	Sheep	Cat	Rabbit
Average Brain Weight as a Percent of a Chimp's Brain Weight	60%	35%	7%	2.5%
Average Brain Weight (grams)				

B. In some cases, a chimpanzee's brain weight is less than that of other mammals. Complete the table by finding the average weight of each mammal's brain. In this case, suppose that a chimpanzee's brain weighs 420 grams.

Animal	Dolphin	Human	Giraffe	Bear
Average Brain Weight as a Percent of a Chimp's Brain Weight	375%	350%	162%	119%
Average Brain Weight (grams)				

C. In some cases, a chimpanzee's brain weight is much more than that of other mammals. Complete the table by finding the average weight of each mammal's brain. In this case, suppose that a chimpanzee's brain weighs 450 grams.

Animal	Opossum	Guinea Pig	Hedgehog	Rat
Average Brain Weight as a Percent of a Chimp's Brain Weight	1.5%	1%	0.8%	0.5%
Average Brain Weight (grams)				

6

Commissions, Taxes, and Tips
Finding the Percent of a Number

Objectives

In this lesson, you will:

- Use a proportion to find the percent of a number.

Key Terms

- commission

Problem 1   Sales Commissions

Salespeople are often paid part of their compensation as a commission. A **commission** is a percent of the total dollar amount that a salesperson sells.

A. A salesperson in a large department store receives a 3% commission on his total sales. If he sells a total of $425, how much will he be paid in commission? Find his commission by first finding 1% of 425 and then using that answer to find 3% of 425. Use a complete sentence to write your answer.

B. We can also write 3% as a fraction: $3\% = \dfrac{\Box}{\Box}$.

We can use this fraction as a ratio to write a proportion that represents this situation. In the proportion, we need to compare the part to the whole in both ratios.

$$\frac{\text{part}}{\text{whole}} = \frac{3}{100} \qquad \frac{\text{part}}{\text{whole}} = \frac{x}{425}$$

We can write the proportion $\dfrac{3}{100} = \dfrac{x}{425}$. Solve the proportion to find the commission.

C. Write and solve a proportion to find the salesperson's commission if he sells $550.

D. Write and solve a proportion to find the salesperson's commission if he sells $325.

1. A company who sells math textbooks has six salespeople. The table lists each person's sales for a particular week. Complete the table by finding each salesperson's commission.

Salesperson	Total Sales	Percent Commission	Commission
Mr. Allen	$2588.25	4%	
Ms. White	$2106.50	2%	
Mr. Ramirez	$4555.00	3%	
Ms. Hunt	$6258.20	5%	
Mr. Lee	$3430.75	4%	
Ms. Todd	$1005.80	2%	

Write a complete sentence to explain the method that you used to find the commissions.

Take Note

When solving problems involving money, you can assume that you should round your answer to the nearest cent.

2. For some items that you buy, sales tax is added to the price of the item. Sales tax is usually calculated as a percent of the price of the item. In a city, the sales tax is 5%. Write and solve a proportion to find the sales tax on each item.

A CD for $10

A video game for $50

A jacket for $115.20

A movie for $25.60

School supplies for $34.30

Groceries for $78.90

© 2008 Carnegie Learning, Inc.

6

Problem 2   Tips

Many restaurant servers make some of their pay from tips. One rule of thumb is that you should leave 15% of the total bill as a tip. Write and solve a proportion to find the amount of the tip that you should leave. Then complete the restaurant bill.

Bill:	$ 25.60
Tip:	$_____
Total:	$_____

Bill:	$ 75.80
Tip:	$_____
Total:	$_____

Bill:	$ 35.98
Tip:	$_____
Total:	$_____

Investigate Problem 2

1. At a restaurant, you and your friend order a meal that costs $24.00. You leave a 20% tip. The sales tax is 6%. What is the total that you spent at the restaurant?

   Write and solve a proportion to find the tip.

   Write and solve a proportion to find the sales tax.

   Find the total that you spent at the restaurant. Use a complete sentence to explain.

2. We have used two methods to find the percent of a number:

   Find 1% and then multiply the result by the percent to find the answer.

   Write and solve a proportion.

   Use either method to find the indicated percent of each number.

   25% of 72   35% of 90

   19% of 400   140% of 60

   250% of 32   12% of 252,020

6

Find It on the Fifth Floor
Finding One Whole, or 100%

Objectives

In this lesson, you will:

- Use a proportion to find a number that corresponds to 100%.

Key Terms

- discount
- markup

Problem 1   Employee Bonuses

An accountant is reviewing a department store's financial statements. However, some of the information is missing from the files. She needs to determine the dollar amount of each employee's total sales based on the employee's bonus. Each employee's bonus is a percent of his or her total sales. Employee names, bonus percents, and bonus amounts are listed in the table. Help the accountant by determining each employee's total sales that result in the bonus amount.

Employee Name	Bonus Percent	Bonus Amount	Total Sales
Kiesha	18%	$540	
Tonya	21%	$768	
Ruth	15%	$650	
Mario	10%	$325	
Joseph	23%	$678	

A. Work with your partner to find Kiesha's total sales. Determine what 1% of the total sales would be by dividing the bonus amount by the bonus percent (in percent form) and then find the total sales by multiplying by 100.

B. Check your answer to Part (A) by writing a proportion. Then solve the proportion to find Kiesha's total sales. Enter Kiesha's total sales in the table.

$$\frac{part}{whole} = \frac{18}{100} \qquad \frac{part}{whole} = \frac{540}{x}$$

Complete the proportion: $\dfrac{\boxed{}}{100} = \dfrac{\boxed{}}{x}$

C. Use either method to complete the table. Show your work below.

6

Investigate Problem 1

1. A manager at the department store keeps track of "points" for each employee. Employees earn points by being on time for work and for keeping the department neat. On a particular day, he gives "smile" points for each time that the employee smiles at a customer. He recorded the smile points that each employee should receive, along with the percent of total points that smile points represented. He had a problem with his computer, though, and the column with the employees' total points was erased. Now he needs to find the total points that each employee has earned. Use proportions to help the manager complete the table.

Employee Name	Smile Points	Percent of Total Points	Total Points
Garrett	15	5%	
Ricardo	26	8%	
Brent	6	2%	
Lin	21	6%	
Danielle	45	12%	

Problem 2   Discount and Markup

In selling, a decrease in the price of an item is called a **discount.** When the price of an item is increased, the increase is called a **markup.** The department store recently had a big sale where the prices of items were marked 25% off of the regular price.

Now that the sale is over, Tremain needs to mark each of the items back up to its original price. The items and their sale prices are listed in the table. Write and solve a proportion to find the original price for each item. Show your work at the left. The first item is done for you.

Item	Sale Price	Original Price
Shirt	$24.00	$32
Pants	$36.00	
Sweater	$59.95	
Suit	$299.00	
Sports coat	$159.95	

$$\text{Shirt} = \frac{\text{part}}{\text{whole}} = \frac{75}{100} \quad \frac{\text{part}}{\text{whole}} = \frac{24}{x}$$

$$\frac{75}{100} = \frac{24}{x}$$
$$75x = 2400$$
$$x = 32$$

A. If the sale price was 25% off of the original price, what percent of the original price is the sale price? Use complete sentences to explain your answer.

Investigate Problem 2

1. The department store realizes it isn't making enough money.
   The store manager decides to mark up prices by 20%.
   All of the tags still have the lower original price on them.
   Find the new price for each item.

Item	Original Price	New Price
Shirts	$22.00	
Pants	$29.00	
Shoes	$65.00	
Jackets	$50.00	

2. The department store orders toasters from a company that produces three different models of toasters. The company has found that the percent of each shipment that is defective differs by model. Model A's defect rate is 2.5%, Model B's defect rate is 1.75%, and Model C's defect rate is 3.2%.

   On a particular shipment, the company forgets to mark the total shipped of each model. You only know that you received 5 defective Model A toasters, 7 defective Model B toasters, and 16 defective Model C toasters. How many of each model was shipped? You can determine the shipment numbers based on the number of defective toasters and the rate for each model. Show all of your work at the left.

3. The Music Department of the department store sold 12 jazz CDs last month. Jazz sales during that month made up 2% of the Music Department's total sales. Using a proportion, find the number of CDs that the store sold during that month.

   Suppose that the store sells 14 jazz CDs during the next month and the percent of sales from jazz CDs is still 2%. What is the total number of CDs that the store will sell?

4. Solve the problem: 25 is 10% of what number?

   You know that 38% of a number is 342. What is the number?

6

6

It's Your Money
Finding Percents Given Two Numbers

Objectives

In this lesson, you will:

- Use a proportion to find percent, given two numbers.
- Find simple interest.

Key Terms

- principal
- simple interest

Problem 1   Your Budget

In order to make a budget, you keep a record of your expenses for a month. You want to make a circle graph of the information so that you can see where your money is going. The table shows the amounts that you spent in each category.

Expense	Amount	Percent of Income
Bus fare	$25	
Lunch at school	$35	
Clothes and shoes	$30	
CDs	$20	
Movie tickets	$15	

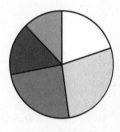

A. Your total income from your part-time job is $125 for the month. For each expense, work with your partner to find the percent of your income that the expense represents using two methods.

The first method is to determine the number that 1% of the income would be and then find how many 1%s there are in each expense. For the "Bus fare" expense you have:

1% of the income: $\frac{1}{100}(125) = \frac{1}{100} = 1.25$

Number of 1%s in bus fare: $\frac{25}{1.25} = \boxed{}$

B. The second method is to write and solve a proportion. Solve the proportion to find the percent of income that the expense represents. For the "Bus fare" expense you have:

$\frac{part}{whole} = \frac{x}{100}$ $\frac{part}{whole} = \frac{25}{125}$

Complete and solve the proportion: $\frac{x}{100} = \frac{\boxed{}}{\boxed{}}$

Enter the percent in the table. Complete the table by finding the percent for each expense. Then enter each expense in the correct place in the circle graph.

6

Investigate Problem 1

1. You make $150 a month at your part-time job. You want to start saving money to put in a savings account. At the end of the month, you put what money you have left into your savings account. Complete the table below to find what percent of your income you are saving and what percent of your income you are spending.

Expense	Amount	Percent of Income
Lunch	$30	
Bus fare	$15	
Shopping	$50	
Movies	$20	
Saved	$35	

2. Three friends are trying to determine which of them is getting the best percent of return on their investment. Each person's total investment and his or her return are listed in the table. Complete the table by calculating the percent returns. Use either method to find the percents.

Person	Total Investment	Total Return	Percent Return
Jefferson	$25,000	$450	
Kate	$22,500	$425	
Liam	$32,000	$525	

Take Note

When you spend money to buy such items as real estate, businesses, or stocks, you are making an investment. If the result of your investment is that you earned more money than you spent, you are seeing a *return on your investment*.

Problem 2   Simple Interest

At a bank, interest is an amount paid by the bank for using your money. The **principal** is the amount of money that you deposit into the bank. **Simple interest** is when interest is paid only as a percent of the principal. To find simple interest, find the product of the principal, the annual interest rate (written as a decimal), and the time in years that the money is in the bank.

Find the amount of simple interest earned for the deposit.

Principal: $300   Time: 15 years

Annual interest rate: 3%   Annual interest rate
                                                                     as a decimal: 0.03

Simple Interest = (Principal)(Annual interest rate)(Time in years)

        = (_____)(_____)(_____)

        = _____

1. Gavin and Susanna have bank accounts at different banks. Gavin's bank has an annual interest rate of 0.04. Susanna's bank has an annual interest rate of 0.03. They want to know whose simple interest will be higher in 5 years. Given the principal for each, find the simple interest for Gavin and Susanna.

Name	Principal	Simple Interest
Gavin	$325	
Susanna	$440	

Who will have the higher simple interest in 10 years?

Who will have the higher simple interest in 15 years?

Find the simple interest after 5 years if Gavin and Susanna's annual interest rates were switched. Who will have the higher simple interest?

2. Join your group with another. Compare your answers to Question 1. Be sure that if you have any answers on which you do not agree, you work together to find out why.

3. The number 40 is what percent of 200?

The number 45 is what percent of 180?

What percent of 250 is 135?

What percent of 120 is 240?

6

So You Want to Buy a Car
Percent Increase and Percent Decrease

Objectives

In this lesson, you will:

● Find the percent of increase of a quantity.
● Find the percent of decrease of a quantity.

Key Terms

● percent increase
● percent decrease

As we have discovered so far in Chapter 6, percents are used in many different situations in daily life including salaries, bonuses, commissions, tips, sales tax, discounts, interest on loans and savings, investment returns, and many others. Many of these can be classified as representing either a *percent increase* or a *percent decrease*.

Problem 1   Car Savings

You can describe a change in quantities using a percent of change. A **percent increase** occurs when a new amount of a quantity is greater than the original amount, such as real estate values that increase by 12% per year. A **percent decrease** occurs when a new amount of a quantity is less than the original amount, such as the value of a car decreasing at 10% per year.

A. You are saving to buy a car. You have a savings account that earns simple interest at a rate of 2.5% per year. This means that for every $100 in the savings account, the bank puts an additional $2.50 into your account at the end of the year. How much interest would you receive in one year if you start with $4000 in your savings account? Work with your partner to find the answer. Show your work below.

B. What is the total amount of money in the account after the interest is added?

C. You can find the percent increase in the amount of money in your savings account. The percent increase is the ratio:

$$\text{percent increase} = \frac{\text{amount of increase}}{\text{original amount}}$$

Complete the ratio to find the percent increase in the amount of money in your savings account after one year if you deposit $5000 at the beginning of the year and have $5150 in the account at the end of the year. Write the ratio as a decimal and then as a percent.

$$\text{percent increase} = \frac{\text{amount of increase}}{\text{original amount}} = \frac{5150 - \boxed{}}{5000} = \frac{\boxed{}}{\boxed{}}$$

$$= \boxed{} = \boxed{}\%$$

6

1. A car dealer advertises a sale on one of last year's models. The original price is $13,000 and the sale price is $10,400. The salesperson is having difficulty determining the discount. Work with your partner to find the discount. Show your work. Write your answer as a complete sentence.

   $13,000 – $10,400 = _____

   Use a ratio to find the percent decrease in the price of the car.

   $$\text{percent decrease} = \frac{\text{amount of decrease}}{\text{original amount}} = \frac{\boxed{} - \boxed{}}{\boxed{}} = \frac{\boxed{}}{\boxed{}}$$

   $$= \boxed{} = \boxed{}\%$$

2. The average price of a gallon of gasoline has changed dramatically since 1940. The table shows the average price for a gallon of gasoline for different 10-year periods. Complete the table by finding the amount of increase and the percent increase from one 10-year period to the next. Show your work at the right.

10-year Period	Price per Gallon
1940	$0.18
1950	$0.27
1960	$0.31
1970	$0.36
1980	$1.22
1990	$1.22
2000	$1.56

Amount of Increase	Percent Increase

3. During which 10-year period was the percent increase the greatest? Write your answer using a complete sentence.

4. Form a group with another partner team. Compare your answers to Questions 2 and 3. Be sure that if you have any answers on which you do not agree, you work together to find out why.

6

5. You decide to purchase a few accessories for your car. The table below lists a number of items, each item's retail price, and each item's sale price. Complete the table by finding the amount of decrease and the percent decrease (discount) of each item. Show your work below.

Item	Retail Price	Sale Price	Amount of Decrease	Discount
Floor mats	$45.00	$38.70		
Seat covers	$36.70	$33.03		
Travel mug	$15.00	$11.25		
Car emergency kit	$89.80	$76.33		
Car cover	$159.80	$111.86		

6. You consider getting a loan to buy a car. The monthly payment amounts for two different loans for three different cars are shown below.

Car	Payments for a 36-month Loan	Payments for a 48-month Loan
Car 1 (new, $18,000)	$582	$448
Car 2 (new, $13,000)	$420	$324
Car 3 (used, $10,000)	$326	$253

What is the percent increase in the monthly payment amount if you buy Car 1 at 36 months instead of Car 3 at 48 months? Use one decimal place in your answer.

What is the percent decrease in the monthly payment amount if you buy Car 2 at 48 months instead of Car 2 at 36 months? Use one decimal place in your answer.

7. For each set of numbers, find the percent of change. Is the percent change a percent increase or a percent decrease?

original: 25   original: 80   original: 120

new: 5   new: 56   new: 240

6

Looking Back at Chapter 6

Key Terms

percent • p. 169
benchmark percent • p. 174
commission • p. 177

discount • p. 182
markup • p. 182
principal • p. 186

simple interest • p. 186
percent increase • p. 189
percent decrease • p. 189

Summary

Writing Percents as Fractions (p. 169)

To write a percent as a fraction, write the percent as a ratio with a denominator of 100. Then simplify the fraction, if possible.

Examples
$23\% = \dfrac{23}{100}$
$75\% = \dfrac{75}{100} = \dfrac{3}{4}$
$56\% = \dfrac{56}{100} = \dfrac{14}{25}$

Writing Percents as Decimals (p. 169)

To write a percent as a decimal, first write the percent as a fraction with a denominator of 100. Then write the fraction as a decimal.

Examples
$46\% = \dfrac{46}{100} = 0.46$
$87\% = \dfrac{87}{100} = 0.87$
$3\% = \dfrac{3}{100} = 0.03$

Writing Decimals as Percents (p. 170)

To write a decimal as a percent, write the decimal as a fraction with a denominator of 100. Then write the fraction as a percent.

Examples
$0.82 = \dfrac{82}{100} = 82\%$
$0.49 = \dfrac{49}{100} = 49\%$
$0.307 = \dfrac{30.7}{100} = 30.7\%$

Writing Fractions as Percents (p. 170)

To write a fraction as a percent, first write the fraction with a denominator of 100. Then write the fraction as a percent. We can also write the fraction as a decimal and then as a percent.

Examples
$\dfrac{5}{25} = \dfrac{20}{100} = 20\%$
$\dfrac{6}{15} = 0.4 = 40\%$

Using Benchmark Percents to Find the Percent of a Number (p. 174)

To find the percent of a number using a benchmark percent, first write the benchmark percent (1%, 10%, etc.) as a fraction and multiply the fraction by the given number. Then multiply the result by the percent you want to find, written as a whole number.

Example
To find 25% of 340, first find 1% of 340 by writing 1% as a fraction and multiplying the result by 340.

$$1\% = \dfrac{1}{100} \qquad \dfrac{1}{100} \times \dfrac{340}{1} = \dfrac{340}{100} = 3.4$$

To find 25% of 340, multiply 1% of 340, which is 3.4, by 25.

$$3.4 \times 25 = 85$$

Using a Proportion to Find the Percent of a Number (p. 177)

To find the percent of a number using a proportion, first write the percent as a fraction with a denominator of 100. Next, write a ratio that compares the percent of the number to the whole number. Finally, write and solve a proportion that uses ratios that compare the parts to the wholes.

Examples   To find the number that is 6% of 750, write and solve a proportion that uses ratios that compare the parts to the wholes.

$$6\% = \frac{6}{100} \qquad\qquad \frac{6}{100} = \frac{x}{750}$$
$$x = 45$$

A salesperson earns a 5% commission on an item that she sold for $225. How much does she earn on the item? Write and solve a proportion that uses ratios that compare the parts to the wholes.

$$5\% = \frac{5}{100} \qquad\qquad \frac{5}{100} = \frac{x}{225}$$
$$x = 11.25$$

Finding a Discounted Price (p. 182)

To find the price for an item that has been discounted, first write the discount percent as a fraction. Then write and solve a proportion that uses ratios that compare the parts to the wholes.

Example   A sweater's original price is $35. The sale price is 20% off of the original price. What percent of the original price is the sale price? What is the sale price of the sweater?

Because the sale price is 20% off, the sale price is 80% of the original price.

$$\frac{80}{100} = \frac{x}{35}$$
$$100x = 2800$$
$$x = 28$$

The sale price of the sweater is $28.

Finding the Markup (p. 183)

To find the price for an item that has been marked up, first write the markup percent as a fraction. Then write and solve a proportion that uses ratios that compare the parts to the wholes.

Example   A department store buys hair dryers at a cost of $4 each. The store then marks up the cost by 25%. What percent of the original price is the markup price?

What is the markup price of a hair dryer?

Because the markup price will be 25% more than the original price, the markup price is 125% of the original price.

$$\frac{125}{100} = \frac{x}{4}$$
$$100x = 500$$
$$x = 5$$

The markup price of a hair dryer is $5.

Finding Percents Given Two Numbers (p. 185)

To answer the question, "The number a is what percent of b?" first find 1% of a. Then, find how many 1%s are in b. Or, you can write and solve the proportion $\frac{x}{100} = \frac{a}{b}$, where x is the percent written as a whole number.

Example   To answer the question, "The number 42 is what percent of 600?" find 1% of 600, then find how many 1%s are in 42.

$$1\% \text{ of } 600 = \frac{1}{100} \times 600 = \frac{600}{100} = 6$$

Because $42 \div 6 = 7$, the number 42 is 7% of 600.

Example   To find the answer to the question, "The number 42 is what percent of 600?" you can write and solve a proportion.

$$\frac{x}{100} = \frac{42}{600}$$

$$600x = 4200$$

$$x = 7$$

So, the number 42 is 7% of 600.

Finding Simple Interest (p. 186)

To find the simple interest paid by a bank, find the product of the principal, the annual interest rate (written as a decimal), and the time in years that the money is in the bank.

Example   You deposit $500 into an account for 3 years that pays 2% annual interest. How much interest does the account earn?

Simple interest = (500)(0.02)(3) = 30

The account earned $30 in simple interest.

Finding a Percent Increase (p. 189)

To find a percent increase, use the following ratio.

$$\text{percent increase} = \frac{\text{amount of increase}}{\text{original amount}}$$

Example   You are saving money to buy a stereo. Last month you had $200 in your bank account. This month you have $230 in your account. The percent increase in the amount of your bank account is $(230 - 200) \div 200 = 0.15 = 15\%$.

Finding a Percent Decrease (p. 190)

To find a percent decrease, use the following ratio.

$$\text{percent decrease} = \frac{\text{amount of decrease}}{\text{original amount}}$$

Example   The stereo you want to buy is on sale. The original price was $270. The sale price is $225. The percent decrease in the price of the stereo, rounded to the nearest tenth of a percent, is $(270 - 225) \div 270 \approx 0.167 = 16.7\%$.

6

Looking Ahead to Chapter 7

Focus   In Chapter 7, you will work with integers. You will add, subtract, multiply, and divide integers. You will also work with number lines, absolute value, and scientific notation.

Chapter Warm-up

Answer these questions to help you review skills that you will need in Chapter 7.

Use mental math to find the product or quotient.

1. 3 × 9

2. 6 × 7

3. 5 × 8

4. 38 ÷ 2

5. 45 ÷ 9

6. 18 ÷ 6

Write the prime factorization of the number.

7. 48

8. 64

9. 56

Read the problem scenario below.

Perry got 93 out of 100 problems correct on his math test. About half of the class scored above 82%.

10. What percent did Perry get on his math test?

11. Was his percent higher or lower than 82%? By how much was his percent higher or lower than 82%?

Key Terms

integer ● p. 199
negative integer ● p. 199
positive integer ● p. 199
number line ● p. 199
profit ● p. 201
loss ● p. 201
sum ● p. 204

integer addition ● p. 206
difference ● p. 209
integer subtraction ● p. 210
product ● p. 211
quotient ● p. 213
absolute value ● p. 215
opposites ● p. 217

additive inverse ● p. 217
power ● p. 219
exponent ● p. 219
power of ten ● p. 219
expanded form ● p. 219
scientific notation ● p. 223
negative exponent ● p. 224

7

Integers

The cent, once a copper coin, is now composed of copper-plated zinc that weighs 2.5 grams for each cent, about 20% less than an older penny. In Lesson 7.5, you will determine how far the mass of a penny is from specification.

7

I Love New York

Negative Numbers in the Real World

7

Objectives

In this lesson, you will:

- Write integers to represent real-life situations.
- Graph integers on a number line.
- Compare integers.

Key Terms

- integer
- negative integer
- positive integer
- number line
- profit
- loss

One of the most important numbers in mathematics is the number zero. It was not until the Middle Ages that people needed a number for "no items." After the concept of zero became widely understood, some mathematicians began to explore numbers less than zero.

In the 1800s, a well-defined system of integers was developed that included consistent rules for addition, subtraction, multiplication, and division. The numbers . . . , –4, –3, –2, –1, 0, 1, 2, 3, 4, . . . are **integers.** Integers include **negative integers** (integers less than zero), zero, and **positive integers** (integers greater than zero). In many situations, you can solve problems more easily by being able to represent quantities using integers.

Problem 1   New York Highs and Lows

Your friend and her family are moving to New York City. She wants to know how cold it gets in the winter there. You help her by finding out the average low temperatures for the winter months.

Month	Dec.	Jan.	Feb.	Mar.
Average low temperature	17°F	–4°F	–2°F	10°F

A. A **number line** is a line that extends in both directions forever with one point that is assigned a value of zero and a given length assigned as one unit. Positive integers are assigned to the units on the right of zero and negative integers to the units on the left of zero. Use the number line below to graph each integer in the table. December is done for you.

```
◄─┼┼┼┼┼┼┼┼┼┼┼┼┼┼┼┼┼┼┼┼┼┼┼┼┼┼┼┼┼◆┼┼┼►
  –10–9–8–7–6–5–4 –3–2 –1  0  1  2  3  4  5  6  7  8  9 10 11 12 13 14 15 16 17 18 19 20
```

B. On the number line, the values of integers increase as you move from left to right. Write the temperatures in order from least to greatest.

C. Use the number line to complete each statement. Use the symbol > for greater than and the symbol < for less than.

–1 ◯ –2   –9 ◯ –5   –3 ◯ 2

12 ◯ –8   0 ◯ –2   7 ◯ 0

Take Note

If a number (other than 0) has no sign, it is a positive integer. You read the integer 10 as "positive ten" instead of just "ten." You read the integer –2 as "negative two."

© 2008 Carnegie Learning, Inc.

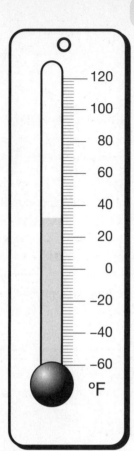

Investigate Problem 1

1. Write each temperature in degrees Fahrenheit as an integer. Use negative integers when necessary.

   Temperature when water freezes: _____

   Temperature outside today: _____

   Hottest temperature last summer: _____

2. In northern Alaska in January, it is sometimes as cold as 40 degrees below zero (in degrees Fahrenheit). On the same day in Death Valley, California, the temperature can be 95 degrees above zero (in degrees Fahrenheit). Write each temperature as an integer. Use the thermometer at the left to find the number of degrees between these temperatures.

3. The highest temperature recorded in New York was 108 degrees above zero (in degrees Fahrenheit) on July 22, 1926, at Troy. The lowest temperature recorded in New York was 52 degrees below zero (in degrees Fahrenheit), recorded on February 18, 1979, at Old Forge. Write each temperature as an integer. Then use the thermometer at the left to find the number of degrees between the temperatures.

Problem 2   On Wall Street

The New York Stock Exchange (NYSE) is located on Wall Street in New York City. At the NYSE, one measure of how well stocks are doing is the Dow Jones Industrial Average. You may have heard on the radio, "The Dow Jones Industrial Average lost 44 points today." Points are the units used to measure the combined gains and losses of stocks.

You can represent a gain in the Dow Jones Industrial Average as a positive integer and a loss as a negative integer. Complete the table by writing each gain or loss as an integer.

Dow Jones Industrial Average		
Date	Gain or Loss	Gain or Loss as an Integer
April 26, 2005	loss of 91 points	
April 27, 2005	gain of 47 points	
April 28, 2005	loss of 128 points	

7

1. The value of a company's stock depends on many factors. One factor is whether a company makes a profit or a loss during a given time period. **Profit** is the amount of money that a company earns after expenses have been subtracted. **Loss** is the amount of money that a company loses because it does not earn enough money to cover its expenses. On a number line a profit is written as a positive integer and a loss is written as a negative integer. Work with your partner to write each profit or loss as an integer.

   A profit of $400: _____   A loss of $234: _____

   A loss of $679,000: _____   A profit of $560: _____

2. A company makes a profit of $5000 one month and a loss of $1000 the next month. Write each amount as an integer. Then plot each integer on the number line below. How many dollars are between the profit and the loss? Use the number line to help you.

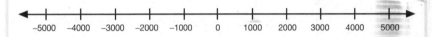

3. Another company had a loss of $500 the first week of the month, a loss of $400 the second week, a profit of $1000 the third week, and a loss of $100 the last week of the month. Write each amount as an integer. Plot the integer representing the first week's loss on the number line below.

   Start at the point you just plotted and move to the left on the number line to represent a loss of $400. At what point are you now on the number line?

   Next, move from the second point you plotted to the right to represent a profit of $1000. At what point are you now on the number line?

   Finally, move from the third point you plotted to the left to represent a loss of $100. At what point are you now on the number line?

   What is the company's total profit or loss for the month? Use a complete sentence to write your answer.

4. Share your answers with another partner team.

Problem 3   New York Heights and Depths

Integers are used to represent height (as the distance above the ground, water, or sea level) and depth (as the distance below the ground, water, or sea level). On the number line height is written as a positive integer and depth is written as a negative integer.

A. Write each height or depth as an integer.

The Hudson River is about 45 feet deep.

The highest point in New York rises 5344 feet above sea level.

B. The Holland Tunnel in New York City is a tunnel that connects the island of Manhattan with New Jersey under the Hudson River. The deepest point of the tunnel is about 90 feet below sea level. The highest point in Manhattan, Bennett Park, is about 270 feet above sea level. Write the lowest point of the Holland Tunnel and the highest point in Manhattan as integers. Then plot each integer on the number line below.

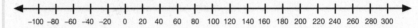

−100 −80 −60 −40 −20 0 20 40 60 80 100 120 140 160 180 200 220 240 260 280 300

C. Suppose you drive from Bennett Park through the tunnel. How many feet are between the highest point that you drove from and the lowest point that you drove through? Use the number line to help you.

Investigate Problem 3

1. You take an elevator up to the 86th Floor Observatory of the Empire State Building in New York City, which is 320 meters above street level. The 102nd Floor Tower, although closed to the public, is about 370 meters above street level. The basement of the building is about 10 meters below street level. The street level is at zero meters. Write the height of the 86th Floor Observatory, the height of the 102nd Floor Tower, and the depth of the basement, and the street level as integers. Then plot each integer on the number line below.

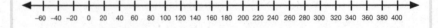

−60 −40 −20 0 20 40 60 80 100 120 140 160 180 200 220 240 260 280 300 320 340 360 380 400

2. Suppose that you could take an elevator from the basement to the 102nd Floor Tower. How many meters are between the highest point that you were in the elevator and the lowest point? Use the number line to help you. Share your answers with another partner team.

7.2 Going Up?
Adding Integers

Objectives

In this lesson, you will:
- Add integers.

Key Terms
- sum
- integer addition

Problem 1 To the Top Floor

A large hotel has a ground floor and 25 floors of guest rooms above street level and 5 floors of parking below street level. The hotel's elevator can stop at every floor. Work with your partner to draw a diagram of the hotel's elevator.

Use your diagram to answer the following questions.

Suppose that the elevator starts at street level, goes up 7 floors, and then goes down 3 floors. On which floor would the elevator be?

Suppose that the elevator starts at street level, goes up 10 floors, and then goes down 12 floors. On which floor would the elevator be?

Suppose that the elevator starts at street level, goes down 4 floors, and then goes up 11 floors. On which floor would the elevator be?

Suppose that the elevator starts at street level, goes down 2 floors, then goes up 5 floors, and finally goes down 3 floors. On which floor would the elevator be?

Investigate Problem 1

1. We can assign positive integers to the floors above street level and negative integers to the floors below street level. Write an integer addition problem that models the elevator's motion in each case below.

   Starts at street level, goes up 7 floors, and then goes down 3 floors.

   Starts at street level, goes up 10 floors, and then goes down 12 floors.

   Starts at street level, goes down 4 floors, and then goes up 11 floors.

   Starts at street level, goes down 2 floors, then goes up 5 floors, and finally goes down 3 floors.

2. Use your diagram of the elevator to help you write a sentence that describes the motion of the elevator modeled by each integer addition problem below. Then find the sum to determine on which floor the elevator stops.

   $(-2) + 20 =$

   $12 + (-7) =$

   $2 + (-5) =$

   $26 + (-20) + (-5) + (-3) =$

3. Join your group with another. Compare the sums that you found in Question 2 with others in your group. Then use complete sentences to explain whether the elevator motion model helped you understand the addition of integers.

In Problem 1, we used the real-life representation of elevator motion
to model integer addition. We can also use an abstract representation,
the number line, to model integer addition.

A. Start at 5. Then move 4 units to the right. Represent this by
graphing 5 on the number line and then drawing an arrow that
starts at 5 and ends 4 units to the right of 5. Where are you on
the number line?

This situation can be written as the sum of two integers. Write
and evaluate an exression that represents this situation.

B. Start at –6. Then move 5 units to the right. Represent this by
graphing –6 on the number line and then by drawing an arrow
that starts at –6 and ends 5 units to the right of –6. Where are
you on the number line?

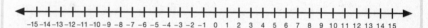

This situation can be written as the sum of two integers. Write
and evaluate an exression that represents this situation.

C. Start at –2. Then move 5 units to the left. Represent this by
graphing –2 on the number line and then by drawing an arrow
that starts at –2 and ends 5 units to the left of –2. Where are you
on the number line?

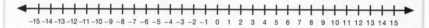

This situation can be written as the sum of two integers. Write
and evaluate an exression that represents this situation.

D. Start at 12. Then move 4 units to the right. Then move 8 units to
the left. Represent this by graphing 12 on the number line, then
by drawing an arrow that starts at 12 and ends 4 units to the
right of 12, and then by drawing arrow 8 units to the left of the
previous ending point. Where are you on the number line?

This situation can be written as the sum of two integers. Write
and evaluate an exression that represents this situation.

7

1. Find each sum. Then write a sentence that describes the movement on the number line that you could use to find the sum.

   (–12) + 15 =

   8 + (–13) =

   (–240) + 300 =

   2450 + (–1500) =

2. **Math Path: Integer Addition**

   Complete the rule below for using a number line to add integers.

   On a number line, move to the _____ when you add a positive integer, and move to the _____ when you add a negative integer.

   Use a number line to find each sum.

   –14 + 1 =

   –11 + 11 =

   9 + (–7) =

   –8 + (–8) =

   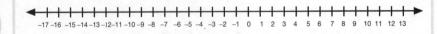

© 2008 Carnegie Learning, Inc.

Test Scores, Grades, and More
Subtracting Integers

7

Objectives

In this lesson, you will:
- Subtract integers.

Key Terms

- difference
- integer subtraction

Problem 1   Correct and Incorrect?

A. On some tests, your final score is found by subtracting the number of incorrect responses from the number of correct responses. For example, if you answered 45 questions correctly and 10 questions incorrectly, your final score would be 35.

How can you represent the number of correct answers using positive integers? Use a complete sentence in your answer.

How can you represent the number of incorrect answers using negative integers? Use a complete sentence in your answer.

B. Work with your partner to answer each question.

Your teacher scores a test that has 30 correct answers and 30 incorrect answers. Write a subtraction problem that models this situation. Then write an integer addition problem that models this situation.

Your teacher scores a test that has 43 correct answers and 27 incorrect answers. Write a subtraction problem that models this situation. Then write an integer addition problem that models this situation.

Your teacher scores a test that has 10 correct answers and 15 incorrect answers. Write a subtraction problem that models this situation. Then write an integer addition problem that models this situation.

Your teacher scores a test that has 22 correct answers and 37 incorrect answers. Write a subtraction problem that models this situation. Then write an integer addition problem that models this situation.

Investigate Problem 1

1. Write a sentence that describes a test that could be modeled by each pair of subtraction and integer addition problems below. Then find the answer to the subtraction problem and the integer addition problem to determine the final score.

   $45 - 23 =$ $(-23) + 45 =$

   $17 - 35 =$ $17 + (-35) =$

2. Model each situation using an integer addition or integer subtraction problem.

   Your score on a test was 15, but you can answer extra questions to change your score. You answer 4 more questions and answer them correctly. What is your new score?

   Your score on a test was 12, but you can answer extra questions to change your score. You answer 5 more questions, but answer them incorrectly. What is your new score?

   Your score on a test was 15, but you can answer extra questions to change your score. You answer 5 more questions and answer them correctly. What is your new score?

   Your score on a test was 25, but you can answer extra questions to change your score. You answer 12 more questions and answer them incorrectly. What is your new score?

3. Write a sentence that describes a test that could be modeled by the integer subtraction problem. Then find the answer to the subtraction problem to determine the final score.

   $15 - 3 =$

   $23 - 7 =$

   $23 - (-7) =$

   $17 - (-35) =$

© 2008 Carnegie Learning, Inc.

4. Form a group with another partner team. Compare the differences that you found in Question 3 with others in your group. Then use complete sentences to explain whether describing a test score helped you to understand subtraction of integers.

Problem 2   Using a Number Line to Subtract Integers

We can use a number line to represent subtraction of integers. Recall from Lesson 7.2 that when you added a negative integer, you moved to the left on the number line. In which direction do you think you should move in order to subtract a positive integer?

A. Start at –4. Then subtract 5. Where are you on the number line?

Write and solve an integer subtraction problem that represents this situation.

B. Start at 10. Then subtract 5. Where are you on the number line?

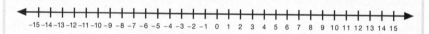

Write and solve an integer subtraction problem that represents this situation.

C. Start at 10. Then subtract –5. Where are you on the number line?

Write and solve an integer subtraction problem that represents this situation.

D. Start at –5. Then subtract –10. Where are you on the number line?

Write and solve an integer subtraction problem that represents this situation.

7

1. For each subtraction problem, find the difference. Then write a sentence that describes the movement on the number line that you could use to solve the problem.

   −18 − 5 =

   8 − (−13) =

   −240 − 300 =

   2450 − (−1500) =

2. **Math Path: Integer Subtraction**

   Complete the rule for using a number line to subtract integers.

   On a number line, move to the _____ when you subtract a positive integer, and move to the _____ when you subtract a negative integer.

   Use a number line to find each difference.

   −11 − 2 =

   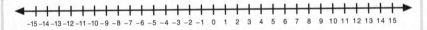

   5 − (−2) =

   −7 − 7 =

   −8 − (−8) =

Checks and Balances
Multiplying and Dividing Integers

Objectives

In this lesson, you will:
- Multiply integers.
- Divide integers.

Key Terms

- product
- quotient

Problem 1   Checking Account

In a bank account, you can use positive integers to represent deposits, or money that you put into the account. You can use negative integers to represent withdrawals, or money that you take out of the account.

A. You have learned that multiplication is repeated addition. For example, if you deposit $8 each week for 5 weeks, you can add the number 8 five times, $8 + 8 + 8 + 8 + 8 = 40$, or you can multiply 8 by 5 to get 40. You decide to open a checking account. The monthly service charge is $4, which you can represent as –4. Write the integer multiplication problem represented by the repeated addition in the table. Then find the total amount that has been taken out of your account at the end of each month.

Month	Repeated Addition	Product	Result
1	(–4)	1 × (–4)	–4
2	(–4) + (–4)	2 × (–4)	–8
3	(–4) + (–4) + (–4)		
4	(–4) + (–4) + (–4) + (–4)		
5	(–4) + (–4) + (–4)+ (–4) + (–4)		
6	(–4) + (–4) + (–4)+ (–4) + (–4) + (–4)		

B. Work with your partner to use repeated addition to find each product.

$-9 \times 6 =$

$7 \times (-11) =$

$-12 \times 7 =$

$13 \times (-5) =$

$9 \times (-1) =$

$-1 \times 6 =$

7

1. Use a complete sentence to describe what happened in part (B) when you multiplied a number by –1 or multiplied –1 by a number.

2. What is the product of (–1) and 5?

   What is the product of (–1), (–1), and 5?

   What do you think is the product of (–1) and (–1)? Use a complete sentence to explain.

3. Find each product.

   $3 \times (-5) =$ $(-1) \times (-5) =$

   $2 \times (-5) =$ $(-2) \times (-5) =$

   $1 \times (-5) =$ $(-3) \times (-5) =$

   $0 \times (-5) =$

   Use the pattern to determine the sign of the product of two negative numbers. Use a complete sentence in your answer.

4. **Math Path: Product of Negative Integers**

   We have seen that a negative number can be written as the product of –1 and a positive number. For example $-6 = -1 \times 6$. Complete the statement to rewrite each number in the multiplication problem below as the product of –1 and a positive number.

   $(-5) \times (-4) = (-1) \times \boxed{} \times (-1) \times \boxed{}$

   Now, complete the statement by using the Commutative Property of Multiplication to rewrite the problem.

   $(-5) \times (-4) = (-1) \times (-1) \times \boxed{} \times \boxed{}$

   You know that $(-1) \times (-1) = \boxed{}$. So, you know that

   $(-4) \times (-5) = \boxed{}$.

5. Find each product.

   $7 \times (-4) =$ $(-9) \times 4 =$

   $(-8) \times (-9) =$ $(-15) \times (-42) =$

Problem 2   Account Balances

A. You have learned that division is repeated subtraction. For example, if you have $28 in your account and you withdraw $7 each week, you can subtract the number 7 from 28 four times until you have a zero balance: $28 - 7 - 7 - 7 - 7 = 0$. You can also divide 28 by 7 to get 4. You are determining the number of 7s there are in 28, which is 4. In a similar way, you can use repeated subtraction to divide integers. For instance, to determine the number of -5s there are in -35, perform repeated subtraction until you get to 0. Complete the table.

Number of –5s	Repeated Subtraction	Result
1	$-35 - (-5)$	-30
	$-35 - (-5) - (-5)$	
	$-35 - (-5) - (-5) - (-5)$	
	$-35 - (-5) - (-5) - (-5) - (-5)$	
	$-35 - (-5) - (-5) - (-5) - (-5) - (-5)$	
	$-35 - (-5) - (-5) - (-5) - (-5) - (-5) - (-5)$	
	$-35 - (-5) - (-5) - (-5) - (-5) - (-5) - (-5) - (-5)$	

How many -5s there are in -35? Use a complete sentence in your answer.

B. Work with your partner to use repeated subtraction to find each quotient.

$-27 \div (-9) =$

$-120 \div (-20) =$

$-45 \div (-5) =$

C. Another way to find the quotient of two integers is to use what we know about multiplying integers. For example, if we divide 24 by 6, the answer is 4 because $6 \times 4 = 24$. Use this reasoning to find each quotient by writing a related multiplication problem. Complete each statement.

$-27 \div (-9) = \boxed{}$ because $-9 \times \boxed{} = -27$.

$-27 \div 9 = \boxed{}$ because $9 \times \boxed{} = -27$.

$-120 \div (-20) = \boxed{}$ because $-20 \times \boxed{} = -120$.

$45 \div (-5) = \boxed{}$ because $-5 \times \boxed{} = 45$.

1. Find each quotient by writing and evaluating a related multiplication problem.

72 ÷ (–4) =

–36 ÷ 4 =

–81 ÷ (–9) =

–45 ÷ (–15) =

2. Math Path: Integer Multiplication and Integer Division

Form a group with another partner team. In your group, complete the rule for multiplying or dividing two integers.
Then write an example of the rule.

The product of two positive integers is a
_____ integer.

The quotient of two positive integers is a
_____ integer.

The product of two negative integers is a
_____ integer.

The quotient of two negative integers is a
_____ integer.

The product of a positive integer and a
negative integer is a _____ integer.

The product of a negative integer and a
positive integer is a _____ integer.

The quotient of a positive integer and a
negative integer is a _____ integer.

The quotient of a negative integer and a
positive integer is a _____ integer.

3. Use the rules you completed in Question 2 to find each product or quotient.

–54 ÷ 6 =   144 ÷ 16 =

55 ÷ (–5) =   –25 × 5 =

–90 ÷ (–15) =   15 × (–6) =

22 × 4 =   –12 × (–5) =

7.5 Weight of a Penny
Absolute Value and Additive Inverse

Objectives

In this lesson, you will:
- Write the absolute value of a number.

Key Terms
- absolute value
- opposites
- additive inverse

Problem 1 A Science Experiment

The average life span of a U.S. coin is 30 years. In science class, you are weighing pennies from different years to determine whether the mass of a penny changes because of wear and tear. According to the U.S. Mint coin specifications, the mass of a penny should be 2.5 grams, which is 2500 milligrams. Your table shows the differences in the masses of 9 pennies from the specification of 2500 milligrams.

Decade	Mass #1	Mass #2	Mass #3
1970s	–13 milligrams	–14 milligrams	–10 milligrams
1980s	–9 milligrams	–6 milligrams	5 milligrams
1990s	9 milligrams	7 milligrams	–2 milligrams

A. In order to determine which pennies are the furthest from the specification, you can write the *absolute value* of each number in the table. The **absolute value** of a number is the distance between the number and 0 on a number line.

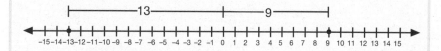

The distance between –13 and 0 is 13, so the absolute value of –13, written as |–13|, is 13. The distance between 9 and 0 is 9, so the absolute value of 9, written as |9|, is 9. Write the absolute value of the number that represents each weight in the table.

Decade	Absolute Value of Mass #1	Absolute Value of Mass #2	Absolute Value of Mass #3
1970s	|–13| = 13	|–14| =	|–10| =
1980s	|–9| =	|–6| =	|5| =
1990s	|9| =	|7| =	|–2| =

B. Which coin is the furthest from specification?

7

1. When the expression inside the absolute value symbol is a sum or difference, we find the sum or difference inside the absolute value symbol first. Then we find the absolute value of the result. Work with your partner to find each absolute value.

   |−6 + 5| = | ⬜ | =

   |−7 − (−11)| = | ⬜ | =

   |−7 − 11| = | ⬜ | =

   |5 − 12| = | ⬜ | =

2. There are times when we need to know the distance between any two numbers on the number line. In Lesson 7.2, we used our elevator model to find the sums of integers. Suppose that the elevator traveled from the tenth floor above street level to the third floor below street level. How many floors did the elevator travel? Use a complete sentence in your answer.

   How many floors did the elevator travel in going from the fifth floor below street level to the seventh floor above street level? Use a complete sentence in your answer.

3. In each case in Question 2, we need to find the number of floors traveled, or the distance traveled. Whenever we find a distance traveled, the answer is expressed as a positive number and can be found taking the absolute value of the difference of two numbers. Find the distance between the numbers by writing an absolute value expression.

Distance between 5 and 10 = | [   ] | =

Distance between –5 and 10 = | [   ] | =

Distance between –54 and –23 = | [   ] | =

4. On a number line, when two integers are the same distance from 0 but on opposite sides of 0, the integers are **opposites.** Graph the integers –8, 5, –3, 0, and 12 on the number line. Then graph the opposite of the integer. Zero is its own opposite.

–15 –14 –13 –12 –11 –10 –9 –8 –7 –6 –5 –4 –3 –2 –1 0 1 2 3 4 5 6 7 8 9 10 11 12 13 14 15

Decide whether the statement below is true or false. Write an example to justify your answer.

Two numbers are opposites if they have the same absolute value but different signs.

5. Math Path: Additive Inverse

In earlier lessons, we used the additive identity 0. The **additive inverse** of a number is the number such that the sum of the given number and its additive inverse is 0 (the additive identity). Work with your partner to complete each addition problem.

[   ] + 6 = 0   –9 + [   ] = 0   –34 + 34 = [   ]

7

Exploring the Moon
Powers of Ten

Objectives

In this lesson, you will:

- Represent numbers using powers of 10.
- Multiply and divide by powers of 10.

Key Terms

- power
- exponent
- power of ten
- expanded form

In earlier chapters, we worked with powers and exponents, expanded form, and the base-ten decimal system. We can now put these different concepts together in order to explore our universe.

Problem 1   *The Earth to the Moon*

A. In Lesson 1.6, we saw that a power is used to represent repeated multiplication. For example, 3×3 can be represented by the power 3^2, where 3 is the base of the power and 2 is the exponent. Work with your partner to complete each power of ten.

$10,000 = 10 \times 10 \times 10 \times 10 = 10^{\boxed{}}$

$1000 = 10^{\boxed{}}$

$100 = 10^{\boxed{}}$

$10 = 10^{\boxed{}}$

$1 = 10^{\boxed{}}$

B. In order to have a consistent system, the power of ten that is equal to 1 is defined to be 10^0. In fact, this is true for any base. When any base is raised to the zero power, it is defined to be 1. Complete each statement.

$5^0 = \boxed{}$ $25^0 = \boxed{}$ $50^{\boxed{}} = 1$ $500^{\boxed{}} = 1$

C. Recall that we can write a number in expanded form using powers of ten. For example, we can write the distance in miles from Earth to the Moon as:

$238,712 = (2 \times 100,000) + (3 \times 10,000) + (8 \times 1000)$
$+ (7 \times 100) + (1 \times 10) + (2 \times 1)$

$= (2 \times 10^5) + (3 \times 10^4) + (8 \times 10^3) + (7 \times 10^2)$
$+ (1 \times 10^1) + (2 \times 10^0)$

Write each number in expanded form using powers of ten.

Diameter of the Moon: 3476 km =

Height of lunar mountains: 25,000 ft =

Moon's surface temperature: 273°F =

1. Write each decimal in expanded form. Remember that the place values to the right of the decimal point are $\frac{1}{10} = 0.1$, $\frac{1}{100} = 0.01$, $\frac{1}{1000} = 0.001$, etc.

   Proportion of gravity of Moon to gravity of Earth:

   0.167 =

   Proportion of the mass of Moon to mass of Earth:

   0.0123 =

   Number of days for Moon to rotate around Earth:

   27.322 =

2. Form a group with another partner team. Compare your answers with others in your group. Then use complete sentences to explain how you wrote each number in expanded form.

3. In keeping with the system of powers of 10, how do you think we can define powers of ten that are less than 1? Use complete sentence to explain your method.

4. Use the method you explained in Question 3 to complete the following powers.

   $10,000 = 10^{\boxed{}}$ $\frac{1}{10} = 10^{\boxed{}}$

   $1000 = 10^{\boxed{}}$ $\frac{1}{100} = 10^{\boxed{}}$

   $100 = 10^{\boxed{}}$ $\frac{1}{1000} = 10^{\boxed{}}$

   $10 = 10^{\boxed{}}$ $\frac{1}{10,000} = 10^{\boxed{}}$

   $1 = 10^{\boxed{}}$

5. Write each number in expanded form using powers of ten.

23.45 =

345.125 =

56,345.987 =

405,378.34 =

6. Write each number as a power of ten.

10,000,000 =   0.000001 =

1,000,000,000 =   0.0000001 =

7. Math Path: Multiplying and Dividing by Powers of Ten

The table shows the product of a number and a power of 10.

10 × 4.5 = 45	0.1 × 4.5 = 0.45
100 × 4.5 = ____	0.01 × 4.5 = ____
1000 × 4.5 = ____	0.001 × 4.5 = ____
10,000 × 4.5 = ____	0.0001 × 4.5 = ____

Write a sentence explaining how the decimal point moves when you multiply by powers of 10 greater than 1 (a whole number).

Write a sentence explaining how the decimal point moves when you multiply by powers of 10 less than 1 (a decimal).

What is the quotient of 1245 and 100?
What is the quotient of 68 and 0.001?

Complete the statements that give rules for dividing by powers of 10.

When you divide by powers of 10 that are greater than 1, you move the decimal point one place to the _____ for each zero in the power of 10.

When you divide by powers of 10 that are less than 1, you move the decimal point one place to the _____ for each decimal place in the power of 10.

8. Use what you learned in Question 7 to find each product or quotient.

89 × 10 =   209 × 0.1 =   155 × 0.01 =

2.9 × 100 =   5.237 × 1000 =   178 × 0.001 =

251 ÷ 100 =   9.265 ÷ 0.10 =   10,454 ÷ 0.001 =

7

7.7 Expanding Our Perspective
Scientific Notation

Objectives

In this lesson, you will:
- Read and write numbers using scientific notation.

Key Terms

- scientific notation
- negative exponent

In the last century, scientists began to unlock the mysteries of the universe by exploring our solar system and galaxy. Through the use of new technologies, scientists also began to explore incredibly small building blocks of matter including cells, molecules, and atoms. Scientists needed to express the very large numbers of our universe and the very small numbers within the subatomic universe as well.

Problem 1 Numbers of the Universe

Scientists began to use a shorthand notation for writing large and small numbers using the powers of ten called **scientific notation.** To use scientific notation, begin by writing the number as a decimal between 1 and 10. Then multiply the decimal by a power of ten.

For example, the distance from the Sun to Earth is approximately 93,000,000 miles. Using scientific notation, we can write this number as $9.3 \times 10,000,000 = 9.3 \times 10^7$.

In the following table are facts about the universe. The very large numbers are written in standard form or using scientific notation. Complete the table.

Description	Standard Form	Scientific Notation
Distance from Earth to the closest star, Proxima Centauri	39,920,000,000,000 km	
Farthest distance from Earth to Pluto	7,528,000,000 km	
Number of stars in the Milky Way		1.0×10^{14}
Farthest distance to outer ring of Saturn from center of planet	480,000 km	
Farthest distance Voyager 1 was from Earth		1.42×10^{10} km
Distance around the Sun (circumference)	4,400,000 km	

Investigate Problem 1

1. Math Path: Negative Exponents

In Lesson 7.6, we found powers of ten for numbers that were less than 1.

$$\frac{1}{10} = 10^{-1} \qquad \frac{1}{100} = 10^{-2} \qquad \frac{1}{1000} = 10^{-3} \qquad \frac{1}{10{,}000} = 10^{-4}$$

The exponents on these powers of ten are **negative exponents.** Complete the statements for each power of 10. The first one is done for you.

$$0.1 = \frac{1}{10} = \frac{1}{10^1} = 10^{-1} \qquad \boxed{} = \frac{1}{100} = \frac{1}{10^{\boxed{}}} = 10^{\boxed{}}$$

$$\boxed{} = \frac{1}{1000} = \frac{1}{10^{\boxed{}}} = 10^{\boxed{}}$$

$$\boxed{} = \frac{1}{10{,}000} = \frac{1}{10^{\boxed{}}} = 10^{\boxed{}}$$

2. Write each number as a power with a negative exponent. Then find the value of the power.

$$\frac{1}{2^3} = \qquad\qquad\qquad \frac{1}{5^2} =$$

$$\frac{1}{4^2} = \qquad\qquad\qquad \frac{1}{3^3} =$$

3. Scientific notation is also used to represent numbers very close to zero. For example, the width of a hydrogen atom is about 0.000000000019253 meters, which can be written in scientific notation as 1.9253×10^{-11} meters.

The table below lists facts about the universe of the atom. The very small numbers are written in standard form or using scientific notation. Complete the table.

Description	Standard Form	Scientific Notation
Width of a human red blood cell	0.000007 m	
Length of microscopic ocean plants called phytoplankton		4.5×10^{-5} m
Width of a grain of sand	0.00012 m	
Diameter of a raindrop	0.003 m	
Thickness of a piece of paper		1.8×10^{-4} m
Diameter of a virus	0.0000001 m	

Looking Back at Chapter 7

Key Terms

integer • p. 199
negative integer • p. 199
positive integer • p. 199
number line • p. 199
profit • p. 201
loss • p. 201
sum • p. 204

integer addition • p. 206
difference • p. 209
integer subtraction • p. 210
product • p. 211
quotient • p. 213
absolute value • p. 215
opposites • p. 217

additive inverse • p. 217
power • p. 219
exponent • p. 219
power of ten • p. 219
expanded form • p. 219
scientific notation • p. 223
negative exponent • p. 224

Summary

Using Integers in Real-Life Situations (p. 199)

Integers allow you to represent quantities in real-life situations in such a way that problems involving these quantities are easier to solve.

Examples   You can represent distances with integers:

loss of 7 yards: –7 yards   5 feet in reverse: – 5 feet

You can represent temperatures with integers:

–35 degrees Fahrenheit   –10 degrees Celsius

Graphing Integers on a Number Line (p. 199)

A number line is a line that extends in both directions forever with one point that is assigned a value of zero and a given length assigned as one unit. To graph an integer, draw a dot on the number line where the integer is represented.

Examples   The integers –1, 2, and 5 are graphed below.

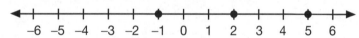

Comparing Integers (p. 199)

To compare integers, graph each integer on a number line. The values of integers increase as you move from left to right.

Examples   Because 1 is to the left of 4 on the number line, 1 < 4.

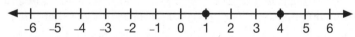

Because 5 is to the right of –3 on the number line, 5 > –3.

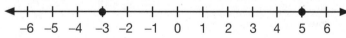

Because –2 is to the right of –6 on the number line, –2 > –6.

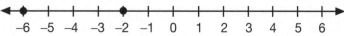

Using a Number Line to Add Integers (p. 205)

To add two integers using a number line, begin by graphing the first integer in the sum.

If the second number in the sum is *positive*, move to the right on the number line the number of units given by the second number.

If the second number in the sum is *negative*, move to the left on the number line the number of units given by the second number.

Example $(-2) + 3 = 1$

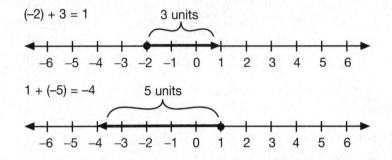

$1 + (-5) = -4$

Using a Number Line to Subtract Integers (p. 209)

To subtract two integers using a number line, begin by graphing the first integer in the difference.

If the second number in the difference is *positive*, move to the left on the number line the number of units given by the second number.

If the second number in the difference is *negative*, move to the right on the number line the number of units given by the second number.

Examples $4 - 7 = -3$

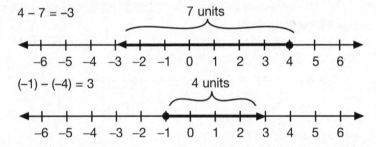

$(-1) - (-4) = 3$

Multiplying and Dividing Integers (p. 214)

Multiplication and division of *positive* integers is the same as with other numbers.

To find a product that involves *negative* integers, first rewrite each negative number as the product of -1 and a positive number. Then find the product using the fact that $(-1) \times (-1) = 1$, when necessary. To divide negative integers, use what you know about multiplying integers.

Examples $(-5) \times 6 = (-1) \times 5 \times 6 = -30$

$(-8) \times (-2) = (-1) \times (-1) \times 8 \times 2 = 16$

$36 \div (-6) = -6$ because $(-6) \times (-6) = 36$

$(-40) \div (-4) = 10$ because $10 \times (-4) = -40$

Finding Absolute Value (p. 215)

To find the absolute value of a number, find the distance between the number and 0 on a number line.

Example $|-4| = 4$ $|3| = 3$

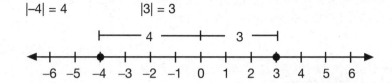

Finding the Absolute Value of a Sum or Difference (p. 216)

To find the absolute value of a sum or difference, first find the sum or difference inside the absolute value. Then find the absolute value of the result.

Examples $|-11 + 6| = |-5| = 5$ $|-8 - (-10)| = |2| = 2$

$|-5 - 17| = |-22| = 22$ $|3 - 9| = |-6| = 6$

Using the Additive Inverse (p. 217)

The additive inverse of a number is the number such that the sum of the given number and its additive inverse is 0.

Examples $4 + \boxed{} = 0$ $\boxed{} + (-16) = 0$ $17 + (-17) = \boxed{}$

$4 + (-4) = 0$ $16 + (-16) = 0$ $17 + (-17) = 0$

Multiplying and Dividing by Powers of Ten (p. 221)

When you multiply a number by a power of ten that is *greater than 1*, move the decimal point of the number one place *to the right* for each zero in the power of ten.

When you multiply a number by a power of ten that is *less than 1*, move the decimal point of the number one place *to the left* for each zero in the power of ten.

When you divide a number by a power of ten that is *greater than 1*, move the decimal point of the number one place *to the left* for each zero in the power of ten.

When you divide a number by a power of ten that is *less than 1*, move the decimal point of the number one place *to the right* for each zero in the power of ten.

Examples $100 \times 0.35 = 35$ $0.01 \times 299 = 2.99$ $10 \times 6.75 = 67.5$

$4.1 \div 0.001 = 4100$ $922 \div 100 = 9.22$ $3 \div 0.1 = 30$

Using Scientific Notation to Write Numbers (p. 224)

To write a number using scientific notation, first write the number as a decimal between 1 and 10. Then multiply the decimal by an appropriate power of ten.

Examples $3{,}600{,}000 = 3.6 \times 10^6$ $45{,}000{,}000{,}000 = 4.5 \times 10^{10}$

$615{,}700 = 6.157 \times 10^5$ $0.0000345 = 3.45 \times 10^{-5}$

$0.00000000042 = 4.2 \times 10^{-10}$ $0.0099 = 9.9 \times 10^{-3}$

Looking Ahead to Chapter 8

Focus
In Chapter 8, you will practice problem-solving techniques. You will learn to solve one-step equations and two-step equations, use the Cartesian coordinate system, and solve problems by using multiple representations.

Chapter Warm-up

Answer these questions to help you review skills that you will need in Chapter 8.

Find the sum or difference.

1. $27 + 94$

2. $\dfrac{3}{4} + \dfrac{4}{6}$

3. $\dfrac{5}{8} - \dfrac{3}{2}$

Find the product or quotient.

4. 2×14

5. $\dfrac{4}{7} \times \dfrac{2}{9}$

6. $\dfrac{3}{7} \div \dfrac{6}{5}$

Use mental math to find the value of the variable.

7. $\dfrac{x}{4} = 3$

8. $10x = 60$

9. $x + \dfrac{1}{3} = \dfrac{2}{3}$

Read the problem scenario below.

Kenneth gets paid $25 a week for delivering newspapers. He wants to save $210 to buy a new bike.

10. Will Kenneth have enough money after 6 weeks?

11. How many weeks will Kenneth have to work to be able to buy the bike?

12. If Kenneth has $\dfrac{1}{3}$ of the money he will need, how much money does Kenneth have?

Key Terms

8

Algebraic Problem Solving

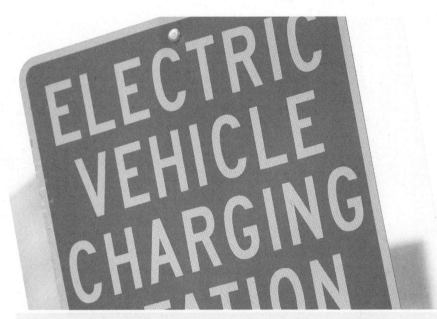

Because they produce no emissions or pollution while parked or running, electric cars are zero-emissions vehicles, or ZEVs. In Lesson 8.7, you will use tables and graphs to determine the distance that an electric car can travel in a certain amount of time.

8

Life in a Small Town
Picture Algebra

Objectives

In this lesson, you will:

- Use picture algebra to represent and solve a problem.

Key Terms

- variable
- equation

Take Note

Recall that we can use a **variable** (a letter or symbol) to represent an unknown value.

In Lesson 1.1, we solved problems by drawing pictures or diagrams to help us understand the relationships between different quantities. In this lesson, you will use this process to solve problems.

Problem 1   The Economy

Suppose that for social studies class, each student must choose a small town and write a report about the town's industry, resources, and economy. The town you choose has three main shops— Gift Gala, the Coffee Stop, and Flowers 'R Us. On a particular day, the shops together earned a total of $432. Gift Gala earned $52 more than Flowers 'R Us. The Coffee Stop earned $32 more than Flowers 'R Us. How much money did each shop earn that day?

A. In the space below, complete the picture to represent the problem. Label the known parts with their values. Do not worry about making the drawing to scale.

Gift Gala	?		
Coffee Stop	?		} 432
Flowers 'R Us	?		

B. Use your picture to find out how much money each shop earned that day.

Gift Gala's earnings:

Coffee Stop's earnings:

Flowers 'R Us' earnings:

C. You can write an *equation* to represent the picture you drew above. An **equation** is a mathematical sentence that you make by placing an equals sign (=) between two expressions. One way to write an equation is to begin by writing the equation with words. One equation that you can write for this problem is:

$$\text{Gift Gala's earnings} + \text{Coffee Stop's earnings} + \text{Flowers 'R Us' earnings} = 432$$

You can label the unknown parts with a variable—use a "g" for Gift Gala's earnings, a "c" for the Coffee Stop's earnings, and an "f" for Flowers 'R Us' earnings. Write the equation above using variables instead of words.

Investigate Problem 1

1. Complete each statement to write two other equations for Problem 1.

   Coffee Stop's earnings = Flowers 'R Us' earnings + ☐

   Gift Gala's earnings = Flowers 'R Us' earnings + ☐

2. Write an equation using variables for each word equation above.

Problem 2   The People

There are two main sections in the town that you are studying, the Hill section and the River section. The town has 1456 people altogether in both sections. The number of people in the Hill section is 256 more than twice the number of people in the River section. How many people live in each section of town?

A. Draw a picture to represent the situation. (Hint: Begin by using a rectangle to represent the River section.) Label the unknown parts with the variable r, where r represents the number of people in the River section, and label the known parts with their values. Do not worry about making the drawing to scale.

B. Use the picture to find out how many people there are in each section of town.

   Number of people in River section:

   Number of people in Hill section:

Investigate Problem 2

1. Complete the statement to write a word equation for Problem 2.

   people in Hill Section

   2(people in River section) + ☐ + (people in River section) = 1456

2. Complete the statement below to write an equation using variables for Problem 2. In the equation, the variable r represents the number of people in the River section.

   ☐r + ☐ + r = 1456

Problem 3 *The Pizza Parlor*

The town has two pizza parlors, Happy Days Pizza and Pizza Palace. On a given day, Happy Days Pizza delivers 35 fewer pizzas than Pizza Palace. Together they deliver a total of 125 pizzas. How many pizzas did each pizza parlor deliver that day?

A. Draw a picture to represent the situation. Label the unknown parts with a variable and the known parts with their values. Do not worry about making the drawing to scale.

B. Use the picture to find out how many pizzas each pizza parlor delivers.

Happy Days' deliveries:

Pizza Palace's deliveries:

C. Use complete sentences to explain how the picture you drew helped you solve the problem.

D. Use a complete sentence to explain how you know that your answers are correct.

Investigate Problem 3

1. Write a word equation to represent Problem 3.

2. Complete the statement to write an equation for Problem 3. In the equation, the variable p represents Pizza Palace's deliveries.

$p + (p - \boxed{}) = \boxed{}$

Form a group with another partner team to solve the more complicated problem below.

Problem 4 — The Agriculture

On one of the farms outside of town, a water tank used for irrigation holds a total of 4568 gallons of water. The tank has three pipes through which the water drains to irrigate three different fields. Pipe B drains twice as much water as Pipe A. Pipe C drains 68 gallons more than Pipe B. Assume that the tank is drained completely before it is refilled. How many gallons does each pipe drain from the tank?

A. Draw a picture to represent the situation. Label the unknown parts with variables and the known parts with their values. Do not worry about making the drawing to scale.

B. Use the picture to find the number of gallons of water that will be drained by each pipe.

Gallons drained by Pipe A:

Gallons drained by Pipe B:

Gallons drained by Pipe C:

C. Use complete sentences to explain how the picture you drew helped you solve the problem.

D. Use complete sentences to explain the mathematical steps you used to solve the problem.

E. Write a word equation to represent Problem 4.

© 2008 Carnegie Learning, Inc.

A company in town makes a special plastic piece that is used in automobiles. The company has five different machines that can produce the piece at different rates. For a particular job, the company needs to produce 2718 pieces.

Machine 2 produces twice as many pieces as Machine 1.

Machine 3 produces 15 more than three times as many pieces as Machine 1.

Machine 4, the oldest machine, produces 7 less pieces than Machine 1.

Machine 5 produces 10 more pieces than Machine 2.

How many pieces should each machine produce?

A. Draw a picture to represent the situation. Label the unknown parts with variables and the known parts with their values. Do not worry about making the drawing to scale.

B. Use the picture to find the number of pieces that each machine should produce.

Number of pieces produced by Machine 1:

Number of pieces produced by Machine 2:

Number of pieces produced by Machine 3:

Number of pieces produced by Machine 4:

Number of pieces produced by Machine 5:

C. Use complete sentences to explain the mathematical steps you used to solve the problem.

D. Write a word equation to represent Problem 5.

8

8.2 Computer Games, CDs, and DVDs
Writing, Evaluating, and Simplifying Expressions

Objectives

In this lesson, you will:
- Evaluate expressions.

Key Terms

- algebraic expression
- evaluate

Algebra is a powerful tool, developed to answer people's needs to solve complicated problems. In algebra, letters are used to represent quantities and to express relationships that hold for the quantities. In Lesson 8.1, we began using algebra. Picture algebra helped us decide the mathematical processes we needed to solve problems. We also used variables to represent unknown quantities.

8

Problem 1   Buying Computer Games, CDs, and DVDs

William is planning to buy a number of items over the Internet. For each item that he buys, he will have to pay a flat fee of $7.50 for shipping and handling.

Item	Price	Shipping and Handling	Total Cost (with Shipping and Handling)
computer game	$29.95	$7.50	
skateboard	$59.25		
comic book collection	$43.50		
book			$54.50
CD			$25.75
DVD	$19.95		

A. Complete the table. In the table, what values changed—price, shipping and handling, or total cost?

B. In the table, what values did not change?

C. Did one value depend on another? Write complete sentences to explain.

D. Use a complete sentence to describe how you find the total cost for an item.

1. Math Path: Algebraic Expressions

An **algebraic expression** is a phrase that uses variables, numbers, and operations. Whenever we perform the same mathematical process over and over again, often we can write an algebraic expression to represent the situation. Write an algebraic expression to represent the total cost in the table. Let the variable p represent the price of the item.

Expression for total cost: _____

Use this expression to calculate the total cost of an item whose price is $15.67. Then use a complete sentence to describe how the expression helped you find the cost.

Problem 2   Renting DVDs

You want to rent DVDs from a local store. The store charges $3 for each DVD, but requires you pay a membership fee of $20.

Number of DVDs	Membership Fee	Total Cost
10		
25		
13		
32		

A. Complete the table to find the total cost of renting DVDs including the membership fee. In the table, what values changed?

B. In the table, what values did not change?

C. Did one value depend on another? Write complete sentences to explain.

D. Write an algebraic expression to represent the total cost of renting DVDs. Let the variable d represent the number of DVDs.

Expression for total cost: _____

Use this expression to calculate the total cost of renting 55 DVDs. Be sure to follow the proper order of operations.

What is the total cost of renting 42 DVDs?

© 2008 Carnegie Learning, Inc.

Take Note

Order of Operations

1. Evaluate expressions inside grouping symbols like ( ) or [ ].
2. Multiply and divide from left to right.
3. Add and subtract from left to right.

Investigate Problem 2

1. You can replace the variables in an algebraic expression with any number. After you replace the variable, you can find the value of, or **evaluate,** the expression.

   Evaluate $t - 8$ when $t = -7, -9,$ and 12.

   Evaluate $4y$ when $y = -3, 0,$ and 5.

   Evaluate $3x - 6$ when $x = -1, 4,$ and 8.

   Evaluate $-2m + 8$ when $m = -5, -3,$ and 10.

   Evaluate $-2.5 + 7.2y$ when $y = -3, 0,$ and 7.

2. Sometimes it is more convenient to use a table to record the results from evaluating an expression. Complete each table.

h	$3h - 5$
2	
−5	
9	
−4	

m	$16 - 5m$
−1	
0	
1	
2	

y	$-5y + 3.55$
1.3	
−2.4	
5.2	
−8.7	
−4.3	

z	$-\dfrac{2}{3}z + 2\dfrac{1}{3}$
6	
−6	
9	
−2	

3. Form a group with another partner team and compare your answers in Question 2. If you have any answers on which you do not agree, work together to find out why.

4. Explain how you evaluated the expressions to the other groups in your class.

5. Finding an algebraic expression that represents a problem is usually the most difficult part of solving these types of problems. Work with your partner to read the following situation and answer the questions.

You have $100 saved and you are spending it at the rate of $10 per week. How much money will you have left after the first week?

How much money will you have left after 4 weeks?

How much money will you have left after 10 weeks?

In this set of questions, what values changed? What values did not change?

Did one value depend on another? Use complete sentences to explain.

Write an algebraic expression to represent the situation above. In your expression, what does the variable represent?

6. Read the following situation and answer the questions.

A local store has 35 computer games in stock and receives 5 more each day. During this time period, no games are sold. How many computer games will the store have in 2 days?

How many computer games will the store have in 10 days?

How many computer games will the store have in 2 weeks?

In this set of questions, what values changed? What values did not change?

Did one value depend on another? Use complete sentences to explain.

Write an algebraic expression to represent this situation. In your expression, what does the variable represent?

Selling Cars
Solving One-Step Equations

Objectives

In this lesson, you will:
- Solve one-step equations.

Key Terms

- solve
- one-step equation

Problem 1   One Day Only

An automobile dealer decided to hold a one-day sale in which the price on every car in stock was immediately reduced by $550. Complete the table below to find the sale price of each model of car.

Model	Regular Price	Sale Price
sedan	$25,890	
coupe	$27,700	
SUV	$35,980	

A. How did you find the sale price given the regular price? Use a complete sentence to explain.

B. Write an expression to represent the sale price given the regular price.

C. Write an equation that you can use to find the regular price of a van. (Hint: Place an equals sign between the expression that you wrote in part (B) and the van's sale price of $19,987.)

Model	Regular Price	Sale Price
van		$19,987
luxury sports car		$55,990

D. Use the equation to find the regular price of the van.

Investigate Problem 1

1. Write an equation that you can use to find the regular price of the luxury sports car in Problem 1. Use complete sentences to explain how you wrote the equation.

2. Use the equation that you wrote above to find the regular price of the luxury sports car. Use a complete sentence to explain how you found your answer.

Problem 2   Your Friendly Car Dealer

You read a report that says that only $\frac{7}{100}$ of all people who own car dealerships in the country are women.

A. There are about 20,000 people who own car dealerships in the country. How many of them are female?

B. In a group of 2000 people who own car dealerships attending a conference, about how many would you expect to be female?

C. How did you find the number of women car dealers, given the total number of car dealers? Use complete sentences to explain your answer.

D. Write an expression to represent the number of women car dealers, given the total number of car dealers.

E. Write an equation that you can use to find the total number of car dealers in a certain city, given that the number of women car dealers in the city is 14. (Hint: Place an equals sign between the expression that you wrote in Part (D) and the number of women car dealers in the city.)

F. Use the equation to find the total number of car dealers in the city.

Investigate Problem 2

1. Math Path: Solutions of Equations

In Problem 1 and Problem 2, you wrote equations to represent particular problem situations. To **solve** each equation, you found the values of the variable that make the equation true. In both problems, solving the equation required only one operation, so the equation is called a **one-step equation.**

What operation is used in each equation?

$$m + 6 = 13 \qquad 19 = x - 10 \qquad \frac{s}{5} = 4.2 \qquad 3y = 15$$

Solve each equation. That is, find the values of the variable that make the equation true. In each case, use a complete sentence to explain how you found the solution.

How does the operation that you used to solve each equation compare to the operation that is actually part of the equation? Use complete sentences to explain.

2. Form a group with another partner team and compare your answers in Question 1. If you have any answers on which you do not agree, work together to find out why.

3. Below is an example of a one-step equation and three different mathematical solutions.

$$z + 6 = 14 \qquad\qquad z + 6 = 14 \qquad\qquad z + 6 = 14$$

$$z + 6 - 6 = 14 - 6 \qquad \underline{-6 = -6} \qquad z + 6 + (-6) = 14 + (-6)$$

$$z + 0 = 8 \qquad\qquad z + 0 = 8 \qquad\qquad z + 0 = 8$$

$$z = 8 \qquad\qquad\quad z = 8 \qquad\qquad\qquad z = 8$$

Explain each solution method and why it works.

4. Use each different solution method in Question 3 to solve each equation.

$x - 8 = 12$ $x - 8 = 12$ $x - 8 = 12$

$5c = 20.5$ $5c = 20.5$ $5c = 20.5$

$b + 75 = 12$ $b + 75 = 12$ $b + 75 = 12$

$\dfrac{v}{4} = 2.3$ $\dfrac{v}{4} = 2.3$ $\dfrac{v}{4} = 2.3$

5. Use any method shown in Question 3 to solve each equation.

$2.45 + b = 5.45$ $6d = 2.46$

$\dfrac{t}{5} = 20.2$ $y \div \dfrac{3}{4} = \dfrac{7}{8}$

$230 = m - 78$ $2.5w = 27.35$

8.4

A Park Ranger's Work Is Never Done
Solving Two-Step Equations

Objectives

In this lesson, you will:
- Solve two-step equations.

Key Terms

- two-step equation
- inverse operations

Many situations can be modeled by equations that need more than one operation to solve them. The equations are called *multi-step equations.* In this lesson, we will work with **two-step equations,** equations that require two operations to solve.

Problem 1 *Building a Walkway*

At a local national park, the park rangers decide that they want to extend a wooden walkway through the forest to encourage people to stay on the path. The existing walkway is 150 feet long. The park rangers believe that they can build the additional walkway at a rate of about 5 feet per hour.

A. How many total feet of walkway will there be after the park rangers work 5 hours?

B. How many total feet of walkway will there be after the park rangers work 7 hours?

C. Define a variable for the amount of time that the rangers will work. Then use the variable to write an expression that represents the total number of feet of walkway built, given the amount of time that the rangers will work.

D. How many hours will the rangers need to work to have a total of 500 feet of walkway completed?

E. Use complete sentences to explain how you found the answer to Part (D).

F. What mathematical operations did you perform to find the answer to Part (D)?

G. Write an equation that you can use to find the amount of time needed for the rangers to have a total of 500 feet of walkway completed. (Hint: Place an equals sign between the expression that you wrote in Part (C) and the total length of the completed walkway.) Then find the value of the variable that will make this equation true.

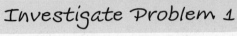

Investigate Problem 1

1. How many hours will the rangers need to work to have a total of 270 feet of walkway completed? Use complete sentences to explain how you found the answer.

   What mathematical operations did you perform to find the answer?

   Use complete sentences to explain why using these mathematical operations gives you the correct answer.

   Write an equation that you can use to find the amount of time it will take to have a total of 270 feet of walkway completed.

   Find the value of the variable that will make this equation true.

2. How many hours will the rangers need to work to have a total of 100 feet of walkway completed? Use a complete sentence to explain how you found the answer.

   What mathematical operations did you perform to find the answer?

   Write an equation that you can use to find the amount of time it will take to to have a total of 100 feet of walkway completed.

   Find the value of the variable that will make this equation true.

3. Form a group with another partner team and compare your answers in Questions 1 and 2. If you have any answers on which you do not agree, work together to find out why.

Part of a park ranger's job is to perform rescue missions for people and animals. Suppose that a bear cub has fallen into an abandoned mine shaft on the park grounds. The cub is 77 feet below the surface of the ground in the mine shaft. A ranger coaxed the cub to climb into a basket attached to a rope and is pulling up the cub at a rate of 7 feet per minute.

A. How many feet below the surface of the ground will the cub be in 6 minutes?

B. How many feet below the surface of the ground will the cub be in 11 minutes?

C. Define a variable for the amount of time spent pulling the cub up the shaft. Then use the variable to write an expression that represents the number of feet below the surface of the ground the cub is, given the number of minutes that the ranger has spent pulling up the cub.

D. In how many minutes will the cub be 14 feet from the surface?

E. Use a complete sentence to explain how you found the answer to Part (D).

F. What mathematical operations did you perform to find the answer to Part (D)?

G. Use complete sentences to explain why using these mathematical operations gives you the correct answer.

H. Write an equation that you can use to find the number of minutes it takes for the cub to be 14 feet below the surface of the ground by setting the expression you wrote in Part (C) equal to 14. Then find the value of the variable that will make the equation true.

1. In how many minutes will the cub be 28 feet from the surface?

2. Use complete sentences to explain how you found the answer to Question 1.

3. What mathematical operations did you perform to find the answer to Question 1?

4. Use complete sentences to explain why using these mathematical operations gives you the correct answer.

5. Write an equation that you can use to find the number of minutes it takes for the cub to be 28 feet below the surface of the ground. Then find the value of the variable that will make the equation true.

6. Math Path: Inverse Operations

In Problems 1 and 2, you needed to perform *inverse operations* to solve the equation. **Inverse operations** are two operations that undo each other. For example, adding 3 and subtracting 3 are inverse operations. Below are two different examples of ways to solve two-step equations. On each line, name the inverse operations. The first one is done for you.

$$2m - 6 = 22$$
$$2m - 6 + 6 = 22 + 6 \qquad \underline{\text{Subtract 6 and add 6.}}$$
$$2m = 28$$
$$\frac{2m}{2} = \frac{28}{2} \qquad \underline{\hspace{5cm}}$$
$$m = 14$$

$$2m - 6 = 22$$
$$\underline{+6 = +6} \qquad \underline{\hspace{5cm}}$$
$$2m = 28$$
$$\frac{2m}{2} = \frac{28}{2} \qquad \underline{\hspace{5cm}}$$
$$m = 14$$

7. Solve each two-step equation. Show your work.

$5v - 34 = 26$ $\qquad\qquad\qquad$ $3x + 7 = 37$

$23 + 4x = 83$ $\qquad\qquad\qquad$ $2.5c - 12 = 13$

$\dfrac{3}{4}x + 2 = 4\dfrac{2}{3}$ $\qquad\qquad\qquad$ $-\dfrac{2}{3}b + \dfrac{2}{5} = 6\dfrac{4}{5}$

$-\dfrac{t}{5} - 9 = 21$ $\qquad\qquad\qquad$ $2 = 2.27 - \dfrac{s}{4}$

$12m - 17 = 139$ $\qquad\qquad\qquad$ $121.1 = -19.3 - 4d$

$-23z + 234 = 970$ $\qquad\qquad\qquad$ $7685 = 345 - 5d$

8

Where's the Point?

Plotting Points in the Coordinate Plane

Objectives

In this lesson, you will:
- Identify points in the coordinate plane.
- Graph points in the coordinate plane.

Key Terms

- Cartesian coordinate system
- *x*-axis
- *y*-axis
- origin
- coordinate plane
- ordered pair
- *x*-coordinate
- *y*-coordinate

In earlier mathematics classes, you may have created graphs such as pictographs and bar graphs to display information. These types of graphs do a good job of showing some information, but fall short of being able to show how one quantity relates to another quantity.

Problem 1   The Cartesian Coordinate System

French mathematician René Descartes devised a method for assigning every point a unique name that describes its location.

A. Take a blank sheet of paper and draw two points somewhere on the paper. Do not allow your partner to see your paper. Turn to your partner and try to describe exactly where the points are on the paper so that your partner can draw two points in the exact same location on his or her paper. Then switch roles and have your partner try to do the same thing with you.

B. Were either of you successful? If so, use complete sentences to explain how you or your partner described the locations of the points.

C. Descartes's method was very straightforward and can be easily duplicated. Use a ruler to measure the distance from the left edge of the paper to the point. Then measure the distance from the bottom of the paper to the point. Now, use those measurements to have your partner duplicate your points on his or her paper. Then switch and have your partner measure and give you the distances to draw his or her points.

D. Were you more successful or less successful using the method in Part (C) than you were using the method in Part (A)? Use complete sentences to explain.

1. Descartes used a similar process to devise his coordinate system that you can duplicate. From the point below, draw a horizontal segment to the right of the point, across the entire width of the box. Then draw a vertical line segment up from the same point across the entire side of the box. Use the length of 1 unit shown below to mark every 1 unit on both lines, starting from the point.

— 1 unit

Does your diagram look similar to your partner's diagram?

2. Place a point anywhere on your diagram. Then have your partner duplicate the point on his or her diagram. Now switch roles and try to duplicate your partner's point. Were you and your partner successful in duplicating the points? Why or why not?
Use complete sentences to explain your answer.

3. **Math Path: Cartesian Coordinate System**

Your work in Questions 1 and 2 is an approximation of how Descartes designed what became known as the **Cartesian coordinate system.** The horizontal number line you drew is the **x-axis** and the vertical number line you drew is the **y-axis.** The point at which they cross is the **origin.** The intersection of these two number lines forms a **coordinate plane.** Label the x-axis, the y-axis, and the origin in the coordinate plane above.

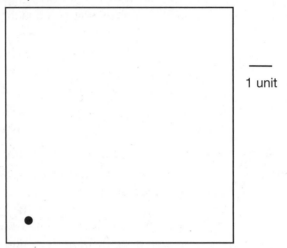

4. Each point on a graph can be represented by an ordered pair. An **ordered pair** consists of two numbers. The first number, called the **x-coordinate,** is the horizontal distance from the origin to the point. The second number, called the **y-coordinate,** is the vertical distance from the origin to the point. The ordered pair is written as (*x*-coordinate, *y*-coordinate). Write the ordered pair of the point that you and your partner drew in Question 2.

5. Usually a coordinate plane is drawn using a grid. The grid helps you to define the ordered pairs of the points. Use the coordinate plane to write the ordered pair that represents each point.

A (_____ , _____)
B (_____ , _____)
C (_____ , _____)
D (_____ , _____)
E (_____ , _____)
F (_____ , _____)
G (_____ , _____)
H (_____ , _____)
I (_____ , _____)
J (_____ , _____)

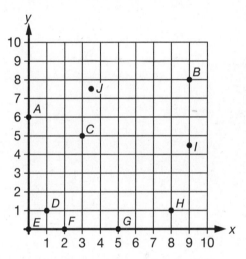

6. Plot each point in the coordinate plane.

A(3, 4)
B(5, 7)
C(0, 3)
D(9, 0)
E(0, 0)
F(2.5, 3.1)
$G\left(3\frac{1}{3}, 4\frac{7}{8}\right)$
$H\left(8\frac{1}{4}, 7\frac{5}{6}\right)$
I(4.25, 7.5)

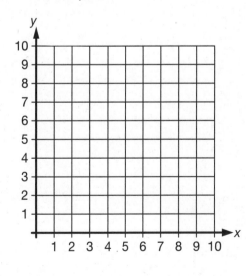

8

Get Growing!
Using Tables and Graphs

Objectives

In this lesson, you will:

- Make a table of values.
- Create a graph of ordered pairs.

Key Terms

- table
- graph

Now that we have a method of representing unique points, we can construct a "picture" or graph of a relationship between two quantities. We can express a relationship in several ways:

- Write an equation.
- Create a table of values.
- Construct a graph.

Problem 1 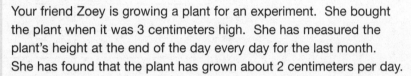 *Height of a Plant*

Your friend Zoey is growing a plant for an experiment. She bought the plant when it was 3 centimeters high. She has measured the plant's height at the end of the day every day for the last month. She has found that the plant has grown about 2 centimeters per day.

A. How high was the plant at the end of the first day? Use a complete sentence in your answer.

B. How high was the plant at the end of the fifth day?

C. How high was the plant after the first week?

D. What quantities are changing? What quantities remain constant? Use complete sentences in your answer.

E. What quantity depends on the other quantity? Use a complete sentence in your answer.

Investigate Problem 1

1. Define a variable for the amount of time in days that Zoey has been measuring the plant.

2. Write an expression that you can use to represent the plant's height in terms of the amount of time in days that Zoey has been measuring it.

3. Use the expression that you wrote in Question 2 and your answers to Parts (A), (B), and (C) in Problem 1 to complete the first six rows of the table.

Time (days)	Height (centimeters)
0	
1	
5	
10	
13	
	33
	45

4. To complete the last two rows of the **table**, write two equations by setting the expression that you wrote in Question 2 equal to each height. Then solve each equation to find the amount of time in days that it takes for the plant to reach each height.

5. Use the grid below to create a **graph** to represent the values in the table. Begin by labeling your axes. Use time for the horizontal axis and height for the vertical axis. The axes are already numbered.

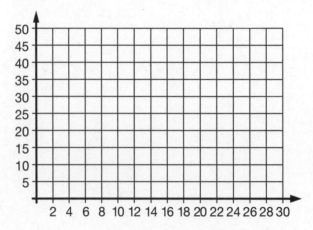

8

6. Write each row in your table in Question 3 as an ordered pair. Note that the *x*-coordinate is the time and the *y*-coordinate is the height.

7. Plot each ordered pair on the prepared grid in Question 5.

8. What do you notice about points that you graphed in the coordinate plane above? Write your answer using a complete sentence.

9. Draw a straight line through the points. How would you describe this line? Write your answer using a complete sentence.

10. Use your graph to answer the following questions. Use complete sentences in your answers.

   When will the height of the plant be 19 centimeters?

   How tall will the plant be in 25 days?

11. How does the graph help you visualize the relationship between the amount of time and the plant height? Use complete sentences to explain.

12. Form a group with another partner team and compare your graphs and your answers to Question 10. If you have any answers on which you do not agree, work together to find out why. Be prepared to share your work with the rest of the class.

Problem 2   *Planting a Garden*

Your friend Julio wants to plant a garden against his house and enclose the garden with 24 feet of fence that he bought. At the right is a diagram of where he wants to plant the garden. The garden will have a fence on two sides.

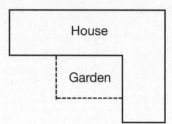

A. Suppose that the width of the garden is 4 feet. In order to have enough fencing to enclose the garden and to use all of the fencing, what length should Julio make the garden? Use a complete sentence in your answer.

B. What is the area of the garden with the dimensions in part (A)? Write your answer using a complete sentence.

C. Suppose that the width of the garden is 6 feet. In order to have enough fencing to enclose the garden and to use all of the fencing, what length should Julio make the garden? What is the area of the garden with these dimensions?

D. Suppose that the width of the garden is 12 feet. In order to have enough fencing to enclose the garden and to use all of the fencing, what length should Julio make the garden? What is the area of the garden with these dimensions?

E. If the area of the garden is 140 square feet, what are the width and length of the garden? Does this question have only one answer? Use complete sentences to explain your answer.

Take Note

You may remember that the area of a rectangle is equal to the number of square units contained in the rectangle. The area can be found by multiplying the length of the rectangle by its width.

© 2008 Carnegie Learning, Inc.

1. In Problem 2, what quantities are changing? What quantities remain constant? Use complete sentences in your answer.

2. What quantity depends on the other quantity? Use a complete sentence in your answer.

8

3. Define a variable for the width of the garden.

4. Write an expression that you can use to represent the area of the garden.

5. Use the expression that you wrote in Question 4 and your answers to Parts (C), (D), and (E) in Problem 2 to complete the table.

Width (feet)	Area (square feet)
0	
4	
6	
12	
	140
	140
18	
20	
24	

6. Write each row in your table in Question 5 as an ordered pair. The x-coordinate is the width and the y-coordinate is the area.

7. Use the grid below to create a graph to represent the values in the table. Begin by labeling your axes. Use width for the horizontal axis and area for the vertical axis. The axes are already numbered.

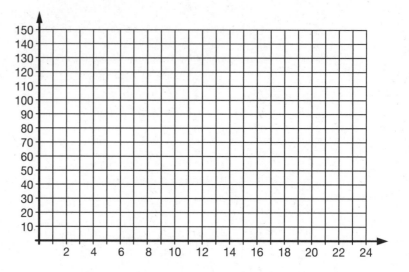

8. Plot each ordered pair on the grid.

9. What do you notice about points that you graphed in the coordinate plane above? Write your answer using a complete sentence.

10. Connect the points with a smooth curve. The result should be an upside down U-shaped curve.

11. Use your graph to answer the following questions.

What are the dimensions of a garden that has an area of 119 square feet?

What is the area of a garden that has a width of 15 feet?

8.7

Saving Energy
Solving Problems Using Multiple Representations

Objectives

In this lesson, you will:

- Use equations, tables, and graphs to solve problems.

Key Terms

- multiple representations

We now have several powerful tools to help us solve complex problems including picture algebra, expressions, equations, tables, and graphs. These tools are **multiple representations,** or different ways of visualizing a problem. Each of these representations is useful in different ways.

Problem 1 · Electric Cars

Your uncle in California drives an electric car. The average speed of his car is 15 miles per hour.

A. How far will your uncle's car travel in 5 hours? Use a complete sentence in your answer.

B. How far will your uncle's car travel in 10 hours? Use a complete sentence in your answer.

C. How far will your uncle's car travel in 30 minutes? Use a complete sentence in your answer.

D. How far will your uncle's car travel in six and one-half hours? Use a complete sentence in your answer.

E. Your uncle drove his car for 135 miles at the average speed. How many hours did he drive? Use a complete sentence in your answer.

1. What are the two quantities that are changing in Problem 1?

2. What quantity depends on the other quantity? Use a complete sentence in your answer.

3. Work on completing the table below by first filling in the names of the quantities in Problem 1 and their units of measure. Then fill in the table with your answers from Problem 1. The other table entries will be filled in later.

	Column 1	Column 2
Quantity Name		
Unit of Measure		
Problem 1, Part (A)	5	
Problem 1, Part (B)	10	
Problem 1, Part (C)		
Problem 1, Part (D)		
Problem 1, Part (E)		135
Question 6		112.5
Question 7		$123\frac{3}{4}$
Expression		

4. Define a variable for the quantity in Column 1. Enter this variable in the "Expression" row of the table under Column 1.

5. Write an expression that you can use to represent the quantity in Column 2 in terms of the quantity in Column 1. Enter this expression in the "Expression" row of the table under Column 2.

6. You want to determine how long it will take the car to travel 112.5 miles. Use the expression you wrote in Question 5 to write an equation that you can solve to find your answer. Then write your answer in the appropriate place in the table.

7. You want to determine how long it will take the car to travel $123\frac{3}{4}$ miles. Use the expression that you wrote in Question 5 to write an equation that you can solve to find your answer. Then write your answer in the appropriate place in the table.

8. Use the grid below to create a graph to represent the values in the table. Begin by labeling your axes. Use time for the horizontal axis and distance for the vertical axis. The axes are already numbered.

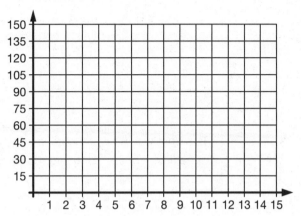

9. Write each row in your table in Question 3 as an ordered pair. Note that the *x*-coordinate is the amount of time that the car traveled and the *y*-coordinate is the distance the car has traveled.

10. Plot each ordered pair on the prepared grid in Question 8.

11. Draw a straight line through the points. How would you describe this line? Write your answer using a complete sentence.

12. Use your equation to answer the following questions.

    Your uncle drove his car for 450 miles at the average speed. How many hours did he drive?

    How far will your uncle's car travel in 29 hours?

13. Join your group with another and compare your graphs and your answers to Question 12. If you have any answers on which you do not agree, work together to find out why. Be prepared to share your work with the rest of the class.

Problem 2 — Energy-Saving Bulbs

When you use energy-efficient light bulbs, you can save up to $4.32 on your monthly electric bill for each bulb that you use (assuming that a bulb burns for 12 hours per day and electricity costs $.30 per kilowatt hour). Suppose that your family's monthly electric bill is $80.

A. What will the electric bill be if you change 2 bulbs to energy-efficient bulbs? Use a complete sentence in your answer.

B. What will the electric bill be if you change 4 bulbs to energy-efficient bulbs? Use a complete sentence in your answer.

C. What will the electric bill be if you change 5 bulbs to energy-efficient bulbs? Use a complete sentence in your answer.

D. If the electric bill is $54.08, how many bulbs were changed to energy-efficient bulbs? Use a complete sentence in your answer.

E. If the electric bill is $45.44, how many bulbs were changed to energy-efficient bulbs? Use a complete sentence in your answer.

Investigate Problem 2

1. What are the two quantities that are changing in Problem 2? Use a complete sentence in your answer.

Investigate Problem 2

2. What quantity depends on the other quantity? Use a complete sentence in your answer.

3. Work on completing the table below by first filling in the names of the quantities in Problem 2 and their units of measure. Then fill in the table with your answers from Problem 2. The other table entries will be filled in later.

	Column 1	Column 2
Quantity Name		
Unit of Measure		
Problem 2, Part (A)	2	
Problem 2, Part (B)	4	
Problem 2, Part (C)	5	
Problem 2, Part (D)		54.08
Problem 2, Part (E)		45.44
Question 6		36.80
Question 7		28.16
Expression		

4. Define a variable for the quantity in Column 1. Enter this variable in the "Expression" row of the table under Column 1.

5. Write an expression that you can use to represent the quantity in the Column 2 in terms of the quantity in Column 1. Enter this expression in the "Expression" row of the table under Column 2.

6. You want to determine how many bulbs were changed to energy-efficient bulbs if the monthly electric bill is $36.80. Use the expression that you wrote in Question 5 to write an equation that you can solve to find your answer. Then write your answer in the appropriate place in the table.

7. You want to determine how many bulbs were changed if the monthly electric bill is $28.16. Use the expression that you wrote in Question 5 to write an equation that you can solve to find your answer. Then write your answer in the appropriate place in the table.

8. Use the grid below to create a graph to represent the values in the table. Begin by labeling your axes. Use the number of bulbs for the horizontal axis and the amount of the electrical bill for the vertical axis. The axes are already numbered.

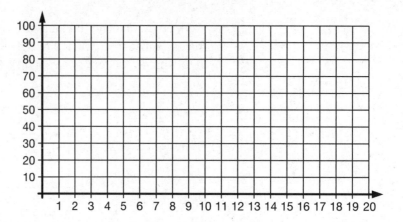

9. Write each row in your table in Question 3 as an ordered pair. Note that the *x*-coordinate is the number of bulbs and the *y*-coordinate is the amount of the electric bill.

10. Plot each ordered pair on the prepared grid in Question 8.

11. Draw a straight line through the points. How would you describe this line? Write your answer using a complete sentence.

12. Use your graph to answer the following questions. Write your answer using a complete sentence.

What will the electric bill be if you change 15 bulbs to energy-efficient bulbs?

If the electric bill is $58.40, how many bulbs were changed?

13. Join your group with another and compare your graphs and your answers to Question 12. If you have any answers on which you do not agree, work together to find out why. Be prepared to share your work with the rest of the class.

Looking Back at Chapter 8

Key Terms

variable • p. 231

equation • p. 231

algebraic expression • p. 238

evaluate • p. 239

solve • p. 243

one-step equation • p. 243

two-step equation • p. 245

inverse operations • p. 248

Cartesian coordinate
    system • p. 252

x-axis • p. 252

y-axis • p. 252

origin • p. 252

coordinate plane • p. 252

ordered pair • p. 253

x-coordinate • p. 253

y-coordinate • p. 253

table • p. 256

graph • p. 256

multiple representation • p. 261

Summary

Using Picture Algebra (p. 231)

You can use a picture or diagram to help you solve word problems. You can also use the picture to write an equation that represents the situation.

Example   On a given day, Pretty Petals and Coral's Florals sell 46 roses altogether. Pretty Petals sells 12 more roses than Coral's Florals. Draw a picture to represent the situation.

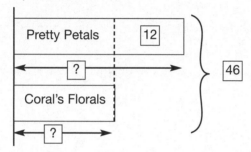

From the picture, you can see that Coral's Florals sold 17 roses and Pretty Petals sold, 17 + 12, or 29 roses.

Because the two shops sold 46 roses altogether, you can write the following word equation.

Number of roses sold + Number of roses sold = 46 roses
    by Pretty Petals   by Coral's Florals

Let *p* represent the number of roses sold by Pretty Petals and *c* represent the number of roses sold by Coral's Florals. A variable equation for the situation is

$p + c = 46.$

Writing Algebraic Expressions (p. 238)

To write an algebraic expression for a situation, use variables, numbers, and operations to represent the situation.

Example   A small pizza costs $6. There is a delivery fee of $1. Let the variable *p* represent the number of pizzas. Use the variable to write the expression for the total cost.

Expression for total cost: 6*p* + 1

Evaluating Algebraic Expressions (p. 239)

To evaluate an algebraic expression, replace the variable with any number and evaluate the expression.

Example   To evaluate $3x - 7$ when $x = 3$, replace x with 3 and evaluate.

$$3 \cdot 3 - 7 = 9 - 7 = 2$$

To evaluate $3x - 7$ when $x = -2$, replace x with -2 and evaluate.

$$3 \cdot (-2) - 7 = -6 - 7 = -13$$

Solving One-Step Equations (p. 243)

To solve an equation, find the value of the variable that makes the equation true. A one-step equation requires one operation to find this value.

Example   To solve the equation $4x = 20$, use one operation to find the value that makes the equation true.

$$\frac{4x}{4} = \frac{20}{4}$$

$$x = 5$$

Solving Two-Step Equations (p. 248)

To solve a two-step equation, find the value of the variable that makes the equation true. Use inverse operations to find this value.

Example   To solve the equation $5y + 3 = 13$, use two operations to find the value that makes the equation true.

$$5y + 3 - 3 = 13 - 3$$

$$5y = 10$$

$$\frac{5y}{5} = \frac{10}{5}$$

$$y = 2$$

Plotting Points in the Coordinate Plane (p. 253)

To plot a point (x, y) in the coordinate plane, start at the origin. First move x units horizontally and then move y units vertically. Draw a point.

Examples   The points (1, 1), (2, 5), (4, 7), and (8, 9) are plotted in the coordinate plane.

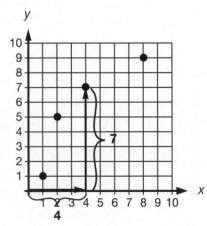

Making a Table of Values (p. 256)

To make a table of values for a situation, first write an expression that represents the situation. In your table, record the quantity names from your expression, the units of measure, and the expression. Then evaluate the expression for different values. Enter these values and the answers in your table.

Example   You have $15. Your parents will give you $5 a week for allowance. You want to write an expression that will represent the amount of money that you will have after a certain number of weeks. Let *t* represent the number of weeks you have been earning an allowance. An expression that represents this situation is $5t + 15$. In your table, let the first column represent the number of weeks and the second column represent the total amount of money you have saved.

Quantity Name	Time	Total Amount of Money
Unit of Measure	Weeks	Dollars
	1	20
	2	25
	3	30
	4	35
	5	40
Expression	t	5t + 15

Constructing a Graph (pp. 256–257)

To construct a graph from a table of values, first label the axes on a grid by using the table values as a guide. Next, write each row of numbers in your table as an ordered pair. Then plot each ordered pair on the grid. Finally, connect the points with a smooth line.

Example

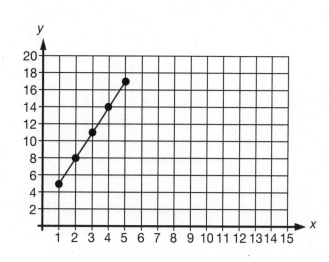

x	y	Ordered Pair
1	5	(1, 5)
2	8	(2, 8)
3	11	(3, 11)
4	14	(4, 14)
5	17	(5, 17)

Looking Ahead to Chapter 9

Focus In Chapter 9, you will work with angles and angle pairs, triangles, quadrilaterals, and other polygons. You will learn to find the lengths of sides and measures of angles. You will also learn how to find a measurement indirectly.

Chapter Warm-up

Answer these questions to help you review skills that you will need in Chapter 9.

Use a ruler to find the length of each line segment below in centimeters.

1. _____

2. _____

Find the sum.

3. 66 + 24

4. 86 + 94

5. 53 + 37

9 **Read the problem scenario below.**

There are 20 marbles in a bag. Nine are red, 4 are orange, 3 are yellow, and the rest are blue.

6. Write a ratio that represents the number of red marbles to the total number of marbles.

7. Write a ratio that represents the number of orange marbles to the total number of marbles.

8. Write a ratio that represents the number of yellow marbles to the total number of marbles.

9. Write a ratio that represents the number of marbles that are not blue to the total number of marbles.

Key Terms

angle p. 273	corresponding angles p. 275	rectangle p. 283
vertex p. 273	vertical angles p. 277	square p. 283
degrees p. 273	adjacent angles p. 277	polygon p. 285
right angle p. 273	triangle p. 279	diagonal p. 285
straight angle p. 273	equilateral triangle p. 280	regular polygon p. 286
acute angle p. 274	isosceles triangle p. 280	irregular polygon p. 286
obtuse angle p. 274	scalene triangle p. 280	similar polygons p. 287
protractor p. 274	acute triangle p. 280	corresponding sides p. 288
complementary angles p. 275	obtuse triangle p. 280	scale factor p. 288
supplementary angles p. 275	right triangle p. 280	corresponding angles p. 289
transversal p. 275	quadrilateral p. 283	similar triangles p. 291
congruent angles p. 275	trapezoid p. 283	indirect measurement p. 291
alternate interior angles p. 275	parallelogram p. 283	congruent polygons p. 295
alternate exterior angles p. 275	rhombus p. 283	congruent p. 295

9

Geometric Figures and Their Properties

The highest flagpole in the world is in North Korea and stands 160 meters tall. In Lesson 9.5, you will use indirect measurement to find the height of a flagpole.

Geometry Introduction

Geometry is the branch of mathematics that studies the size and shape of things. The basic building blocks of geometry are points, lines, and planes. In this chapter, you will explore angles and polygons consisting of rays and line segments. You will also learn to make decisions about whether polygons are mathematically similar or exactly the same.

The following terms are common geometric terms that you should remember from earlier mathematics courses.

A *point* represents a position in space with no size.

Point *A* is represented by this dot.

A *line* is a collection of points that extend infinitely in opposite directions. A line is named using two points on the line. For example, line *BC* is shown.

A *line segment* is a piece of a line with two endpoints. A line segment is named by its two endpoints. For example, line segment *XY* is shown.

X •———————————• Y

A *ray* extends forever in one direction with one endpoint. A ray is named by its endpoint and another point on the ray. For example, ray *ST* is shown.

S •————————————→ T

A *plane* is a flat surface with no thickness that extends forever in two dimensions.

Figuring All of the Angles
Angles and Angle Pairs

Objectives

In this lesson, you will:

- Determine measures of angles.
- Identify special angle pairs.

Key Terms

- angle
- vertex
- degrees
- right angle
- straight angle
- acute angle
- obtuse angle
- protractor
- complementary angle
- supplementary angle
- transversal
- congruent angles
- alternate interior angles
- alternate exterior angles
- corresponding angles
- vertical angles
- adjacent angles

Problem 1 · Pizza Angles

Your aunt is opening an Italian restaurant. You volunteer to help her on the weekends. One of your jobs is to slice the pizzas as they come out of the oven. You notice that the pieces have a smaller or larger angle at the center of the slice depending on the number of pieces into which the customer wants a pizza cut.

Imagine that the sides of a slice of pizza are two different rays with the same endpoint. These rays connect to form an **angle.** The endpoint is called the **vertex** of the angle.

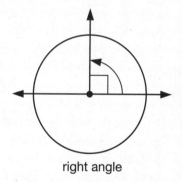

The angle in the figure at the right has several names: ∠B, ∠ABC, and ∠CBA. Notice that when you use three letters to name an angle, the vertex is always the middle letter.

The measure of an angle gives the size of the opening between its sides. The unit used to measure angles is **degrees** (°).

Imagine that you slice an extra-large round pizza into 360 equal pieces. The angle of each slice measures one degree (1°). There are 360° around a point (in this case, the center of the pizza).

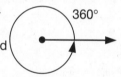

The angle formed by a slice that is one quarter of the pizza measures 90°. This is a **right angle,** and is shown by placing a corner, ⌐, at its vertex.

The angle formed by a slice that is one half of the pizza is a **straight angle.** Determine the measure of a straight angle. Use a complete sentence to explain how you determined the measure.

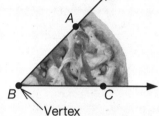

right angle

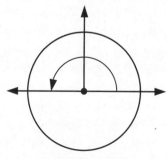

straight angle

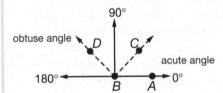

Investigate Problem 1

1. Angles that measure less than 90° are **acute angles.** Angles that measure between 90° and 180° are **obtuse angles.** The obtuse angle in the diagram below is ∠ABD. Name the acute angle.

2. You can measure angles using a tool called a **protractor.** Align the center of the protractor with the vertex of the angle. Each line on the protractor has two measures—one for an acute angle and one for an obtuse angle.

Measuring an acute angle   Measuring an obtuse angle

A right angle, which measures 90°, is a useful benchmark, or reference angle. If you compare your angle to a right angle and identify it as acute or obtuse *before* using a protractor to measure it, you will not be confused by which mark to use on the protractor. Would you estimate the measure of the angle at the left to be 40° or 140°? Use a complete sentence to explain your reasoning.

Use your protractor to measure the angles below. Don't forget to first identify each angle as *right*, *acute*, or *obtuse*. Record the angle measures in the table.

Angle	Type of Angle	Measure
∠ACR		
∠ACN		
∠RCN		
∠ACE		
∠ECG		
∠ECI		

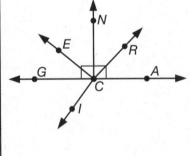

3. Compare your measurements with your partner. If you have an angle measure that is more than 2° greater or less than your partner's measure of the same angle, measure the angle again together.

© 2008 Carnegie Learning, Inc.

4. Math Path: Complementary and Supplementary Angles

What is the sum of the measure of ∠ACR and the measure of ∠RCN?

Two angles whose sum is 90° (a right angle) are **complementary angles.** Which pairs of angles in the figure in Question 2 are complementary angles?

Two angles whose sum is 180° (a straight angle) are **supplementary angles.** Which pairs of angles in the figure in Question 2 are supplementary angles?

5. Math Path: Special Pairs of Angles

In the figure below, parallel lines *k* and *m* are cut by line *n*, called a **transversal.** When a transversal intersects two parallel lines, certain pairs of angles are formed that have equal measures. When angles have equal measures, the angles are said to be **congruent angles.**

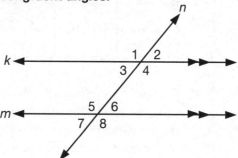

∠3 and ∠6 are **alternate interior angles.**

∠4 and ∠5 are alternate interior angles.

∠1 and ∠8 are **alternate exterior angles.**

∠2 and ∠7 are alternate exterior angles.

What do you notice about these angle pairs? Use a complete sentence in your answer.

The following angle pairs are **corresponding angles.**

∠1 and ∠5   ∠3 and ∠7

∠2 and ∠6   ∠4 and ∠8

What do you notice about these angle pairs? Use a complete sentence in your answer.

9

Problem 2 — Getting an Angle on Angles

Your aunt wants you to help her make new tables for the restaurant. You create a drawing of your design for the new tables. In the drawing, the top of the table, represented by line *t*, is parallel to the bench, represented by line *b*. The brace is represented by line *n*.

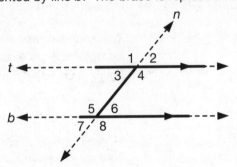

A. Use your protractor to measure all of the angles in the drawing and record them in the table. Remember to estimate before measuring.

Angle	Measure	Angle	Measure
∠1		∠5	
∠2		∠6	
∠3		∠7	
∠4		∠8	

Take Note

The symbol "*m* ∠ 1" means "the measure of angle 1."

B. Complete the table at the right. What do you notice about these angle measures? Use complete sentences to describe your findings.

Sums of Angles	
$m \angle 1 + m \angle 2$	
$m \angle 3 + m \angle 4$	
$m \angle 1 + m \angle 3$	
$m \angle 2 + m \angle 4$	
$m \angle 5 + m \angle 6$	
$m \angle 7 + m \angle 8$	
$m \angle 5 + m \angle 7$	
$m \angle 6 + m \angle 8$	

C. Compare your observations with those of your partner. Are your observations the same or different?

D. Create a new set of angles at the right using two parallel lines and a transversal. Label the angles formed. Have your partner measure all of the angles.

1. **Math Path: Vertical and Adjacent Angles**

A pair of opposite angles formed by two intersecting lines are **vertical angles.** Vertical angles have equal measures. Angles that share a side are **adjacent angles.**

Name all of the vertical angles in the drawing in Problem 2.

Name all of the adjacent angles in the drawing in Problem 2.

2. In the figure, line *k* is parallel to line *m*. Find the measures of all of the angles without using your protractor.

$m \angle 1 =$

$m \angle 2 =$

$m \angle 3 =$

$m \angle 4 =$

$m \angle 5 =$

$m \angle 6 =$

$m \angle 7 =$

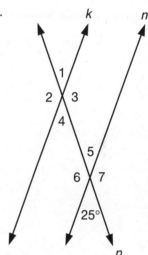

3. Find the measures of all of the angles in the figure without using your protractor.

$m \angle 1 =$

$m \angle 2 =$

$m \angle 3 =$

$m \angle 4 =$

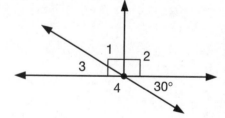

4. Find the measures of all of the angles in the figure without using your protractor.

$m \angle 1 =$

$m \angle 2 =$

$m \angle 3 =$

$m \angle 4 =$

$m \angle 5 =$

$m \angle 6 =$

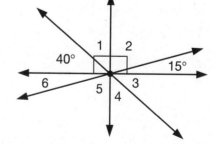

9

9.2 A Collection of Triangles
Classifying Triangles

Objectives

In this lesson, you will:

- Classify triangles by their side lengths.
- Classify triangles by their angle measures.

Key Terms

- triangle
- congruent sides
- equilateral triangle
- isosceles triangle
- scalene triangle
- acute triangle
- obtuse triangle
- right triangle

Take Note

When the lengths of the sides of a triangle are equal, they are marked with a dash.

Problem 1   Classifying Stamps

Most postage stamps are shaped as rectangles or squares. In some rare cases though, world governments have issued stamps shaped as triangles. A **triangle** is a figure that has three sides and three angles. In 1997, the United States issued its first triangular stamp.

Your cousin collects rare triangular stamps. The outlines of the stamps are shown below. Help your cousin by sorting the triangles that represent the stamps into groups so that each group is described by one characteristic. You can refer to the triangle by the letter.

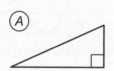
A

B

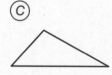
C

D

E

F

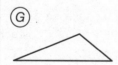
G

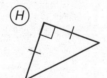
H

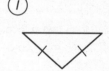
I

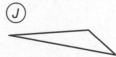
J

Group	Triangles	Characteristics
1		
2		
3		
4		

1. In the table in Problem 1, did some of the triangles fit into more than one category? If so, which ones?

2. Math Path: Classifying Triangles

We can classify triangles by their side lengths. Just as congruent angles have the same measure, **congruent sides** have the same length.

  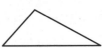

An **equilateral triangle** has three congruent sides.

An **isosceles triangle** has two congruent sides.

A **scalene triangle** has no congruent sides.

We can also classify triangles by their angles.

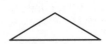 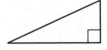

An **acute triangle** has three acute angles

An **obtuse triangle** has one obtuse angle.

A **right triangle** has one right angle.

Cut out three exact copies of the same triangle. Label the angles *A*, *B*, and *C*.

Arrange the three triangles so that one of each of angle *A*, angle *B,* and angle *C* are next to each other.

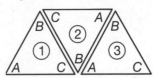

What do you notice? Write your answer using a complete sentence.

Did you get the same result as others in your group? Use complete sentences to explain.

© 2008 Carnegie Learning, Inc.

Take Note

Triangles can be named using the three vertices of the triangle in any order.

Triangle *ABC*, Triangle *BCA*, or Triangle *CAB*.

Take Note

In an isosceles triangle, the angles opposite the congruent sides have the same measure. In an equilateral triangle, all three angles have the same measure.

3. The straight line that is formed by angle *A*, angle *B*, and angle *C* is a visual representation of the fact that the sum of the measures of the three angles in a triangle is always 180°. Find the measure of the missing angle(s) in each triangle.

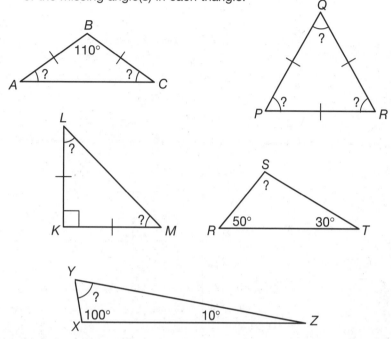

Problem 2   Stamp Design

Decide whether it is possible to design a stamp that has each shape described below. If it is possible, draw an example. If it is not possible, explain why.

A right isosceles triangle   An acute isosceles triangle

An obtuse scalene triangle   An equilateral right triangle

An obtuse isosceles triangle   A scalene right triangle

An equilateral acute triangle   An obtuse equilateral triangle

Investigate Problem 2

1. With your partner, use a ruler to measure and mark 2 inches on a straw or piece of spaghetti. Cut the straw or piece of spaghetti into the 2-inch length. Repeat this process to make pieces whose lengths are whole inches from 3 inches up to 12 inches.

   For each set in the table below, toss a pair of number cubes three times. Record the three numbers in the table under "Side Lengths." These numbers represent the lengths of the sides of a triangle. Use your straws or pieces of spaghetti to attempt to form a triangle with these side lengths. Record whether or not you can form a triangle.

	Side Lengths	Do the Side Lengths Form a Triangle? (Yes or No)
Set 1		
Set 2		
Set 3		
Set 4		
Set 5		
Set 6		
Set 7		

   What do you notice about the sets that form a triangle?
   What do you notice about the sets that do not form a triangle?
   Use complete sentences to record your observations.

The Signs Are Everywhere
Quadrilaterals and Other Polygons

Objectives

In this lesson, you will:

- Classify quadrilaterals.
- Classify polygons.
- Find angle measures in polygons.

Key Terms

- quadrilateral
- trapezoid
- parallelogram
- rhombus
- rectangle
- square
- polygon
- diagonal
- regular polygon
- irregular polygon

Take Note

Quadrilaterals can be named using the four vertices by either listing them in order clockwise or counterclockwise.

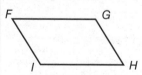

Quadrilateral *FGHI* or Quadrilateral *FIHG*

Problem 1 *Shapes of Signs*

You are teaching a bicycle safety course to a group of third graders. You want the class to learn the road signs that are put up for bicyclists. You tell them that there are standard shapes for road signs. Some of these shapes are *quadrilaterals.* A **quadrilateral** is a closed figure with four sides and four angles. Like triangles, quadrilaterals are classified by their sides and angles.

Warning signs   **Regulation signs**   **Guide signs**   **Recreational area signs**

A. A **trapezoid** is a quadrilateral with exactly one pair of parallel sides. Which types of road signs, if any, appear to be trapezoids?

B. A **parallelogram** is a quadrilateral in which both pairs of opposite sides are parallel. Which types of road signs, if any, appear to be parallelograms?

C. A **rhombus** is a parallelogram with four sides of equal length. Which types of road signs, if any, appear to be rhombuses?

D. A **rectangle** is a parallelogram with 4 right angles. Which types of road signs, if any, appear to be rectangles?

E. A **square** is a parallelogram with 4 sides of equal length and 4 right angles. Which types of road signs, if any, appear to be squares?

1. Write as many names as you can for quadrilateral *CLMS*.

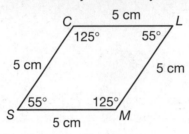

Write five names for quadrilateral *ROCK*.

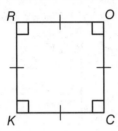

Write as many names as you can for quadrilateral *STAR*.

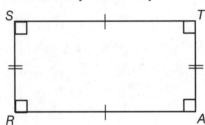

2. Work with your partner to answer each question. If your answer is "no," then draw a quadrilateral to justify your answer.

Are all rectangles parallelograms?

Are all parallelograms rectangles?

Are all squares rectangles?

Are all rectangles squares?

Are all rhombuses squares?

Are all squares rhombuses?

Are all quadrilaterals parallelograms?

Are all parallelograms quadrilaterals?

Problem 2   *Pay Attention to the Signs*

You want to teach your students to recognize other common road signs. Except for circular signs, almost all road signs are polygons. A **polygon** is a closed figure whose sides are line segments. Polygons can be classified by the number of their sides.

The prefix "penta-" means "five." Which road signs are pentagons?

The prefix "octa-" means "eight." Which road signs are octagons?

Investigate Problem 2

1. In Lesson 9.2, we learned that the sum of the measures of the angles of a triangle is 180°. What about the sum of the measures of the angles of other polygons? We can use triangles to help find this sum. A **diagonal** is a line segment in a polygon that connects two vertices that are not connected by a side. When you draw a diagonal in the quadrilateral below, you can see that the quadrilateral is made up of two triangles.

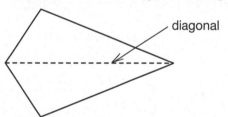

diagonal

Because the sum of the measures of the angles of each triangle above is 180°, the sum of the measures of the angles of a quadrilateral is 2 × 180° or 360°. At the left, draw each polygon listed in the table. Then complete the table.

Polygon	Number of Sides	Number of Triangles	Sum of the Measures of the Angles of the Polygon
Quadrilateral	4	2	2 × 180° or 360°
Pentagon	5		
Hexagon	6		
Heptagon	7		
Octagon	8		
Nonagon	9		
Decagon	10		

2. **Math Path: Regular Polygons**

In a **regular polygon,** all of the sides have the same length and all of the angles have the same measure. A polygon that is not regular is **irregular.** What are the measures of each angle of a regular pentagon? Use complete sentences to explain.

What are the measures of each angle of a regular hexagon? Use complete sentences to explain.

What are the measures of each angle of a regular octagon? Use complete sentences to explain.

3. Find the measure of the missing angle of each polygon. For each polygon, explain your reasoning.

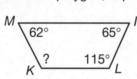

$m \angle K = $ _____ $m \angle L = $ _____

$m \angle B = $ _____

4. In Lesson 9.2, we learned that the length of the third side of a triangle is always less than the sum of the lengths of the other two sides. Does this apply to quadrilaterals? Does the length of the fourth side of a quadrilateral always have to be less than the sum of the lengths of the other three sides? Work with your partner to write an explanation of your thinking.

How Does Your Garden Grow?
Similar Polygons

Objectives

In this lesson, you will:

- Determine whether polygons are similar.

Key Terms

- similar polygons
- corresponding sides
- scale factor
- corresponding angles

If you have ever built a scale model of a car or an airplane or enlarged a picture on a photocopy machine, you have used similar polygons.

Problem 1   Drawing a Landscaping Plan

After reading a book about landscape design, you want to design two large flower beds that are the same shape but different sizes. You use rectangles to represent the flower beds. Polygons that have the same shape but not necessarily the same size are **similar polygons.** Complete the table to investigate the properties of similar polygons.

	Length, ℓ (units of longer side)	Width, w (units of shorter side)	Ratio of Width to Length $\frac{w}{\ell}$
A			
B			
C			
D			
E			
F			
G			
H			

1. Group the rectangles that have equal ratios of width to length. How many different groups do you have? What can you say about the rectangles in each group? Write your answer using a complete sentence.

2. **Math Path: Scale Factor**

   Corresponding sides of figures are in corresponding positions in different figures. A **scale factor** is the ratio of the lengths of the corresponding sides of two figures that are similar. You find the scale factor by taking the ratio of the lengths of the corresponding sides of the new figure to the original figure. A scale factor greater than 1 means that the original figure has been enlarged to form the new figure. A scale factor between 0 and 1 means that the original figure has been reduced to form the new figure. What are the scale factors of the similar rectangles?

   To enlarge rectangle C to rectangle D, the scale factor is _____.

   To reduce rectangle E to rectangle B, the scale factor is _____.

   To enlarge rectangle G to rectangle H, the scale factor is _____.

   To reduce rectangle H to rectangle G, the scale factor is _____.

   To enlarge rectangle B to rectangle E, the scale factor is _____.

3. Give an example of two squares and find the ratio of the sides of the squares. Do you think that all squares are similar to all other squares? Use complete sentences to explain why or why not.

4. The quadrilateral *MATH* is similar to the quadrilateral *POLG*. Complete each statement to find the ratios of the lengths of the corresponding sides.

$$\frac{MA}{PO} = \frac{\Box}{\Box} \qquad \frac{AT}{OL} = \frac{\Box}{\Box} \qquad \frac{TH}{LG} = \frac{\Box}{\Box} \qquad \frac{HM}{GP} = \frac{\Box}{\Box}$$

Use complete sentences to explain what you discovered about the ratios of the lengths of the corresponding sides of similar polygons.

Take Note

When naming two figures that are similar, the vertices should be written in order so that they correspond. In Question 4, point *M* corresponds to point *P*, point *A* corresponds to point *O*, etc.

9

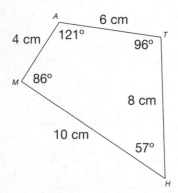

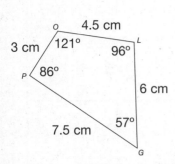

5. **Corresponding angles** of two figures are angles that are in corresponding positions in both figures. Write the measures of corresponding angles in quadrilateral *MATH* and quadrilateral *POLG*.

   $m \angle M$: $m \angle A$: $m \angle T$: $m \angle H$:

   $m \angle P$: $m \angle O$: $m \angle L$: $m \angle G$:

   Use complete sentences to explain what you discovered about the measures of corresponding angles of similar polygons.

Problem 2   Campaign Posters

Your community has a gardening club, and you decide to run for president of the club. You want to make different sized posters with your smiling picture and hang them throughout the community.

A. Your best picture is 3 inches by 4 inches. You want each poster that you make to be similar to the original photo. What sizes of posters can you make? Complete the table.

Size	Scale Factor
3 in. × 4 in.	1

Elect Mary President of the Gardening Club!

B. Choose one of the sizes from your table. For that size, show that the poster and the original photo are similar. (You can assume that all of the angles of the poster and the original photo are right angles.) Use complete sentences in your answer.

9

Investigate Problem 2

1. After you are elected, you plan to have a contest to design a poster that will encourage people in the community to plant trees. The rules of the contest will state that the design should be drawn on a small sheet of paper that is 3 inches by 9 inches. What sizes of poster paper should you buy to enlarge the poster so that it is similar to the drawing and has the same proportions? Show mathematically whether the sizes in the table will work.

Poster Paper	
Length	Width
1 ft	3 ft
6 in.	12 in.
12 in.	36 in.
16 in.	48 in.
9 in.	36 in.

2. Triangle *CAT* is similar to triangle *DOG*. Find the missing lengths.

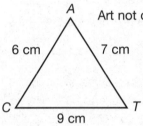
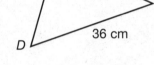

Art not drawn to scale.

DO = _____   *GO* = _____

3. Draw two quadrilaterals that are similar to the quadrilateral below so that one uses a scale factor of 2 and another uses a scale factor of 3.

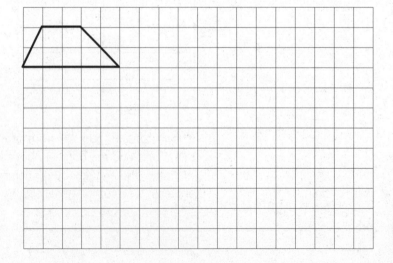

Shadows and Mirrors
Indirect Measurement

Objectives

In this lesson, you will:
- Use similar triangles to find measurements indirectly.

Key Term

- similar triangles
- indirect measurement

Problem 1   Height

You can use **similar triangles** to measure the height of a flagpole, telephone pole, or any object that is not easily measured directly. This type of measurement is called **indirect measurement.**

A. On a sunny day, hold a meter stick so that it makes a right angle with the ground. Measure the length of the meter stick's shadow. Next, measure the length of the flagpole or telephone pole's shadow. Use your measurements to label the diagram.

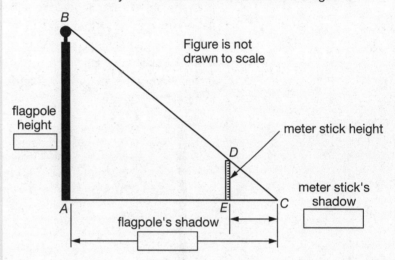

Figure is not drawn to scale

flagpole height

meter stick height

meter stick's shadow

flagpole's shadow

B. In the diagram, name the triangles that are similar. Discuss with your partner how you know that the triangles are similar.

C. In Lesson 9.4, we saw that the ratios of the lengths of the corresponding sides of similar polygons are equal. Use this fact to complete the proportion below. Then solve the proportion to find the height of the flagpole.

$$\frac{\text{Height of flagpole}}{\text{Height of meter stick}} = \frac{\text{Length of flagpole's shadow}}{\text{Length of meter stick's shadow}}$$

$$\frac{?}{1 \text{ meter}} = \frac{\boxed{} \text{ meters}}{\boxed{} \text{ meter(s)}}$$

Investigate Problem 1

1. Suppose that your meter stick casts a 0.5-meter shadow and the flagpole casts a 6-meter shadow. Draw and label the similar triangles involved. Then write and solve a proportion to find the approximate height of the flagpole.

2. A second method for indirectly measuring the height of a flagpole is to use a mirror. Have your partner measure you from the ground to your eye level. Then measure a convenient distance from the base of the flagpole to a level spot. Place the mirror flat on the ground at that level spot. Now, back up from the mirror until you can see the top of the flagpole in the mirror. Mark the spot at which you are standing. Then measure the distance from the mirror to that spot. Use your measurements to label the diagram.

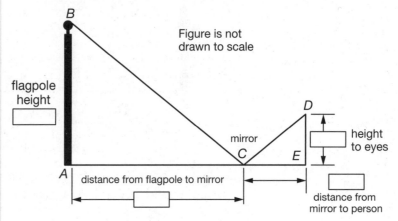

Use the diagram to write and solve a proportion to find the height of the flagpole.

$$\frac{\text{Height of flagpole}}{\text{Height to eyes}} = \frac{\boxed{}}{\boxed{}}$$

$$\frac{?}{\boxed{}\ \text{meters}} = \frac{\boxed{}\ \text{meters}}{\boxed{}\ \text{meters}}$$

The height of the flagpole is _____ meters.

3. Suppose that you used the method in Question 2 and found the measurements below. Use similar triangles to find the height of the flagpole.

height to eyes = 150 centimeters

distance from mirror to person = 100 centimeters

distance from flagpole to mirror = 600 centimeters

4. Miguel and Bill want to measure the length of a lake in Carnegie Park. On a diagram, they mark this length as segment *DE*. To indirectly measure the length, first they locate a point *A* from which they can see the edge of the lake on both sides at point *D* and point *E*. From point *A*, they use chalk to mark straight lines to both edges of the lake. Then they stake points *B* and *C* so that the line that they mark from point *B* to point *C* is parallel to segment *DE*. Then they measure the distances as shown in the diagram. How long is the lake?

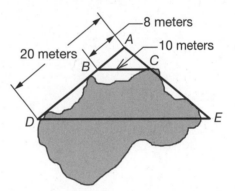

Use complete sentences to describe how you found the length of the lake. Then share your solution with another partner team.

9

9.6 A Geometry Game
Congruent Polygons

Objectives

In this lesson, you will:

- Use properties of congruent and similar polygons.
- Determine whether polygons are congruent.

Key Terms

- congruent polygons
- congruent

In Lesson 9.4, we saw that polygons that have the same shape but not necessarily the same size are similar polygons. **Congruent polygons** are polygons that have the same shape and the same size.

Problem 1   Designing a Geometry Game

Because congruent polygons have the same size and shape, their corresponding sides are congruent. That is, the lengths of their corresponding sides are equal. Likewise, the corresponding angles of congruent polygons are **congruent.** That is, the measures of corresponding angles are equal. Congruent polygons have a scale factor of 1.

Design a geometry game board using triangles and rectangles. Include the following on your game board on the next page.

- A triangle congruent to triangle *ABC*
- A triangle similar to triangle *ABC* with a scale factor of 0.5
- A triangle similar to triangle *ABC* with a scale factor of 1.5
- A rectangle congruent to rectangle *DEFG*
- A rectangle similar to rectangle *DEFG* with a scale factor of 0.5
- A rectangle similar to rectangle *DEFG* with a scale factor of 2
- A rectangle congruent to rectangle *HIJK*
- A rectangle similar to rectangle *HIJK* with a scale factor of 0.5
- A rectangle similar to rectangle *HIJK* with a scale factor of 2.5

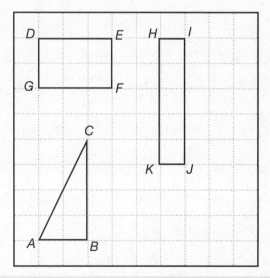

Investigate Problem 1

1. Form a group with another partner team. Each partner team should use the game board that they designed. Take turns asking the questions to each team below. If a team answers the question correctly, they can color in the polygon that pertains to that question. The team with the most polygons colored in at the end of the allowed time wins the game.

- The measure of ∠B is about 26.6°. What is the measure of the angle that corresponds to angle B in the triangle that is congruent to triangle ABC?

- The length of IJ is 5 units. What is the length of the corresponding side in the rectangle with a scale factor of 2.5?

- The measure of ∠A is about 63.4°. What is the measure of the angle that corresponds to angle A in the triangle that is similar to triangle ABC with a scale factor of 1.5?

- The length of DG is 2 units. What is the length of the corresponding side in the rectangle with a scale factor of 0.5?

- The ratio of the length of the shorter side of a rectangle to the longer side is 0.2. Is this rectangle similar to rectangle DEFG or rectangle HIJK?

- The length of side BC is 4 units. What is the length of the corresponding side in the triangle with a scale factor of 0.5?

- The measure of ∠F is 90°. What is the measure of the angle that corresponds to angle F in the rectangle that is similar to rectangle DEFG with a scale factor of 2?

- The perimeter of a rectangle is the distance around the rectangle. What is the perimeter of the rectangle that is similar to rectangle HIJK with a scale factor of 0.5?

- What is the perimeter of the rectangle that is congruent to rectangle DEFG?

2. If time permits, add a right triangle, triangle LMN, to your game board with side lengths of 3 units, 4 units, and 5 units, like the one at the right. Then add a similar, but not congruent, triangle and a congruent triangle to the board. Work with your partner to design additional questions that you can ask the other partner team about the triangles. Then continue to play the game using the questions that you created.

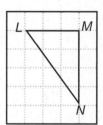

Looking Back at Chapter 9

Key Terms

angle ● p. 273
vertex ● p. 273
degrees ● p. 273
right angle ● p. 273
straight angle ● p. 273
acute angle ● p. 274
obtuse angle ● p. 274
protractor ● p. 274
complementary angles ● p. 275
supplementary angles ● p. 275
transversal ● p. 275
congruent angles ● p. 275
alternate interior angles ● p. 275
alternate exterior angles ● p. 275

corresponding angles ● p. 275
vertical angles ● p. 277
adjacent angles ● p. 277
triangle ● p. 279
equilateral triangle ● p. 280
isosceles triangle ● p. 280
scalene triangle ● p. 280
acute triangle ● p. 280
obtuse triangle ● p. 280
right triangle ● p. 280
quadrilateral ● p. 283
trapezoid ● p. 283
parallelogram ● p. 283
rhombus ● p. 283

rectangle ● p. 283
square ● p. 283
polygon ● p. 285
diagonal ● p. 285
regular polygon ● p. 286
irregular polygon ● p. 286
similar polygons ● p. 287
corresponding sides ● p. 288
scale factor ● p. 288
corresponding angles ● p. 289
similar triangles ● p. 291
indirect measurement ● p. 291
congruent polygons ● p. 295
congruent ● p. 295

Summary

Finding Measures of Angles (p. 274)

To determine the measure of an angle, use a protractor. Align the center of the protractor with the vertex of the angle. Each line on the protractor has two measures—one for an acute angle and one for an obtuse angle.

Example

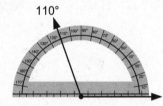

110°

The measure of the angle is 110°.

Identifying Acute, Right, and Obtuse Angles (p. 274)

Angles that measure less than 90° are acute angles. Angles that measure between 90° and 180° are obtuse angles. Angles that measure exactly 90° are right angles.

Examples

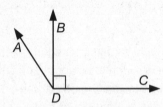

∠ADB is an acute angle.

∠BDC is a right angle.

∠ADC is an obtuse angle.

Identifying Complementary and Supplementary Angles (p. 275)

Two angles whose sum is 90° are complementary angles. Two angles whose sum is 180° are supplementary angles.

Examples

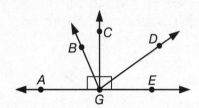

∠AGB and ∠BGC are complementary.

∠AGC and ∠CGE are supplementary.

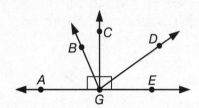

Identifying Special Pairs of Angles (p. 275, 277)

The pairs of angles formed by parallel lines that are cut by a transversal include alternate interior angles, alternate exterior angles, and corresponding angles. Vertical angles are a pair of opposite angles formed by two intersecting lines. Each of these special pairs of angles are congruent. Angles that share a side are adjacent angles and are not necessarily congruent.

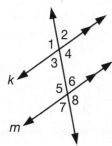

Examples The pairs of alternate interior angles are ∠4 and ∠5 and ∠3 and ∠6.

The pairs of alternate exterior angles are ∠1 and ∠8 and ∠2 and ∠7.

The pairs of corresponding angles are ∠1 and ∠5, ∠2 and ∠6, ∠3 and ∠7, and ∠4 and ∠8.

The pairs of vertical angles are ∠1 and ∠4, ∠2 and ∠3, ∠5 and ∠8, and ∠6 and ∠7.

The pairs of adjacent angles are ∠1 and ∠2, ∠2 and ∠4, ∠4 and ∠3, ∠3 and ∠1, ∠5 and ∠6, ∠6 and ∠8, ∠8 and ∠7, and ∠7 and ∠5.

Finding Measures of Angles Without Using a Protractor (p. 276–277)

To find the measures of all the angles without using a protractor, use what you know about pairs of angles.

Examples ∠1 and the angle that measures 110° are vertical angles. So, $m\angle 1 = 110°$.

∠1 and ∠2 are supplementary angles. So, $m\angle 2 = 180° - 110° = 70°$.

∠2 and ∠3 are vertical angles. So, $m\angle 3 = 70°$.

∠4 and ∠1 are corresponding angles. So, $m\angle 4 = 110°$.

∠5 and ∠3 are alternate interior angles. So, $m\angle 5 = 70°$.

∠5 and ∠6 are vertical angles. So, $m\angle 6 = 70°$.

∠4 and ∠7 are vertical angles. So, $m\angle 7 = 110°$.

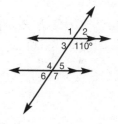

Classifying Triangles by Side Lengths (p. 280)

An equilateral triangle has three congruent sides. An isosceles triangle has exactly two congruent sides. A scalene triangle has no congruent sides.

Examples

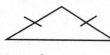

The triangle has exactly two congruent sides. So, the triangle is isosceles.

The triangle has three congruent sides. So, the triangle is equilateral.

The triangle has no congruent sides. So, the triangle is scalene.

Classifying Triangles by Angles (p. 280)

An acute triangle has three acute angles. An obtuse triangle has one obtuse angle. A right triangle has one right angle.

Examples

 The triangle has 3 acute angles.
So, the triangle is acute.

The triangle has 1 right angle.
So, the triangle is right.

 The triangle has 1 obtuse angle.
So, the triangle is obtuse.

Classifying Quadrilaterals (p. 283)

To classify each quadrilateral below, identify it by its angles and sides.

Examples

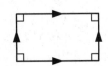 The quadrilateral has exactly one pair of parallel sides. So, the quadrilateral is a trapezoid.

The quadrilateral is a parallelogram with four sides of equal length. So, the quadrilateral is a rhombus.

The quadrilateral is a parallelogram with four right angles. So, the quadrilateral is a rectangle.

Classifying Polygons (p. 285)

To name a polygon, count the number of its sides.

Examples

 The polygon has 8 sides.
So, the polygon is an octagon.

 The polygon has 5 sides.
So, the polygon is an pentagon.

Identifying Regular and Irregular Polygons (p. 286)

In a regular polygon, all of the sides have the same length and all of the angles have the same measure. A polygon that is not regular is irregular.

 The polygon's sides all have the same length and the angles all have the same measure. So, the polygon is regular.

 The polygon's sides do not all have the same length and all the angles do not have the same measure. So, the polygon is irregular.

Identifying Similar and Congruent Polygons (p. 287)

Two polygons are similar if they have the same shape, but not necessarily the same size. Two polygons are congruent if they have the same size and shape. To determine whether polygons with the same shape are similar, find the ratios of the lengths of the corresponding sides. If the polygons are similar, all of the ratios will be the same.

Example

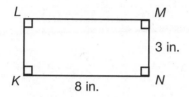

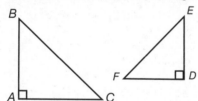

$$\frac{AD}{KN} = \frac{BC}{LM} = \frac{16 \text{ in.}}{8 \text{ in.}} = 2$$

$$\frac{AB}{KL} = \frac{DC}{NM} = \frac{6 \text{ in.}}{3 \text{ in.}} = 2$$

Because the ratios are equal, the rectangles are similar.

Identifying Corresponding Angles and Corresponding Sides (p. 288–289)

The corresponding sides of two congruent or similar figures are the sides that are in corresponding positions. The corresponding angles of two congruent or similar figures are the angles that are in corresponding positions.

Example

Triangle *ABC* is similar to triangle *DEF*.

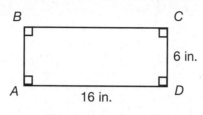

The corresponding sides of the triangles are sides *AB* and *DE*, sides *BC* and *EF*, and sides *CA* and *FD*.

The corresponding angles of the triangles are ∠*A* and ∠*D*, ∠*B* and ∠*E*, and ∠*C* and ∠*F*.

Using Indirect Measurement (p. 291)

To measure a length indirectly, create two similar triangles and then write and solve a proportion that uses the ratios of the corresponding lengths of the similar triangles.

Example

You want to measure the height of a tree in your backyard.

To measure it indirectly, you make a right angle with a meter stick and the ground and line up the end of the meter stick's shadow with the end of the tree's shadow.

The shadow of the meter stick is 0.5 meter and the shadow of the tree is 5 meters. Now use a proportion to solve for the height of the tree.

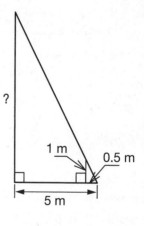

$$\frac{\text{Height of tree}}{\text{Height of meter stick}} = \frac{\text{Length of tree's shadow}}{\text{Length of meter stick's shadow}}$$

$$\frac{x}{1 \text{ meter}} = \frac{5 \text{ meters}}{0.5 \text{ meter}}$$

$$0.5x = 5$$

$$x = 10$$

The height of the tree is 10 meters.

Looking Ahead to Chapter 10

Focus
In Chapter 10, you will find perimeters of rectangles, find circumferences of circles, and find the areas of rectangles, circles, parallelograms, triangles, trapezoids, and composite figures. You will find squares and square roots of numbers, and use the Pythagorean theorem to solve problems.

Chapter Warm-up

Answer these questions to help you review skills that you will need in Chapter 10.

Use mental math to find the sum.

1. $27 + 94$

2. $13 + 45$

3. $9 + 5 + 21$

Find the product.

4. 3.4×5.7

5. 9.1×2.6

6. 1.52×7.8

Evaluate the power.

7. 9^2

8. 20^2

9. 45^2

Write as many names as you can for the quadrilateral.

10.

11.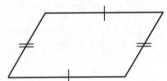

12.

Your aunt is using the triangle to make a quilt. Describe the triangle as acute, right, or obtuse.

13.

14.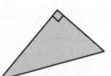

15.

Key Terms

perimeter ● p. 305

area ● p. 305

circle ● p. 311

center ● p. 311

radius ● p. 311

diameter ● p. 311

circumference ● p. 312

pi ● p. 312

composite figure ● p. 318

square ● p. 321

perfect square ● p. 321

square root ● p. 321

radical sign ● p. 321

radicand ● p. 321

leg ● p. 325

hypotenuse ● p. 325

Pythagorean theorem ● p. 325

converse ● p. 329

Pythagorean triple ● p. 332

10

Area and the Pythagorean Theorem

A skate park may contain half pipes, quarter pipes, banked ramps, stairs, and other objects so that skateboarders can do tricks. In Lesson 10.3, you will use what you know about area to help design a skate park for a city.

10

10

All Skate!

Perimeter and Area

Objectives

In this lesson, you will:
- Find perimeters of rectangles.
- Find areas of rectangles.
- Determine the effect on perimeter and area of changing dimensions.

Key Terms
- perimeter
- area

The **perimeter** of a closed figure is the distance around the figure. Perimeter is measured in linear units, such as feet or centimeters. The **area** of a closed figure is the number of square units needed to cover the figure. Area is measured in square units, such as square feet or square centimeters.

Problem 1 Skating Rink

At Starlight Middle School, students construct a roller skating rink in the shape of a rectangle each day during lunch period. They form the frame around the outside of the rink with interlocking framing pieces that are each one meter long and form the floor with tiles that each cover one square meter.

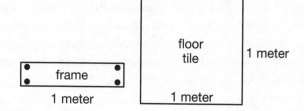

Because the students don't want to always skate in the same configuration, they build a different rectangular rink each day. The school has 36 flooring tiles. Complete the table to find the number of different rectangular rinks that the students can construct using the 36 tiles. For each rectangular rink, how many pieces of framing will they need around the outside of the rink to hold it together? If you need to, draw diagrams of the rinks in the space at the left.

Rectangles with an Area of 36 Square Meters		
Length	**Width**	**Number of Framing Pieces Needed (Perimeter)**

10

1. What patterns do you notice in the table in Problem 1? Compare your thinking with your partner's.

2. Work with your partner to write a formula that you can use to find the area of any rectangle.

3. Work with your partner to write a formula that you can use to find the perimeter of any rectangle.

4. Form a group with another partner team. Compare the formulas that you found for area and perimeter.

5. On Monday, for the individual speed-skating competition, it is important to have as much space as possible for students to stand around the edges of the rink to watch the speed trials. Which rectangle should the students build so that the standing room around the edges of the rink is as large as possible (that is, which rectangle has the maximum perimeter)?

6. On Wednesday, there is an "everybody skate" and very few students watch. Which rectangle should the students build so that the standing room around the edges of the rink is as small as possible (that is, which rectangle has the minimum perimeter)? Write a complete sentence to explain your thinking.

7. On Friday, the nearby elementary school borrows some of the framing pieces so that the students are left with only 24 pieces of framing. Find the number of different sizes of rectangular skating rinks the students can build using all 24 pieces of framing. How many flooring tiles will they need to use? Complete the table.

Rectangles with a Perimeter of 24 Meters		
Length	Width	Number of Flooring Tiles Needed (Area)

10

8. What patterns do you notice in the table in Question 7? Write your answer using a complete sentence.

9. Do the formulas that you found in Questions 2 and 3 for area and perimeter work for these rectangles? List two examples for area and two examples for perimeter showing whether they work or not.

10. Which rectangle should the students build if they want the greatest amount of skating area? Write your answer using a complete sentence.

11. What are the length and width of the rink that the students should build if they want the least amount of skating area for individual practice? Write your answer using a complete sentence.

12. Use the results of Questions 5, 6, 10, and 11 to answer each question. Use complete sentences.

   Given a rectangle with a fixed area, how can you maximize the perimeter and how can you minimize the perimeter?

   Given a rectangle with a fixed perimeter, how can you maximize the area and how can you minimize the area?

13. Suppose that the students have 48 square tiles and use all of them to build a rectangular rink. What are the length and width of the rink with the largest perimeter? What are the length and width of the rink with the smallest perimeter?

14. Suppose that the students have 48 framing pieces and use all of them to build a rectangular rink. What are the length and width of the rink with the largest area? What are the length and width of the rink with the smallest area?

10

In Lesson 9.4, you learned about scale factors and similar figures. Let's look at what happens to the perimeter and area of similar figures.

Problem 2   *Pizza Disaster*

Starlight Middle School does not have enough skates for all of the students. The Student Council decides to sell pizza at lunch to raise money for extra skates. The personal size pizzas that they are selling are rectangular with dimensions of 4 inches by 6 inches. The perimeter of each pizza is decorated with toppings of sausage or mushrooms.

In order to make more money, Alex decides that making pizzas with the same shape but with dimensions that are twice the size, three times the size, and four times the size would bring in more money. Alex made the poster shown on the right.

4 inches
6 inches

Pizza Extravaganza	
Size	Price
Personal size	$2
Personal size × 2	$4
Personal size × 3	$6
Personal size × 4	$8

A. At the end of the day, Alex was totally confused. They had used up the week's supply of pizza dough and toppings, but they had not made that much more money. Mr. Hadley, the math teacher, took one look at the sign and shook his head. "Remember what you learned in math class this year?" He advised Alex to complete the table. Help Alex by finding the perimeter and area of each pizza size. Then find the scale factor of the bigger pizzas to the personal size pizza.

Size	Dimensions	Perimeter	Area	Scale Factor
Personal size				
Personal size × 2				
Personal size × 3				
Personal size × 4				

B. Alex realized that the personal size × 2 pizza was not twice as big as he had planned. Look at the table and discuss with your partner what you think went wrong with Alex's plan.

1. How do the area and perimeter change compared to how the scale factor changes? Write your answer using a complete sentence.

2. How much greater is the area of the personal size × 3 pizza than the personal size pizza? How much greater is the area of the personal size × 4 pizza than the personal size pizza?

3. How many times greater is the perimeter of the personal size × 3 pizza than the personal size pizza? How many times greater is the perimeter of the personal size × 4 pizza than the personal size pizza?

4. How do the answers to Questions 2 and 3 relate to the scale factor? Write your answer using a complete sentence.

5. What dimensions could Alex have used to make a pizza with an area twice as large as the personal size pizza? Write your answer using a complete sentence.

6. What dimensions could Alex have used to make a pizza with an area three times as large as the personal size pizza? Write your answer using a complete sentence.

7. What dimensions could Alex have used to make a pizza with an area four times as large as the personal size pizza? Write your answer using a complete sentence.

8. The personal size pizza feeds one person. How many students should Alex's personal size × 2 pizza feed?

   How many students should Alex's personal size × 3 pizza feed?

   How many students should Alex's personal size × 4 pizza feed?

10

9. The personal size pizza feeds one person for $2. What prices should Alex have charged for each of the larger pizzas? Complete the poster with the new prices.

Pizza Extravaganza	
Size	**Price**
Personal size	$2
Personal size × 2	
Personal size × 3	
Personal size × 4	

10. Suppose that Alex had made a personal size × 10 pizza using his method from Part (A). How many times greater is the perimeter of the personal size × 10 pizza than the personal size pizza?

    How many times greater is the area of the personal size × 10 pizza than the personal size pizza?

    How many students would the personal size × 10 pizza feed?

11. Alex also thought he would make a pizza using his method from Part (A) but with dimensions that are one half of the size for dieters and charge $1. What would the dimensions of this personal size × $\frac{1}{2}$ pizza be?

    What would the area of the personal size × $\frac{1}{2}$ pizza be?

    What would the perimeter of the personal size × $\frac{1}{2}$ pizza be?

12. How do the area and perimeter of the personal size × $\frac{1}{2}$ pizza relate to the scale factor? Write your answer using a complete sentence.

13. Alex learned an important and costly lesson with the pizza disaster. Write several complete sentences explaining how the area and perimeter of scaled figures relate to the scale factor.

14. Complete the sentence: If two figures are similar and the scale factor is 5, the area of the larger figure is _____ times the area of the smaller figure and the perimeter of the larger figure is _____ times the perimeter of the smaller figure.

Round Food Around the World
Circumference and Area of a Circle

Objectives

In this lesson, you will:

- Find circumferences of circles.
- Find areas of circles.

Key Terms ·

- circle
- center
- radius
- diameter
- circumference
- pi

Problem 1   Round Bread

A **circle** is a figure that consists of all points in a plane that are the same distance from a fixed point, called the **center** of the circle. The distance from the center to any point on the circle is the **radius** of the circle. The distance across the circle through the center is the **diameter** of the circle. The radius of a circle is one half of the diameter of the circle.

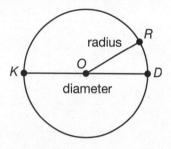

Point *O* is the center of the circle.

Segment *OR* is a radius of the circle.

Segment *KD* is a diameter of the circle.

The length of segment *KO* is one half of the length of segment *KD*.

In many countries of the world, bread is in the shape of a circle. Complete the table by finding the radius or the diameter of the type of bread.

Part of the World	Name of Bread	Radius	Diameter
Middle East	pita	5 inches	
Latin America	tortilla		8 inches
Ireland	soda bread	4 inches	
India	chapati		12 inches
Ethiopia	iniera	10 inches	

10

Investigate Problem 1

1. In Lesson 10.1, we learned that the perimeter is the distance around a figure. The distance around a circle has a special name—the **circumference.**

   Form a group with another partner team. Use string and a ruler or a tape measure to find the distance around several circular objects (the circumference). Then measure the distance across the object through the center (the diameter). Record your measurements in the table.

Object	Circumference, C	Diameter, d	Ratio of Circumference to Diameter, $\frac{C}{d}$

2. The ratio $\frac{C}{d}$ is called **pi** (pronounced "pie") and is written using the Greek letter π. Compare your results with those of your group members. Is the ratio $\frac{C}{d}$ close to the approximate value of π, which is 3.14? Write your answer using a complete sentence.

3. Press the π key on a calculator. Use a complete sentence to describe what the calculator shows.

4. Write a formula for the circumference C of a circle that uses π and the diameter d.

5. Write a formula for the circumference C of a circle that uses π and the radius r.

A strudel is a German pastry that is made by first layering fruit between thin sheets of dough and then baking. You and your cousin are making strudel. You make the strudel in the shape of circle, but then decide that it should be in the shape of a rectangle. What can you do?

A. Each member of your group should create a diagram of the strudel by cutting a circle out of paper. Then divide the circle into eight or more pie-shaped congruent sections (sections of equal size and shape).

B. Cut out each pie-shaped section. Then rearrange the sections into a single figure, as shown.

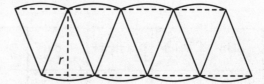

C. The figure that you formed is approximately a parallelogram. You can form a rectangle from the parallelogram.

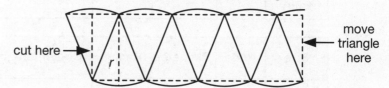

cut here →   ← move triangle here

D. So, you can cut the strudel and make a rectangle from a circle. We can use the formula for the area of a rectangle to develop the formula for the area of a circle. The radius is the height of the rectangle. The length of the rectangle is half of the circumference of the circle. Write a formula for the area of a circle using π and r. Use a complete sentence to explain how you found the formula.

E. Compare your formula with the formulas of others in your group.

10

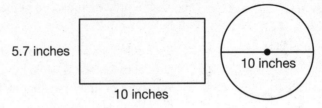

1. Two strudels are shown below. The perimeter of the rectangular strudel is about the same as the circumference of the round strudel. Which strudel has the greater area?

5.7 inches

10 inches

10 inches

10 inches

Area of rectangular strudel:

Area of circular strudel:

2. Collect the prices of small, medium, and large pizzas from two pizza restaurants. You will also need the diameters, in inches, of the pizzas. Use the information you collect to complete the tables below.

Size	Price	Diameter	Radius	Circumference	Area	Price per Square Inch
Small						
Medium						
Large						

Size	Price	Diameter	Radius	Circumference	Area	Price per Square Inch
Small						
Medium						
Large						

3. For each restaurant, determine which size of pizza is the lowest cost per person. Use complete sentences to explain your reasoning.

City Planning
Areas of Parallelograms, Triangles, Trapezoids, and Composite Figures

Objectives

In this lesson, you will:

- Find areas of triangles, parallelograms, and trapezoids.
- Find areas of composite figures.

Key Terms

- composite figures

Take Note

A parallelogram is described by its height and the length of its base.

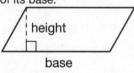

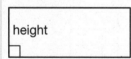

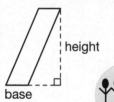

Problem 1   Areas of Parallelograms

In the city where Starlight Middle School is located, the city planners want to build a skating park. The shape of the park is a parallelogram, shown at the right. What is the area of the park?

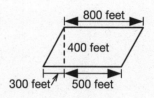

A. Below is a family of parallelograms. Find the area of each parallelogram.

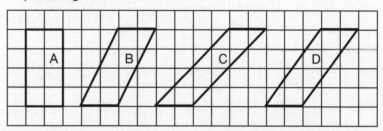

Area of parallelogram A: Area of parallelogram B:

Area of parallelogram C: Area of parallelogram D:

B. What patterns do you see in the areas of the family of parallelograms? Write a complete sentence to explain why they would be called a family.

C. Form a group with another partner team. Each person in your group should draw a parallelogram (that is not a rectangle) on a piece of grid paper. Record the base, height, area, and perimeter of your parallelogram. Cut your parallelogram in two pieces so that it can be reassembled into a rectangle. Record the length, width, perimeter, and area of the new rectangle that you formed.

Parallelogram	Rectangle
Base:	Length:
Height:	Width:
Area:	Area:
Perimeter:	Perimeter:

10

Investigate Problem 1

1. In Part (C), what relationship do you see between the area of the rectangle and the area of the original parallelogram? Write a complete sentence to describe the relationship.

2. Use what you discovered to find the area of the park in Problem 1.

3. The measures of the length and width of the rectangle you formed are the same as the measures of the base and height of the original parallelogram. Write the formula for finding the area of any parallelogram.

4. Is the perimeter of the parallelogram the same as the perimeter of the rectangle in Part (C)? Use complete sentences to explain.

Problem 2   Areas of Triangles

A. On the grid below, draw 5 triangles that have the same area as triangle ABC.

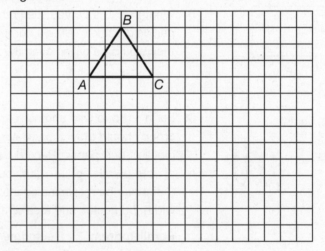

B. Write the length of the base and the height of each triangle on the grid.

C. What do all of these triangles have in common besides their areas? Use complete sentences to explain.

10

Investigate Problem 2

1. As with a parallelogram, a triangle is described by the length of its base and its height.

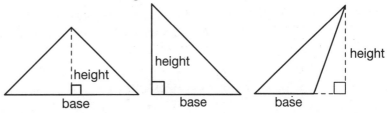

In your group, each person should draw a triangle on a sheet of grid paper. Record the base and height of the triangle. Cut out the triangle and trace it to make another copy of your triangle. Cut out the copy of the triangle. Piece together your two triangles to form a parallelogram. Record the base and height of the parallelogram.

How do the length of the base and height of the parallelogram compare to those of the original triangle? Write your answer using complete sentences.

2. In your group, each person should draw and cut out a parallelogram. Then cut it into two congruent triangles. What conclusions can you make about the area of a triangle and the area of a parallelogram? Use a complete sentence to write your answer.

3. How do you think the formula for the area of a triangle is related to the formula for the area of a parallelogram? Use a complete sentence to write your answer.

4. In your group, each person should cut out two congruent trapezoids. Rearrange the trapezoids to form a parallelogram.

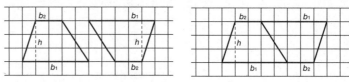

5. Use what you know about finding the area of a parallelogram to find the area of a trapezoid. Write the formula for the area of a trapezoid using the variables b_1, b_2, and h.

A **composite figure** is a figure that can be divided into several common figures. For instance, the composite figure at the right can be divided into a rectangle and a triangle.

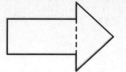

To find the area of a composite figure, find the area of each common figure that makes up the composite figure and then add the areas.

Problem 3   Areas of Composite Figures

A city planner has been given the task of designing several new and unique features to be placed throughout the city. The city wants to add several new flower gardens. Find the area of each new flower garden.

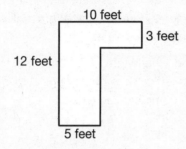

Area of first rectangle:

Area of second rectangle:

Area of composite figure:

Area of triangle:

Area of half of circle:

Area of composite figure:

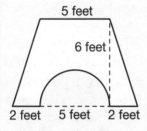

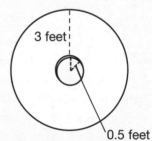

Area of trapezoid:

Area of half of circle:

Area of composite figure:

Area of larger circle:

Area of smaller circle:

Area of composite figure:

1. The city wants to build a swimming pool. The new design that uses half circles on the ends is shown below. Find the swimming pool's area.

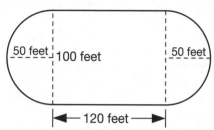

2. The city planner needs to design stages for two different parks in the city. Find the area of each stage.

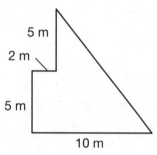 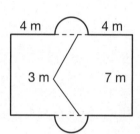

3. The children of the city are excited because the city is planning two new playgrounds. Find the area of each playground.

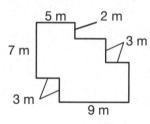 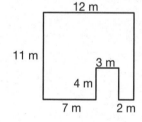

10

© 2008 Carnegie Learning, Inc.

10.4 Sports Fair and Square
Squares and Square Roots

Objectives

In this lesson, you will:
- Find squares of numbers.
- Find and estimate square roots of numbers.

Key Terms

- square
- perfect square
- square root
- radical sign
- radicand

Problem 1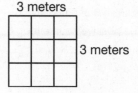

A judo match is held on a square mat that has an area of 676 square feet. How can you find the length of the side of the mat?

A. Find the area of each square below.

1 meter

1 meter

Area = ___ square meter

2 meters

2 meters

Area = ___ square meters

3 meters

3 meters

Area = ___ square meters

B. How does the area of each square relate to the length of its side? Write your answer using a complete sentence.

C. We can write this relationship as the **square** of a number:

$$1^2 = 1 \qquad 2^2 = 4 \qquad 3^2 = 9 \qquad 4^2 = 16$$

Write the squares of the next seven whole numbers. These numbers are called **perfect squares.**

D. The factors that are multiplied to form a perfect square are called *square roots.* A **square root** of a number is one of the two identical factors of the number. Perfect squares have integers as their square roots. For instance, the square roots of 36 are 6 and −6 because (6)(6) = 36 and (−6)(−6) = 36. So, every positive number has two square roots, a positive square root and a negative square root. We write a square root using the **radical sign** $\sqrt{\ }$. A radical sign indicates the positive square root of a number.

$$\sqrt{1} = 1 \qquad \sqrt{4} = 2 \qquad \sqrt{9} = 3 \qquad \sqrt{16} = 4$$

Write the square root of each perfect square.

$$\sqrt{121} = \qquad \sqrt{169} = \qquad \sqrt{400} =$$

E. The square root of 676 is the length of the side of the judo mat. Find $\sqrt{676}$ to find the length of the side of the mat.

10

Investigate Problem 1

1. Most numbers do not have integers for their square roots. To estimate the (positive) square root of a number that is not a perfect square, begin by finding the two perfect squares closest to the number so that one is less than the number and one is greater than the number. Then use trial and error to find the best estimate for the square root.

Estimate $\sqrt{10}$ to the nearest tenth.

Nine is the closest perfect square less than 10 and 16 is the closest perfect square greater than 10.

So, $\sqrt{10}$ is between $\sqrt{9}$ = _____ and $\sqrt{16}$ = _____. Now estimate the square root to the nearest tenth by choosing numbers between 3 and 4 and finding the square of these numbers to determine which one is the best estimate.

(3.1)(3.1) = _____   (3.2)(3.2) = _____

Which number's square is closer to 10?

So, $\sqrt{10}$ ≈ ____. The symbol ≈ means **"approximately equal to."**

2. Estimate $\sqrt{39}$ to the nearest tenth.

____ is a perfect square less than 39 and ____ is a perfect square greater than 39.

So, $\sqrt{39}$ is between _____ and _____.

$\sqrt{39}$ ≈ ____

3. Estimate $\sqrt{27}$ to the nearest tenth.

____ is a perfect square less than 27 and ____ is a perfect square greater than 27.

So, $\sqrt{27}$ is between _____ and _____.

$\sqrt{27}$ ≈ ____

4. Estimate $\sqrt{60}$ to the nearest tenth.

____ is a perfect square less than 60 and ____ is a perfect square greater than 60.

So, $\sqrt{60}$ is between _____ and _____.

$\sqrt{60}$ ≈ ____

Take Note

You can write the square roots of 36 as ±6, meaning positive 6 and negative 6. The positive square root, 6, is called the *principal square root* of 36.

5. For each number, race your partner to estimate the square root of the number. You may use a calculator, but you may not use the calculator's square root key. When you complete a number, see whether you or your partner has a closer estimate by squaring each of your estimates.

$\sqrt{79} \approx$

$\sqrt{135} \approx$

$\sqrt{2} \approx$

$\sqrt{30} \approx$

6. Explain how you found your estimates to your partner.

7. Why don't negative numbers have square roots? Use a complete sentence to explain your answer.

Problem 2   Square Sports Arenas

Each sport below is played on a square mat. Find the dimensions of each mat given its area. Write your answer using a complete sentence.

Gymnastics

1600
square feet

Wrestling

1521
square feet

Boxing

484
square
feet

Judo

576
square
feet

10

1. Find the area of a square whose perimeter is 40 feet.
   Use complete sentences to explain how your found the area.

2. Find the area of a square whose perimeter is 64 inches.
   Write your answer using a complete sentence.

3. Find the perimeter of a square whose area is 81 square meters.
   Use complete sentences to explain how you found the perimeter.

4. Find the perimeter of a square whose area is 256 square meters.
   Write your answer using a complete sentence.

5. For a judo competition, an instructor needs to create two square
   competition areas. She needs to purchase 1089 square feet of
   tatami mats to cover the floor of Area A and 184 feet of tape to
   mark the outside edge of the Area B. Which competition area is
   bigger? Use complete sentences to explain how you determined
   the bigger area.

6. Use the square root key of your calculator to find the square root
   of each number to the nearest hundredth.

   $\sqrt{5}$ ≈ $\sqrt{7}$ ≈

   $\sqrt{19}$ ≈ $\sqrt{32}$ ≈

   $\sqrt{56}$ ≈ $\sqrt{78}$ ≈

Are You Sure It's Square?
The Pythagorean Theorem

Objectives

In this lesson, you will:
- Prove the Pythagorean theorem.
- Use the Pythagorean theorem to solve problems.

Key Terms

- leg
- hypotenuse
- Pythagorean theorem

The Pythagorean theorem is one of the best known theorems in mathematics. It is named for Pythagoras, a Greek mathematician that lived in approximately 500 B.C. Although Pythagoras is given credit for discovering the theorem, the ancient Babylonians, Chinese, and Egyptians understood it and used it to construct their buildings and land boundaries.

Problem 1   Is It Square?

Your family is building a rectangular cabin that has a length of 40 feet and a width of 30 feet. You need to make sure to set the posts at the four corners. How do you know that the cabin is in the shape of a rectangle and not a parallelogram?

A rectangle can be divided into two right triangles. The sides that form the right angle are called the **legs.** The side opposite of the right angle is the **hypotenuse.**

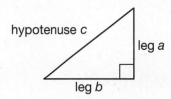

The **Pythagorean theorem** is a formula that relates the lengths of the three sides of a right triangle. It states that if a and b are the lengths of the legs of a right triangle and c is the length of the hypotenuse, then

$$a^2 + b^2 = c^2.$$

You measure the hypotenuse of your cabin and find it to be 50 feet in length. Fill in the boxes to show that the Pythagorean theorem is true for the dimensions of your cabin.

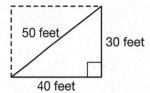

$$a^2 + b^2 = c^2$$

$$\boxed{}^2 + \boxed{}^2 = \boxed{}^2$$

$$\boxed{} + \boxed{} = \boxed{}$$

$$\boxed{} = \boxed{}$$

Write the Pythagorean theorem in your own words.

1. Use the Pythagorean theorem to find the distance from point C to point B in the coordinate plane. Use a complete sentence to explain how you found the distance.

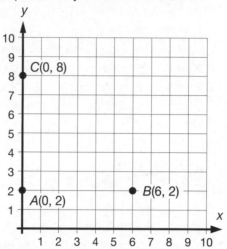

2. There is a special relationship that exists between the squares of the lengths of the sides of a right triangle. Use graph paper to draw an isosceles right triangle. Draw squares on each side of the triangle as shown. Then in each of the two smaller squares, draw the diagonals. Cut out the two smaller squares. Then cut those squares into fourths along the diagonals. Fit these pieces on top of the larger square.

Recall that an isosceles right triangle is a right triangle whose legs have the same length.

10

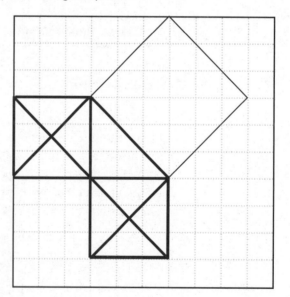

3. On graph paper, draw a right triangle that has one leg that is 3 units in length and one leg that is 4 units in length. Draw a square on the hypotenuse of the triangle as shown. Cut out a 3-unit by 3-unit square and a 4-unit by 4-unit square from the same graph paper. Then cut the two squares into strips that are either 4 units by 1 unit or 3 units by 1 unit, and individual squares of 1 unit by 1 unit. Arrange the strips and squares on top of the square along the hypotenuse.

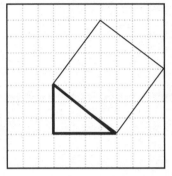

What is the relationship between the area of the squares you cut out and the area of the square you drew? Use a complete sentence to write your answer.

4. On graph paper, draw a right triangle so that the length of one leg is twice the length of the other leg. Draw a square along each leg of the triangle as shown. Cut out the smaller square. Then cut out the larger square and cut it into four congruent triangles as shown. Draw a square along the hypotenuse.

Arrange the smaller square and the triangles to exactly cover the square that lies along the hypotenuse.

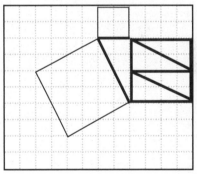

Does the special relationship between the legs and the hypotenuse hold? Use a complete sentence to explain.

10

5. Does the Pythagorean theorem work for triangles that are not right triangles? Use complete sentences to explain your reasoning.

10

A Week at Summer Camp
Using the Pythagorean Theorem

Objectives

In this lesson, you will:

- Use the converse of the Pythagorean theorem.
- Find Pythagorean triples.

Key Terms

- converse
- Pythagorean triple

Problem 1   *Morning of Day One*

In Lesson 10.5, we learned the Pythagorean theorem:

If a triangle is a right triangle, then $a^2 + b^2 = c^2$.

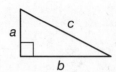

The **converse** of a theorem is created when the if-then parts of the theorem are exchanged. Switch the if-then parts of the Pythagorean theorem and complete the statement below, which is the converse of the Pythagorean theorem.

If _____, then **the triangle is a _____ triangle.**

A. In the morning of Day 1 at summer camp, you are playing a game of baseball. The catcher has a chance to get a player out who is trying to steal second base. How far must the catcher throw the ball if she is on home plate throwing to the player on second base? Write your answer using a complete sentence.

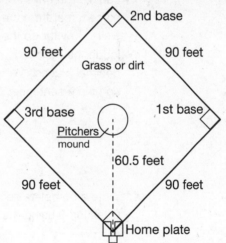

B. Did you use the Pythagorean theorem or its converse to solve the problem? Use complete sentences to explain.

10

1. In the afternoon of Day 1 at summer camp, you are scheduled for wood-working class. You are making a table with a length of 40 inches and a width of 25 inches. You measure the diagonal of the table to be 45 inches. Is the table rectangular?
That is, does the table have corners that are right angles?
Write your answer using a complete sentence.

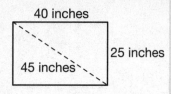

2. Did you use the Pythagorean theorem or its converse to solve Question 1? Write a complete sentence to explain.

3. In the morning of Day 2 at summer camp, you are helping wash the windows of your cabin. You have an 18-foot ladder that you place 5 feet from the base of the cabin wall. How far up the wall will the top of the ladder be? Round your answer to two decimal places. Write your answer using a complete sentence.

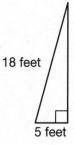

4. Write a complete sentence explaining how you answered Question 3 using the Pythagorean theorem.

5. In the afternoon of Day 2 at summer camp, you take a hike, walking 12 kilometers north and then 9 kilometers east. How many kilometers must you hike to get back to your starting point along the path shown?

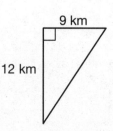

6. In the morning of Day 3 at summer camp, you use material to make camp pennants. How many square inches of material did you use to make your pennant, shown at the right? Write your answer using a complete sentence.

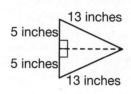

13 inches
5 inches
5 inches
13 inches

7. In the afternoon of Day 3 at summer camp, you take a rafting trip. When you are 40 miles from camp on your raft, how far are you from the lighthouse? Use the map at the right to help you. Write your answer using a complete sentence.

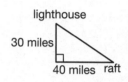

lighthouse
30 miles
40 miles raft

Problem 2   Evening of Day Three

10

A. When you return from your rafting trip, you find that you have locked yourself out of your cabin. The only open window is on the second floor 24 feet above the ground. You find an adjustable ladder nearby, but there's a bush along the edge of the cabin, so you have to place the ladder 10 feet from the cabin. What length of ladder do you need to reach the window? Write your answer using a complete sentence.

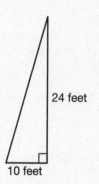

24 feet
10 feet

B. Write the Pythagorean theorem as it relates to the situation in Part (A). What do you notice about the lengths of the sides of the right triangle shown?

1. Math Path: Pythagorean Triples

You may have noticed in part (B) of Problem 2 that all of the side lengths of the right triangle were integers. The set of three positive integers a, b, and c that satisfy the equation $a^2 + b^2 = c^2$ is a **Pythagorean triple.** For example, the integers 3, 4, and 5 form a Pythagorean triple because $3^2 + 4^2 = 5^2$. Form a group with another partner team. Find as many Pythagorean triples as you can.

2. Each group should take turns sharing their Pythagorean triples with the rest of the class. Keep a class list on the board or some other space that everyone in the class can see. Look for patterns in the list. Use a complete sentence to explain what you notice.

3. In the afternoon of Day 4 at summer camp, you ride a bicycle 8 miles north and then 5 miles west. Draw a diagram to represent the situation. What is the shortest distance to the nearest tenth of a mile that you must travel to return to the camp? Write your answer using a complete sentence.

4. In the evening of Day 4 at summer camp, you plan to sleep out in a tent. The tents are triangular in shape and are constructed so that the cloth that forms the tent is 10 feet long. The bottom of the tent is 6 feet wide. What is the height of the pole that you need to hold the tent in place? Write your answer using a complete sentence.

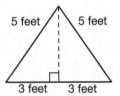

5. In the morning of Day 5 at summer camp, you help your camp counselor move a large round table into the dining hall. The door to the dining hall is 8 feet high and 3 feet wide. The table measures 8.5 feet in diameter. Your counselor decides that it is impossible to fit the table through the door, so he gives up. Explain to him how it is possible to move the table through the door. Draw a diagram to represent the situation. Write your answer using complete sentences.

6. In the afternoon of Day 5 at summer camp, you watch several workers at the camp construct a new ramp for water skiing on the lake. You take a peek at the blueprint for the ramp, shown at the right. How long must the workers make the ramp? Write your answer using a complete sentence.

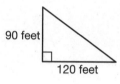

7. On the morning of the last day at camp, your grandmother comes to pick you up. You want to show her how much your swimming has improved, so you swim across the camp pool diagonally 10 times. A diagram of the pool is shown at the right. How far do you swim to impress your grandmother? Write your answer using a complete sentence.

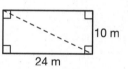

10

© 2008 Carnegie Learning, Inc.

Looking Back to Chapter 10

Key Terms

perimeter ● p. 305

area ● p. 305

circle ● p. 311

center ● p. 311

radius ● p. 311

diameter ● p. 311

circumference ● p. 312

pi ● p. 312

composite figure ● p. 318

square ● p. 321

perfect square ● p. 321

square root ● p. 321

radical sign ● p. 321

radicand ● p. 321

leg ● p. 325

hypotenuse ● p. 325

Pythagorean theorem ● p. 325

converse ● p. 329

Pythagorean triple ● p. 332

Summary

Finding Perimeters of Rectangles (p. 305)

To find the perimeter of a rectangle, find the distance around the rectangle. You can also multiply 2 by the rectangle's length and 2 by the rectangle's width, and add the products.

Example

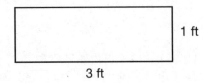

1 ft

3 ft

Perimeter = 3 + 1 + 3 + 1 = 8 feet

Perimeter = 2*l* + 2*w* = 2(3) + 2(1) = 6 + 2 = 8 feet

Finding Areas of Rectangles (p. 305)

To find the area of a rectangle, multiply the length of the rectangle by the width of the rectangle.

Example

2 cm

10 cm

Area = $l \times w$

= 10 × 2

= 20 square centimeters

Finding Circumferences of Circles (p. 312)

To find the circumference of a circle, multiply the radius of the circle by 2π. You can use 3.14 for π.

Example   Circumference = $2\pi r$

Circumference = $2\pi(3)$

≈ 2(3.14)(3)

= 18.84 inches

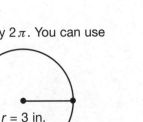

r = 3 in.

Finding Areas of Circles (p. 313)

To find the area of a circle, multiply the square of the radius by π.

Example

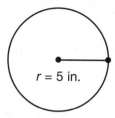

$r = 5$ in.

Area $= \pi r^2$

Area $= \pi (5)^2$

$\approx (3.14)(25)$

$= 78.5$ square inches

Finding Areas of Parallelograms (p. 315)

To find the area of a parallelogram, multiply the height of the parallelogram by the length of its base.

Example

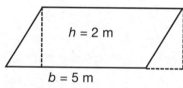

$h = 2$ m

$b = 5$ m

Area $= bh$

Area $= 5(2)$

$= 10$ square meters

Finding Areas of Triangles (p. 317)

To find the area of a triangle, multiply $\dfrac{1}{2}$ of the base of the triangle by the triangle's height.

Example

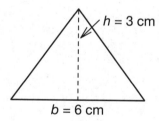

$h = 3$ cm

$b = 6$ cm

Area $= \dfrac{1}{2}bh$

Area $= \dfrac{1}{2}(6)(3)$

$= 9$ square centimeters

10

Finding Areas of Trapezoids (p. 317)

To find the area of a trapezoid, multiply $\frac{1}{2}$ of the sum of the bases of the trapezoid by the height of the trapezoid.

Example

$b_1 = 3$ ft

$h = 2$ ft

$b_2 = 5$ ft

$$\text{Area} = \frac{1}{2}(b_1 + b_2)h$$

$$\text{Area} = \frac{1}{2}(3 + 5)(2)$$

$$= \frac{1}{2}(8)(2)$$

$$= 8 \text{ square feet}$$

Finding Areas of Composite Figures (p. 318)

To find the area of a composite figure, find the area of each common figure that makes up the composite figure and then add the areas.

Example

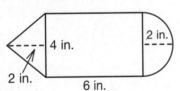

4 in.

2 in.

2 in.

6 in.

Area of triangle = $\frac{1}{2}(4)(2) = 4$ square inches

Area of rectangle = $4 \times 6 = 24$ square inches

Area of half of circle = $\frac{1}{2}(\pi)(2^2) \approx \frac{1}{2}(3.14)(4) = 6.28$ square inches

Area of composite figure = $4 + 24 + 6.28 = 34.28$ square inches

Finding Squares of Numbers (p. 321)

To find the square of a number, multiply the number by itself.

Example   To find the square of 3, multiply 3 by itself.

$3 \times 3 = 3^2 = 9$

So, the square of 3 is 9.

Finding Square Roots of Numbers (p. 321)

To find the square roots of a number that is a perfect square, find the identical factors of the number. One factor is the square root.

Example

The number 49 is a perfect square. To find the square roots of 49, you know that (7)(7) = 49 and that (–7)(–7) = 49. So, the square roots of 49 are 7 and –7.

The positive square root is $\sqrt{49} = 7$.

To estimate the positive square root of a number that is not a perfect square, begin by finding two perfect squares, one less than the number and one greater than the number. Then use trial and error to estimate the square root.

Example

To estimate $\sqrt{18}$, you know that 16 is the closest perfect square less than 18 and 25 is the closest perfect square greater than 18. So, $\sqrt{18}$ is between $\sqrt{16} = 4$ and $\sqrt{25} = 5$.

(4.1)(4.1) = 16.81

(4.2)(4.2) = 17.64

(4.3)(4.3) = 18.49 } So, $\sqrt{18}$ is between 4.2 and 4.3.

You can estimate $\sqrt{18} \approx 4.25$.

Using the Pythagorean Theorem (p. 325)

The Pythagorean theorem states that if a and b are the lengths of the legs of a right triangle and c is the length of the hypotenuse, then $a^2 + b^2 = c^2$.

Example

Triangle ABC is a right triangle. To find the distance from point A to point C, you can use the Pythagorean theorem.

The distance from A to B is 5 units.

The distance from B to C is 4 units.

Let the variable c represent the distance from A to C. Then substitute values into the Pythagorean theorem.

$5^2 + 4^2 = c^2$

$41 = c^2$

$c = \sqrt{41} \approx 6.4$

So, the distance from point A to point C is about 6.4 units.

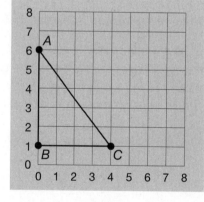

You can use the converse of the Pythagorean theorem to show that a triangle is a right triangle. If $a^2 + b^2 = c^2$, then the triangle is a right triangle.

Finding Pythagorean Triples (p. 332)

To find a Pythagorean triple, find any three integers that satisfy the equation $a^2 + b^2 = c^2$.

Examples

The integers 5, 12, and 13 are a Pythagorean triple because $5^2 + 12^2 = 13^2$.

The integers 20, 21, and 29 are a Pythagorean triple because $20^2 + 21^2 = 29^2$.

10

Looking Ahead to Chapter 11

Focus   In Chapter 11, you will find probabilities of different types of events and analyze data. You will investigate the mean, the median, the mode, and range of data sets. You will also learn several ways to represent data, such as frequency tables, histograms, stem-and-leaf plots, box-and-whisker plots, and circle graphs.

Chapter Warm-up

Answer these questions to help you review skills that you will need in Chapter 11.

Find the quotient. Then write the answer as a percent.

1. $12 \div 48$

2. $45 \div 50$

3. $21 \div 63$

Find the product.

4. $\dfrac{2}{3} \times \dfrac{4}{5}$

5. $\dfrac{1}{7} \times \dfrac{8}{3}$

6. $\dfrac{6}{14} \times \dfrac{7}{2}$

Solve the proportion.

7. $\dfrac{20}{30} = \dfrac{x}{360}$

8. $\dfrac{15}{20} = \dfrac{x}{360}$

9. $\dfrac{19}{152} = \dfrac{x}{360}$

Read the problem scenario below.

Lindsey wants to buy a new mountain bike. The cost of the bike that she wants is $250. She has 30% of the money for the bike.

10. How much money does Lindsey have?

11. What percent would Lindsey have if she had $225?

Key Terms

outcome   p. 341
event   p. 341
probability of an event   p. 341
favorable outcome   p. 341
sample space   p. 342
random   p. 342
theoretical probability   p. 343
experimental probability   p. 343

complementary events   p. 344
compound event   p. 345
independent event   p. 346
dependent event   p. 346
mean   p. 351
median   p. 352
mode   p. 352
range   p. 352

histogram   p. 357
frequency table   p. 358
stem-and-leaf plot   p. 363
box-and-whisker plot   p. 367
upper quartile   p. 367
lower quartile   p. 367
circle graph   p. 372

11

Probability and Statistics

The total number of steel and wooden roller coasters in North America is 748. In Lesson 11.6, you will use a data display called a box-and-whisker plot to analyze data about roller coasters.

11

Sometimes You're Just Rained Out
Finding Simple Probabilities

Objectives

In this lesson, you will:

- Find the probability of an event.

Key Terms

- outcome
- event
- probability of an event
- favorable outcome
- sample space
- random
- theoretical probability
- experimental probability
- complementary events

Probability is a part of our daily lives. For instance, when the weatherperson says that there is a 30% chance of rain, or the sportscaster says that Herman is batting 0.300, probability is involved. Because probability is used so frequently in everyday life, it is important to know how to correctly interpret questions like the following.

- If the weatherperson says that the probability of rain is 30%, should you cancel your plans to attend the baseball game?

- If Herman's batting average is 0.300, is it likely that he will get a hit?

Problem 1   A Baseball Game

Your real baseball game was rained out, so you are indoors playing a board game about baseball. In the game, you take turns rolling a number cube to move around the board. On one of your turns, you roll a 6. Rolling a 6 is an *outcome of an event*. An **outcome** is one possible result. An **event** is a collection of outcomes. For example, rolling a number cube and getting a 1, 2, 3, 4, 5, or 6 is an event. The chance that the event will happen is the **probability of the event.** You can find a probability of an event by finding the ratio of the number of **favorable outcomes** (the outcomes that you want) to the number of possible outcomes.

$$\text{Probability} = \frac{\text{Number of favorable outcomes}}{\text{Number of possible outcomes}}$$

A. In any situation, which is bigger, the number of favorable outcomes or the number of possible outcomes? Use a complete sentence to explain.

B. Can the number of favorable outcomes and the number of possible outcomes be the same? If so, what would the probability be? Use complete sentences to explain.

C. What is the largest probability? What is the smallest probability? In each case, use complete sentences to explain your reasoning.

1. Work with your partner and use a single number cube marked with 1, 2, 3, 4, 5, and 6 on its faces.

Roll the cube once. How many different numbers is it possible to roll?

What is the number of possible outcomes of rolling a number cube once?

List all of the possible outcomes. The set of all possible outcomes is called the **sample space.**

You want to roll a 1. How many favorable outcomes are there?

What is the probability of rolling a 1?

What is the probability of rolling a 2?

What is the probability of rolling a 6?

How many even numbers can you roll?

What is the probability of rolling an even number?

What is the probability of rolling an odd number?

What is the probability of rolling a prime number?

What is the probability of rolling a number greater than 4?

What is the probability of rolling a number greater than or equal to 2?

2. Roll the number cube 30 times. In the table, record the number of times each number is rolled in the first row. The other rows will be filled out later.

Number	1	2	3	4	5	6
Number of Times the Number is Rolled (with Your Partner)						
Number of Times the Number is Rolled (in Your Group)						
Number of Times the Number is Rolled (in Your Class)						

3. Form a group with another partner team. Share the number of times each number is rolled with your group. Add the numbers of both partner teams together and record them in the table.

4. Each group should take turns sharing the number of times each number is rolled with the entire class. Add the numbers of all groups together and record them in the table.

5. Math Path: Theoretical and Experimental Probability

A **theoretical probability** is a probability based on knowing all of the possible outcomes that are equally likely to occur. An **experimental probability** is based on performing an experiment in the same way many times, each of which is called a trial. Each time that the desired event occurs is called a success. You can find the experimental probability by taking the ratio of the actual number of successes to the number of trials. For instance, if you rolled a 1 on the number cube seven times times, your experimental probability is

$$\text{Experimental probability} = \frac{\text{Number of successes}}{\text{Number of trials}} = \frac{7}{30}.$$

6. Complete the table to show the theoretical and experimental probabilities of rolling each number. Base the experimental probabilities on the class results in Question 2.

Number	1	2	3	4	5	6
Theoretical Probability of Rolling the Number						
Experimental Probability of Rolling the Number						

7. Does your experimental probability match your theoretical probability? Discuss your answer with your partner.

Take Note

The probabilities that you found in Question 1 are *theoretical probabilities*. The ratio of the number of times that you roll a 1 to the number of trials is the *experimental probability*.

11

In your baseball card collection, you have a total of 60 cards. You have cards from four teams—the Astros, the Cardinals, the Mets, and the Pirates. For each team, you have 5 outfielders' cards and 10 infielders' cards. Suppose that you pick a single card from the deck at random (without looking).

A. If you want to choose a Mets card, how many favorable outcomes are there? What is the sample space for the problem?

B. What is the probability of choosing a Mets card?

C. What is the probability of choosing an outfielders' card?

Investigate Problem 2

1. **Math Path: Complementary Events**

   Two events are **complementary** when one event or the other event can occur, but both events can not occur at the same time. The sum of the probabilities of two complementary events is 1. So, to find the probability of not choosing an outfielders' card, subtract the probability of choosing an outfielders' card from 1. What is the probability of not choosing an outfielders' card?

2. A standard deck of playing cards has 52 cards in 4 suits. Clubs and spades are printed in black. Hearts and diamonds are printed in red. Each suit has 13 cards—an ace, a king, a queen, a jack, and numbered cards from 2 through 10. Suppose that you choose a single card from the deck at random.

   What is the probability of choosing a diamond?

   What is the probability of choosing a red card?

   What is the probability of choosing a face card (king, queen, or jack)?

   What is the probability of choosing a numbered card less than 7?

3. Let us now re-examine the statements from page 341.

   If the weatherperson says that the probability of rain is 30%, should you cancel your plans to attend the baseball game? Use a complete sentence to explain.

   If Herman's batting average (probability of getting a hit) is 0.300, is it likely that he will he get a hit? Use a complete sentence to explain.

11

11.2 Socks and Marbles
Finding Probabilities of Compound Events

Objectives

In this lesson, you will:
- Understand independent and dependent events.
- Find the probability of a compound event.

Key Terms

- compound event
- independent event
- dependent event

In Lesson 11.1, you found the probabilities of single events. **Compound events** consist of two or more events. For instance, flipping a coin and getting heads and rolling a number cube and getting a 4 is a compound event.

Problem 1   Socks in a Drawer

Suppose that you have a drawer of different colored individual socks. You know that there are 6 blue socks, 10 brown socks, and 4 black socks.

A. You reach in the drawer without looking and pull out a sock.

What is the probability that the sock is blue?

What is the probability that the sock is brown?

What is the probability that the sock is black?

B. Suppose you pull out a brown sock. Then you pull out another sock without putting the brown sock back.

What is the probability that the second sock is brown? Is the probability the same as or different from the probability of pulling out a brown sock in Part (A)? Explain your reasoning using a complete sentence.

C. Suppose that you pull out a brown sock. Then you pull out another sock, but this time you put the brown sock back in the drawer first.

What is the probability that the second sock is brown? Is the probability the same as or different from the probability of pulling out a brown sock in Part (A)? Explain your reasoning using a complete sentence.

11

1. The process that was used in Part (B) of Problem 1 is called "sampling without replacement." The process that was used in Part (C) of Problem 1 is called "sampling with replacement." Do you see why? Use complete sentences to explain.

2. **Math Path: Independent and Dependent Events**

   There are two types of compound events. **Independent events** are events in which the outcome of one event does not affect the outcome of the other event. **Dependent events** are events in which the outcome of one event does affect the outcome of the other event.

   Decide whether the compound events are independent or dependent.

   spinning a spinner and landing on blue and rolling a number cube and getting a 1

   spinning two different spinners, both landing on red

   choosing two cards from a standard deck without replacing the first card and getting two face cards

3. When you sample with replacement, are the events independent or dependent?

4. When you sample without replacement, are the events independent or dependent?

5. In Part (C) of Problem 1, the probability of pulling two brown socks by pulling out a sock, replacing it, and then pulling out a second sock can be found by multiplying the probabilities of the single events. Are these two events independent or dependent?

   Complete the statement to find the probability.

   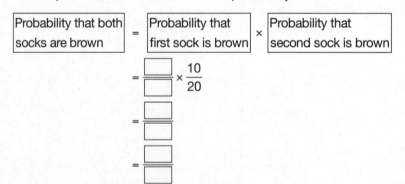

6. Use the result of Question 5 to write a rule for finding the probability of two independent events.

7. In Part (B) of Problem 1, you can find the probability of pulling two brown socks out of the drawer by pulling out a sock and then pulling out a second sock without replacing the first. You need to multiply the probability of the first event by the probability of the second event, given that the first event occurred. Are these two events independent or dependent?

Complete the statement to find the probability.

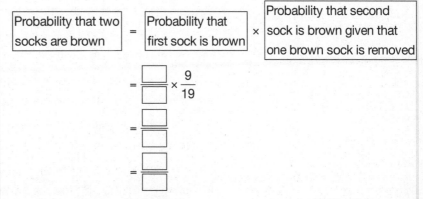

8. Use the result of Question 7 to write a rule for finding the probability of two dependent events.

9. Use the results of Questions 6 and 8 to find each probability.

What is the probability of pulling two blue socks out of the drawer if you pull out a blue sock and then pull out a second sock without putting the first one back?

What is the probability of pulling two black socks out of the drawer if you pull out a black sock and then pull out a second sock without putting the first one back?

What is the probability of pulling one black sock and one blue sock out of the drawer if you sample without replacement?

What is the probability of pulling one brown sock and one blue sock out of the drawer if you sample without replacement?

Suppose that you are conducting an experiment of pulling a sock from a drawer, not replacing it, and then pulling a second sock from the drawer. Out of 38 trials, about how many times would you expect to pull a pair of brown socks?

About how many times would you expect to pull pairs of socks out of the drawer in order to pull 1 pair of brown socks? Use a complete sentence to explain.

Take Note

You can use a theoretical probability to determine a result you might get from conducting an experiment by multiplying the number of trials of the experiment by the theoretical probability.

11

Suppose that you have a bag of marbles containing 4 green marbles, 5 red marbles, 7 white marbles, and 9 yellow marbles.

A. You reach in the bag without looking and pull out a marble.

What is the probability that the marble is green?

What is the probability that the marble is red?

What is the probability that the marble is white?

What is the probability that the marble is yellow?

B. Suppose that you pull out a red marble from the bag and then pull out another marble without replacing the red marble.

What is the probability of pulling out a red marble, not replacing it and then pulling out a green marble?

What is the probability of pulling out a red marble, not replacing it and then pulling out a red marble?

What is the probability of pulling out a red marble, not replacing it and then pulling out a white marble?

What is the probability of pulling out a red marble, not replacing it and then pulling out a yellow marble?

C. Which probabilities in part (A) and part (B) are the same? Which probabilities are different? Use the idea of independent and dependent events to explain why. Write your explanation using complete sentences.

D. Suppose that you pull out a red marble from the bag, but this time you put the red marble back in the bag before you pull out a second marble.

What is the probability that the second marble is green?

What is the probability that the second marble is red?

What is the probability that the second marble is white?

What is the probability that the second marble is yellow?

E. Which probabilities in part (A) and part (D) are the same? Which probabilities are different? Use the idea of independent and dependent events to explain why. Write your explanation using complete sentences.

1. What is the probability of pulling two red marbles from the bag if you pull one red marble, put it back into the bag, and then pull a second red marble?

2. What is the probability of pulling two red marbles from the bag if you pull one red marble and then pull a second red marble without putting the first red marble back?

3. What is the probability of pulling two green marbles from the bag if you pull one green marble and then pull a second green marble without putting the first green marble back?

4. What is the probability of pulling two white marbles from the bag if you pull one white marble and then pull a second white marble without putting the first white marble back?

5. What is the probability of pulling two yellow marbles out of the bag if you pull one yellow marble and then pull a second yellow marble without putting the first yellow marble back?

6. Use the results of Questions 1–5 to write complete sentences to explain how pulling a marble without putting it back changes the probability of pulling a second marble of the same color.

7. What is the probability of pulling one yellow marble and one green marble if you sample without replacement?

8. What is the probability of pulling one red marble and one green marble if you sample without replacement?

9. If you pull three marbles, what is the probability that you pull a red marble, a green marble, and a yellow marble if you sample without replacement?

11

11.3

What Do You Want to Be?
Mean, Median, Mode, and Range

Objectives

In this lesson, you will:

- Find the mean, median, mode, and range of a set of data.

Key Terms

- mean
- median
- mode
- range

There are many instances in which people need to work with large amounts of data. For example, principals work with student test scores and insurance brokers base their policy rates on the number of car accidents in different cities. In each case, someone must work with a large amount of information in the form of numbers.

Problem 1   You Want to Be a Teacher!

As a teacher, one of your responsibilities is to assess how well your students have learned the material that you have taught. Suppose that you gave a test to the 15 students in your class. The test scores for the 20-point test are listed below.

5, 14, 17, 18, 9, 11, 11, 14, 17, 8, 5, 20, 19, 5, 14

A. Did your students do well on this test? Use a complete sentence to explain why or why not.

B. One number that is often used to describe a set of data is the *mean,* or arithmetic average of the data. The **mean** is the sum of the data values divided by the number of items in the data set. What is the mean of the test scores?

C. Approximately what percent of the scores is above the mean?

D. Now that you have found the mean of the test scores, do you have a better understanding of how well the students did on the test? Explain your answer using a complete sentence.

11

© 2008 Carnegie Learning, Inc.

Take Note

When you have an even number of items in a data set, you can find the **median** by finding the mean of the middle two numbers. For instance, for the data set 2, 3, 5, 6, 8, 9, the median is the mean of 5 and 6, which is $\frac{5+6}{2}$, or 5.5.

Take Note

Sometimes, a set of data will have more than one mode. For example, the data set 3, 6, 2, 5, 2, 1, 0, 6, is bimodal. The numbers 2 and 6 are the modes of the data.

1. A second number that is used to describe a set of data is the *median* of the data. The **median** is the middle score of the data, found by listing all the scores in order and finding the score exactly in the middle. What is the median test score?

2. Does the median provide you with a better understanding of how well your students did on the test? Use a complete sentence to explain why or why not.

3. A third number that is used to describe a set of data is the *mode* of the data. The **mode** is the number in the data set that appears most often. What is the mode of the scores, that is, the test score that appears the greatest number of times in the list?

4. One additional measure that is useful in analyzing data sets is the *range* of the data set. The **range** is the difference between the greatest number and the least number in the data set. What is the range of the test scores?

5. Suppose that you want to own a shoe store. You need to be able to make decisions about what sizes of shoes to order.

   To help you learn about the "average" shoe size, your teacher will find and record the shoe size of each student in your class and then divide the sizes into two groups. One group will be all of the girls' sizes and the other group will be all of the boys' sizes.

   Find the mean shoe size for all of the students in your class.

   Find the mean shoe size for the boys.

   Find the mean shoe size for the girls.

6. Find the median shoe size for all of the students in your class.

   Find the median shoe size for the boys.

   Find the median shoe size for the girls.

11

7. Find the mode of the shoe sizes for all of the students.

Find the mode of the shoe sizes for the boys.

Find the mode of the shoe sizes for the girls.

8. Find the range of the shoe sizes for all of the students.

Find the range of the shoe sizes for the boys.

Find the range of the shoe sizes for the girls.

9. What does the mean tell you about the shoe sizes?

What does the median tell you about the shoe sizes?

What does the mode tell you about the shoe sizes?

What does the range tell you about the shoe sizes?

10. If you need to order shoes at your shoe store, how could you use the mean to make decisions? How could you use the median? How could you use the mode? How could you use the range? Write your answers using complete sentences.

11. If you were to pick a student at random based on the data that were collected, what is the probability the student's shoe size is a 7?

What is the probability the student's shoe size is a 13?

12. What shoe size would have the highest probability of being the shoe size of a student selected at random? Use a complete sentence to explain.

11

As the Chief Executive Officer (CEO) of a large corporation, you need to make decisions about the salaries of your employees. The table shows the salaries of different categories of employees at your corporation and the number of people in each category.

Category	Salary	Number
Chief Executive Officer (CEO)	$150,000	1
Chief Financial Officer (CFO)	$125,000	1
Vice Presidents (VP)	$100,000	2
Managers	$55,000	6
Group Leaders	$30,000	10
Workers	$25,000	80

Management is considered to be the managers, the VPs, the CFO, and the CEO.

A. Find the mean salary of all of the employees.

Find the mean salary of the management.

B. Find the median salary of all of the employees.

Find the median salary of the management.

C. Find the mode of the salaries of all of the employees.

Find the mode of the salaries of the management.

D. Find the range of the salaries of all of the employees.

Find the range of the salaries of the management.

E. What does the mean tell you about the salaries of the corporation's employees? What does the median tell you? What does the mode tell you? Write your answers using complete sentences.

1. If you were in charge of negotiating raises for the group leaders and workers, how could you use the mean, median, mode, or range to argue for more money? Use complete sentences to explain your reasoning.

2. If you were the CEO in charge of negotiating with the group leaders and workers, how could you use the mean, median, mode, or range to argue to keep the salaries the same? Use complete sentences to explain your reasoning.

3. If you choose an employee at random based on the information in the table, what is the probability that the person's salary is $55,000?

   What is the probability that the person's salary is more than $40,000?

   What is the probability that the person's salary is less than $35,000?

4. Compare your answers to Questions 1–3. Be sure that if you have any answers on which you do not agree, you work together to find out why. Be prepared to share your work with the rest of the class.

11

Get the Message?

Histograms

Objectives

In this lesson, you will:

- Interpret histograms.
- Create frequency tables and histograms.

Key Terms

- histogram
- frequency table

Bar graphs are useful when we observe small data sets. For large data sets or data with a wide range of values, there is another type of graph that allows us to "see" interesting trends or characteristics of the data. This graph is called a *histogram*. A **histogram** displays numerical data that has been organized into equal intervals.

Problem 1   Text Messaging

You can use a cellular phone to send and receive messages in a text format. In a recent study, ten male and female teenagers sent and received text messages. The average number of messages sent per day by each participant is shown below.

3.0, 2.8, 4.0, 3.7, 3.4, 3.0, 0.9, 4.1, 3.3, 1.7

A. The graph below is a bar graph of the data.

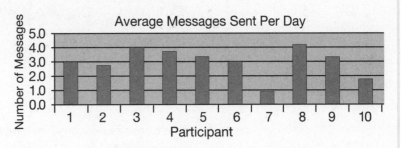

B. What does each bar represent? Write your answer using a complete sentence.

C. What information does the bar graph help us to "see" about the data set? What conclusions can we make based on this graph? Use complete sentences to explain.

1. Math Path: Frequency Tables

You can use a **frequency table** to help you to organize data into intervals. The number of values that fall in the interval is the frequency of the interval. Complete the frequency table using the data in Problem 1. Make a tally mark (|) in the interval column each time that a data value falls in that interval. Then total the tally marks to find the frequency. The tally mark for the first value, 3.0, has been recorded for you.

Data Intervals	0.0–0.9	1.0–1.9	2.0–2.9	3.0–3.9	4.0–4.9
Tally						
Frequency					

2. Below is a histogram that displays the data in the frequency table above.

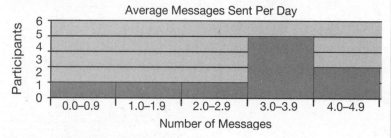

What does each bar represent?

What does the horizontal axis represent? What does the vertical axis represent?

3. What information does the histogram in Question 2 help us to "see" about the data set? What conclusions can we make based on this graph? Use complete sentences to explain.

4. Using the histogram, can you "see" in which interval the mean would be?

Can you "see" in which interval the median would be?

Can you "see" in which interval the mode would be?

11

Problem 2   Length of a Phone Call

You are trying to determine how much time you spend on each call that you receive on your cellular phone. The data below are the number of minutes that you were on the phone for 25 calls that you made last week.

48, 33, 23, 28, 17, 12, 38, 43, 34, 25, 33, 37,

17, 22, 21, 39, 12, 45, 48, 17, 9, 52, 5, 17, 44

A. How many intervals of equal size do you need to represent the data? Write your answer using a complete sentence. (Remember that not all intervals must have data.)

Complete the frequency table below for the data using the intervals you chose. Use only as many columns as you need. To complete the table, use tally marks to list each occurrence in an interval. Then total the tally marks and write the frequency for each interval.

Data Intervals							
Tally							
Frequency							

B. Use the frequency table to construct a histogram below.

First, draw and label the horizontal and vertical axes.

Next, place the intervals on the horizontal scale.

Next, label the vertical scale, beginning with zero and ending with a number large enough to include all of the frequencies in the table.

Next, draw a bar to represent the frequency of each interval.

Finally, add a title to the histogram.

11

State or District	Number of Post Offices
AK	184
AL	558
AR	582
AZ	198
CA	1056
CO	381
CT	233
DC	1
DE	53
FL	457
GA	606
HI	72
IA	892
ID	226
IL	1225
IN	716
KS	603
KY	785
LA	468
MA	398
MD	394
ME	433
MI	822
MN	734
MO	912
MS	407
MT	312
NC	741
ND	341
NE	479
NH	227
NJ	520
NM	286
NV	85
NY	1513
OH	996
OK	576
OR	332
PA	1711
RI	51
SC	360
SD	338
TN	533
TX	1409
UT	176
VA	809
VT	270
WA	443
WI	718
WV	759
WY	176

Investigate Problem 2

1. What does each bar in your histogram in Problem 2 represent?

   What does the horizontal axis represent? What does the vertical axis represent?

2. What information does the histogram in Problem 2 help us to "see" about the data set? What conclusions can we make based on this graph? Use complete sentences to explain.

3. Using the histogram, can you "see" in which interval the mean would be?

   Can you "see" in which interval the median would be?

   Can you "see" in which interval the mode would be?

Problem 3   Snail Mail Messages

At the left is a table that lists all of the states and the District of Columbia and the number of primary U.S. post offices that are in the state or district.

Construct a frequency table for the data.

11

1. Use the frequency table to construct a histogram of the data.

2. What does each bar represent?

What does the horizontal axis represent? What does the vertical axis represent?

3. What information does the histogram in Question 1 help us to "see" about the data set? What conclusions can we make based on this graph? Use complete sentences to explain.

4. Using the histogram, can you "see" in which interval the mean would be?

Can you "see" in which interval the median would be?

Can you "see" in which interval the mode would be?

11

11.5 Go for the Gold!
Stem-and-Leaf Plots

Objectives

In this lesson, you will:
- Interpret stem-and-leaf plots.
- Create stem-and-leaf plots.

Key Terms

- stem-and-leaf plot

Whenever we work with data sets, it is helpful to try to "picture" or display the data in a meaningful way in order to "see" some interesting patterns that are not obvious when the data is in a list.

Problem 1 · Gold Medals

You are planning on following the next Olympics very closely on television. In order to better understand the games, you do some research and list the numbers of gold medals that the United States has won in the Summer Olympic Games in different years.

35, 40, 44, 37, 36, 83, 34, 33, 45, 36, 34, 32, 40,

38, 24, 41, 22, 45, 41, 25, 23, 12, 78, 20, 11

A. Order the data. Then find the mean, median, mode, and range of the data.

The mean is _____. The median is _____.

The mode is _____. The range is _____.

B. A **stem-and-leaf plot** is a data display that helps you to see the spread of the data. The *leaves* of the data are made from the digits with the least place value. The *stems* of the data are made from the remaining digits in the greater place values. Each data point is listed once in the plot. Complete the plot. The first data point, 11, is done for you.

Take Note

To display data points like 175 and 5.4 in a stem-and-leaf plot, remember that the leaf is the digit with the least place value. So, 175 is displayed as 17 | 5 and 5.4 is displayed as 5 | 4.

```
0 |
1 | 1
2 |
3 |
4 |
5 |
6 |
7 |
8 |          1 | 1 = _____ medals
```

C. Be sure to include a key that indicates what the stems and leaves indicate. Complete the key in your stem-and-leaf plot.

11

1. Circle the mean of the data in the stem-and-leaf plot in Problem 1. Draw a square around the median of the data. Place a triangle around the mode of the data.

2. Does displaying the data in this form make it easier to "see" any trends or interesting patterns that were not obvious from the list in Problem 1? Use a complete sentence to explain why or why not.

3. How would you describe the number of gold medals that the United States has won over the years? Use a complete sentence to explain your answer.

4. Form a group with another partner team. Compare your answers to Questions 1–3. Be sure that if you have any answers on which you do not agree, you work together to find out why.

Problem 2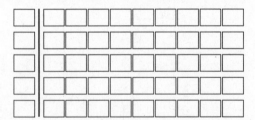

The heights (in centimeters) of 8 female gymnasts on the U.S. Olympic team are listed below.

145, 147, 152, 152, 152, 155, 155, 170

A. Construct a stem-and-leaf plot of the data. Use only as many boxes as you need. Include a key with your plot.

B. Circle the mean of the data in the stem-and-leaf plot in Part (A). Draw a square around the median of the data. Place a triangle around the mode of the data.

C. How would you describe the gymnasts' heights? Use a complete sentence to explain your answer.

11

1. You want to understand how diving scores work in the Olympics. Judges award raw scores on a scale of 1 to 10. This score is then multiplied by the degree of difficulty of the dive. The raw scores from 5 judges for 6 different dives by a diver in an Olympic trial are shown below.

7.8, 6.5, 6.8, 7.0, 7.5, 8.0, 7.8, 7.9, 8.2, 8.7,

5.5, 5.9, 5.4, 5.5, 5.8, 8.7, 8.8, 8.8, 9.0, 8.9,

7.6, 7.5, 7.0, 7.0, 7.4, 6.6, 6.9, 7.3, 7.2, 7.0

Use the space at the left to order the data. Then construct a stem-and-leaf plot of the data. Include a key with your plot.

2. Circle the mean of the data in the stem-and-leaf plot. Draw a square around the median of the data. Place a triangle around the mode of the data.

3. Does displaying the data in this form make it easier to "see" any trends or interesting patterns that were not obvious from the list above? Use a complete sentence to explain why or why not.

4. How would you describe the scores of the diver for the six dives? Use a complete sentence to explain your answer.

5. Form a group with another partner team. Compare your answers to Questions 1–4. Be sure that if you have any answers on which you do not agree, you work together to find out why. Be prepared to share your stem-and-leaf plot with the entire class.

11

11

All About Roller Coasters
Box-and-Whisker Plots

Objectives

In this lesson, you will:
- Interpret box-and-whisker plots.
- Create box-and-whisker plots

Key Terms

- box-and-whisker plot
- upper quartile
- lower quartile

We have found a number of ways to display data in an effort to "see" the data. Histograms help us to quantify large groups of data, and stem-and-leaf plots can indicate trends. We are now going to look at another data display, a box-and-whisker plot, that can help us see how spread out the data are and how much the data are clustered around the mean.

Problem 1   Ride Til You Drop

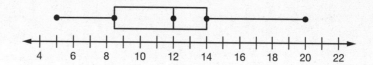

Your class visits an amusement park for a day. Each class member rides only the roller coasters. Each of you keeps track of the number of times that you ride. In a **box-and-whisker plot,** a number line is used to show how data are distributed. The box-and-whisker plot below represents the number of times that each class member rode a roller coaster that day.

A. What is the lowest number in the data set?

What is the highest number in the data set?

B. The vertical line inside the box represents the median of the data. What is the median of the data?

C. The point in the box directly to the right of the median represents the median of the upper half of the data. The median of the upper half of the data is called the **upper quartile.** What is the value of the upper quartile?

D. Similarly, the point in the box directly to the left of the median represents the median of the lower half of the data. The median of the lower half of the data is called the **lower quartile.** What is the value of the lower quartile?

E. The horizontal lines on both ends of the box are called whiskers. What do the dots at the end of the whiskers represent?

11

Investigate Problem 1

1. The box-and-whisker plot divides the data set into how many parts? Use a complete sentence to explain how you know.

2. Can you tell how many numbers are in the data set? Use a complete sentence to explain.

3. What do you know about the fraction of the data set that is represented by each of the parts of the box-and-whisker plot? Use a complete sentence to explain.

4. Look at the box-and-whisker plot again. Use complete sentences to write any conclusions that you can make about the data in the data set.

5. Form a group with another partner team. Compare your answers to Parts (A)–(E) in Problem 1 and Questions 1–4. Be sure that if you have any answers on which you do not agree, you work together to find out why.

Problem 2   Coasters with the Greatest Drop

The drop of a roller coaster is the biggest drop in height experienced on the roller coaster. The box-and-whisker plot represents the drop of the 10 roller coasters in the United States that hold the record for the greatest drop.

Greatest Drop of Roller Coasters

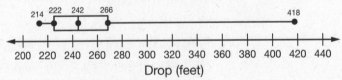

214 222 242 266   418

200 220 240 260 280 300 320 340 360 380 400 420 440
Drop (feet)

A. Look at the box-and-whisker plot. Each whisker represents about what fraction of the data?

B. About what fraction of the data is represented by the large box?

11

Problem 3   *Upside Down!*

On a roller coaster, an inversion is when a rider is turned completely upside down. The numbers of inversions of the top 30 roller coasters with inversions are listed below.

14, 13, 11, 20, 11, 17, 13, 13, 26, 11, 13, 19, 13, 31, 17,
19, 11, 11, 15, 18, 12, 17, 16, 15, 14, 13, 12, 11, 13, 11

A. List the numbers of inversions from least to greatest.

Find the median.

Find the upper quartile by finding the median of the upper half of the data (all of the numbers above the median).

Find the lower quartile by finding the median of the lower half of the data (all of the numbers below the median).

Into how many parts has the data been divided?

B. What is the highest number of inversions?

What is the lowest number of inversions?

Create a number line on the line at the bottom of the page that includes numbers in the range of the data (the highest and lowest number of inversions).

C. Locate the median on the number line. About an inch above the number line, draw a dot for the median and label its value.

Locate the upper quartile on the number line. About an inch above the number line, draw a dot for the upper quartile and label its value.

Locate the lower quartile on the number line. About an inch above the number line, draw a dot for the lower quartile and label its value.

D. Locate the lowest data value on the number line. About an inch above the number line, draw a dot for the lowest data value and label its value.

Locate the highest data value on the number line. About an inch above the number line, draw a dot for the highest data value and label its value.

E. Draw a box with sides at both quartiles.

Draw a vertical line through the median.

Draw a "whisker" to the highest data value and a "whisker" to the lowest data value.

Take Note

Recall that when there is an even number of data points, you find the median by finding the mean of the two middle numbers.

11

1. Is the box-and-whisker plot you constructed in Problem 3 similar to the one in Problem 1? Use a complete sentence in your answer.

2. Look at the box-and-whisker plot that you made. Use complete sentences to write any conclusions that you can make about the data in the data set.

3. Form a group with another partner team. Compare your box-and-whisker plots. Be sure that if the plots do not look similar that you work together to find out why. Be prepared to share your box-and-whisker plot with the rest of the class.

4. The box-and-whisker plots below show the speeds of the top 10 fastest wooden roller coasters and the top 10 fastest steel roller coasters.

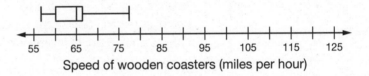

Speed of wooden coasters (miles per hour)

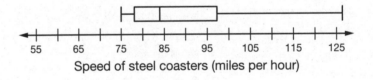

Speed of steel coasters (miles per hour)

5. About what fraction of the steel roller coasters have speeds that are greater than 100 miles per hour? Write your answer using a complete sentence.

6. Three-fourths of the wooden roller coasters are slower than approximately what speed? Write your answer using a complete sentence.

7. Are any of the wooden roller coasters as fast as the steel roller coasters? Use a complete sentence to explain.

11

What's Your Favorite Flavor?
Circle Graphs

Objectives

In this lesson, you will:
- Interpret circle graphs.
- Create circle graphs.

Key Terms

- circle graphs

Besides histograms, stem-and-leaf plots, and box-and-whisker plots, there are several other ways of displaying data in order to "see" the data. One way of displaying data that you may already know is a bar graph.

Problem 1   One Scoop or Two?

The table shows the most popular ice cream flavors sold at a local ice cream shop.

Frozen Yogurt Flavors	Cherry	Chocolate	Vanilla	Peach	Other
Number of Scoops Sold	200	300	340	120	40

A. Construct a bar graph of this information in the space provided.

Most Popular Frozen Yogurt Flavors

Number of Scoops Sold

B. Which was the most popular flavor?

Which was the least popular flavor?

Use a complete sentence to write any conclusions you can make using the bar graph.

11

1. Complete the table below. First, for each flavor, write the amount of the flavor as a fraction of the total number of scoops sold. Then write the fraction as a decimal and then as a percent.

Frozen Yogurt Flavors	Cherry	Chocolate	Vanilla	Peach	Other
Number of Scoops Sold	200	300	340	120	40
Fraction of Total					
Fraction of Total as a Decimal					
Percent of Total					

2. At the right is a *circle graph* of the most popular frozen yogurt flavors. A **circle graph** is a data display that represents data as parts of a whole. Label each section with the percent that the section represents.

Most Popular Frozen Yogurt Flavors
- Cherry
- Chocolate
- Vanilla
- Peach
- Other

3. How does the circle graph enable you to "see" the data differently than the bar graph? Use a complete sentence to explain your answer.

4. When you construct a circle graph, the area of the sections of the circle are based on the percents of each category of data. Remember that there are 360 degrees in a circle. For each flavor, write and solve a proportion to find the number of degrees in each section that will represent the flavor. The first one is done for you.

Cherry: $\dfrac{200}{1000} = \dfrac{x}{360}$ $x = 72$ degrees

Chocolate:

Vanilla:

Peach:

Other:

Problem 2 How Much is Enough Frozen Yogurt?

The table below shows the average amount of frozen yogurt eaten per person per year in the top six countries that eat the most frozen yogurt.

A. Complete the table below. First, for each country, write the amount of frozen yogurt eaten per person as a fraction of the total amount eaten by all countries. Then write the fraction as a decimal and then as a percent.

Country	New Zealand	U.S.	Australia	Finland	Sweden	Canada
Amount Eaten per Person (liters)	27	19	18	14	12	10
Fraction of Total Amount Eaten						
Fraction of Total as a Decimal						
Percent of Total						

B. Use the percents from your table to construct a circle graph below. Be sure to include a key to the graph or label each section with the name of a country.

11

Looking Back at Chapter 11

Key Terms

outcome • p. 341

event • p. 341

probability of an event • p. 341

favorable outcome • p. 341

sample space • p. 342

random • p. 342

theoretical probability • p. 343

experimental probability • p. 343

complementary events • p. 344

compound event • p. 345

independent event • p. 346

dependent event • p. 346

mean • p. 351

median • p. 352

mode • p. 352

range • p. 352

histogram • p. 357

frequency table • p. 358

stem-and-leaf plot • p. 363

box-and-whisker plot • p. 367

upper quartile • p. 367

lower quartile • p. 367

circle graph • p. 372

Summary

Finding Probabilities of Events (p. 341)

To find the probability of an event, find the ratio of the number of favorable outcomes to the number of possible outcomes.

Example   To find the probability that if a coin is flipped, it will land heads up, find the ratio of the number of heads on a coin to the number of faces on a coin.

$$\text{Probability} = \frac{\text{Number of heads}}{\text{Number of faces}} = \frac{1 \text{ head}}{2 \text{ faces}} = \frac{1}{2}$$

So, the probability that if a coin is flipped, it will land heads up is $\frac{1}{2}$.

Finding Probabilities of Complementary Events (p. 344)

Two events are complementary if one event or the other can occur, but not both. The sum of the probabilities of two complementary events is 1.

Example   To find the probability of pulling an ace from a standard deck of cards, find the ratio of the number of aces in a deck to the number of cards in a deck.

$$\text{Probability} = \frac{\text{Number of aces}}{\text{Number of cards}} = \frac{4 \text{ aces in a deck}}{52 \text{ cards in a deck}} = \frac{4}{52} = \frac{1}{13}$$

So, the probability of pulling an ace from a standard deck of cards is $\frac{4}{52}$, or $\frac{1}{13}$. You can use this to find the probability of not pulling an ace from a standard deck by subtracting the probability of pulling an ace from 1. So, the probability of not pulling an ace is $1 - \frac{1}{13} = \frac{12}{13}$.

Finding Probabilities of Independent Events (p. 346)

To find the probability of independent events, multiply the probability of the first event by the probability of the second event.

Example

A bag of markers contains 5 red, 9 orange, and 6 yellow markers. You can find the probability of choosing a red marker, replacing it, and then choosing an orange marker by multiplying the probability of choosing a red marker by the probability of choosing an orange marker.

$$\text{Probability} = \boxed{\text{probability of choosing red}} \times \boxed{\text{probability of choosing orange}}$$

$$= \frac{5}{20} \times \frac{9}{20}$$

$$= \frac{45}{400} = \frac{9}{80}$$

So, the probability of first choosing a red marker, replacing it, and then choosing an orange marker is $\frac{9}{80}$.

Finding Probabilities of Dependent Events (p. 347)

To find the probability of dependent events, multiply the probability of the first event by the probability of the second event, given that the first event occurred.

Example

To find the probability of choosing a red marker, then choosing an orange marker, without replacing the red marker, multiply the probability of choosing a red marker by the probability of choosing an orange marker, given that a red marker had already been removed.

$$\text{Probability} = \frac{5}{20} \times \frac{9}{19} = \frac{45}{380} = \frac{9}{76}$$

So, the probability of choosing a red marker, then an orange marker is $\frac{9}{76}$.

Finding the Mean and Median (pp. 351, 352)

To find the mean of a set of data, add all of the data values and divide by the number of items in the data set. To find the median of a set of data, arrange the items in order from smallest to largest and find the item that is exactly in the middle of the list.

Example

The scores of your class on a 25-point math quiz are listed below.

20, 13, 16, 24, 25, 19, 17, 11, 18, 22, 24, 23, 16, 20, 16

To find the mean, add the scores and divide by 15.

$$\text{mean} = \frac{20 + 13 + 16 + 24 + 25 + 19 + 17 + 11 + 18 + 22 + 24 + 23 + 16 + 20 + 16}{15} = \frac{284}{15} = 18\frac{14}{15}$$

So, the mean score of the class is $18\frac{14}{15}$.

Example

To find the median quiz score, arrange the numbers in order from smallest to largest. Then find the number in the middle.

11, 13, 16, 16, 16, 17, 18, ⑲, 20, 20, 22, 23, 24, 24, 25

The median score is 19.

11

Finding the Mode and Range (p. 352)

To find the mode of a set of data, find the number that appears most often in the data set.

Example To find the mode of the quiz scored from the previous page, find the number that appears most often.

11, 13, (16, 16, 16,) 17, 18, 19, 20, 20, 22, 23, 24, 24, 25

The number 16 appears three times, more than any other. So the mode is 16.

To find the range of a set of data, find the difference between the greatest number and the least number in the data set.

Example To find the range of the quiz scores, find the greatest score and least score and subtract.

Range = greatest – least = 25 – 11 = 14

So, the range of the quiz scores is 14.

Creating Histograms (p. 359)

To create a histogram, first make a frequency table. Then place intervals along the horizontal axis and number the vertical axis. Draw a bar at each interval to represent the frequency at that interval. Be sure to add a title to the histogram.

Example A group of 15 people recorded the average number of emails that they receive per day, listed below.

4.0, 3.2, 5.0, 2.5, 4.0, 5.3, 2.0, 6.2, 1.8, 2.0, 4.5, 3.0, 1.7, 3.1, 2.6

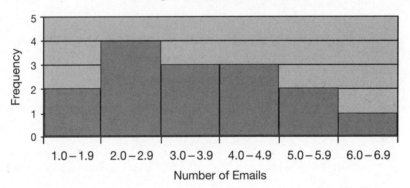

Creating a Stem-and-Leaf Plot (p. 363)

To create a stem-and-leaf plot, use the digits with the least place value as the leaves and the remaining digits with greater place values as the stem. Be sure to include a key that indicates what the stems and leaves represent.

Example
Everyone in your class reaches into their pockets to see how much change they have. The amounts, in cents, are 15, 48, 92, 72, 50, 75, 70, 18, 85, 95, 42, 25, 63, 59, 87, 13, 55, 75, 99, and 25. A stem-and-leaf plot of the data is shown.

1	3 5 8
2	5 5
3	
4	2 8
5	0 5 9
6	3
7	0 2 5 5
8	5 7
9	2 5 9

2 | 5 = 25 cents

Creating a Box-and-Whisker Plot (p. 367)

A box-and-whisker plot uses a number line to show how data are distributed.

Example
The heights of each of your classmates in inches are 62, 58, 67, 68, 68, 72, 66, 65, 60, 61, 64, 67, and 64.

To create the box-and-whisker plot, find the median, the upper quartile, and the lower quartile. Then plot these points on a number line, and draw a box between the upper quartile and the lower quartile.

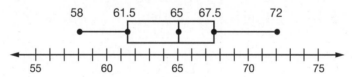

Creating Circle Graphs (p. 372)

To create a circle graph, first find the percents of each of the data items. Then, find how many degrees each data item will represent.

Example
To see what pizza toppings are your town's favorites, you gather information from the local pizzeria. Of the total pizzas that the pizzeria sells, 27.5% are cheese, 37.5% are pepperoni, 20% are mushroom, 7.5% are sausage, and 7.5% are other.

To find the number of degrees in the circle graph needed to represent each topping, write and solve a proportion. A circle graph is shown.

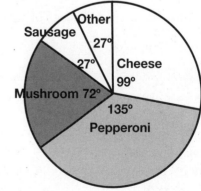

Looking Ahead to Chapter 12

Focus   In Chapter 12, you will work with volume and surface area of three-dimensional figures. You will learn about prisms, pyramids, cones, cylinders, and spheres. You will also design nets and construct top, side, and front views of three-dimensional objects.

Chapter Warm-up

Answer these questions to help you review skills that you will need in Chapter 12.

Find the product.

1. $3 \times 4 \times 2.5$

2. $6.5 \times 9 \times 9$

3. $11 \times 2 \times 5$

Evaluate the expression. Use 3.14 for π.

4. 30π

5. $2\pi(15)$

6. $\pi(4)^2$

Read the problem scenario below.

Jacob is running for class president and is making posters for his campaign. He wants to make the posters in different shapes. Below are three posters that Jacob made.

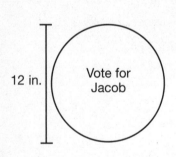

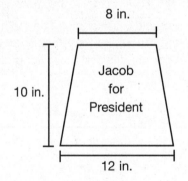

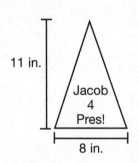

7. Write the name of the shape of each poster below it.

8. What is the area of each poster? Use 3.14 for π.

9. How many square inches of paper did Jacob use to make all three posters?

Key Terms

prism • p. 381
face • p. 381
base • p. 381
height • p. 381
vertex • p. 381
edge • p. 381
solid • p. 382

polyhedron • p. 382
pyramid • p. 382
cylinder • p. 382
cone • p. 383
sphere • p. 383
cube • p. 385
volume • p. 386

surface area • p. 387
sphere • p. 401
hemisphere • p. 403
net • p. 405
scale factor • p. 409
scaled • p. 409
similar solids • p. 409

12

12

Volume and Surface Area

There are in excess of 10,000 different packages and containers to choose from in the average supermarket, including both food and non-food items. In Lesson 12.4, you will design containers that have the greatest volume and use the least amount of material.

12

Your Friendly Neighborhood Grocer
Three-Dimensional Figures

Objectives

In this lesson, you will:

- Identify three-dimensional figures.

Key Terms

- prism
- face
- base
- height
- vertex
- edge
- solid
- polyhedron
- pyramid
- cylinder
- cone
- sphere

Take Note

The prism in the middle of the figures above is called a *rectangular* prism.

In Chapters 9 and 10, you studied two-dimensional figures. These two-dimensional figures are used to form figures in three dimensions.

Problem 1   Packing Meat

Suppose that a butcher in a grocery store needs to package ground meat. He needs to decide between the three packages below.

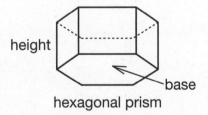

A. Which package would stack better in the display case and why? Which package would roll better in a packaging machine and why? Write your answers using complete sentences.

B. The figures above in the center and on the right are *prisms*. A **prism** is a three-dimensional figure consisting of flat surfaces called **faces**. Two of the faces are parallel and congruent polygons called **bases**. The other faces are rectangles. The **height** of a prism is the length of a segment that is perpendicular to the bases and joins the bases. A prism is named for the shape of its bases.

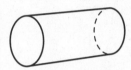

height

base

hexagonal prism

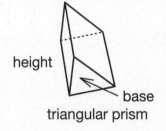

height

base

triangular prism

Mark an X on each face of the hexagonal and triangular prisms. A **vertex** of a prism is the point where three faces of the prism intersect. Draw a dot on each vertex. An **edge** is where two faces of a prism intersect in a line. Draw a line on each edge.

12

1. The prisms in Problem 1 are part of a group of **solids,** or three-dimensional figures, called *polyhedrons.* A **polyhedron** is a solid that has faces that are polygons. Another type of polyhedron is a *pyramid.* A **pyramid** is a solid that has triangular faces that meet at one point, a common vertex. The base of a pyramid is a polygon. A pyramid is named for the shape of its base. The height of a pyramid is the length of the segment from the common vertex to the base such that the segment is perpendicular to the base.

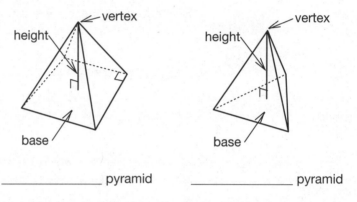

_____ pyramid   _____ pyramid

Decide whether each pyramid above is a rectangular pyramid or a triangular pyramid. Write your answers on the lines. Then use complete sentences to explain your answers.

2. One of the butcher's possible packages in Problem 1 was not a polyhedron but a *cylinder.* A **cylinder** is a solid that has two congruent parallel bases that are circles. Many groceries are packaged in cylinders. The height of the cylinder is the length of a segment that is perpendicular to the bases and joins the bases.

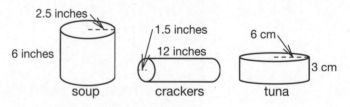

What is the height of each cylinder?

What is the radius of each cylinder?

What is the diameter of each cylinder?

12

3. Two other solids that are not polyhedrons are a *cone* and a *sphere.* A **cone** is a solid that has one circular base and one vertex. A **sphere** is the set of all points in space that are the same distance from a center point. Identify each item below as a prism, cone, sphere, or cylinder.

4. Explain to your partner the similarities and differences between cones and pyramids.

5. Identify buildings or other objects in your environment that are shaped like these five geometric solids—prisms, pyramids, cylinders, cones, and spheres. Keep an ongoing list of your findings in the margin at the left.

6. **Math Path: Euler's Formula**

In 1752, Swiss mathematician Leonhard Euler (pronounced "oiler") stated a formula that related the number of faces, vertices, and edges of geometric solids whose faces are polygons. Use toothpicks and clay to build each polyhedron. Then complete the table.

Take Note

Remember that a *face* of a polyhedron is any flat surface of the polyhedron, a *vertex* is a point where three faces of a polyhedron intersect, and an *edge* is the line formed when two faces of a polyhedron intersect.

		Solid	Number of Edges, E	Number of Faces, F	Number of Vertices, V
Polyhedrons	Prisms	triangular			
		rectangular			
		pentagonal			
		hexagonal			
	Pyramids	triangular			
		rectangular			
		pentagonal			
		hexagonal			

Do you see a pattern or relationship? State your pattern or relationship using words or variables.

Do you think this relationship works for all pyramids and prisms? Discuss this with your group.

12

12

Carnegie Candy Company
Volumes and Surface Areas of Prisms

Objectives

In this lesson, you will:

- Find volumes of rectangular and triangular prisms.
- Find surface areas of rectangular and triangular prisms.

Key Terms

- cube
- volume
- surface area

Problem 1   Candy Cubes

The Carnegie Candy Company decides to make mathematical candy packages. The company makes caramels in the shape of a *cube*. A **cube** is a special prism with faces that are all congruent squares, as shown at the right. The caramel cubes are 1 inch by 1 inch by 1 inch.

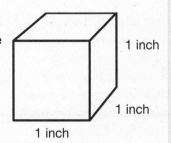

1 inch

1 inch

1 inch

A. Although most candy companies package their candies in bags or long rectangular boxes, the Carnegie Candy Company packages their caramels in cubic packages. Because of this, they can only make packages of certain sizes. What sizes can they make, and how many caramels will be in each package? Complete the table.

Size of Package (cubic inches)	Number of Caramels
1 × 1 × 1	1
2 × 2 × 2	8
3 × 3 × 3	
4 × 4 × 4	
5 × 5 × 5	
⋮	⋮
s × s × s	

B. A package contains 216 caramels. How are the caramels arranged in the package? Use a complete sentence to explain.

C. A package contains 7^3 caramels. How many caramels are layered on each face? Write your answer using a complete sentence.

12

1. Math Path: Volume

The **volume** of a solid is the amount of space occupied by the solid, or the capacity of the solid. You can think of volume as the number of unit cubes that will fit into a three-dimensional shape. A unit cube has a length, width, and height of 1 unit and is the basic unit of measurement for volume.

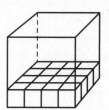

One strategy for finding the volume of a rectangular prism is to count the number of layers of unit cubes it takes to fill the rectangular prism. The number of unit cubes in a layer is the same as the area of the base. So, the number of unit cubes in a rectangular prism (the volume) is the area of the base multiplied by its height. Find the volume of the cube at the right.

In all prisms, the volume is the area of the base B multiplied by the height h. This is written mathematically as

Volume of a prism $= B \times h$.

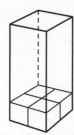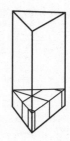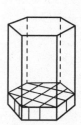

If the prism is a rectangular prism, then the area of the base is equal to the length of the base times the width of the base and the formula becomes

Volume of a rectangular prism $= \square \times w \times h$.

2. Find the volume of each rectangular prism.

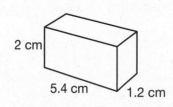

2 cm

5.4 cm 1.2 cm

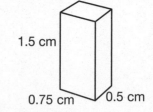

1.5 cm

0.75 cm 0.5 cm

$V = \square \times w \times h$

$= \boxed{} \times \boxed{} \times \boxed{}$

$= \boxed{}$ cubic centimeters

$V = \times w \times h$

$= \boxed{} \times \boxed{} \times \boxed{}$:

$= \boxed{}$ cubic centimeters

12

Cheaper By the Dozen

The Carnegie Candy Company has a special order for 2 dozen caramels packaged together in a box that is a rectangular prism. They have a problem, though. The company always packages their caramels in cubes and 24 is not the cube of an integer. They need to find all of the possible dimensions of a box that would hold exactly 24 cubic caramels.

A. Use sugar cubes or some other type of cube to find all of the possible arrangements of 24 cubes.

B. Complete the table. Note that you may or may not need all of the rows. Do not use the last column yet. This will be completed later.

Length	Width	Height	Volume (cubic units)	

How many different arrangements did you find?

Were all of the volumes of the boxes equal to 24?

C. Because the designers are designing a new box that they have never used before, the box needs to be as inexpensive as possible so that they can make a profit. Because the material used to make the boxes is very expensive (bright colored foil), the company needs to be sure that they make the *surface area* of the box as small as possible. The **surface area** is the sum of all of the areas that form the surface of the solid. In this case, the surface area is the area of all six faces—top, bottom, left side, right side, front, and back.

12

1. **Math Path: Surface Area**

   Label the last column of your table "Surface Area (square units)." Surface area is measured in square units because each face is a two-dimensional figure.

   To find the surface area, you can count the square units on each face of your box. Or, you can sketch each box and find the area of each face and then add the areas. Complete the table.

2. Which box in the table had the smallest surface area? How would you describe its shape? Use a complete sentence to explain why it had the smallest surface area.

3. Write the formula for finding the volume of any rectangular prism.

4. Write the formula for finding the surface area of any rectangular prism.

5. Using what you decided as the best way to package 24 caramels, how would you package 36 caramels to make the surface area of the box as small as possible? Explain your answer using a complete sentence.

6. How would you package 48 caramels to make the surface area of the box as small as possible? Explain your answer using a complete sentence.

7. On March 14 (Pi Day), the Carnegie Company wants to package the caramels in a box that has the same volume and surface area. Is this possible? Use a complete sentence to explain your thinking mathematically.

12

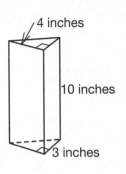

8. The Carnegie Candy Company is deciding whether to begin selling chocolate milk at their store in containers that are triangular prisms. The milk could pour from a hole in one corner of the top. What is the volume of the container of milk shown at the right? Write a complete sentence to explain how you used the formula for the volume of a prism to find the volume of milk in the container.

9. Find the surface area of the milk container. Write a complete sentence that explains how you found the answer.

10. What is the volume of a box of your favorite cereal? Measure the length, width, and height of the box. Then calculate the volume. Write your answer using a complete sentence.

11. Find the surface area of a box of your favorite cereal. Write a complete sentence that explains how you found the answer.

12. A certain kind of imported chocolate comes in packages that are shaped like triangular prisms, as shown below. What is the volume of chocolate that the container could hold? Write your answer using a complete sentence.

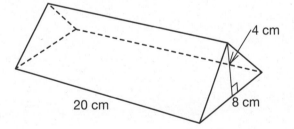

12

The Playground Olympics
Volumes and Surface Areas of Cylinders

Objectives

In this lesson, you will:

- Find volumes of cylinders.
- Find surface areas of cylinders.

Key Terms

- volume
- surface area

Problem 1   *Lemonade Dilemma*

Walnut Grove Middle School holds an annual event called the Playground Olympics. This year the student council is planning to sell lemonade during the event. The group wants to use a drink dispenser instead of selling cans of lemonade. They decide to measure the height and diameter of a typical lemonade can. The group wants to find the volume of the can.

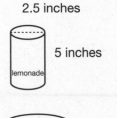

2.5 inches

5 inches

lemonade

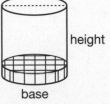

height

base

A. To find the volume of a cylinder, imagine filling the cylinder completely with unit cubes and parts of unit cubes. The volume of a cylinder is the number of unit cubes that it holds. We can use the same method that we used for finding the volume of a prism. That is, we can multiply the area of the base (one layer of unit cubes) by the height (the number of layers of unit cubes that the cylinder holds).

Because the base of a cylinder is always a circle, the area of the base is πr^2 where r is the radius. The formula becomes

Volume of a cylinder = $B \times h = \pi r^2 h$.

Find the volume of lemonade that the can holds. Use 3.14 for π.

B. The student council decides to design a cylindrical cup that will hold one half as much lemonade as a can and also a cylindrical cup that will hold twice as much lemonade as a can. Form a group with another partner team. In your group, design cylindrical cups with different dimensions that will have one half of the volume of a typical can and cylindrical cups with different dimensions that will hold twice the volume of a typical can.

C. Share your results with other groups in your class. Record the different cup sizes that were found.

12

1. The class president thinks that the student council should also design a cup that holds 3 times as much as a typical lemonade can. What possible dimensions could this cup have? Draw and label your design for this "Giant Gulp" cup.

2. At the Playground Olympics, the Pep Club plans on selling souvenir tennis balls with the school logo stamped on each ball. Tennis balls are 6 centimeters in diameter. Design several containers to hold the tennis balls. Sketch each container and label the dimensions.

   Design a cylindrical container that will hold 1 tennis ball.

   Design a cylindrical container that will hold 4 tennis balls.

   Design a cylindrical container that will hold 8 tennis balls.

   Design a container in the shape of a rectangular prism that will hold 1 tennis ball.

   Design a container in the shape of a rectangular prism that will hold 4 tennis balls.

   Design a container in the shape of a rectangular prism that will hold 8 tennis balls.

   Complete the table below.

Number of Tennis Balls	Cylinder			Rectangular Prism		
	Height (cm)	Radius (cm)	Volume (cm³)	Height (cm)	Area of Base (cm²)	Volume (cm³)
1						
4						
8						

3. Form a group with another partner team. Compare your containers with your group's containers. Did everyone in your group design the same containers? How were the containers different?

Problem 2 · *Can Do!*

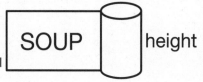

Recall from Lesson 12.2 that the surface area is the sum of the areas that form the surface of a three-dimensional figure. The label of a can covers the surface of the can that is not circular. If you cut the label from a can, you can see that the label is a rectangle.

A. The width of the rectangle is the height of the can. Because the label wraps around the can, the length of the rectangle is the circumference of the can. The surface area of the can is the area of the rectangle plus the area of the two circular bases.

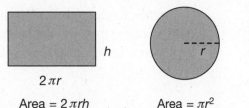

$2\pi r$

Area = $2\pi rh$ Area = πr^2 Area = πr^2

Surface Area of a Cylinder = $2(\pi r^2) + 2\pi rh$

Find the surface area of a can with a radius of 3.5 inches and a height of 6 inches. Use 3.14 for π.

B. Manufacturers try to design containers that hold a maximum amount of product (soft drinks, soup, etc.) but use a minimum amount of surface material (plastic, paper, tin, etc.) They measure a can's efficiency rating by dividing the surface area (SA) by the volume (V) and determining the ratio $\dfrac{SA}{V}$.

In your group, bring several cans from home or ask the employees in the cafeteria to borrow some cans for this investigation. Measure the radius and height of each can. Then determine the volume and surface area of each can. Finally, calculate the ratio $\dfrac{SA}{V}$. Use the table below to organize your work.

Type of Can	Height (cm)	Radius (cm)	Volume (cm³)	Surface Area (cm²)	$\dfrac{SA}{V}$

© 2008 Carnegie Learning, Inc.

12

Lesson 12.3 • Volumes and Surface Areas of Cylinders   **393**

1. Which cans in part (B) were the most efficient? Which cans were the least efficient? Write complete sentences to explain your findings.

2. Label each can with its efficiency rating. Line the cans up across the front of the classroom from least efficient to most efficient. What has the greatest effect on the volume of a cylinder, doubling the radius or doubling the height? Use a complete sentence to explain your reasoning.

What has the greatest effect on the surface area of a cylinder, doubling the radius or doubling the height? Use a complete sentence to explain your reasoning.

3. Wrapping paper comes on rolls and is measured in square feet. If you have the three presents below to wrap for the Playground Olympics prizes, will you have enough paper? Use complete sentences to write a paragraph that explains how you found your answer.

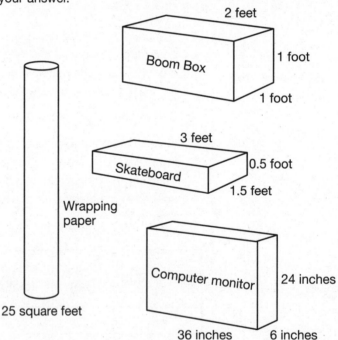

2 feet
Boom Box
1 foot
1 foot

3 feet
Skateboard
0.5 foot
1.5 feet

Wrapping paper

25 square feet

Computer monitor
24 inches
36 inches
6 inches

12

12.4 The Rainforest Pyramid
Volumes of Pyramids and Cones

Objectives

In this lesson, you will:
- Find volumes of pyramids.
- Find volumes of cones.

Key Terms

- pyramid
- cone

In Lesson 12.1, we looked at pyramids and cones. If a prism and a pyramid have congruent bases and the same height, will they have the same volume? If a cylinder and a cone have congruent circular bases and the same height, will they have the same volume?

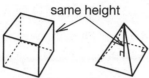

same height   same height

congruent bases   congruent bases

Problem 1   Selling Popcorn

A middle school class is selling popcorn to raise money for a class trip to the Rainforest Pyramid in Galveston, Texas. The students would like to use one of the four types of containers shown above to hold the popcorn. Some of the students think that if the heights of the four containers are the same, then the volumes of the four containers will be the same. Other students think that there may be a difference.

In your group, investigate the volumes of these pairs of solids. You will need a hollow prism and a hollow pyramid with the same base and height, and a hollow cylinder and a hollow cone with the same base and height. You can use rice, sand, or water to investigate these volumes. Be sure to use a box or another container under your shapes to catch the spills. Follow the steps below.

Step 1: Fill your pyramid with sand, rice, or water. Then very carefully pour the contents of the pyramid into the prism. About how much of your prism is filled?

Repeat Step 1 until the prism is filled. How many times did you pour the volume of your pyramid into the prism to fill the prism?

Step 2: Fill your cone with sand, rice, or water. Very carefully pour the contents into the cylinder. About how much of the cylinder is filled?

Repeat Step 2 until the cylinder is filled. How many times did you pour the volume of your cone into the cylinder to fill the cylinder?

12

1. Compare your group's results with the results of other groups in your class. Were the results similar for the two pairs of solids? Write a complete sentence to explain.

2. Complete the statements below to summarize your investigation in Problem 1.

    The volume of a pyramid is _____ of the volume of a prism if the pyramid and the prism have congruent bases and the same height.

    The volume of a cone is _____ of the volume of a cylinder if the cone and the cylinder have congruent circular bases and the same height.

3. An organization's profit is the difference between its income and its expenses. Which price for the popcorn will bring the most profit? Use complete sentence to explain your reasoning.

    Jumbo size popcorn $3   **Medium size popcorn $2**

    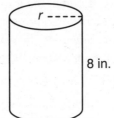   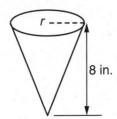

4. Determine a fair pricing scheme for selling popcorn in a cylindrical container and a cone-shaped container if the containers have the same height and congruent bases. Write your answer using complete sentences.

5. What would be a fair pricing scheme for selling popcorn in a rectangular prism-shaped container and a pyramid-shaped container that have the same height and congruent bases? Write your answer using complete sentences.

12

Problem 2

In Problem 1, we discovered that if a rectangular prism and a pyramid have congruent bases and the same height, then the pyramid's volume is $\frac{1}{3}$ of the rectangular prism's volume. This is true for all pyramids. So,

$$\text{Volume of a pyramid} = \frac{1}{3}B \times h$$

where B is the area of the base and h is the height.

The Rainforest Pyramid in Galveston, Texas, is a building that is 100 feet high and has a square base with sides that are 200 feet in length. What is the volume of this building? Show your work below. Then write your answer using a complete sentence.

Investigate Problem 2

1. The height of the Great Pyramid of Giza is 480 feet and its square base has a side length of 750 feet. What is the volume of the Great Pyramid? Show your work at the left. Then write your answer using a complete sentence.

2. The Transamerica Building in San Francisco, California, is also a square pyramid. It is 853 feet tall and its square base has an area of 2025 square feet. Find the volume of the Transamerica Building to the nearest cubic foot. Show your work at the left. Then write your answer using a complete sentence.

3. The pyramid arena in Memphis, Tennessee, is 321 feet tall and has a square base that is 300 feet on each side. What is the volume of this arena? Show your work at the left. Then write your answer using a complete sentence.

12

Problem 3   Cups or Cones?

In Problem 1, we discovered that if a cone and a cylinder have congruent bases and the same height, then the cone's volume is $\frac{1}{3}$ of the cylinder's volume. This is true for all cones. So,

$$\text{Volume of a cone} = \frac{1}{3}B \times h = \frac{1}{3}\pi r^2 h$$

where r is the radius and h is the height.

Take Note

The **height** of a cone is the length of the segment from the common vertex to the base such that the segment is perpendicular to the base.

A. The middle school class wants to plan a trip for next year, so the class president decides that it would be much more profitable to sell soft ice cream on hot days rather than to continue selling popcorn. The class needs to order containers to hold the ice cream, so they order the cups and cones, shown below.

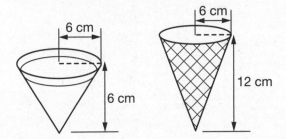

The class president says, "Let's charge $1 for the cup and $2 for the cone, because the cone is twice as tall as the cup." The class treasurer says, "No way—both the cone and the cup have the same volume, so we have to charge the same amount, $2 for each." Who is right, the president or the treasurer? Find the volume of the cup and the volume of the cone.

Volume of cup =

Volume of cone =

B. What would be a fair price to charge for each? Write a complete sentence to explain your answer.

C. Change the dimensions of the cup so that the new cup has the same volume as the cone.

New dimensions of cup:

height =   diameter =

D. Change the dimensions of the cone so that the new cone has the same volume as the original cup.

New dimensions of cone:

height =   diameter =

1. The fourth grade class at the elementary school decided that the middle school was selling ice cream so they should sell popcorn. They gathered all of the old containers that no one else was using. They found cones, cylinders, and boxes shaped like rectangular prisms.

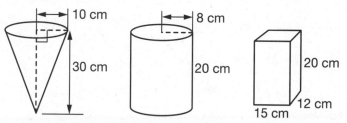

The prices they decided on were:

cone: $2.50

cylinder: $3.75

rectangular prism: $3.50

Which container gives customers the best buy for their money? Use the volume of each container to explain your answer. Use complete sentences in your explanation.

Volume of cone:

Volume of cylinder:

Volume of rectangular prism:

12

2. Use an 8.5-inch by 11-inch sheet of paper to design a container. The container should have the greatest volume possible. You may cut and tape the paper together to form a three-dimensional figure. You may use only one sheet of paper.

   Record all of the dimensions of your container and the volume of your container. Be sure to write down any diagrams, tables, or equations that you used to help you solve the problem.

Each group should present their container to the class, explaining their process and their conclusions.

Which group's container had the largest volume?

What was the shape of the container with the largest volume?

What was the volume of this container?

What patterns did you notice with all of the containers designed? Write your answer using complete sentences.

12

What on Earth?

Volumes and Surface Areas of Spheres

Objectives

In this lesson, you will:

- Find volumes of spheres.
- Find surface areas of spheres.

Key Terms

- sphere
- hemisphere

A *sphere* is a very common geometric figure. You may know it by its most common name of "ball." You can describe a sphere by giving its radius.

Problem 1   Earth's Volume

Earth is not a perfect *sphere*, but it has been formed by gravitational forces into a spherical shape. Scientists in ancient Greece and Egypt determined that Earth was round by observing the shadow of Earth as it passed across the moon during a lunar eclipse. Eratosthenes, a scientist from Alexandria, Egypt, who lived during the third century B.C., actually estimated the circumference of Earth.

A. To determine the volume of a sphere, let's compare it to the volume of a cylinder. Using clay or modeling dough, make a sphere with a diameter of 3 inches.

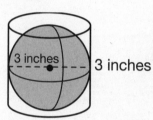

Wrap a strip of plastic around the sphere (a transparency sheet will work). Then trim the plastic so that it is as tall as the sphere you made.

Tape the plastic together tightly to form a cylinder with an open top and bottom.

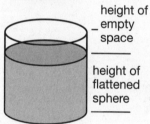

Next, flatten the sphere so that it fits snugly in the bottom of the cylinder.

Measure the following dimensions.

height of the cylinder = _____

height of the flattened sphere = _____

height of the empty space in the cylinder = _____

What relationship do you notice?

B. The volume of the sphere is about what fractional part of the volume of the cylinder? Write your answer using a complete sentence.

12

Investigate Problem 1

1. If your experiment worked out perfectly, you would find that the volume of a sphere is $\frac{2}{3}$ of the volume of a cylinder with the same diameter.

   Volume of a sphere = $\frac{2}{3}$(Volume of a cylinder) = $\frac{2}{3}(\pi r^2 h)$

   Remember that the height of the cylinder is equal to the diameter of the sphere, so the height of the cylinder is $2r$. We can substitute $2r$ for the height into the equation.

   Volume of a sphere = $\frac{2}{3}\pi r^2(2r) = \frac{4}{3}\pi r^3$

   Find the volume of the sphere that you made in Problem 1.

2. Think about the earlier investigation that you did in which you investigated the relationship between a cone and a cylinder. Both cones and spheres are related to cylinders. Find the volumes of the three figures below. Use 3.14 for π.

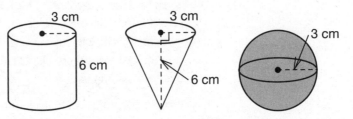

   Volume of cylinder: _____ cubic centimeters

   Volume of cone: _____ cubic centimeters

   Volume of sphere: _____ cubic centimeters

3. How do the volumes compare? Use mathematics to explain. Write your answer using a complete sentence.

4. Earth has a diameter of about 7926 miles and a surface area of about 197 million square miles.

   What is the circumference of Earth at the equator?

   Circumference of Earth: _____ miles

   What is the volume of Earth?

   Volume of Earth: _____ cubic miles

© 2008 Carnegie Learning, Inc.

12

5. Eratosthenes estimated the circumference of Earth to be about 28,750 miles. How far off was his estimate? Write your answer using a complete sentence.

6. **Math Path: Hemisphere**

   A **hemisphere** is exactly half of a sphere. An igloo is shaped like a hemisphere. What is the volume of the space of an igloo with an inside diameter of 50 feet?

   If a tepee shaped like a cone has the same volume as the igloo, what are the possible dimensions of the tepee?

   A nomadic tent used in the Sahara desert is shaped like a triangular prism. If this tent had the same volume as the igloo, what would its dimensions be?

   An adobe house is shaped like a rectangular prism. What would the dimensions of the adobe house be if the house had the same volume of space as the igloo?

7. A Native American hogan was a more permanent dwelling than a tepee, which could be easily rolled up and transported. A hogan is shaped like a rectangular prism with a rectangular pyramid on top. What is the volume of a typical hogan as shown at the right?

   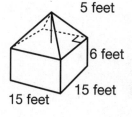

8. A yurt is a dwelling used by nomadic tribes in Mongolia. It is very weather-resistant and can be easily transported by folding it. It is shaped like a cylinder with a cone on top. What is the volume of a typical yurt as shown at the right? Use 3.14 for π.

   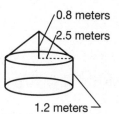

Problem 2   Another House on Earth

A geodesic dome is used by many people as an energy-efficient home. Richard Buckminster Fuller created the geodesic dome. A geodesic dome is approximately a hemisphere.

A. What is the volume of a geodesic dome that has a circular base with a diameter of 40 feet? Write your answer using a complete sentence and explain your reasoning.

B. We want to determine the amount of material needed to make a geodesic dome roof. We need to find the surface area of the geodesic dome, a hemisphere. We cannot flatten out the surface of a sphere to easily measure its surface area, but we can investigate the formula for the surface area of a sphere.

Choose a ball similar in size to a tennis ball. Measure its diameter.

Construct 5 paper circles with the same diameter as the ball. Tape the circles to the surface of the ball with no overlaps. This is somewhat difficult and you will need to cut the circles to fill in the gaps. Use each circle's area completely before you start using another circle.

How many circles did you use to completely cover the ball with no overlap?

Investigate Problem 2

1. If this wrapping of the sphere is done perfectly, you will find that it takes exactly 4 circles to cover the sphere. The formula for the surface area of a sphere is 4 times the area of a circle with the same radius.

   Surface area of a sphere = $4\pi r^2$

   Find the surface area of the geodesic dome in part (A) above.

2. Find the volume and surface area of each type of sports ball.

Type of Ball	Diameter	Volume	Surface Area
ping-pong	40 millimeters		
golf ball	1.5 inches		
baseball	7.5 centimeters		
bowling ball	8.6 inches		

12

Engineers and Architects
Nets and Views

Objectives

In this lesson, you will:

- Design nets for three-dimensional figures.
- Construct side, front, and top views of three-dimensional objects.

Key Terms

- net

Packaging engineers design crates, barrels, and other containers by designing nets. A **net** is a two-dimensional pattern that you can fold to form a three-dimensional figure.

Problem 1   *Creating Shipping Boxes*

A shipping company is shipping 1000 computer monitors by boat. Each monitor is in the shape of a cube with a side length of 1 foot. A well-designed box will hold a computer monitor in place with no extra space. One **net** for the box is shown below.

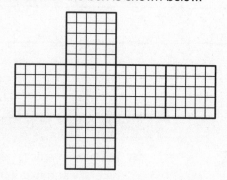

A. Help the company design a box to hold the computer monitor by drawing several other nets that would fold to make a box. Use graph paper to design your nets.

B. Cut out each net that you designed in one piece. Fold each net into a 1-cubic-foot box. Form a group with another partner team. How many different nets were produced by your group?

C. Nets can also help us to calculate the surface area of three-dimensional figures. A net is a two-dimensional representation of the surface area of a figure.

The shipping company must also design steel shipping containers (with lids) to hold the shipping boxes. They need to have three sizes of containers. A small container will hold 8 boxes, a medium container will hold 24 boxes, and a large container will hold 36 boxes. The containers need to be designed to use the steel as efficiently as possible. Design the most efficient container for each of the three sizes. Write a complete sentence that explains why your design is the most efficient.

12

D. Sketch the nets that you designed.

E. For each container, record its dimensions, the surface area of each face of the container, and the total surface area of each container in the table.

Number of Boxes	Dimensions of Most Efficient Container	Total Surface Area (square feet)
8		___ + ___ + ___ + ___ + ___ + ___ + = _____
24		___ + ___ + ___ + ___ + ___ + ___ + = _____
36		___ + ___ + ___ + ___ + ___ + ___ + = _____

Investigate Problem 1

1. Bring in an empty cereal box from home. Cut it apart very carefully and fold it flat. This is the net that the cereal manufacturer designed for your brand of cereal. Measure the dimensions of the net.

   What is the surface area of your cereal box?
   _____ square _____

   What is the volume of your cereal box?
   _____ cubic _____

2. Bring in a can of food from home. Measure the dimensions of your can. Then make a net for your can.

   What is the surface area of your can?
   _____ square _____

   What is the volume of your can?
   _____ cubic _____

3. Design a net for a cylinder that would have enough volume to hold the contents of your cereal box. Label the cylinder's dimensions.

   What is the surface area of your cylinder?
   _____ square _____

   What is the volume of your cylinder?
   _____ cubic _____

4. For each net below, name the solid that can be formed.

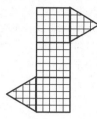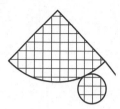

5. Draw four nets for four different geometric figures. Label the dimensions of the net. Trade nets with your partner and name the figure represented by the nets. Check each other's work.

Problem 2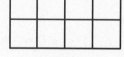

Although we live in a three-dimensional world, we often represent objects in our world using two-dimensional images, drawings, or pictures. Architects create plans for buildings on blueprints that show every aspect of the building—front, back, right side, left side, top, and bottom. Construction crews use these two-dimensional plans to construct the three-dimensional structure.

Use sugar cubes or some other type of cube to construct a model of the building shown at the right. How many cubes were used to construct this model?

Imagine that you are standing directly in front of this building. What do you see? Choose the view that represents the front view and label it.

Is the back view the same?

Imagine that you are standing above the building looking down. What is the top view of the building? Choose the view that represents the top view and label it.

Is this the same as the bottom view? The bottom view is often called the floor plan.

Now imagine that you are looking directly at the left side. What is this left side view? Choose the view that represents the side view and label it.

Is the right side view the same?

What is the surface area of this building in square units?

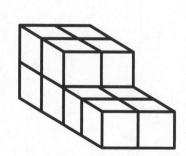
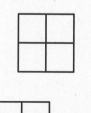

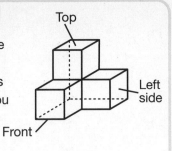

1. Draw the six views of the model of the building shown at the right. You may want to model the building with cubes to help you visualize the views that you cannot directly see.

Top **Front** **Left side**

Right side **Bottom** **Back**

2. An architect designed this building called "hexagon." Draw the six views of the building.

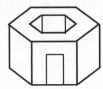

Top **Front** **Left side**

Right side **Bottom** **Back**

12

Double Take

Similar Solids

Objectives

In this lesson, you will:

- Compare volumes of similar solids.
- Compare surface areas of similar solids.

Key Terms

- scale factor
- scaled
- similar solids

In Lesson 9.4 we learned that corresponding angles in similar figures are congruent and that corresponding sides are proportional. Recall that figures can be scaled up or scaled down by a **scale factor**.

Problem 1   Peanuts and Sports Drinks

Three-dimensional objects can also be **scaled** up or scaled down. A model car is a scaled-down version of the real object. The model is mathematically similar to the original object. Every detail is in proportion.

A. **Similar solids** are solids that have the same shape but not necessarily the same size. Use what you know about cubes, spheres, and cylinders to decide whether each statement is true or false. For each statement, write a complete sentence that explains your reasoning.

Not all cubes are similar.

All prisms are similar.

All spheres are similar.

Not all cylinders are similar.

12

B. Two polyhedrons are similar if their corresponding bases are similar and the lengths of their corresponding heights are proportional. Two cones or cylinders are similar if the ratio of their radii equals the ratio of their heights.

Bill and Rick own a concession stand near a baseball park. Bill and Rick sell a sports drink and peanuts at the baseball games. Every week they try different marketing strategies to attract more business.

This week they decide to give everyone twice as much sports drink and twice as many peanuts for the same price as last week. They order boxes and cups with dimensions that are twice the dimensions of the boxes and cups that they used the week before. By super-sizing everything, they hope to sell twice as much. Here are the dimensions of last week's and this week's containers.

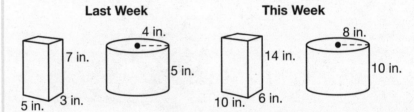

Last Week	This Week

Bill took one look at the new containers and said, "They are huge. Are you sure that they hold twice as much?" Rick said, "I'm positive. I scaled them up by 2. Every dimension is twice as much." All the spectators, even the players, wanted to buy these new super-sized containers for the old prices.

Before second inning was over, Bill and Rick sold out and they had a lot less money than they had at any other game. They were puzzled and couldn't figure out what went wrong. The baseball coach was also their math teacher. He asked them to calculate the volume of last week's containers and the volume of the new scaled-up containers from this week. Help Bill and Rick find the volume of each container from last week and this week.

Volume of last week's peanut container: _____

Volume of scaled-up peanut container: _____

Volume of last week's sports drink container: _____

Volume of scaled-up sports drink container: _____

© 2008 Carnegie Learning, Inc.

12

1. How do the volumes compare? Use a complete sentence in your answer.

2. Was the volume also scaled up by 2? Use a complete sentence to explain.

3. What should Bill and Rick have charged for their scaled-up containers? Write a complete sentence to explain your reasoning.

4. For both the peanut and the sports drink containers, write the ratio of the volume of last week's containers to the volume of the super-sized containers.

Peanuts: $\dfrac{\text{Volume of last week's container}}{\text{Volume of scaled-up container}} = \dfrac{\boxed{}}{\boxed{}} = \dfrac{\boxed{}}{\boxed{}}$

Sports drink: $\dfrac{\text{Volume of last week's container}}{\text{Volume of scaled-up container}} = \dfrac{\boxed{}}{\boxed{}} = \dfrac{\boxed{}}{\boxed{}}$

5. How many of last week's containers fit into the scaled-up containers for peanuts?

How many of last week's containers fit into the scaled-up containers for sports drink?

How does this number relate to the scale factor 2? Write a complete sentence that explains your reasoning mathematically.

6. Are last week's containers and the scaled-up containers similar? Are the ratios of the corresponding dimensions the same?

Ratios of peanuts containers:

length: $\dfrac{5 \text{ in.}}{10 \text{ in.}} = \dfrac{\boxed{}}{\boxed{}}$

width: $\dfrac{3 \text{ in.}}{6 \text{ in.}} = \dfrac{\boxed{}}{\boxed{}}$

height: $\dfrac{7 \text{ in.}}{14 \text{ in.}} = \dfrac{\boxed{}}{\boxed{}}$

Ratio of sports drink containers:

height: $\dfrac{5 \text{ in.}}{10 \text{ in.}} = \dfrac{\boxed{}}{\boxed{}}$

radius: $\dfrac{4 \text{ in.}}{8 \text{ in.}} = \dfrac{\boxed{}}{\boxed{}}$

12

7. Bill and Rick had to pay four times as much for the scaled-up containers. That also cut into their profits. Bill thought that maybe they had been overcharged, but Rick thought that they should calculate the surface area of the four containers before they complained.

Surface area of last week's peanut container: _____

Surface area of scaled-up peanut container: _____

Surface area of last week's sports drink container: _____

Surface area of scaled-up sports drink container: _____

8. How do the surface areas compare? Use a complete sentence in your answer.

9. Was the surface area of the scaled-up containers twice the surface area of last week's containers? Use a complete sentence to explain.

10. For both the peanut and the sports drink containers, write the ratio of the surface area of last week's containers to the surface area of the super-sized containers.

Peanuts: $\dfrac{\text{Surface area of last week's container}}{\text{Surface area of scaled-up container}} = \dfrac{\boxed{}}{\boxed{}} = \dfrac{\boxed{}}{\boxed{}}$

Sports drink: $\dfrac{\text{Surface area of last week's container}}{\text{Surface area of scaled-up container}} = \dfrac{\boxed{}}{\boxed{}} = \dfrac{\boxed{}}{\boxed{}}$

11. How do the numbers in Question 10 relate to the scale factor 2? Write a complete sentence that explains your reasoning mathematically.

12. If Bill and Rick had truly wanted to enlarge the containers so that they would hold twice as much, what should they have done? Design a peanut container and a sports drink container that do hold twice as much. Record the dimensions and sketch the containers at the left.

13. Form a group with another partner team. In your group, discuss how the volume and the surface area of a geometric solid change as each of its dimensions is doubled, tripled, quadrupled, and so on.

12

Looking Back at Chapter 12

Key Terms

prism • p. 381
face • p. 381
base • p. 381
height • p. 381
vertex • p. 381
edge • p. 381
solid • p. 382

polyhedron • p. 382
pyramid • p. 382
cylinder • p. 382
cone • p. 383
sphere • p. 383
cube • p. 385
volume • p. 386

surface area • p. 387
sphere • p. 401
hemisphere • p. 403
net • p. 405
scale factor • p. 409
scaled • p. 409
similar solids • p. 409

Summary

Identifying Three-Dimensional Figures (p. 381)

Prisms and pyramids are three-dimensional solids called polyhedrons and are named for the shape of their bases. Other solids are cylinders, cones, and spheres.

Examples

    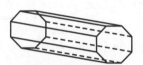

Triangular Prism   **Rectangular Pyramid**   **Octagonal Prism**

Finding Volumes of Prisms (p. 386)

To find the volume of a prism, multiply the area of the base by the height of the prism.

Examples

   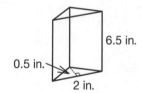

Volume = $\ell \times w \times h$

Volume = $3 \times 1.5 \times 4$

= 18 cubic feet

Volume = $B \times h$

Volume = $\left(\dfrac{1}{2} \times 2 \times 0.5 \right) \times 6.5$

= 3.25 cubic inches

Finding Surface Areas of Rectangular Prisms (p. 387)

To find the surface area of a rectangular prism, find the sum of the areas of the surfaces of the prism.

Example

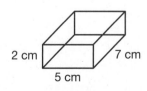

Area of bases = 2(2 × 5) = 2 × 10 = 20 square centimeters
Area of sides = 2(2 × 7) = 2 × 14 = 28 square centimeters
Area of sides = 2(5 × 7) = 2 × 35 = 70 square centimeters
Surface Area = 20 + 28 + 70 = 118 square centimeters

12

Finding Surface Areas of Triangular Prisms (p. 389)

To find the surface area of a triangular prism, find the sum of the areas of the surfaces of the prism.

Example

Area of bases = $2(\frac{1}{2} \times 6 \times 4) = 2 \times 12 = 24$ square feet

Area of sides = $2(5 \times 8) = 2 \times 40 = 80$ square feet

Area of bottom = $6 \times 8 = 48$ square feet

Surface Area = $24 + 80 + 48 = 152$ square feet

Finding Volumes of Cylinders (p. 391)

To find the volume of a cylinder, multiply the area of the circular base by the height of the cylinder. You can use 3.14 for π.

Example

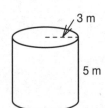

Volume = $\pi r^2 h$

Volume = $\pi (3)^2(5)$

$\approx 3.14(9)(5)$

$= 141.3$ cubic meters

Finding Surface Areas of Cylinders (p. 393)

To find the surface area of a cylinder, find the sum of the areas of the circular bases and the area of the rectangle that forms the side of the cylinder. You can use 3.14 for π.

Example

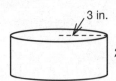

Area of bases = $2\pi r^2 \approx 2(3.14)(3^2) = 56.52$ sq. in.

Area of rectangle = $2\pi rh \approx 2(3.14)(3)(2) = 37.68$ sq. in.

Surface Area = $37.68 + 56.52 = 94.2$ sq. in.

Finding Volumes of Pyramids (p. 396)

To find the volume of a pyramid, multiply one third of the area of the base by the height.

Example

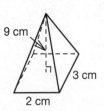

Volume = $\frac{1}{3}B \times h = \frac{1}{3}(2 \times 3) \times 9$

$= 18$ cubic centimeters

Finding Volumes of Cones (p. 396)

To find the volume of a cone, multiply one third of the area of the circular base by the height of the cone. You can use 3.14 for π.

Example

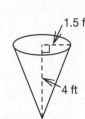

Volume = $\frac{1}{3}B \times h = \frac{1}{3}\pi r^2 h$

Volume $\approx \frac{1}{3}(3.14)(1.5)^2(4)$

$= 9.42$ cubic feet

12

Finding Volumes and Surface Areas of Spheres (p. 401)

To find the volume of a sphere, use the formula: To find the surface area of a sphere, use the formula:

$$\text{Volume of a sphere} = \frac{4}{3}\pi r^3.$$ $$\text{Surface Area} = 4\pi r^2.$$

You can use 3.14 for π.

Example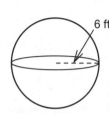

$$\text{Volume} = \frac{4}{3}\pi r^3$$

$$\text{Volume} \approx \frac{4}{3}(3.14)(6)^3$$

$$= 904.32 \text{ cubic feet}$$

$$\text{Surface Area} = 4\pi r^2$$

$$\text{Surface Area} \approx 4(3.14)(6)^2$$

$$= 452.16 \text{ square feet}$$

Constructing Views of Three-Dimensional Objects (p. 407)

To construct different views of a three-dimensional object, imagine that you are looking directly at the top, front, or side of the object.

Examples

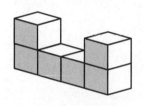 **Side View**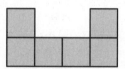

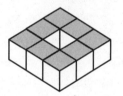 **Front View**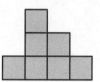

Top View

Determining Whether Solids are Similar Solids (p. 409)

To determine whether two solids are similar, find the ratios of their corresponding dimensions. If the ratios of all corresponding dimensions are the same, the solids are similar.

Example

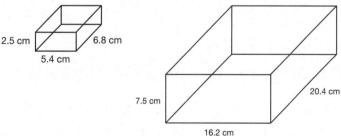

$$\frac{2.5 \text{ cm}}{7.5 \text{ cm}} = \frac{1}{3}$$

$$\frac{5.4 \text{ cm}}{16.2 \text{ cm}} = \frac{1}{3}$$

$$\frac{6.8 \text{ cm}}{20.4 \text{ cm}} = \frac{1}{3}$$

Because the ratios are the same, the solids are similar.

12

Looking Ahead to Chapter 13

Focus   In Chapter 13, you will work with linear functions and learn about function notation. You will use the slope and x- and y-intercepts to graph linear functions and to write linear equations in slope-intercept form. You will also create scatter plots and find lines of best fit.

Chapter Warm-up

Answer these questions to help you review skills that you will need in Chapter 13.

Write each ratio as a fraction.

1. Two of my five pens are red.

2. Seventeen of the thirty math students are girls.

Write each rate as a fraction.

3. Paul used 20 gallons of gas to drive 500 miles.

4. A 13-ounce can of coffee costs $3.25.

Evaluate the expression when $x = 4$.

5. $4x + 2$

6. $5(x - 9)$

7. $\dfrac{x}{2} - 7$

Read the problem scenario below.

Kelly has $600 in the bank. She just bought a cellular phone and must pay $30 each month to her cellular phone company.

8. Using the variable m to represent months, write an expression to show how much money Kelly will have in the bank after she starts paying her cellular phone bill.

9. How much money will she have after 3 months?

10. How much money will Kelly have after 8 months?

11. How many months can she pay for her phone before she runs out of money?

Key Terms

13

Linear Functions

Rock climbers who use only their hands, feet, and other body parts to make upward progress are "free-climbing," using ropes and other gear only for protection.   In Lesson 13.2, you will use a linear function to determine your height at different times when rock climbing.

13

Running a Tree Farm

Relations and Functions

Objectives

In this lesson, you will:

- Use tables and graphs to represent functions.
- Use function notation.

Key Terms

- relation
- input
- output
- function
- input-output table
- independent variable
- dependent variable
- domain
- range
- function notation

In Chapter 8, when we were solving problems using multiple representations, we were actually establishing relationships between two quantities. In this lesson, we will also express relationships in many ways—with words, using an algebraic expression, making a table, and using a graph.

Problem 1 · Planting Seedlings

A **relation** is the mathematical term for any set of ordered pairs. The first coordinate of an ordered pair in a relation is called the **input** and the second coordinate is called the **output**. A relation is a **function** if for every input you have exactly one output.

A. On your tree farm, you can find many situations in which a function would be helpful. For example, you might want to describe the relationship between the ages of the trees you have growing. We can express a function in several ways.

In words: The saplings in a new planting are four years younger than the trees in the previous planting.

Write the words to express the perimeter of the square planting box in terms of the side length of the box.

B. Using an algebraic expression: You can express the age of the saplings in a new planting as $t - 4$, where t is the age in years of the trees in the previous planting.

Suppose you measure two trees. The first tree's height is 3 feet more than 4 times the second tree's height. Write an expression to represent the first tree's height in terms of the second tree's height.

Write four ordered pairs that satisfy this relationship.

Problem 1 Planting seedlings

C. Making a table: The **input-output table** shows the relationship between the input value, the age of a tree in the previous planting, and the output value, the age of a sapling in a new planting.

Age of Tree (years) (t)	Function s = t – 4	Age of Sapling (years) (s)
5	s = 5 – 4 = 1	1
6	s = 6 – 4 = 2	2
7	s = 7 – 4 = 3	3
8	s = 8 – 4 = 4	4

A tree farm is having a sale. The regular prices and the sale prices are shown in the table. Write each row of numbers in the table as an ordered pair. Then use a complete sentence to explain how the regular price and the sale price are related.

Regular Price	Sale Price
$20	$10
$30	$15
$50	$25
$200	$100

D. Using a graph: The graph shows the relationship between the age of a tree and the age of a sapling. The *x*-coordinate is the age of a tree. The *y*-coordinate is the age of a sapling.

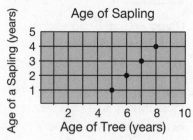

E. The values in the table at the left are plotted as ordered pairs in the graph at the right. Use a complete sentence to explain how the circumference of a tree is related to its diameter.

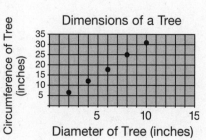

x	y
2	6.28
4	12.57
6	18.85
8	25.13
10	31.40

1. A function is a special relation in which every *x*-coordinate is paired with one and only one *y*-coordinate. A function relates two quantities, so it is often written as a mathematical sentence using two variables. For instance, you can write "The first tree's height is 3 more than 4 times the second tree's height" as $y = 3 + 4x$, where *x* represents the second tree's height and *y* represents the first tree's height.

Decide whether each relation below is a function. In each case, write a complete sentence explaining your reasoning.

The cost of any item is 1.07 times its sales price.

One number is the square root of another number.

(3, 4), (6, 7), (–2, –7), (–3, –7)

(–3, 5), (9, 2), (–5, –7), (–3, –9)

2. The word "function" is often used to describe a relationship. For example, a tree's height is a function of its age. The number of trucks we will need is a function of the number of trees we will be hauling. With most functions, the two quantities are related in such a way that the value of one quantity depends on the value of the other quantity. The **independent variable** represents the input values of the function and the **dependent variable** represents the output values. For each function below, identify the independent variable and the dependent variable.

The amount of money that a tree farmer earns is a function of the number of trees that he sells.

The water height in an irrigation pond rises 2 inches for every day with a good rain.

A tree grows 3 feet each month.

Your salary at a tree farm is $30,000 per year and increases by $600 each year.

Seedlings cost $29.95 per case of one hundred with a shipping charge of $10.

13

3. Math Path: Domain and Range

For a function, the set of all input values is given the mathematical name **domain** and the set of all output values is given the name **range.** Suppose that you are buying fertilizer for the tree farm. Each bag of fertilizer covers 1000 square feet. You can haul up to 6 bags in your truck. The input-output table for the function that relates the number of bags of fertilizer to the number of square feet covered is shown below.

Bags of Fertilizer	Coverage (square feet)
1	1000
2	2000
3	3000
4	4000
5	5000
6	6000

The function that describes this relationship is $y = 1000x$, where x is the number of bags of fertilizer and y is the number of square feet covered.

What is the domain of the function?

What is the range of the function?

4. Math Path: Function Notation

In addition to writing functions in terms of the independent and dependent variables, we can also use **function notation** to write a function. For instance, we can write the function $y = 1000x$ using function notation as $f(x) = 1000x$.

You read the symbol $f(x)$ as "f of x" or "the function of f at x." Rewrite each function below using function notation.

$y = x + 12$ $\qquad\qquad$ $y = 0.75x$ $\qquad\qquad$ $y = 4$

You can find the value of a function for a certain number by substituting the number into the function. To find the value of $f(x) = 1000x$ when $x = 6$, substitute 6 for x and simplify:

$f(x) = 1000x$
$f(6) = 1000(6)$
$f(6) = 6000$

Find the value of each function when $x = 5$.

$f(x) = 50x$ $\qquad\qquad$ $f(x) = 9 - x$ $\qquad\qquad$ $f(x) = x - 10$
$f(5) =$ $\qquad\qquad\qquad$ $f(5) =$ $\qquad\qquad\qquad$ $f(5) =$

> **Take Note**
>
> In the function notation at the right, f is the name of the function, x represents the domain, and $f(x)$ represents the range.

Scaling a Cliff
Linear Functions

Objectives

In this lesson, you will:

- Make input-output tables for linear functions.
- Graph linear functions.

Key Terms

- linear function

When you graph the input and output values of some functions, the graph forms a straight line. A function whose graph is a straight line is a **linear function.** In this lesson, we will examine linear functions to determine some of their properties.

Problem 1   Rock Climbing

You and your friends are rock climbing a vertical cliff along a beach. You have been climbing for a while and are currently 36 feet above the beach when you stop on a ledge to have a snack and then begin climbing again. You can climb about 12 feet in height each hour.

A. How high will you have climbed above the beach in 1 hour after you begin climbing again? Use a complete sentence in your answer.

B. How high will you have climbed above the beach in 2 hours after you begin climbing again?

C. How high will you have climbed above the beach in 180 minutes after you begin climbing again? Use a complete sentence in your answer.

D. How high will you have climbed above the beach in 210 minutes after you begin climbing again?

E. Which quantities are changing? Which quantities remain constant? Use complete sentences in your answers.

F. Which quantity depends on the other quantity? Use a complete sentence in your answer.

Investigate Problem 1

1. Complete the table below by first filling in the names of the quantities in Problem 1 and their units of measure. Then fill in the table with your answers from Problem 1. The rest of the table will be completed later.

	Column 1	Column 2
Quantity Name		
Unit of Measure		
Problem 1, Part (A)	1	
Problem 1, Part (B)	2	
Problem 1, Part (C)		
Problem 1, Part (D)		
Question 4		84
Question 5		96
Question 6		108
Expression		

2. Define a variable for the quantity in Column 1. Enter this variable in the "Expression" row under Column 1.

3. Write an expression that you can use to represent the quantity in Column 2 in terms of the quantity in Column 1. Enter this expression in the "Expression" row under Column 2.

4. How long will it be until you have climbed to 84 feet above the beach? Use the expression that you wrote in Question 3 to write an equation that you can solve to find your answer. Then write your answer in the appropriate place in the table.

5. How long will it be until you have climbed to 96 feet above the beach? Use the expression that you wrote in Question 3 to write an equation that you can solve to find your answer. Then write your answer in the appropriate place in the table.

6. How long will it be until you have climbed to 108 feet above the beach? Use the expression that you wrote in Question 3 to write an equation that you can solve to find your answer. Then write your answer in the appropriate place in the table.

7. You will use the grid below to create a graph to represent the values in the table. Begin by labeling your axes. Use the first quantity from the table for the horizontal axis and the second quantity for the vertical axis. The axes are already numbered.

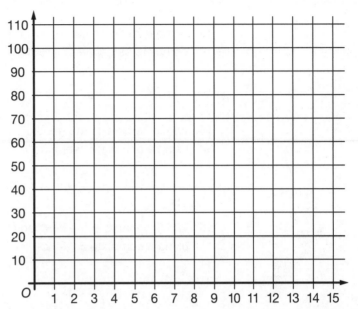

8. Write each row of numbers in your table as an ordered pair. Note that the *x*-coordinate is the amount of time that you have been climbing since you started climbing after your snack and the *y*-coordinate is the total height you have climbed so far.

9. Plot each ordered pair on the prepared grid in Question 7.

10. What do you notice about the points you graphed on the coordinate plane above? Write your answer using a complete sentence.

11. Draw a straight line through the points. How would you describe this line? Write your answer using a complete sentence.

13

12. Is the relation shown in the graph a function? Use a complete sentence to explain why or why not.

13. Is the relation shown in the graph a linear function? Use a complete sentence to explain why or why not.

14. Which variable is the dependent variable? Write your answer using a complete sentence.

15. Which variable is the independent variable? Write your answer using a complete sentence.

16. Describe what happens to the value of the dependent variable each time the independent variable increases by 1. Use a complete sentence in your answer.

17. Describe what happens to the value of the dependent variable when the independent variable increases by 2. Use a complete sentence in your answer.

18. Compare the values of the dependent variable when the independent variable is 1 and 6. Describe how the dependent variable changes in relation to the independent variable.

19. Form a group with another partner team and compare your graphs and your answers to Questions 12 through 18. If you have any answers on which you do not agree, work together to find out why. Be prepared to share your answers with the rest of the class.

Biking Along
Slope and Rates of Change

Objectives

In this lesson, you will:

- Find the slope of a line as a ratio.
- Find the slope of a line as a rate of change.

Key Terms

- rise
- run
- slope
- rate of change

In Lesson 13.2, we worked with linear functions. In this lesson, we will explore some of the special properties of linear functions.

Problem 1   Biking Uphill

You and your friend are taking a week-long trip on your bicycles. On the first day, you come to a hill that has a sign that says "8% grade." You tell your friend that this means that the hill has a vertical change of 8 feet for every 100 feet change in horizontal distance. The vertical change is the **rise** of the hill and the horizontal change is the **run.**

A. The diagram shows the grade of the hill. Fill in the boxes to indicate the rise and the run of the hill.

B. As you go up the hill, the ratio of the vertical change to the horizontal change has a special name. It is called the **slope** of the hill. Complete the statement to find the slope of the line that represents the hill.

$$\text{slope} = \frac{\text{rise}}{\text{run}} = \frac{\boxed{}\ \text{feet}}{\boxed{}\ \text{feet}} = \frac{\boxed{}}{\boxed{}}$$

C. When you are biking up this hill, the slope of the line that represents the hill is positive. After a short break at the top of the hill, you bike down the other side of the hill. Describe the sign of the slope of the line that represents your ride downhill. Use complete sentences to explain your reasoning.

D. Use the definition of slope to find the slope of the line that represents when you are biking on ground that is completely level. Use a complete sentence to explain.

Problem 2 *Setting the Pace*

You and your friend know from previous bicycle trips that you can bike at a rate of about 8 miles per hour.

A. How far will you go in 2 hours? Use a complete sentence in your answer.

B. How far will you go in 3 hours? Use a complete sentence in your answer.

C. How far will you go in 6 hours? Use a complete sentence in your answer.

D. How far will you go in 420 minutes? Use a complete sentence in your answer.

E. Which quantities are changing? Which quantities remain constant? Use complete sentences in your answers.

F. Which quantity depends on the other quantity? Use a complete sentence in your answer.

G. Complete the table below by first filling in the names of the quantities and their units of measure. Then fill in the table with your answers from Parts (A) through (D). The rest of the table will be completed later.

	Column 1	Column 2
Quantity Name		
Unit of Measure		
Problem 2, Part (A)	2	
Problem 2, Part (B)	3	
Problem 2, Part (C)	6	
Problem 2, Part (D)		
Question 3		44
Question 4		164
Expression		

1. Define a variable for the quantity in Column 1. Enter this variable in the "Expression" row of the table under Column 1.

2. Write an expression that you can use to represent the quantity in Column 2 in terms of the quantity in Column 1. Enter this expression in the "Expression" row of the table under Column 2.

3. How long will it take you to bike 44 miles? Use the expression that you wrote in Question 2 to write an equation that you can solve to find your answer. Then write your answer in the appropriate place in the table.

4. How long will it take you to bike 164 miles? Use the expression that you wrote in Question 2 to write an equation that you can solve to find your answer. Then write your answer in the appropriate place in the table.

5. You will use the grid below to create a graph to represent the values in the table. Begin by labeling your axes. Use the first quantity from the table for the horizontal axis and the second quantity for the vertical axis. The axes are already numbered.

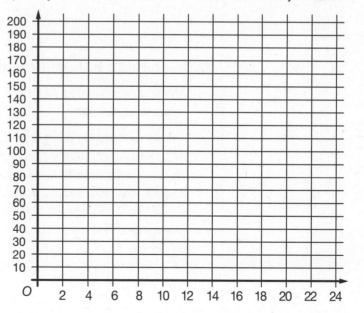

13

6. Write each row of numbers in your table as an ordered pair. Note that the x-coordinate is the amount of time you biked and the y-coordinate is the distance you traveled.

7. Plot each ordered pair on the prepared grid in Question 5.

8. What do you notice about the points you graphed on the coordinate plane? Write your answer using a complete sentence.

9. Draw a straight line through the points. How would you describe this line? Write your answer using a complete sentence.

10. Is the relation shown in the graph a linear function? Use a complete sentence to explain why or why not.

11. As the time increased, what happened to the distance? Use a complete sentence to explain.

12. **Math Path: Rate of Change**

As the time increased by 1 hour, by how much did the distance increase or decrease?

As well as describing the ratio of rise to run, slope can also be used to describe the rate of increase (or decrease) of the distance per 1 hour that you biked. This rate is a **rate of change** that can be described by slope when the units of measure on the x-axis and the y-axis are different. What is the slope of the line? Use the graph to help you. Write a complete sentence to explain your answer.

What units of measure are used for the slope in this problem?

Investigate Problem 2

13. Form a group with another partner team and compare your graphs and your answers to Questions 9 through 12. If you have any answers on which you do not agree, work together to find out why.

Problem 3   *Funding the Trip*

You have saved $100 for your bike trip. You are spending money at the rate of $12.50 per day.

A. How much money will you have left after 1 day? Use a complete sentence in your answer.

B. How much money will you have left after 3 days? Use a complete sentence in your answer.

C. How much money will you have left after 5 days? Use a complete sentence in your answer.

D. Which quantities are changing? Which quantities remain constant? Use complete sentences in your answers.

E. Which quantity depends on the other quantity? Use a complete sentence in your answer.

F. Complete the table below by first filling in the names of the quantities and their units of measure. Then fill in the table with your answers from Parts (A) through (C). The rest of the table will be completed later.

	Column 1	Column 2
Quantity Name		
Unit of Measure		
Problem 3, Part (A)	1	
Problem 3, Part (B)	3	
Problem 3, Part (C)	5	
Question 3		50
Question 4		0
Expression		

Investigate Problem 3

1. Define a variable for the quantity in Column 1. Enter this variable in the "Expression" row of the table under Column 1.

2. Write an expression that you can use to represent the quantity in Column 2 in terms of the quantity in Column 1. Enter this expression in the "Expression" row of the table under Column 2.

3. How long will it be until you have $50 left? Use the expression that you wrote in Question 2 to write an equation that you can solve to find your answer. Then write your answer in the appropriate place in the table.

4. How long will it be until you have no money left? Use the expression that you wrote in Question 2 to write an equation that you can solve to find your answer. Then write your answer in the appropriate place in the table.

5. You will use the grid below to create a graph to represent the values in the table. Begin by labeling your axes. Use the first quantity from the table for the horizontal axis and the second quantity for the vertical axis. The axes are already numbered.

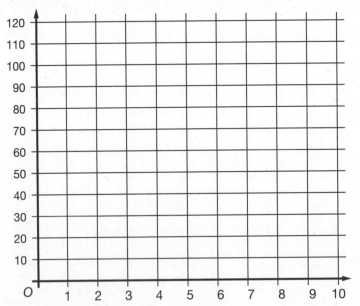

13

6. Write each row of numbers in your table as an ordered pair. Note that the x-coordinate is the amount of time and the y-coordinate is the amount of money you have left.

7. Plot each ordered pair on the prepared grid in Question 5.

8. What do you notice about the points you graphed on the coordinate plane? Write your answer using a complete sentence.

9. Draw a straight line through the points. How would you describe this line? Write your answer using a complete sentence.

10. Is the relation shown in the graph a linear function? Use a complete sentence to explain why or why not.

11. As the time increased, what happened to the amount of money that you had left? Use a complete sentence to explain.

12. As the time increased by 1 day, by how much did the amount of money that you had left increase or decrease?

13. What is the slope of the line? Use the graph to help you. Write a complete sentence to explain your answer.

14. What units of measure are used for the slope in this problem?

15. Join your group with another and compare your graphs and your answers to Questions 9 through 14. If you have any answers on which you do not agree, work together to find out why. Be prepared to share your answers with the rest of the class.

13

Let's Have a Pool Party!
Finding Slope and y-Intercepts

Objectives

In this lesson, you will:

● Find *x*- and *y*-intercepts of a line.

Key Terms

● *x*-intercept
● *y*-intercept

We have used several different representations for linear functions including words, tables, equations, and graphs. In each of these representations, it is often important to be able to find two special points on the line—where the line crosses the *x*-axis and where the line crosses the *y*-axis.

Problem 1 *Draining the Pool*

Your friend wants to have a pool party, but she needs to drain and clean her pool first. The pool holds 6800 gallons of water, and can be drained at a rate of 20 gallons per minute.

A. How many gallons of water will be in the pool after 5 minutes? Use a complete sentence in your answer.

B. How many gallons of water will be in the pool after 30 minutes? Use a complete sentence in your answer.

C. How many gallons of water will be in the pool after 60 minutes? Use a complete sentence in your answer.

D. Which quantities are changing? Which quantities remain constant? Use complete sentences in your answers.

E. Which quantity depends on the other quantity? Use a complete sentence in your answer.

Investigate Problem 1

1. Complete the table below by first filling in the names of the quantities and their units of measure. Then fill in the table with your answers from Parts (A) through (C). The rest of the table will be completed later.

	Column 1	Column 2
Quantity Name		
Unit of Measure		
Problem 1, Part (A)	5	
Problem 1, Part (B)	30	
Problem 1, Part (C)	60	
Question 4		4200
Question 5		
Question 6		
Question 7		
Expression		

2. Define a variable for the quantity in Column 1. Enter this variable in the "Expression" row under Column 1.

3. Write an expression that you can use to represent the quantity in Column 2 in terms of the quantity in Column 1. Enter this expression in the "Expression" row under Column 2.

4. How long will it take until the pool has 4200 gallons of water left in it? Use the expression that you wrote in Question 3 to write an equation that you can solve to find your answer. Then write your answer in the appropriate place in the table.

5. How long will it take until the pool is half full? Use the expression that you wrote in Question 3 to write an equation that you can solve to find your answer. Then write your answer in the appropriate place in the table.

6. How long will it take until the pool is one quarter full? Use the expression that you wrote in Question 3 to write an equation that you can solve to find your answer. Then write your answer in the appropriate place in the table.

7. How long will it take until there are only 10 more minutes left to drain the pool? (Hint: Determine the number of gallons that can be drained from the pool in 10 minutes.) Use the expression that you wrote in Question 3 to write an equation that you can solve to find your answer. Then write your answer in the appropriate place in the table.

13

8. You will use the grid below to create a graph to represent the values in the table. Begin by labeling your axes. Use the first quantity from the table for the horizontal axis and the second quantity for the vertical axis. The axes are already numbered.

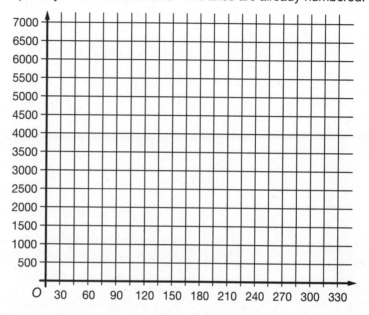

9. Write each row of numbers in your table as an ordered pair. Note that the *x*-coordinate is the amount of time that the pool is draining and the *y*-coordinate is the number of gallons of water left in the pool.

10. Plot each ordered pair on the prepared grid in Question 8.

11. Draw a straight line through the points. Be sure to draw the line so that it intersects both the *x*-axis and the *y*-axis.

12. Is the relation shown in the graph a linear function? Use a complete sentence to explain why or why not.

13. As the time increased, what happened to the amount of water in the pool? Use a complete sentence to explain.

14. As the time increased by 1 minute, by how much did the amount of water in the pool increase or decrease? Use a complete sentence to explain.

15. What is the slope of the line? Use the graph to help you. Write a complete sentence to explain your answer.

16. What units of measure are used for the slope in this problem?

17. Math Path: *x*- and *y*-Intercepts

The ***x*-intercept** of a graph is the *x*-coordinate of the point where the graph crosses the *x*-axis. The ***y*-intercept** of a graph is the *y*-coordinate of the point where the graph crosses the *y*-axis.

Use your graph to find the point where the graph crosses the *x*-axis. Write the point as an ordered pair. What does this point represent in the problem? Use a complete sentence in your answer.

What is the *x*-intercept?

Use your graph to find the point where the graph crosses the *y*-axis. Write the point as an ordered pair. What does this point represent in the problem? Use a complete sentence in your answer.

What is the *y*-intercept?

Use complete sentences to explain what you notice about the ordered pairs that include the *x*- and *y*-intercepts.

18. Form a group with another partner team and compare your graphs and your answers to Questions 12 through 17. If you have any answers on which you do not agree, work together to find out why. Be prepared to share your work with the rest of the class.

Problem 2 · Identifying Slopes and Intercepts

For each representation of a linear function below, find the slope and x- and y-intercepts.

A.

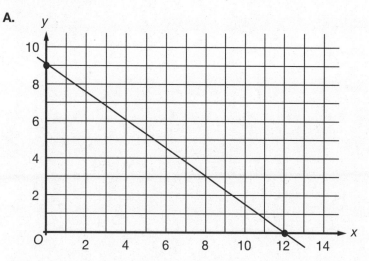

Slope = _____ (Hint: the slope in this case is negative.)

x-intercept = _____

y-intercept = _____

B.

x	y
0	0
1	4
3	12
4	16

Write each row of numbers in the table as an ordered pair.

You can use the coordinates of two points to find the slope of the line through the points. Let the point (x_1, y_1) be the point (1, 4) and (x_2, y_2) be the point (3, 12). Complete the ratio below to find the slope of the line through the points.

$$\text{slope} = \frac{(y_2 - y_1)}{(x_2 - x_1)} = \frac{\boxed{} - \boxed{}}{\boxed{} - \boxed{}} = \frac{\boxed{}}{\boxed{}}$$

Slope = _____

x-intercept = _____

y-intercept = _____

13

13

What's for Lunch?

Using Slope and Intercepts to Graph Lines

13

Objectives

In this lesson, you will:

- Graph lines using slopes and intercepts.
- Use the slope-intercept form of the equation of a line.

Key Terms

- linear equation
- slope-intercept form

Now that we can find the slope and intercepts of a linear function, we can use them in order to graph linear functions more easily.

Problem 1   Lunch Plan A

Your school has three different plans for buying school lunches. In Plan A, you pay $2 per day for a hot lunch. A linear function that models the total amount that you pay for Plan A is $y = 2x$, where x is the number of days that you buy lunch.

A. The slope of the linear function is 2. This means that every time the value of the independent variable increases by 1 unit, the value of the dependent variable increases by 2 units. What happens to the value of the dependent variable if the value of the independent variable *decreases* by 1 unit? Write your answer using a complete sentence.

B. By how many units would the value of the dependent variable increase or decrease if the value of the independent variable *increases* by 4 units? Write your answer using a complete sentence.

C. By how many units would the value of the dependent variable increase or decrease if the value of the independent variable *decreases* by 4 units? Write your answer using a complete sentence.

1. Below is the graph of the linear function $y = 2x$.

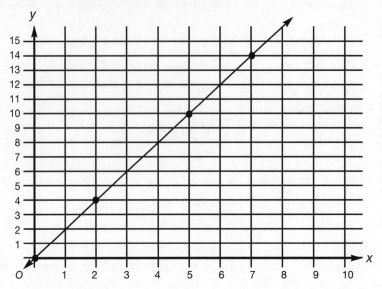

What are the x- and y-intercepts? Write your answer using a complete sentence.

2. Place your pencil on the point on the line where $x = 2$. Move your pencil one unit to the right. This represents an increase of the independent variable by one unit. By how many units up or down do you need to move your pencil to get back to the line? Write your answer using a complete sentence.

3. Repeat the process in Question 2, starting at the point on the line where $x = 6$. Use a complete sentence to describe what you notice.

4. Repeat the process in Question 2, starting at another point on the line. What can you conclude? Write your answer using a complete sentence.

Problem 2   Lunch Plan B

In your school's lunch Plan B, you pay a weekly fee of $10 that goes into your account. When you buy lunch, $2 per day is subtracted from your account balance. A linear function that models the total amount that you have in your account in Plan B is $y = 10 - 2x$, where x is the number of days that you buy lunch.

A. The slope of the linear function is –2. This means that every time the value of the independent variable increases by 1 unit, the value of the dependent variable decreases by 2 units. What happens to the value of the dependent variable if the value of the independent variable *decreases* by 1 unit? Write your answer using a complete sentence.

B. By how many units would the value of the dependent variable increase or decrease if the value of the independent variable *increases* by 4 units?

C. By how many units would the value of the dependent variable increase or decrease if the value of the independent variable *decreases* by 4 units?

Investigate Problem 2

1. Below is the graph of the linear function $y = 10 - 2x$.

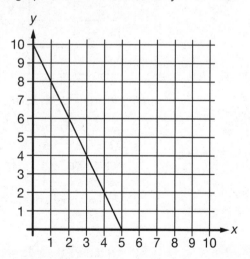

What are the *x*- and *y*-intercepts? Write your answer using a complete sentence.

Investigate Problem 2

2. Place your pencil on the point on the line where $x = 2$. Move your pencil one unit to the right. This represents an increase of the independent variable by one unit. By how many units up or down do you need to move your pencil to get back to the line? Write your answer using a complete sentence.

3. Repeat the process in Question 2, starting at the point on the line where $x = 4$. Use a complete sentence to describe what you notice.

4. Repeat the process in Question 2, starting at another point on the line. What can you conclude? Write your answer using a complete sentence.

5. Complete the table to find the money in your account each week for lunch Plan B when buying lunch for different numbers of days.

x	y
0	
1	
3	
5	

6. Math Path: Linear Equation

Write each row of numbers in the table as an ordered pair. These ordered pairs are said to be solutions of the *linear equation* $y = 10 - 2x$. In a **linear equation** in two variables, the variables are raised to the first power (such as t, not t^2) and appear only once.

7. Compare the y-intercept that you found in Question 1 and the slope from Part (A) with the equation $y = 10 - 2x$. What do you notice? Write your answer using a complete sentence.

Take Note

Although all linear equations are functions, not every equation is a function. You will discover this in a later math course.

8. Math Path: Slope-Intercept Form

When you graph the equation $y = 10 - 2x$, the graph is a straight line. This equation can also be written as $y = -2x + 10$. When an equation is written in this form, it is said to be in *slope-intercept form*. When a linear equation is written in the form $y = mx + b$, it is in **slope-intercept form.**

What do you think the variable m represents in the equation $y = mx + b$? Write your answer using a complete sentence.

What do you think the variable b represents in the equation $y = mx + b$? Write your answer using a complete sentence.

9. Use a complete sentence to explain why you think that the form $y = mx + b$ is called the slope-intercept form.

10. What is the slope of a line whose equation is $y = -3x + 24$? Write your answer using a complete sentence.

11. What is the y-intercept of a line whose equation is $y = -3x + 24$? Write your answer using a complete sentence.

12. Evaluate the expression to complete the table.

	x	y
Expression	x	$-3x + 24$
	1	
	2	
	3	
	4	
	5	
	6	

13. Write each row of numbers in the table as an ordered pair. Then plot each ordered pair below.

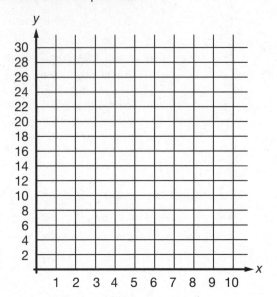

14. Find the slope and the *y*-intercept from the graph. Then compare these with the slope and the *y*-intercept from Questions 10 and 11. Write your findings using a complete sentence.

15. You can also find the *x*-intercept of a line by substituting a 0 into the equation for *y* and solving for *x*. You can find the *y*-intercept in a similar way—substitute a 0 into the equation for *x* and solve for *y*. Use this method to find the *x*- and *y*-intercepts for the graph of the equation $y = 3x - 6$ by completing the boxes.

x-intercept:

$y = 3x - 6$

$0 = 3x - 6$

$\boxed{} = 3x$

$\boxed{} = x$

y-intercept:

$y = 3x - 6$

$y = 3(0) - 6$

$y = 0 - \boxed{}$

$y = \boxed{}$

Use this method to find the *x*- and *y*-intercepts for the graph of the equation $y = -7x + 14$.

In your school's lunch Plan C, you pay a monthly fee of $25 that goes into your account. When you buy lunch, you pay only $.50 per day. A linear function that models the total amount that you pay for Plan C is $y = 25 + 0.5x$, where x is the number of days that you buy lunch.

A. On the grid below, graph the y-intercept of the graph of the equation $y = 25 + 0.5x$.

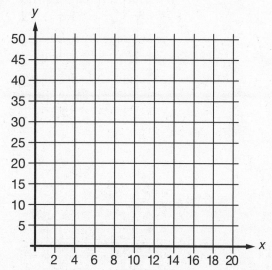

B. The slope of the line is 0.5. What happens to the value of y when x increases by 1 unit? Write your answer using a complete sentence.

C. Place your pencil on the y-intercept. Move your pencil two units to the right. Then based on your slope, move your pencil the correct number of units up or down. What are the coordinates of the point that you land on? Draw the point.

D. Repeat the process in Part (C) two more times to draw two additional points. What are the coordinates of the points?

Draw a line through your points and the y-intercept.

Investigate Problem 3

Use the method outlined in Problem 3 to graph each linear equation written in slope-intercept form.

$y = 3x + 5$

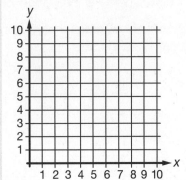

$y = 5x$

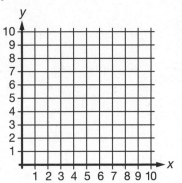

$y = -4x + 7$

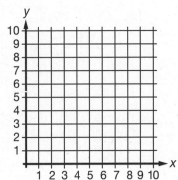

$y = 2.5x$

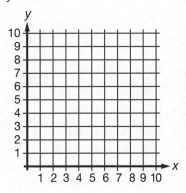

$y = -1.5x + 5$

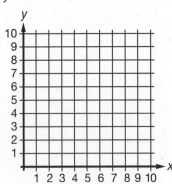

$y = 2x + 4$

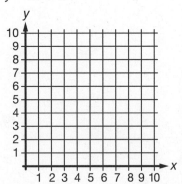

13.6 Healthy Relationships
Finding Lines of Best Fit

Objectives

In this lesson, you will:

- Create scatter plots of data.
- Find a line of best fit for a set of data.

Key Terms

- scatter plot
- line of best fit

Linear functions are very useful models of many everyday situations, as we have seen in the last few lessons. They can also be used to model sets of data approximately, when the points do not all lie on a straight line.

Problem 1   The Leonardo Da Vinci Problem

Leonardo Da Vinci was a famous artist and mathematician who discovered a unique relationship between the height of a person and the span of the person's arms.

A. Your teacher has taped two meter sticks together for each group. Use the taped meter sticks to measure each person's height and the distance between the tips of the person's longest fingers with his or her arms spread wide. The second measurement is called a person's arm span.

Record the measurements to the nearest centimeter in the table.

Group Member's Name	Height (centimeters)	Arm Span (centimeters)

B. Write each row of numbers in the table as an ordered pair. Note that the x-coordinate is the height and the y-coordinate is the arm span.

C. Each group should share their data with the entire class. Take turns writing your group's ordered pairs so that the class can see them.

© 2008 Carnegie Learning, Inc.

13

1. Use the grid below to create a graph of all of the ordered pairs collected in your class. Begin by labeling the horizontal axis as "Height (centimeters)" and the vertical axis as "Arm Span (centimeters)." The axes are already numbered. The graph is called a *scatter plot*. A **scatter plot** is a graph that shows how two sets of data are related.

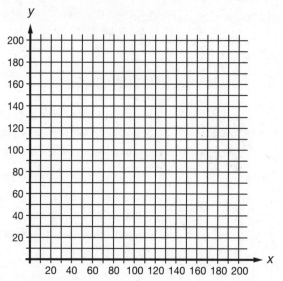

2. Use a complete sentence to describe the shape of the graph of all of the data points.

3. Does the pattern of the points taken as a group increase or decrease as you move from left to right? Write your answer using a complete sentence.

4. As a group, decide where to draw a line through the points that would best "fit" the data, called the *line of best fit*. The **line of best fit** is the line that is very close to most of the points. Use a ruler to draw the line. Be sure to extend the line so that it intersects the *x*-axis and the *y*-axis.

5. What is the *y*-intercept of your "line of best fit?" Write your answer using a complete sentence.

6. Beginning at the *y*-intercept, move one grid line to the right. How many units must you go up or down to get back to the line? Write your answer using a complete sentence.

7. What does the ratio of the number in Question 6 to the number 1 represent? Write your answer using a complete sentence.

8. Using the ratio in Question 7 and the *y*-intercept, write an equation of the line of best fit.

9. Using the equation you wrote in Question 8, answer the following questions.

   If a person's height is 100 centimeters, what is the person's arm span?

   If a person's height is 50 centimeters, what is the person's arm span?

   If a person's height is 75 centimeters, what is the person's arm span?

   If a person's arm span is 100 centimeters, what is the person's height?

10. Write each answer to Question 9 as an ordered pair. Remember that the *x*-coordinate is the height and the *y*-coordinate is the arm span.

11. Add the ordered pairs from Question 10 to your graph using a pen or pencil of a different color. How well do these points fit in with the original data set? Write your answer using a complete sentence.

12. Do you think that your line is a "good" model of the data? Use a complete sentence to explain your reasoning.

13. What are the advantages of having a model, that is, having an equation of the line of best fit, for this set of data? Write your answer using a complete sentence.

Take Note

The data in a scatter plot are said to have a positive relationship when the line that models the data has positive slope, a negative relationship when the line that models the data has negative slope, and no relationship when a line should not be used to model the data.

Investigate Problem 1

14. In a scatter plot, the two sets of data that are graphed can have a positive relationship, a negative relationship, or no relationship. Under each graph below, write either "positive relationship," "negative relationship," or "no relationship."

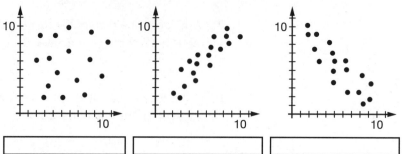

Problem 2 *Children's Proportions*

The ratio of the height of a child's head (from the chin to the top of the head) to the child's total height changes as the child grows older. For instance, the ratio of an infant's head height to his or her total height is about 1 to 3. The ratio of an adult's head height to his or her total height is about 1 to 7.

For a project for health class, you want to prove that this is true, so you measure the total height and the head height of 10 children of different ages in your neighborhood. The table lists the data that you collect.

Age of Child (years)	Head Height (centimeters)	Total Height (centimeters)	Ratio of Head Height to Total Height
12	22.8	152	0.15
2	19.8	90	0.22
14	23.1	165	0.14
13	22.2	148	0.15
5	22.8	114	0.20
10	22.4	140	0.16
3	20.2	101	0.20
6	20.9	110	0.19
9	21.6	135	0.16
7	18.0	100	0.18

At the left, write each row of numbers in the table as an ordered pair. Note that the *x*-coordinate is the age and the *y*-coordinate is the ratio of the head height to the total height.

13

1. Use the grid below to create a graph of all of the ordered pairs in Problem 2. Begin by labeling the horizontal axis as "Age (years)" and the vertical axis as "Ratio of Head Height to Total Height." The axes are already numbered.

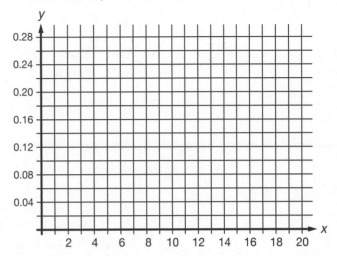

2. Use a complete sentence to describe the shape of the graph of all of the data points.

3. Does the pattern of the points taken as a group increase or decrease as you move from left to right? Write your answer using a complete sentence.

4. With your partner, decide where to draw a line through the points so that it is the line of best fit. Then use a ruler to draw the line. Be sure to extend the line so that it intersects the *y*-axis.

5. What is the *y*-intercept of your "line of best fit"? Write your answer using a complete sentence.

13

6. Beginning at the *y*-intercept, move one unit to the right. How many units must you go up or down to get back to the line? Write your answer using a complete sentence.

7. What does the ratio of the number in Question 6 to the number 1 represent? Write your answer using a complete sentence.

8. Using the ratio in Question 7 and the *y*-intercept, write an equation of the line of best fit.

9. Use the equation you wrote in Question 8 to answer the following questions.

   If a little girl is 4 years old, what is the ratio of the girl's head height to her total height?

   If a boy is 8 years old, what is the ratio of the boy's head height to his total height?

   If a girl is 16 years old, what is the ratio of the girl's head height to her total height?

   If the ratio of a boy's head height to his total height is 0.13, how old is the boy?

10. Write each answer to Question 9 as an ordered pair. Remember that the *x*-coordinate is the age and the *y*-coordinate is the ratio of the head height to the total height.

11. Add the ordered pairs from Question 10 to your graph using a pen or pencil of a different color. How well do these points fit in with the original data set? Write your answer using a complete sentence.

12. Do you think that your line is a "good" model of the data? Use a complete sentence to explain your reasoning.

© 2008 Carnegie Learning, Inc.

Looking Back at Chapter 13

Key Terms

relation • p. 419
input • p. 419
output • p.419
function • p. 419
input-output table • p. 420
independent variable • p. 421
dependent variable • p. 421

domain • p. 422
range • p. 422
function notation • p. 422
linear function • p. 423
rise • p. 427
run • p. 427
slope • p. 427

rate of change • p. 430
x-intercept • p. 438
y-intercept • p. 438
linear equation • p. 444
slope-intercept form • p. 445
scatter plot • p. 450
line of best fit • p. 450

Summary

Determining Whether Relations are Functions (p. 421)

A function is a special relation in which every x-coordinate is paired with one and only one y-coordinate.

 **Examples**

The relation represented by the ordered pairs (1, –1), (2, 3), (1, –3), (–4, 2) is not a function because the x-coordinate 1 is paired with the y-coordinates –1 and –3.

The relation represented by the ordered pairs (–2, 4), (–1, 1), (1, 1), (2, 4) is a function because all of the x-coordinates are paired with one and only one y-coordinate.

Using Function Notation (p. 422)

To write an equation using function notation, replace the dependent variable y with the notation $f(x)$, which is read as "f of x" or "the function of f at x."

 Examples

Original equation:	$y = 3 + x$	$y = 4x - 10$	$y = 6 - (x + 2)$
Function notation:	$f(x) = 3 + x$	$f(x) = 4x - 10$	$f(x) = 6 - (x + 2)$

Finding Slope (p. 427)

To find the slope as a ratio, divide the rise, or vertical change, by the run, or horizontal change.

 Example

To find the slope of the ski hill, divide the change in vertical distance by the change in horizontal distance.

$$\text{Slope} = \frac{\text{rise}}{\text{run}}$$

$$\text{Slope} = \frac{75 \text{ feet}}{150 \text{ feet}}$$

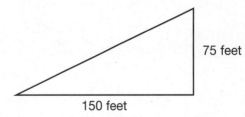

75 feet

150 feet

So, the slope of the ski hill is $\frac{75}{150}$, or $\frac{1}{2}$.

Using Slope to Describe a Rate of Change (p. 430)

To use slope to describe a rate of change, divide the amount of change in the *y*-coordinates by the amount of change in the *x*-coordinates. The *x*-coordinates and the *y*-coordinates will have different units.

Example   Linda swam 400 meters in 8 minutes.

$$\text{Slope} = \frac{400 \text{ meters}}{8 \text{ minutes}} = 50$$

Finding x- and y-Intercepts (p. 438)

The *x*-intercept is the point where the graph crosses the *x*-axis and the *y*-intercept is the point where the graph crosses the *y*-axis.

Example   The graph of $y = -2x + 9$ is shown below.

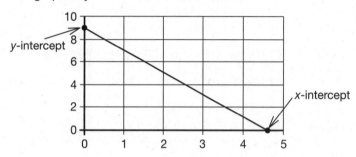

The graph crosses the *x*-axis at $\left(\frac{9}{2}, 0\right)$. The graph crosses the *y*-axis at $(0, 9)$. So, the *x*-intercept is $\frac{9}{2}$ and the *y*-intercept is 9.

Graphing Lines Using Slopes and Intercepts (p. 444)

To graph a linear equation, write the linear equation in slope-intercept form. Identify the slope and graph the *y*-intercept. Place your pencil on the *y*-intercept. Then choose a value for *x* and move that many units to the left or right. Based on the slope, move your pencil the correct number of units up or down and draw a point. Repeat this process until you have enough points to draw a straight line.

Example   For the linear equation $y = -3x + 9$, the slope is -3 and the *y*-intercept is 9.

Place your pencil on the *y*-intercept 9. Then choose the value $x = 1$ and move 1 unit to the right and 3 units down because the slope is -3.

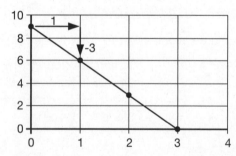

Finding the Equation of a Line from a Graph (p. 445)

To find the equation of a line from its graph, first identify the *y*-intercept. Then choose two convenient points on the line. To find the slope, use the two points in the slope equation. Then use the slope and *y*-intercept to write the equation of the line in slope-intercept form.

Example   From the graph, you can see that the *y*-intercept is 6. Choose Point A (2, 4) as (x_1, y_1) and Point B (4, 2) as (x_2, y_2).

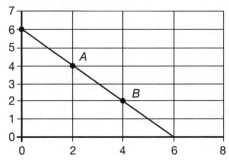

$$\text{Slope} = \frac{y_2 - y_1}{x_2 - x_1} = \frac{2 - 4}{4 - 2} = \frac{-2}{2} = -1$$

So, the equation of the line is $y = -1x + 6 = -x + 6$.

Creating Scatter Plots of Data (p. 450)

To create a scatter plot of data, graph the data as ordered pairs.

Example   The relationship between height and weight of women is shown below as a scatter plot.

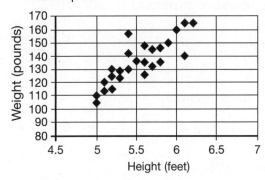

Finding a Line of Best Fit (p. 450)

To find a line of best fit for a set of data, draw a straight line that is very close to most of the points. Be sure that the line intersects the *x*-axis and the *y*-axis.

Example   The line of best fit for the data that shows the relationship between height and weight of women is shown in the graph.

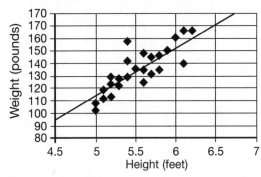

Looking Ahead to Chapter 14

Focus　In Chapter 14, you will learn about different number systems, working with rational numbers, irrational numbers, and real numbers. You will also learn about the properties of number systems, including the distributive property.

Chapter Warm-up

Answer these questions to help you review skills that you will need in Chapter 14.

14

Perform the indicated operation.

1. $\dfrac{3}{4} + 2\dfrac{5}{8}$

2. $\dfrac{5}{9} \times 1\dfrac{3}{4}$

3. $\dfrac{6}{7} \div \dfrac{9}{2}$

Evaluate the power.

4. 9^2

5. 3^4

6. 5^3

Write each number as a power with a negative exponent.

7. $\dfrac{1}{3^2}$

8. $\dfrac{1}{5^4}$

9. $\dfrac{1}{2^4}$

Solve the equation. Write your answer as a decimal.

10. $4x - 12 = 45$

11. $75 - 6y = 36$

12. $14z + (4 - 38) = 85$

13. Write the number that is the additive inverse of –8.

14. Write the number that is the multiplicative inverse of $\dfrac{4}{3}$.

Write an example of each property.

15. Associative Property of Multiplication

16. Commutative Property of Multiplication

© 2008 Carnegie Learning, Inc.

Key Terms

natural number　●　p. 462

whole number　●　p. 462

integer　●　p. 463

rational number　●　p. 465

power　●　p. 467

terminating decimal　●　p. 472

repeating decimal　●　p. 472

bar notation　●　p. 472

irrational number　●　p. 474

real number　●　p. 475

Venn diagram　●　p. 475

distributive property　●　p. 481

© 2008 Carnegie Learning, Inc.

14

Number Systems

Since 1983, cellular telephones have changed from being expensive pieces of equipment used by businesspeople to low-cost items used by people of all ages, including children. In Lesson 14.2, you use powers of rational numbers to determine the number of people in the U.S. who own cellular phones.

14

Is It a Bird or a Plane?
Rational Numbers

Objectives

In this lesson, you will:

- Use a number line to compare and order rational numbers.
- Learn about types of numbers and their properties.
- Perform operations with rational numbers.

Key Terms

- natural number
- whole number
- integer
- rational number

Take Note

Because paper is typically sold in 500-sheet quantities, a paper's weight is determined by the weight of 500 sheets of the paper. So, 500 sheets of 20-pound paper weighs 20 pounds.

In this lesson, we will explore several sets of numbers and their properties.

Problem 1   A Science Experiment

Your science class is conducting an experiment to see how the weight of a paper airplane affects the distance that it can fly. Your class is divided into two groups. Group 1 uses a yard stick to measure the distances that an airplane flies and Group 2 uses a meter stick. Group 2 then takes their measurements in meters and converts them to feet. The results of the experiment are shown in the table.

Type of Paper	Group 1 Measurements	Group 2 Converted Measurements
20-pound paper	$13\frac{7}{8}$ feet	13.9 feet
28-pound paper	$14\frac{3}{8}$ feet	14.4 feet

A. For each type of paper, your science class needs to compare the Group 1 measurement to the Group 2 converted measurement. In Lesson 4.6, we learned how to write a fraction as a decimal. Write $13\frac{7}{8}$ as a decimal.   Write $14\frac{3}{8}$ as a decimal.

B. On the number line below, graph the Group 1 measurements written as decimals and the Group 2 converted measurements.

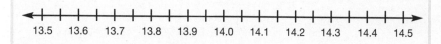

13.5 13.6 13.7 13.8 13.9 14.0 14.1 14.2 14.3 14.4 14.5

Investigate Problem 1

1. Use the number line to determine which group's flight traveled farther for the 20-pound paper and for the 28-pound paper. Write your answers using complete sentences.

Problem 2 · Natural Numbers, Whole Numbers, and Integers

Fractions and decimals belong to a special set of numbers that you will learn about in Problem 3. This set includes other numbers that you already know—natural numbers, whole numbers, and integers.

A. The first set of numbers that you learned when you were very young was the set of counting numbers, or **natural numbers.** This set of numbers consists of the numbers that we use to count objects: 1, 2, 3, 4, 5, … .

How many counting numbers are there?

Does it make sense to ask which counting number is the largest? Use a complete sentence to explain why or why not.

Why do you think this set of numbers is called the natural numbers? Write your answer using a complete sentence.

B. You have used the set of **whole numbers** since grade school. This set is made up of the set of natural numbers and the number 0, the additive identity. Why is zero the additive identity? Write your answer using a complete sentence.

Other than being used as the additive identity, how else is zero used in the set of whole numbers? Write your answer using a complete sentence.

Use a complete sentence to explain why having zero makes the set of whole numbers more useful than the set of natural numbers.

Take Note

In the list

  1, 2, 3, 4, 5, …

the dots at the end of the list mean that the list of numbers goes on without end.

C. In Chapter 7, you used another set of numbers, the *integers*. This set includes all of the whole numbers and their additive inverses.

What is the additive inverse of a number? Write a complete sentence to explain your answer.

We wrote 1, 2, 3, 4, 5, ... to represent the set of natural numbers. Represent the set of integers. Remember to use three dots to show that the numbers go on without end in both directions.

Does it make sense to ask which integer is the smallest or which integer is the largest? Use a complete sentence to explain why or why not.

14

Investigate Problem 2

1. **Math Path: Properties of Numbers and Their Operations**

When we perform operations such as addition or multiplication on the numbers in a set, the operations could produce a number that is also in the system. When this happens, the set is said to be *closed* under the operation.

The set of integers is said to be closed under the operation of addition. This means that for every two integers a and b, the sum $a + b$ is also an integer.

Are the natural numbers closed under addition? Write an example to support your answer.

Are the whole numbers closed under addition? Write an example to support your answer.

2. Consider the operation of subtraction. Are the natural numbers closed under subtraction? Write an example to support your answer.

Are the whole numbers closed under subtraction? Write an example to support your answer.

Are the integers closed under subtraction? Write an example to support your answer.

Are any of these sets closed under multiplication? Write examples to support your answers.

Are any of these sets closed under division? Write examples to support your answer.

3. In earlier lessons, we learned about the additive inverse, the multiplicative inverse, the additive identity, and the multiplicative identity.

Which of these does the set of natural numbers have, if any? Use a complete sentence to explain.

Which of these does the set of whole numbers have, if any? Use a complete sentence to explain.

Which of these does the set of integers numbers have, if any? Use a complete sentence to explain.

A **rational number** is a number that can be written in the form $\frac{a}{b}$, where a and b are both integers and b is not equal to 0.

A. Does the set of rational numbers include the set of whole numbers? Write an example to support your answer.

$$\boxed{} = \frac{\boxed{}}{\boxed{}}$$

B. Does the set of rational numbers include the set of integers? Write an example to support your answer.

$$\boxed{} = \frac{\boxed{}}{\boxed{}}$$

C. Does the set of rational numbers include all fractions? Write an example to support your answer.

$$\frac{\boxed{}}{\boxed{}}$$

D. Does the set of rational numbers include all decimals? Write an example to support your answer.

$$\boxed{} = \frac{\boxed{}}{\boxed{}}$$

We will examine the answer to Part (D) in more detail in Lesson 14.3. In that lesson we will determine which decimal numbers can be written exactly as fractions.

Investigate Problem 3

1. Is the set of rational numbers closed under addition? Write an example to support your answer.

Is the set of rational numbers closed under subtraction? Write an example to support your answer.

Is the set of rational numbers closed under multiplication? Write an example to support your answer.

Is the set of rational numbers closed under division? Write an example to support your answer.

2. Does the set of rational numbers have an additive identity?
Write an example to support your answer.

Does the set of rational numbers have a multiplicative identity?
Write an example to support your answer.

Does the set of rational numbers have an additive inverse?
Write an example to support your answer.

Does the set of rational numbers have a multiplicative inverse?
Write an example to support your answer.

3. You can add, subtract, multiply, and divide rational numbers in
much the same way that you did using integers. Perform the
indicated operation.

$1.5 + (-8.3) =$ $\qquad$ $-12.5 - 8.3 =$

$-\dfrac{1}{2} - \dfrac{3}{4} =$ $\qquad$ $2\dfrac{1}{2} + \left(-3\dfrac{7}{8}\right) =$

$-2.0 \times (-3.6) =$ $\qquad$ $6.75 \times (-4.2) =$

$-\dfrac{2}{3} \times \dfrac{3}{8} =$ $\qquad$ $-3\dfrac{3}{4} \times \left(-2\dfrac{3}{5}\right) =$

$-1.5 \div 4.5 =$ $\qquad$ $-2.1 \div (-3.5) =$

$-\dfrac{2}{5} \div \dfrac{3}{10} =$ $\qquad$ $-1\dfrac{3}{8} \div \left(-2\dfrac{2}{5}\right) =$

How Many Times?
Powers of Rational Numbers

Objectives

In this lesson, you will:
- Find powers of rational numbers.
- Multiply and divide powers of rational numbers.

Key Terms

- power

In Lesson 1.6, we learned that a **power** is a number written using a base and an exponent that represents repeated multiplication.

base   exponent

$$4^5 = 4 \times 4 \times 4 \times 4 \times 4$$

power

Problem 1   How Many Times More Cellular Phones?

In 1985, there were about 5^8 people in the United States who owned a cellular phone. By 2002, that number had grown to about 5^{12} people. How many times greater was the number of people who owned a cellular phone in 2002 than in 1985?

A. To find the value of each **power**, you can write 5^8 and 5^{12} as repeated multiplication and multiply.

$$5^8 = 5 \times 5 \times 5 \times 5 \times 5 \times 5 \times 5 \times 5 =$$

$$5^{12} = 5 \times 5 \times 5 \times 5 \times 5 \times 5 \times 5 \times 5 \times 5 \times 5 \times 5 \times 5 =$$

To answer the question, you could divide the value of 5^{12} by the value of 5^8 above, but in this lesson, we will learn an easier way!

B. The number of people who owned cellular phones in 1985 is actually closer to $\left(\dfrac{49}{10}\right)^8$ people. To find this number, let's begin by finding the values of some easier powers by writing each power first as repeated multiplication and then multiplying.

$$\left(\dfrac{2}{3}\right)^2 = \left(\dfrac{2}{3}\right)\left(\dfrac{2}{3}\right) = \qquad\qquad \left(\dfrac{2}{3}\right)^3 =$$

$$\left(\dfrac{2}{3}\right)^4 = \qquad\qquad\qquad\qquad \left(\dfrac{2}{3}\right)^5 =$$

C. What can you conclude about finding the value of a power whose base is a rational number? Write a complete sentence to explain.

1. Use the results of Part (C) of to complete each statement.

$$\left(\frac{3}{4}\right)^3 = \frac{3^{\square}}{4^{\square}} = \frac{\square}{\square} \qquad \left(\frac{1}{6}\right)^3 = \frac{1^{\square}}{6^{\square}} = \frac{\square}{\square} \qquad \left(\frac{3}{5}\right)^4 = \frac{3^{\square}}{5^{\square}} = \frac{\square}{\square}$$

2. Find the value of each power by first writing it as repeated multiplication and then multiplying.

$(-1)^3 =$ $(-1)^4 =$ $(-1)^5 =$

$(-1)^6 =$ $(1)^3 =$ $(1)^{100} =$

3. What can you conclude about finding the value of a power of –1? What can you conclude about finding the value of a power of 1? Write complete sentences to explain.

4. Use your results from Part (B) and Question 2 to find the value of each power.

$$\left(-\frac{2}{3}\right)^2 = \qquad\qquad \left(-\frac{2}{3}\right)^3 =$$

$$\left(-\frac{2}{3}\right)^4 = \qquad\qquad \left(-\frac{2}{3}\right)^5 =$$

5. In Lesson 7.7, we learned about negative exponents. Recall that

$$0.01 = \frac{1}{100} = \frac{1}{10^2} = 10^{-2}.$$

Use what you have learned to complete each statement to find the value of the power.

$$(2)^{-3} = \frac{1}{2^{\square}} = \frac{\square}{\square} \qquad (10)^{-3} = \frac{1}{10^{\square}} = \frac{\square}{\square} \qquad (-3)^{-2} = \frac{1}{(-3)^{\square}} = \frac{\square}{\square}$$

6. Use what you have learned from Questions 1 and 5 to complete each statement.

$$\left(\frac{5}{6}\right)^{-2} = \frac{5^{\square}}{6^{\square}} = \frac{\frac{1}{5^{\square}}}{\frac{1}{6^{\square}}} = \frac{\frac{1}{\square}}{\frac{1}{\square}} = \frac{\square}{\square}$$

$$\left(\frac{3}{4}\right)^{-3} = \frac{3^{\square}}{4^{\square}} = \frac{\frac{1}{3^{\square}}}{\frac{1}{4^{\square}}} = \frac{\frac{1}{\square}}{\frac{1}{\square}} = \frac{\square}{\square}$$

14

A. Find the value of each product of powers by first writing each power as repeated multiplication and then multiplying.

$(3)^2(3)^3 =$ $\qquad$ $(2)^3(2)^4 =$

$(-5)(-5)^3 =$ $\qquad$ $(-10)^4(-10)^3 =$

$$\left(\frac{1}{4}\right)^2\left(\frac{1}{4}\right)^3 =$$ $\qquad$ $$\left(-\frac{4}{5}\right)^2\left(-\frac{4}{5}\right)^3 =$$

B. What conclusion can you make about multiplying powers? Write your answer using a complete sentence.

C. Complete the statement below to illustrate the conclusion that you wrote in Part (B).

$a^b a^c = a^{\boxed{}}$

D. Do you think that this rule applies to multiplying powers with integer exponents? To decide, first find the value of the product of powers below by writing each power as repeated multiplication and multiplying.

$$(5)^{-2}(5)^{-1} = \left(\frac{1}{5^{\boxed{}}}\right)\left(\frac{1}{5^{\boxed{}}}\right) = \left(\frac{1}{\boxed{}}\right)\left(\frac{1}{\boxed{}}\right) = \frac{1}{\boxed{}}$$

Apply your rule from part (C) to find the value of the product.

$$(5)^{-2}(5)^{-1} = 5^{\boxed{}} = \frac{\boxed{}}{\boxed{}} = \frac{\boxed{}}{\boxed{}}$$

E. Use the example above to write a complete sentence that explains your answer.

Investigate Problem 2

1. Find the value of each product of powers.

$(3)^{-2}(3)^3 =$ $\qquad$ $(2)^{-2}(2)^{-3} =$

$(-1)^{-5}(-1)^3 =$ $\qquad$ $(10)^{-5}(-10)^5 =$

$$\left(\frac{3}{4}\right)^{-2}\left(\frac{3}{4}\right)^{-2} =$$ $\qquad$ $$\left(-\frac{1}{2}\right)^{-5}\left(-\frac{1}{2}\right)^7 =$$

Problem 3   Dividing Powers

A. Find the value of each quotient of powers by first writing the division problem as a multiplication problem using integer exponents. Then apply what you learned in Problem 2 to multiply the powers. The first one is done for you.

$$\frac{(3)^2}{(3)^3} = (3)^2 \times (3)^{-3} = 3^{2+(-3)} = 3^{-1} = \frac{1}{3}$$

$$\frac{(-5)^3}{(-5)} =$$

B. What conclusion can you make about dividing powers? Write your answer using a complete sentence.

C. Complete the equation below to illustrate the conclusion that you wrote in Part (B).

$$\frac{a^b}{a^c} = a^{\boxed{}} , \; a \neq 0$$

Investigate Problem 3

1. Find the value of each quotient of powers.

$$\frac{(-3)^3}{(-3)^2} =$$ $$\frac{(3)^{-2}}{(3)^3} =$$

$$\frac{(-10)^4}{(-10)^{-3}} =$$ $$\frac{(2)^{-2}}{(2)^{-3}} =$$

$$\frac{(10)^{-5}}{(10)^5} =$$ $$\frac{\left(-\frac{4}{5}\right)^3}{\left(-\frac{4}{5}\right)^2} =$$

2. Remember in Problem 1 that we wanted to find out how many times greater the number of cellular phone owners was in 2002 than in 1985. We can find this number by writing the quotient $\frac{5^{12}}{5^8}$. Use what you learned in Problem 3 to find this quotient.

Do you agree that this is much easier than multiplying out the numerator and denominator and then dividing?

Sew What?
Irrational Numbers

Objectives

In this lesson, you will:

- Identify decimals as terminating or repeating.
- Write repeating decimals as fractions.
- Identify irrational numbers.

Key Terms

- terminating decimal
- repeating decimal
- bar notation
- irrational number

You have worked with some numbers that are not rational numbers. For example, $\sqrt{2}$ and $\sqrt{5}$ are not the square roots of perfect squares and cannot be written in the form $\dfrac{a}{b}$, where a and b are both integers.

Problem 1   Making a Quilt

Your aunt is making a quilt. The pattern pieces are right triangles with the dimensions shown.

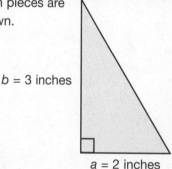

$b = 3$ inches

$a = 2$ inches

A. Is it possible to exactly measure the length of the hypotenuse? Use the Pythagorean theorem by filling in the blanks below. Then use a complete sentence to explain your answer.

$$a^2 + b^2 = c^2$$
$$2^2 + 3^2 = c^2$$
$$\boxed{} = c^2$$
$$\sqrt{\boxed{}} = c$$

B. Even though we often approximate square roots using a decimal, most square roots are irrational numbers. Because all rational numbers can be written as a/b where a and b are integers, they can be written as a terminating decimal (e.g. $\dfrac{1}{4}$ = 0.25) or a repeating decimals (e.g., $\dfrac{1}{3}$ = 0.333....). All other decimals are irrational numbers.

Convert the fraction to a decimal by dividing the numerator by the denominator. Continue to divide until you see a pattern.

$$\dfrac{1}{3} = \qquad 3\overline{)1}$$

C. Use a complete sentence to describe the pattern that you observed in Part (B).

14

D. Convert each fraction to a decimal by dividing the numerator by the denominator. Continue to divide until you see a pattern.

$\dfrac{5}{6} =$ 6⟌5‾‾‾‾

$\dfrac{2}{9} =$ 9⟌2‾‾‾‾

$\dfrac{9}{11} =$ 11⟌9‾‾‾‾

$\dfrac{3}{22} =$ 22⟌3‾‾‾‾

E. These decimal representations are called *repeating decimals*. Use a complete sentence to explain why.

Investigate Problem 1

1. Math Path: Terminating and Repeating Decimals

A **terminating decimal** is a decimal that has a last digit. For instance, the decimal $0.125 = \dfrac{125}{1000} = \dfrac{1}{8}$ is a terminating decimal.

A **repeating decimal** is a decimal with digits that repeat in sets of one or more. We can use two different notations to represent repeating decimals. One notation is to write the decimal, including one set of digits that repeat, and place a bar over the repeating digits. This is called **bar notation.**

$\dfrac{1}{3} = 0.\overline{3}$

$\dfrac{7}{22} = 0.3\overline{18}$

Another notation is to write the decimal, including two sets of the digits that repeat, and using dots to indicate repetition.

$\dfrac{1}{3} = 0.33\ldots$

$\dfrac{7}{22} = 0.31818\ldots$

Write each repeating decimal that you found in Part (D) using both notations.

$\dfrac{5}{6} =$

$\dfrac{2}{9} =$

$\dfrac{9}{11} =$

$\dfrac{3}{22} =$

2. Some repeating decimals represent common fractions, such as $\frac{1}{3}$, $\frac{2}{3}$, and $\frac{1}{6}$, and are used often enough that we recognize the fraction by its decimal representation. For most repeating decimals, though, you cannot recognize the fraction that the decimal represents. For instance, can you tell which fraction is represented by the repeating decimals 0.44… or $0.\overline{09}$?

Both of these repeating decimals represent fractions that you have used. We can use algebra to find the fraction that is represented by the repeating decimal 0.44… . First, write an equation by setting the decimal equal to a variable that will represent the fraction.

$w = 0.44…$

Next, multiply both sides of the equation by a power of 10. The exponent on the power of 10 is equal to the number of decimal places until the decimal begins to repeat. In this case, the decimal begins repeating after 1 decimal place, so the exponent on the power of 10 is 1. Because $10^1 = 10$, multiply both sides by 10.

$10w = 4.4…$

Next, subtract the first equation from the second equation.

$$\begin{array}{r} 10w = 4.44… \\ -w = 0.44… \\ \hline 9w = 4 \end{array}$$

Finally, solve the equation by dividing both sides by what number? So, what fraction is w?

3. Complete the steps to find the fraction that is represented by 0.0909… .

$w = 0.0909…$ $\qquad$ $100w = 9.0909…$ $\qquad$ $100w = 9.0909…$

$$\begin{array}{r} 100w = 9.0909… \\ -w = 0.0909… \\ \hline \boxed{}\,w = \boxed{} \end{array}$$

$w = \dfrac{\boxed{}}{\boxed{}} = \dfrac{\boxed{}}{\boxed{}}$

4. Repeat the procedure above to write the fraction that represents each repeating decimal.

0.55… = $\qquad\qquad\qquad\qquad$ 0.0505… =

$0.\overline{12}$ = $\qquad\qquad\qquad\qquad$ $0.\overline{36}$ =

Problem 2 *Sewing a Tablecloth*

Your aunt wants to sew a round tablecloth with lace trim. The diameter of the tablecloth must be 70 inches. Your aunt wants to know how much trim to purchase.

A. In Lesson 10.2, we found the circumference of a circle. What number should your aunt multiply the diameter of the tablecloth by in order to know how many inches of lace trim to purchase? Write your answer using a complete sentence.

B. In Lesson 10.2, we used an approximation of the number π to find the circumference of a circle. Even though we used this approximation, the number π is a decimal with a never-ending number of digits that do not repeat. Decimals that do not repeat and do not terminate are said to be *irrational numbers.* An **irrational number** is a number that cannot be written in the form $\dfrac{a}{b}$, where a and b are both integers and $b \neq 0$.

C. The most famous irrational number is π. Throughout history, π has been calculated to hundreds and thousands of decimal places. In fact, one way that the speed of computers is measured is based on how fast the computer can calculate the digits of π. Another irrational number is $\sqrt{6}$. This number must be between which two whole numbers?

Use a calculator find each power.

$2.1^2 =$ $2.2^2 =$ $2.3^2 =$

$2.4^2 =$ $2.5^2 =$ $2.6^2 =$

Which of the bases above must $\sqrt{6}$ be between?

Continue the process above for the hundredths place.

$2.41^2 =$ $2.42^2 =$ $2.43^2 =$

$2.44^2 =$ $2.45^2 =$ $2.46^2 =$

Continue the process above for the thousandths place. Are the numbers you are squaring getting close to $\sqrt{6}$?

$2.445^2 =$ $2.446^2 =$ $2.447^2 =$

$2.448^2 =$ $2.449^2 =$ $2.450^2 =$

D. Find $\sqrt{6}$ using the calculator. Do you see any digits repeating in a pattern?

What can you conclude about the square roots of numbers that are not perfect squares? Write your answer using a complete sentence.

© 2008 Carnegie Learning, Inc.

Worth 1000 Words
Real Numbers and Their Properties

Objectives

In this lesson, you will:

- Classify numbers in the real number system.
- Understand the properties of real numbers.

Key Terms

- real number
- Venn diagram

Take Note

The Venn diagram was introduced in 1881 by John Venn, British philosopher and mathematician.

Problem 1   Picturing the Real Numbers

Combining the set of rational numbers and the set of irrational numbers produces the set of **real numbers.** You can use a **Venn diagram** to represent how the sets within the set of real numbers are related.

A. First, at the top of the large rectangle, write the label "Real Numbers." This entire rectangle represents the set of real numbers.

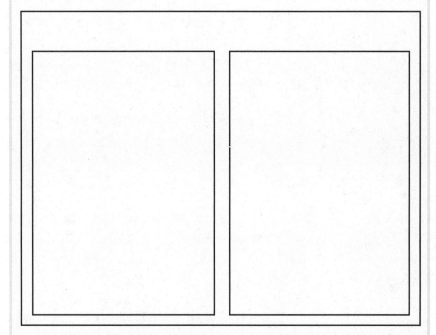

B. Label the smaller rectangle at the right "Irrational Numbers."

C. Label the top of the smaller rectangle at the left "Rational Numbers."

D. Inside the rectangle that represents rational numbers, draw a large circle. Inside the circle, at its top, write the label "Integers."

E. Inside the circle that represents integers, draw a smaller circle. Inside the circle, at its top, write the label "Whole Numbers."

F. Inside the circle that represents the whole numbers, draw a smaller circle. Inside this circle, write the label "Natural Numbers." Your Venn diagram that represents the real number system is complete.

14

Use your Venn diagram in Problem 1 to decide whether each of the following statements is true or false. Write complete sentences to explain your reasoning.

1. A whole number is sometimes an irrational number.

2. A real number is sometimes a rational number.

3. A whole number is always an integer.

4. A negative integer is always a whole number.

5. A rational number is sometimes an integer.

6. A square root is always an irrational number.

7. A fraction is never an irrational number.

8. A decimal is sometimes an irrational number.

The real numbers, together with their operations and properties, form the real number system. You have already encountered many of the properties of the real number system in various lessons. Let's review these properties.

A. Closure: A set of numbers is said to be closed under an operation if the result of the operation on two numbers in the set is another member of the set. For instance, the set of integers is closed under addition. This means that for every two integers a and b, the sum $a + b$ is also an integer.

For any real numbers a and b, is $a + b$ a real number? Is the set of real numbers closed under addition? Write an example to support your answer.

For any real numbers a and b, is $a - b$ a real number? Is the set of real numbers closed under subtraction? Write an example to support your answer.

For any real numbers a and b, is $a \times b$ a real number? Is the set of real numbers closed under multiplication? Write an example to support your answer.

For any real numbers a and b, is $a \div b$ a real number? Is the set of real numbers closed under division? Write an example to support your answer.

B. Additive Identity: An additive identity is a number such that when you add it to a second number, the sum is equal to the second number.

For any real number a, is there a real number such that $a + (\text{the number}) = a$? What is the number?

Does the set of real numbers have an additive identity? Write an example to support your answer.

C. Multiplicative Identity: A multiplicative identity is a number such that when you multiply it by a second number, the product is equal to the second number.

For any real number a, is there a real number such that $a \times (\text{the number}) = a$? What is the number?

Does the set of real numbers have a multiplicative identity? Write an example to support your answer.

14

14

D. Additive Inverse: Two numbers are additive inverses if their sum is the additive identity.

For any real number a, is there a real number such that $a +$ (the number) $= 0$? What is the number?

Does the set of real numbers have an additive inverse?
Write an example to support your answer.

E. Multiplicative Inverse: Two numbers are multiplicative inverses if their product is the multiplicative identity.

For any real number a, is there a real number such that $a \times$ (the number) $= 1$? What is the number?

Does the set of real numbers have a multiplicative inverse?
Write an example to support your answer.

F. Commutative Property of Addition: Changing the order of two or more addends in an addition problem does not change the sum.

For any real numbers a and b, is $a + b = b + a$?
Write an example to support your answer.

G. Commutative Property of Multiplication: Changing the order of two or more factors in a multiplication problem does not change the product.

For any real numbers a and b, is $a \times b = b \times a$?
Write an example to support your answer.

H. Associative Property of Addition: Changing the grouping of the addends in an addition problem does not change the sum.

For any real numbers a, b and c, is $(a + b) + c = a + (b + c)$?
Write an example to support your answer.

I. Associative Property of Multiplication: Changing the grouping of the factors in a multiplication problem does not change the product.

For any real numbers a, b, and c, is $(a \times b) \times c = a \times (b \times c)$?
Write an example to support your answer.

J. Properties of Equality:

Reflexive Property of Equality:

For any real number a, $a = a$.

Write an example of the property.

Symmetric Property of Equality:

For any real numbers a and b, if $a = b$, then $b = a$.

Write an example of the property.

The Transitive Property of Equality:

For any real numbers a, b, and c, if $a = b$ and $b = c$, then $a = c$.

Write an example of the property.

Choose one of the properties of equality and write a complete sentence to explain the property.

Investigate Problem 2

1. For each problem, identify the property that is represented.

   $234 + (-234) = 0$ $-4 \times (3 \times 5) = (-4 \times 3) \times 5$

   $-24 \times 1 = -24$ $-67 \times 56 = 56 \times (-67)$

   $-456 + 34 = 34 + (-456)$ $4 \times 0.25 = 1$

   If $5 = (-1)(-5)$ then $(-1)(-5) = 5$.

   If $c = 5 \times 7$ and $35 = 70 \div 2$, then $c = 70 \div 2$.

   $a + (4 + c) = (a + 4) + c$ $\left(-\dfrac{3}{4}\right)\left(-\dfrac{4}{3}\right) = 1$

   $-2\dfrac{3}{4} \times 1 = -2\dfrac{3}{4}$ $\left(-\dfrac{3}{4}\right) + \left(\dfrac{4}{3} + 5\right) = \left(-\dfrac{3}{4} + \dfrac{4}{3}\right) + 5$

14

The House That Math Built
The Distributive Property

Objectives

In this lesson, you will:

- Understand the distributive property.

Key Terms

- distributive property

Problem 1 Carpeting

A contractor needs to determine the number of square feet of carpeting that is needed to cover the great room and the master suite shown in the floor plan. The great room is 22 feet by 17 feet and the master suite is 13 feet by 17 feet.

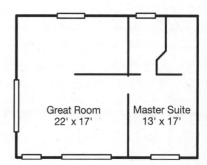

Great Room
22' x 17'

Master Suite
13' x 17'

A. How would you help the contractor find the area of the great room and the master suite? Write your answer using a complete sentence.

B. In Part (A), there are two ways to find the area of the great room and the master suite. You could find the area of each room and then add to get the total area.

Total area in square feet = (17 × 22) + (17 × 13)

$= \boxed{} + \boxed{} = \boxed{}$

Or, you could multiply the width by the total length of both rooms.

Total area in square feet = 17 × (22 + 13)

$= 17 \times \boxed{} = \boxed{}$

C. Finding the area in these two ways is an example of the **distributive property.** This property is useful in simplifying complicated expressions. The *Distributive Property of Multiplication Over Addition* distributes multiplication over addition. It says that you can multiply a number and a sum by first multiplying the number by each addend of the sum and then adding the products. For example, 5(3 + 7) = 5(3) + 5(7).

Find the value of the left side of the equation above by adding and then multiplying.

$5(3 + 7) = 5(\boxed{}) = \boxed{}$

Find the value of the right side of the equation above by multiplying and then adding.

$5(3) + 5(7) = \boxed{} + \boxed{} = \boxed{}$

14

1. The *Distributive Property of Multiplication Over Subtraction* distributes multiplication over subtraction. It says that you can multiply a number and a difference by first multiplying the number by each part of the difference and then subtracting the products. Write an equation that illustrates this property below. Then find the value of each side of the equation.

2. The *Distributive Property of Division Over Addition* distributes division over addition. It says that you can divide a sum by a number by first dividing each addend by the number and then adding the quotients. Write an equation that illustrates this property below. Then find the value of each side of the equation.

3. The *Distributive Property of Division Over Subtraction* distributes division over subtraction. It says that you can divide a difference by a number by first dividing each part of the difference by the number and then subtracting the quotients. Write an equation that illustrates this property below. Then find the value of each side of the equation.

4. Use the distributive property to evaluate each expression. Show your work.

$14(10 + 1) =$ $\qquad$ $6(9 + x) =$

$-2(2 + 17) =$ $\qquad$ $-7(5x + 6) =$

$4(20 - 6) =$ $\qquad$ $9(x - 5) =$

$-2(14 - 8) =$ $\qquad$ $-1(1 - x) =$

$\dfrac{(27 + 6)}{9} =$ $\qquad$ $\dfrac{(125 + 25x)}{5} =$

$\dfrac{(300 - 21)}{3} =$ $\qquad$ $\dfrac{(8x - 44)}{4} =$

$\dfrac{(-45 + 72)}{-9} =$ $\qquad$ $\dfrac{(-36 - 6x)}{2} =$

5. For each equation, identify the property used in each step. For example:

$5(3+7)-34 = 4(9-7)+8$	Given problem
$15+35-34 = 4(9-7)+8$	Distributive Property of Multiplication Over Addition
$15+35-34 = 36-28+8$	Distributive Property of Multiplication Over Subtraction
$(15+35)-34 = (36-28)+8$	Group
$50-34 = 8+8$	Addition and subtraction
$16 = 16$	Reflexive Property of Equality

$2(8x+89) = \dfrac{(24-8)}{8}$ _____

$16x+178 = \dfrac{(24-8)}{8}$ _____

$16x+178 = \dfrac{24}{8} - \dfrac{8}{8}$ _____

$16x+178 = 3-1$ _____

$16x+178 = 2$ _____

$16x+178-178 = 2-178$ _____

$16x = -176$ _____

$\dfrac{16x}{16} = \dfrac{-176}{16}$ _____

$x = -11$ _____

$20+(x+6)+7 = 3(6+5)+x$ _____

$20+x+(6+7) = 3(6+5)+x$ _____

$20+x+13 = 3(6+5)+x$ _____

$x+(20+13) = 3(6+5)+x$ _____

$x+33 = 3(6+5)+x$ _____

$x+33 = 3(6)+3(5)+x$ _____

$x+33 = 18+15+x$ _____

$x+33 = (18+15)+x$ _____

$x+33 = 33+x$ _____

$x+33 = x+33$ _____

14

Looking Back at Chapter 14

Key Terms

natural number ● p. 462
whole number ● p. 462
integer ● p. 463
rational number ● p. 465

power ● p. 467
terminating decimal ● p. 472
repeating decimal ● p. 472
bar notation ● p. 472

irrational number ● p. 474
real number ● p. 475
Venn diagram ● p. 475
distributive property ● p. 481

Summary

Comparing Rational Numbers Using a Number Line (p. 461)

To compare rational numbers, write each rational number as a decimal and plot the numbers on a number line. The number furthest to the right is greatest number.

Example   To compare the numbers $\frac{5}{2}$ and $-\frac{7}{4}$, rewrite each rational number as a decimal. Then plot each decimal on a number line.

$$\frac{5}{2} = 2.5 \qquad\qquad\qquad -\frac{7}{4} = -1.75$$

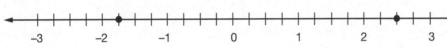

So, $\frac{5}{2}$ is greater than $-\frac{7}{4}$.

Performing Operations with Rational Numbers (p. 465)

To add, subtract, multiply, and divide rational numbers, use what you know about adding, subtracting, multiplying, and dividing integers and fractions.

Examples
$$3\frac{1}{7} + \left(-\frac{5}{7}\right) = \frac{22}{7} + \left(-\frac{5}{7}\right) \qquad\qquad -\frac{4}{3} \div \frac{7}{5} = -\frac{4}{3} \times \frac{5}{7}$$
$$= \frac{17}{7} \qquad\qquad\qquad\qquad\qquad = -\frac{20}{21}$$

Finding Powers of Rational Numbers (p. 467)

To find the value of a power whose base is a rational number, use the rule $\left(\dfrac{a}{b}\right)^c = \dfrac{a^c}{b^c}$.

Examples
$$\left(\frac{4}{7}\right)^2 = \frac{4^2}{7^2} = \frac{16}{49} \qquad\qquad \left(\frac{3}{2}\right)^5 = \frac{3^5}{2^5} = \frac{243}{32}$$

$$\left(\frac{9}{14}\right)^{-3} = \frac{9^{-3}}{14^{-3}} = \frac{\dfrac{1}{9^3}}{\dfrac{1}{14^3}} = \frac{\dfrac{1}{729}}{\dfrac{1}{2744}} = \frac{2744}{729}$$

Finding Products of Powers (p. 469)

To find the product of powers, use the rule $a^b a^c = a^{b+c}$.

Examples $(4)^3 (4)^5 = (4)^{3+5} = 4^8$ $\left(\dfrac{1}{8}\right)^2 \left(\dfrac{1}{8}\right)^3 = \left(\dfrac{1}{8}\right)^5$

$\left(\dfrac{3}{4}\right)^{-5} \left(\dfrac{3}{4}\right)^{-1} = \left(\dfrac{3}{4}\right)^{-5+(-1)} = \left(\dfrac{3}{4}\right)^{-6}$ $(12)^2 (12)^{-9} = (12)^{-7}$

Finding Quotients of Powers (p. 470)

To find the quotient of powers, use the rule $\dfrac{a^b}{a^c} = a^{b-c}$, $a \neq 0$.

Examples $\dfrac{(5)^6}{(5)^3} = (5)^{6-3} = 5^3$ $\dfrac{(-4)^3}{(-4)^5} = (-4)^{3-5} = (-4)^{-2}$

$\dfrac{\left(\dfrac{2}{9}\right)}{\left(\dfrac{2}{9}\right)^{-2}} = \left(\dfrac{2}{9}\right)^{1-(-2)} = \left(\dfrac{2}{9}\right)^3$ $\dfrac{(7)^{-1}}{(7)^6} = (7)^{-1-6} = (7)^{-7}$

Identifying Decimals as Terminating or Repeating (p. 472)

To identify a decimal as terminating or repeating, determine whether the decimal has a last digit or digits that repeat in sets.

Examples $\dfrac{5}{8} = 0.625$ The decimal has a last digit 5, so it is a terminating decimal.

$\dfrac{2}{11} = 0.1818\ldots$ The decimal repeats the set of digits "18," so it is a repeating decimal. You can write this decimal using bar notation as $0.\overline{18}$.

Writing Repeating Decimals as Fractions (p. 473)

To write a repeating decimal as a fraction, first write an equation by setting the decimal equal to a variable that will represent the fraction. Then multiply both sides of the equation by a power of ten. Subtract the first equation from the second equation and solve.

Example   To write $0.22\ldots$ as a fraction, first write the equation $x = 0.22\ldots$.
Then multiply both sides by 10 and subtract the original equation.
Finally, solve for x.

$$x = 0.22\ldots$$
$$10x = 2.22\ldots$$
$$-x = 0.22\ldots$$
$$9x = 2$$
$$x = \dfrac{2}{9}$$

So, the decimal $0.22\ldots$ is equal to the fraction $\dfrac{2}{9}$.

Identifying Irrational Numbers (p. 474)

An irrational number is a number than cannot be written in the form $\frac{a}{b}$. Decimals that do not repeat and do not terminate are irrational numbers.

Examples   The number $\sqrt{2}$ = 1.4142135623... is an irrational number because it does not terminate and does not repeat.

The number 2.457457457457 is a rational number because it repeats.

Classifying Numbers (p. 475)

To classify a number in the real number system, determine whether the number belongs to the set of rational or irrational numbers. If the number is a rational number, then decide whether it belongs to the set of natural numbers, whole numbers, or integer numbers.

Examples   The number –3.7 is a real number belonging to the set of rational numbers.

The number 7 is a real number belonging to the set of rational numbers. This number also belongs to the set of integer numbers, the set of whole numbers, and the set of natural numbers.

The number 6.54384972469... is a real number belonging to the set of irrational numbers.

Identifying Properties of Real Numbers (p. 477)

Use the properties you have learned to identify the property that is being used in each statement.

Examples   For real numbers a and b, the number $a - b$ is a real number.

Closure: This statement is true because the set of real numbers is closed under subtraction.

$4 + (-4) = 0$

Additive Inverse: Two numbers are additive inverses if the sum of the numbers is the additive identity 0.

$(3 \times 5) \times 9 = 3 \times (5 \times 9)$

Associative Property of Multiplication: Changing the grouping of the factors in a multiplication problem does not change the product.

Using the Distributive Property (p. 481)

You can use the distributive property as another way to solve multiplication and division problems involving addition and subtraction.

Examples

$$5(3 + 4) = 5(3) + 5(4)$$
$$= 15 + 20$$
$$= 35$$

$$\frac{(34 + 6y)}{4} = \frac{34}{4} + \frac{6y}{4}$$
$$= \frac{17}{2} + \frac{3}{2}y$$

Looking Ahead to Chapter 15

Focus   In Chapter 15, you will work with transformations. You will learn to plot points in the four-quadrant Cartesian coordinate system and to create and use scale drawings and models. You will learn to graph translations, rotations, reflections, and dilations in the coordinate plane.

Chapter Warm-up

Answer these questions to help you review skills that you will need in Chapter 15.

Plot each point in the coordinate plane.

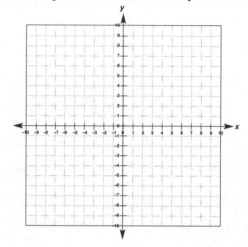

1. (5, 4)

2. (1, 9)

3. (3, 0)

4. (0, 6)

Solve the proportion.

5. $\dfrac{3 \text{ black cars}}{5 \text{ red cars}} = \dfrac{x \text{ black cars}}{15 \text{ red cars}}$

6. $\dfrac{5 \text{ pens}}{x \text{ pencils}} = \dfrac{12 \text{ pens}}{15 \text{ pencils}}$

7. $\dfrac{2 \text{ weeds}}{7 \text{ flowers}} = \dfrac{8 \text{ weeds}}{x \text{ flowers}}$

Find the slope and *y*-intercept of the graph of the equation.

8. $y = 3x - 1$

9. $y = 0.5x + 6$

10. $y = -4x - 3$

Read the problem below.

11. Allen is ordering his school pictures. The smallest size is 2 inches by 3 inches. What size would the pictures be if they were enlarged by a scale factor of 3?

Key Terms

ordered pair • p. 491
x-coordinate • p. 491
y-coordinate • p. 491
quadrant • p. 492
scale drawing • p. 497
scale • p. 499
scale model • p. 501

translation • p. 503
transformation • p. 503
pre-image • p. 505
image • p. 505
rotation • p. 506
center of rotation • p. 506
angle of rotation • p. 506

reflection • p. 509
line of reflection • p. 509
dilation • p. 513
scale factor • p. 513
multiple transformation • p. 515

15

Transformations

One cup of healthy soil contains more than 6 billion living organisms. In Lesson 15.1, you use a complete Cartesian coordinate system to make a map of what lives in dirt.

15

15.1 Worms and Ants
Graphing in Four Quadrants

Objectives

In this lesson, you will:

- Understand the four quadrants of a coordinate plane.
- Identify and plot points in a coordinate plane.

Key Terms

- ordered pair
- *x*-coordinate
- *y*-coordinate
- quadrant

In Lesson 8.5, we learned about the Cartesian coordinate system developed by René Descartes. However, we have been using only a part of the coordinate plane—the part that uses only positive numbers.

Problem 1   What Lives in Dirt?

In science class, you are conducting an experiment to learn about what lives in dirt. Your class goes outside and chooses a plant in a nearby garden. Next, you dig up a 20-inch by 20-inch square of dirt, with the plant located at the center of the square. Then you use string to mark every inch of the area and create a grid of the space. Finally, you record each living thing that you find in the dirt. The graph of what you find living in the dirt is shown.

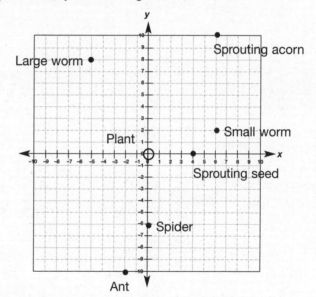

This graph shows the complete Cartesian coordinate system. Recall that the Cartesian coordinate system is formed from two perpendicular number lines (the *x*- and *y*-axes) that intersect at a point called the origin. Just as we learned earlier, each point on the graph can be represented by an **ordered pair** with an **x-coordinate,** which represents the horizontal distance from the origin to the point, and a **y-coordinate,** which represents the vertical distance from the origin to the point. The plant stalk is located at the point (0, 0). Write the ordered pairs of the location of each living thing.

Ant: _____   Small worm: _____

Large worm: _____   Sprouting acorn: _____

Spider: _____   Sprouting seed: _____

1. The axes divide the coordinate plane into four separate regions called **quadrants.** The quadrants are numbered using Roman numerals. The numbering of the quadrants is counterclockwise, beginning with the region at the top right. The quadrants are shown in the coordinate plane below.

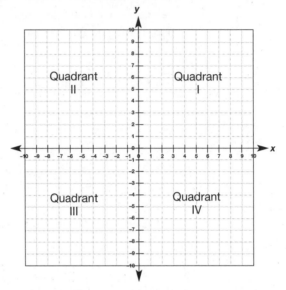

15

Choose four points, one from each quadrant. Then, for each point, determine whether the *x*-coordinate and *y*-coordinate of its ordered pair is positive or negative.

Quadrant I: *x*-coordinate: *y*-coordinate:

Quadrant II: *x*-coordinate: *y*-coordinate:

Quadrant III: *x*-coordinate: *y*-coordinate:

Quadrant IV: *x*-coordinate: *y*-coordinate:

Take Note

If the *x*-coordinate or *y*-coordinate of an ordered pair is zero, then the point lies on an axis and is not located in any of the quadrants.

2. Graph each ordered pair in the coordinate plane below. Identify the quadrant in which the point represented by the ordered pair lies.

(5, 7)

(−5, 7)

(5, −7)

(−5, −7)

(0, 7)

(4, 0)

(−6, 0)

(0, −3)

(2.5, 5.5)

(−3.25, 5)

(9.75, −0.5)

(−3.5, −5.5)

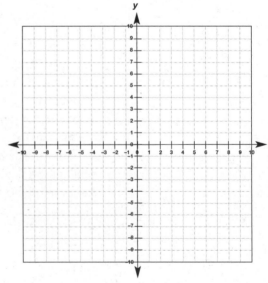

For 15 minutes, you watch an ant walking across your 20-inch by 20-inch grid. The ant begins at the point (–2, –10). Every 3 minutes, you record the *x*- and *y*-coordinates that represent the ant's position. The coordinates are shown in the table.

x-coordinate	*y*-coordinate
–2	–10
0	–6
2	–2
4	2
6	6
8	10

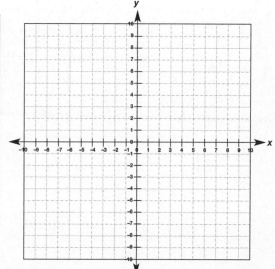

A. Write each row of numbers in the table as an ordered pair. Plot the ordered pairs in the coordinate plane above.

B. Draw a line through the points. Does the line appear to represent a linear function? Use a complete sentence to explain your answer.

C. Find the slope of the line through the points. Show your work below.

D. What is the *y*-intercept of the line?

E. Use the slope and *y*-intercept to write an equation of the line. Write a complete sentence to explain how you wrote the equation.

1. Each table that follows is a representation of a linear function. For each linear function, write the rows of numbers in the table as ordered pairs. Plot the ordered pairs and draw a line through the points. Find the slope and the x- and y-intercepts of the line. Then use the slope and y-intercept to write an equation of the line.

x-coordinate	y-coordinate
−8	−3
−5	0
−2	3
1	6
4	9

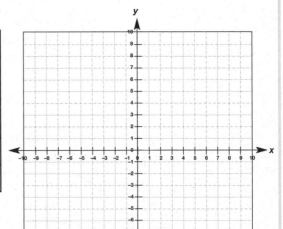

slope:

x-intercept:

y-intercept:

equation of line: _____

x-coordinate	y-coordinate
−3	−9
−1	−5
1	−1
3	3
5	7

slope:

x-intercept:

y-intercept:

equation of line: _____

15

x-coordinate	y-coordinate
–3	9
–1	5
1	1
3	–3
5	–7

slope:

x-intercept:

y-intercept:

equation of line: _____

2. For each of the following linear functions, find the slope and the x- and y-intercepts. Plot the x-intercept and the y-intercept. Beginning at the y-intercept, use the slope to find another point on the line. Finally, draw a line through the points.

y = x + 3

slope:

x-intercept:

y-intercept:

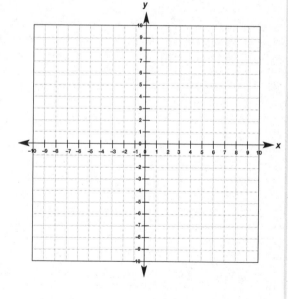

$y = 3x - 1$

slope:

x-intercept:

y-intercept:

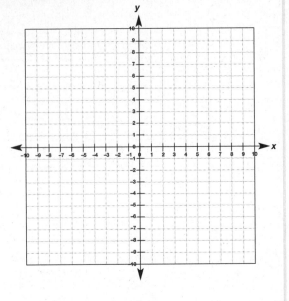

$y = -2x + 5$

slope:

x-intercept:

y-intercept:

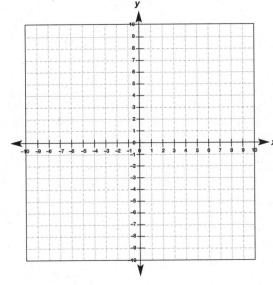

$y = -2.5x + 1$

slope:

x-intercept:

y-intercept:

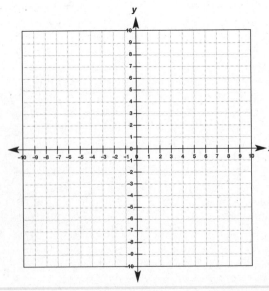

15

15.2 Maps and Models
Scale Drawings and Scale Models

Objectives

In this lesson, you will:

- Make and use scale drawings and scale models.

Key Terms

- scale drawing
- scale
- proportion
- scale model

As people began to explore the world and discover new oceans and land formations, making accurate maps for others to read became very important. In fact, mapmakers were held in such high esteem that the American continents were named after Italian mapmaker Amerigo Vespucci.

Problem 1   Social Studies: Making Maps

Maps are really just *scale drawings*. In Lesson 9.4, we learned about similar polygons that are the same shape but not the same size. A **scale drawing** is a drawing similar to an object but is either larger or smaller than the actual object.

A. Suppose that you are writing a report for a project about Tennessee and want to include a map. The map that you find is too large, so you want to make it smaller. Drawing the map smaller is making a scale drawing. One way to make a scale drawing is shown below.

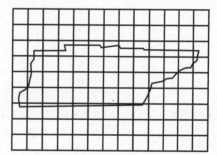

First, draw a grid over the original object. To create a copy that is smaller (or larger) than the original, create a grid with the same number of squares that are proportionally smaller (or larger) than the original grid's squares. Then copy each portion of the object contained in an original square into the corresponding square of the smaller (or larger) grid.

B. Reduce the drawing of Tennessee by using the grid of smaller squares below.

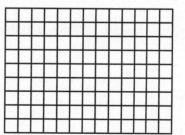

1. Enlarge the drawing of Tennessee by using the grid of larger squares below.

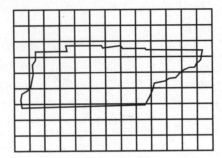

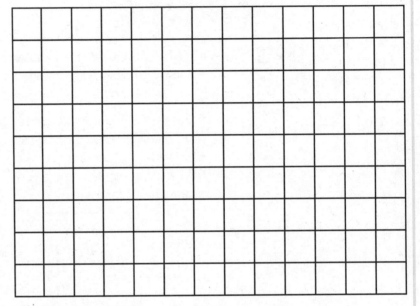

2. To double the size of a map, we can use a grid that has dimensions that are two times the dimensions of the grid on the original map. If we want to make a map that is 10 times larger, what should the dimensions of the new grid be compared to the grid that we place over the original map? Write your answer using a complete sentence.

3. If we want to make a map that is one fifth of the size of the original map, what should the dimensions of the new grid be compared to the grid that we place over the original map? Write your answer using a complete sentence.

Problem 2 *Scale of a Map*

Learning how to read maps and scale drawings is very useful whether you are traveling on vacation, looking at house plans, or designing new machines. The key of a map or drawing tells us the scale of the map or drawing. On the next page is a map of the United States. The *scale* of the map is located at the top right of the map. The **scale** is the ratio of the given length on the drawing to the actual length.

A. The scale on the U.S. map gives a specific length that represents 200 miles or 330 kilometers on the map. The scale at the right is copied from the map. Use a centimeter ruler to measure the scale. On the map, how many centimeters represent 330 kilometers? Write your answer using a complete sentence.

```
0    200 mi
├───────┤
0    330 km
```

B. On the map, how many centimeters represent 200 miles? Write your answer using a complete sentence.

15

Investigate Problem 2

Take Note

Recall that a **proportion** is an equation that states that two ratios or rates are equal.

1. Two cities are 600 kilometers apart. How far apart should they be on the map? Use a proportion based on the scale of the map to help you.

2. The distance between two cities on the map is 3 centimeters. Approximately how far apart in miles are they actually? Use a proportion based on the scale of the map to help you.

3. Use a centimeter ruler to measure the distances between each pair of cities on the map on the following page. Then use a proportion to find the actual distance between the cities. Complete the table.

City 1	City 2	Distance on Map (centimeters)	Actual Distance (kilometers)	Actual Distance (miles)
Washington, D.C.	St. Louis, MO			
Washington, D.C.	Los Angeles, CA			
Seattle, WA	Chicago, IL			
Miami, FL	Portland, OR			
Boston, MA	Phoenix, AZ			
Denver, CO	Atlanta, GA			

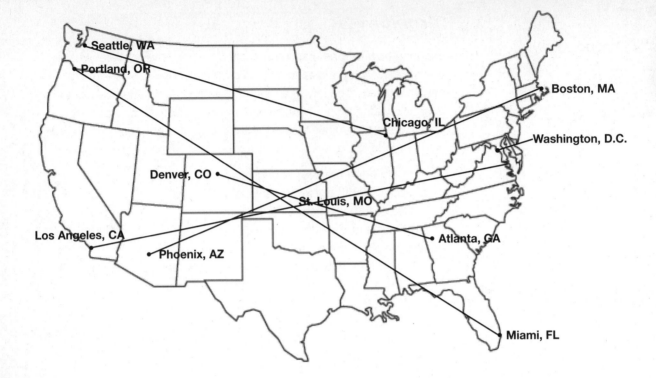

A **scale model** is a three-dimensional object that is similar to an actual object but is either larger or smaller than the actual object.

A. For your project on Tennessee, you want to make a scale model of the Tennessee State Capitol. The building is 170 feet tall. You want your model to be 17 inches tall. Complete the proportion to find the scale you should use to make the model. Write your answer using a complete sentence.

$$\frac{1 \text{ inch}}{\boxed{} \text{ feet}} = \frac{17 \text{ inches}}{170 \text{ feet}}$$

B. The length of the Tennessee State Capitol is 232 feet. According to the scale you determined in part (A), how long should you make the model? Use a proportion to help you.

C. The width of the Tennessee State Capitol is 124 feet. According to the scale you determined in part (A), how wide should you make the model? Use a proportion to help you.

15

Investigate Problem 3

1. You want to make a large model of the Tennessee state bird, the mockingbird. The bird is approximately 24 centimeters long and its wingspan is approximately 36 centimeters. Determine the model bird's length and its wingspan if you use a scale in which 0.5 meter is equal to 1 centimeter.

2. Write a complete sentence to describe how you determined the model bird's length.

3. Write a complete sentence to describe how you determined the model bird's wingspan.

15

Designer Mathematics
Sliding and Spinning

Objectives

In this lesson, you will:

- Graph translations in a coordinate plane.
- Graph rotations in a coordinate plane.

Key Terms

- translation
- transformation
- pre-image
- image
- rotation
- center of rotation
- angle of rotation

You may have had to move things such as a sofa and chair in your living room. Usually you move these heavy objects by pushing or sliding them. In mathematics, when a figure is moved by sliding it, the action is called a *translation*. A **translation** is the movement of a figure from one place to another without turning it. Translations are an example of a class of actions called **transformations** that we can perform on objects. These actions cause one object to be "transformed" into another.

Problem 1   *No, Put It Here!*

Suppose that your house has been selected in a contest to be completely redesigned by an interior designer. The designer makes a drawing of the furniture in your room, shown in the coordinate plane at the right.

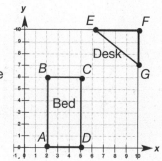

A. Write the coordinates of the corners of each piece of furniture.

   Bed: *A:*   Desk: *E:*

          B: *F:*

          C: *G:*

          D:

B. Suppose that the designer wants to slide the bed so that corner *A* is at the point (2, 3). Draw the bed in its new location in the coordinate plane. What are the new coordinates of the other corners?

   A: (2, 3)   *B:*   *C:*   *D:*

C. Suppose that the designer wants to slide the desk so that corner *E* is at the point (6, 7). Draw the desk in its new location in the coordinate plane. What are the new coordinates of the other corners?

   E: (6, 7)   *F:*   *G:*

15

1. A single translation involves sliding an object either vertically or horizontally a specific number of units. The direction of the translation is indicated by the sign of the number of units. In a vertical translation, a *positive* number indicates a slide *up* and a *negative* number indicates a slide *down*. In a horizontal translation, a *positive* number indicates a slide *right* and a *negative* number indicates a slide *left*.

Perform a vertical translation of +5 units on the square shown. Draw the square in its new position and label it 5*V*.

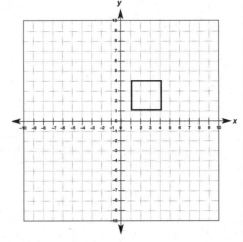

Perform a horizontal translation of –6 units on the original square. Draw the square in its new position and label it –6*H*.

Perform a vertical translation of –1 unit on the original square. Draw the square in its new position and label it –1*V*.

Perform a horizontal translation of +4 units on the original square. Draw the square in its new position and label it 4H.

2. Perform each translation below on the triangle shown. Then draw each new triangle and label it in a manner similar to the way you labeled the squares in Question 1.

Translate the triangle –3 units vertically.

Translate the original triangle +6 units horizontally.

Translate the original triangle +7 units vertically.

Translate the original triangle –3 units horizontally.

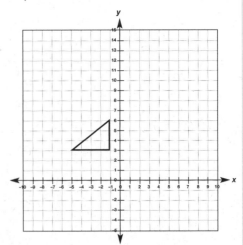

3. Each non-shaded figure below has been translated to a new position. The translated figure is the shaded figure. Describe each translation.

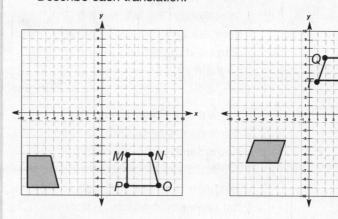

Translation of trapezoid:

Translation of parallelogram:

Take Note

In a vertical translation, only the *y*-coordinate is changed. In a horizontal translation, only the *x*-coordinate is changed.

Take Note

To "add" two ordered pairs, add the *x*-coordinates and add the *y*-coordinates. For example, (1, 2) + (3, 4) = (1 + 3, 2 + 4) = (4, 6).

4. The original figure in a translation is called the **pre-image** and the figure in the new position is called the **image.** The vertices of an image can be found as follows.

Vertical translation up: add a positive number to the *y*-coordinate

Vertical translation down: add a negative number to the *y*-coordinate

Horizontal translation to the right: add a positive number to the *x*-coordinate

Horizontal translation to the left: add a negative number to the *x*-coordinate

Complete the steps below to find the coordinates of the vertices of the images from Question 3. The first vertex is done for you.

Trapezoid	Pre-image	Add (–12, 0).	Image
M	(3, –5)	(3 + (–12), –5 + 0)	(–9, –5)
N			
O			
P			

Parallelogram	Pre-image	Add (–9, –10).	Image
Q			
R			
S			
T			

Suppose that the designer
selects a new painting for your
room. You hang the painting
as shown on the left, but the
designer says that it was really
supposed to be hung as shown
on the right.

Original painting   **Rotated painting**

When the designer turned the
painting, she performed a *rotation*.
A **rotation** is a transformation in
which a figure is turned about a
fixed point. The point is called
the **center of rotation**. Rotations
can be either clockwise (positive
rotations) or counterclockwise

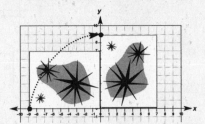

(negative rotations). The **angle of rotation** is the number of degrees
through which the rotation occurs. For example, the rotation that the
designer performed on the painting is shown in the coordinate plane.

A. Complete the statement to describe the rotation.

The rotation is a _____ degree rotation _____
                                                   (clockwise or counterclockwise)
about the origin.

Perform the following rotations on the square below.

B. Rotate the square +90°
(clockwise) about the origin.
Draw the square in its new
position and label it with the
number of degrees positive
or negative that it rotated.

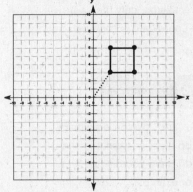

C. Rotate the original square
−180° (counterclockwise)
about the origin. Draw the
square in its new position
and label it with the number
of degrees positive or negative
that it rotated.

D. Rotate the original square −90° about the origin. Draw the
square in its new position and label it with the number of degrees
positive or negative that it rotated.

E. Rotate the original square +270° about the origin. Draw the
square in its new position and label it with the number of degrees
positive or negative that it rotated.

© 2008 Carnegie Learning, Inc.

15

Investigate Problem 2

1. Perform each rotation below on the triangle shown. Then draw each new triangle and label it with the number of degrees positive or negative that it rotated.

   Rotate the original triangle +90° about the origin.

   Rotate the original triangle –270° about the origin.

   Rotate the original triangle –180° about the origin.

   Rotate the original triangle –90° about the origin.

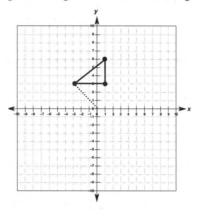

2. Each figure below has been rotated to a new position. The non-shaded figure is the *pre-image* (the original figure) and the shaded figure is the *image* (the translated figure). Describe each transformation.

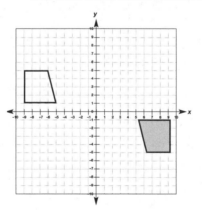
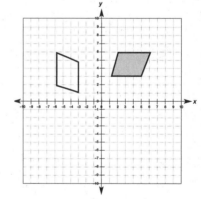

   The trapezoid was rotated _____ degrees about the origin.

   The parallelogram was rotated _____ degrees about the origin.

15

Secret Codes
Flipping, Stretching, and Shrinking

Objectives

In this lesson, you will:

- Graph reflections in a coordinate plane.
- Graph dilations in a coordinate plane.

Key Terms

- reflection
- line of reflection
- dilation
- scale factor

A third type of transformation is called a *reflection* because it is similar to looking at a reflection in a mirror. A **reflection** of a figure is a mirror image that is produced by flipping the figure over a line called the **line of reflection.**

Problem 1   Is It Still a Word?

You and your friends are using a secret code called a "mirror cipher." To write a message, you print each capital letter backwards and the words in order backwards. To decipher (figure out) the message, you just hold it up to a mirror. You are wondering which words are still words when you write them using the mirror cipher.

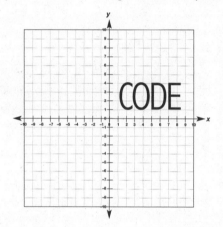

A. In order to perform a reflection of an object you must have a line to reflect in. Suppose that you reflect the word "CODE" in the *y*-axis. Is the reflection still a word? Use a complete sentence to explain.

B. Suppose that you reflect the word "CODE" in the *x*-axis. Is the reflection still a word? Use a complete sentence to explain.

1. Use the blank coordinate plane at the right to determine which capital letters look the same when reflected in a horizontal line such as the *x*-axis.

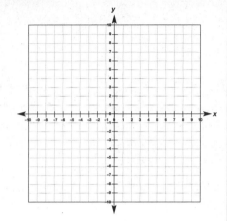

2. Use the blank coordinate plane at the right to determine which capital letters look the same when reflected in a vertical line such as the *y*-axis.

15

3. Write a secret message that can be deciphered when another person holds a mirror on a horizontal line. Write your message below.

4. Write a secret message that can be deciphered when another person holds a mirror on a vertical line. Write your message below.

5. Form a group with another partner team. Exchange your messages and use a mirror to decipher them. Write the other partner team's messages below.

© 2008 Carnegie Learning, Inc.

6. The triangle below is reflected in the line *m*. Notice that if you were to place a mirror perpendicular to the surface on the line *m* and looked into it you would see exactly what you would see without the mirror. The original △*ABC* is reflected in the line *m* to form △*A'B'C'*, read as "triangle *A* prime, *B* prime, *C* prime."

In the figure, the original triangle is called the *pre-image* and the reflected triangle is called the *image*.

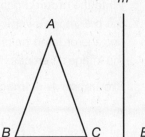

7. Find the image of the quadrilateral at the right when it is reflected in the *x*-axis. Label the vertices of the image.

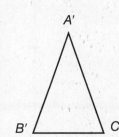

Write the ordered pairs of the pre-image's vertices and the ordered pairs of the image's vertices.

Pre-image	Image
A:	A':
B:	B':
C:	C':
D:	D':

Compare the *x*-coordinates of the pre-image's vertices with the *x*-coordinates of the image's vertices. Are they the same or are they opposites?

Compare the *y*-coordinates of the pre-image's vertices with the *y*-coordinates of the image's vertices. Are they the same or are they opposites?

Write a complete sentence that explains how the coordinates of the pre-image's vertices and the image's vertices of a reflection in the *x*-axis are related.

8. Find the image of the rhombus at the right when it is reflected in the y-axis. Label the vertices of the image.

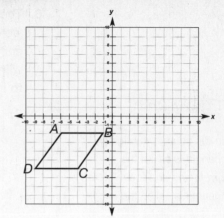

Write the ordered pairs of the pre-image's vertices and the ordered pairs of the image's vertices.

Pre-image	Image
A:	A′:
B:	B′:
C:	C′:
D:	D′:

Compare the x-coordinates of the pre-image's vertices with the x-coordinates of the image's vertices. Are they the same or are they opposites?

Compare the y-coordinates of the pre-image's vertices with the y-coordinates of the image's vertices. Are they the same or are they opposites?

Write a complete sentence that explains how the coordinates of the pre-image's vertices and the image's vertices of a reflection in the y-axis are related.

9. Find the image of the rectangle at the right when it is reflected in the line $x = -1$. Label the vertices of the image. How are the coordinates of the pre-image's vertices and the image's vertices related?

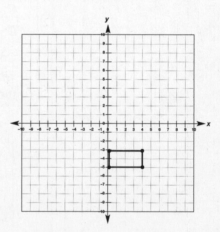

10. Find the image of the rectangle above when it is reflected in the line $y = 2$. Label the vertices of the image. How are the coordinates of the pre-image's vertices and the image's vertices related?

11. Each figure below has been reflected to a new position. The non-shaded figure is the pre-image and the shaded figure is the image. Draw the line in which the pre-image has been reflected to produce the image.

Problem 2   *Word Art*

You are creating a flyer to announce a meeting of the Cipher Club. You use a word processing program that allows you to stretch or shrink the words. For instance, you can change the words below to a larger size.

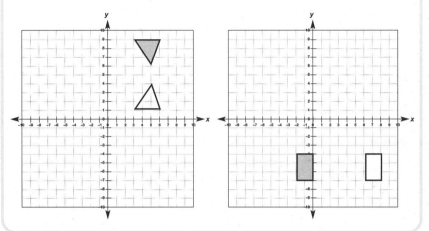

Meeting at 4 p.m.

Meeting at 4 p.m.

This type of transformation is called a *dilation*. A **dilation** reduces or enlarges the size of a figure proportionally. Scale drawings are a type of dilation. The new figure produced by a dilation is *similar* to the original figure. For all other transformations, the new figure produced is *congruent* to the original figure.

A. The words above were changed by a certain factor, called the **scale factor** of the dilation. Use a centimeter ruler to measure the height of the "M" in both figures. Then complete the statement below to find the scale factor.

$$\text{Scale factor} = \frac{\text{Height of larger M}}{\text{Height of smaller M}} = \frac{\boxed{} \text{ cm}}{\boxed{} \text{ cm}} = \boxed{}$$

Problem 2   Word Art

B. A scale factor *greater than 1* produces a new figure that is *larger* than the original. A scale factor *less than 1* produces a new figure that is *smaller* than the original. Find the scale factor that was used to obtain the shaded rectangle from the non-shaded rectangle.

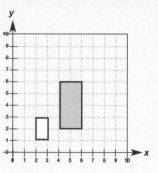

$$\text{Scale factor} = \frac{\text{Height of image}}{\text{Height of pre-image}} = \frac{\boxed{}\ \text{units}}{\boxed{}\ \text{units}} = \boxed{}$$

Investigate Problem 2

1. Dilations have a *center of dilation.* The corresponding vertices of the original and dilated figures should lie on the same line drawn from the center of dilation. The center of the dilation of the rectangles at the right is (0, 0). How do the coordinates of the original figure's vertices compare to the new figure's vertices?

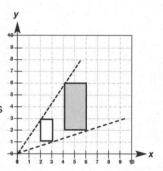

2. Dilate the quadrilateral below by a scale factor of 2 using the origin as the center of dilation. Label the vertices of the image.

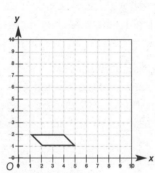

3. Dilate the trapezoid below by a scale factor of $\frac{1}{3}$ using the origin as the center of dilation. Label the vertices of the image.

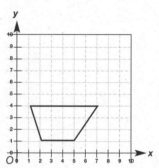

15.5 A Stitch in Time

Multiple Transformations

Objectives

In this lesson, you will:

- Graph multiple transformations in the coordinate plane.

Key Terms

- multiple transformation

By using *multiple transformations*, we can transform a figure into a similar figure anywhere in the coordinate plane. A **multiple transformation** is any combination of two or more translations, rotations, reflections, and dilations.

Problem 1 Programming a Cross Stitch Pattern

You are writing a computer program to automatically generate a cross-stitch pattern based on a single design element. The design element is the triangle at the right.

A. You place the bottom left corner of the pre-image of the design element at (–5, –5). Then you instruct the program to perform transformations on the design element as shown below. What two transformations would you need to perform on the design element to transform it into the design in the first quadrant?

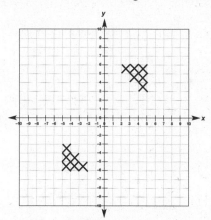

B. In which order would the transformations have to be performed? Write your answer using a complete sentence.

C. Is there more than one way to perform these transformations? Use a complete sentence to explain your answer

1. In the figure at the right, what two transformations would you need to perform on △*ABC* to transform it into △*A'B'C'*?

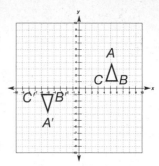

   In which order would the transformations have to be performed? Write your answer using a complete sentence.

   Is there more than one way to transform △*ABC* into △*A'B'C'*? Use a complete sentence to explain your answer.

2. Compare △*A'B'C'* in Question 1 to △*A'B'C'* shown at the right. How is the series of transformations from Question 1 different from the series of transformations in this question? Write your answer using a complete sentence.

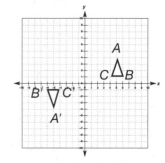

   How many transformations would you need to perform on △*ABC* to transform it into △*A'B'C'*?

   Is there more than one way to transform △*ABC* into △*A'B'C'*? Use a complete sentence to explain your answer.

3. The scale factor of trapezoid *ABCD* to trapezoid *A'B'C'D'* is $\frac{1}{2}$.

   How many transformations would you need to perform on trapezoid *ABCD* to transform it into trapezoid *A'B'C'D'*?

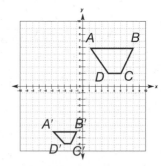

   Is there more than one way to transform *ABCD* into trapezoid *A'B'C'D'*? If so, list at least two ways.

15

4. In the coordinate plane below, perform the following transformations on rectangle *KEYS*. Label the vertices of the final image.

First, perform a vertical translation of +3 on rectangle *KEYS*.

Then reflect rectangle *KEYS* in the *y*-axis.

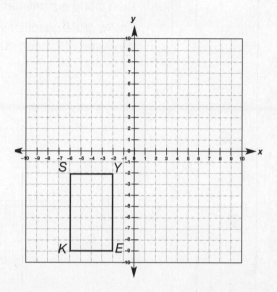

5. In the coordinate plane below, perform the following transformations on rhombus *BITS*. Label the vertices of the final image.

First, perform a horizontal translation of −2 on rhombus *BITS*.

Next, reflect rhombus *BITS* in the *x*-axis.

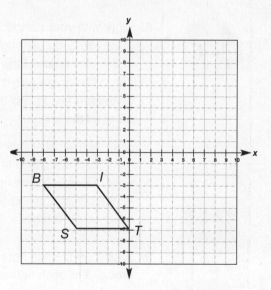

15

6. In the coordinate plane below, perform the following transformations on quadrilateral *BUGS*. Label the vertices of the final image.

First, perform a horizontal translation of –4 on quadrilateral *BUGS*.

Next, reflect quadrilateral *BUGS* in the line $x = 1$.

Then rotate quadrilateral *BUGS* –180° about the origin.

Finally, dilate quadrilateral *BUGS* using a scale factor of 2 with the center of dilation at the origin.

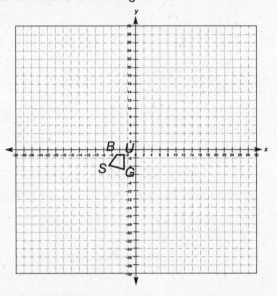

7. Form a group with another partner team and compare your answers to Questions 4 through 6. If you have any answers on which you do not agree, work together to find out why. Be prepared to share your answers with the rest of the class.

8. Work with your partner to draw two congruent figures in the coordinate plane at the right. Designate one figure as the pre-image and the other as the image.

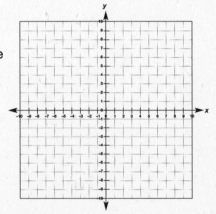

Draw two similar figures in the coordinate plane at the right. Designate one figure as the pre-image and the other as the image.

9. Exchange the two figures with the other partner team in your group. For each figure, list the transformations needed to transform the pre-image into the image.

Image is congruent to pre-image:

Image is similar to pre-image:

Looking Back at Chapter 15

Key Terms

ordered pair   p. 491
x-coordinate   p. 491
y-coordinate   p. 491
quadrant   p. 492
scale drawing   p. 497
scale   p. 499
scale model   p. 501

translation   p. 503
transformation   p. 503
pre-image   p. 505
image   p. 505
rotation   p. 506
center of rotation   p. 506
angle of rotation   p. 506

reflection   p. 509
line of reflection   p. 509
dilation   p. 513
scale factor   p. 513
multiple transformation   p. 515

Summary

Graphing in Four Quadrants of a Coordinate Plane (p. 492)

The x- and y-axes divide the coordinate plane into four quadrants. To identify the quadrant in which a point lies, determine whether the x-coordinate and y-coordinate are positive or negative.

Examples

The point (3, 9) lies in Quadrant I because both the x-coordinate and y-coordinate are positive.

The point (–7, 5) lies in Quadrant II because the x-coordinate is negative and the y-coordinate is positive.

The point (–4, –1) lies in Quadrant III because both the x-coordinate and y-coordinate are negative.

The point (6, –10) lies in Quadrant IV because the x-coordinate is positive and the y-coordinate is negative.

Plotting Points in a Coordinate Plane (p. 493)

To plot a point in a coordinate plane, move x units to the right or left from the origin. Then, from that point, move y units up or down. Draw the point.

Example

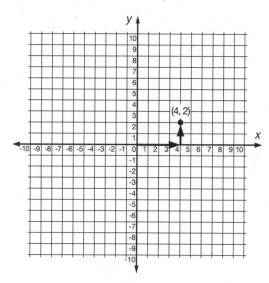

To plot the point (4, 2), start at the origin and move 4 units to the right then 2 units up.

Making Scale Drawings (p. 497)

To make a scale drawing, first draw a grid over the original object. Then create a grid with the same number of squares that are proportionally larger or smaller than the original grid's squares. Finally, copy each square from the original grid into the corresponding square of the larger or smaller grid.

Example

Original Grid

Scale Drawing

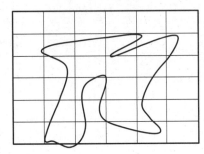

Making Scale Models (p. 501)

To make a scale model of a three-dimensional object, use proportions to find the scale.

Example

For a school project, you are making a model of the Washington Monument. The actual height of the monument is 169 meters. You want your model to be 13 centimeters tall. To determine the scale to use, write and solve a proportion.

$$\frac{1 \text{ cm}}{x \text{ m}} = \frac{13 \text{ cm}}{169 \text{ m}}$$

$$169 = 13x$$

$$13 = x$$

So, the scale that you want to use for your model is:
1 centimeter = 13 meters.

Graphing Translations in a Coordinate Plane (p. 505)

To graph a translation in a coordinate plane, slide the object either vertically or horizontally a specific number of units.

Examples

A horizontal translation of −3 units moves the rectangle 3 units to the left.

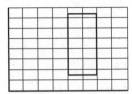 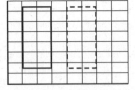

A vertical translation of 4 units moves the triangle up 4 units.

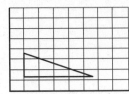 

Graphing Rotations in a Coordinate Plane (p. 506)

To graph a rotation in a coordinate plane, turn the object, either clockwise or counterclockwise, about a fixed point a certain number of degrees.

Example   To rotate the parallelogram below –90 degrees, turn the object about the origin in the counterclockwise direction.

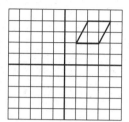 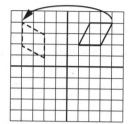

Graphing Reflections in a Coordinate Plane (p. 509)

To graph a reflection in a coordinate plane, flip the image over a line of reflection.

Example   To graph the reflection of the image below about the *y*-axis, flip the image over the *y*-axis.

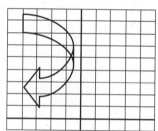 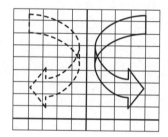

Graphing Dilations in a Coordinate Plane (p. 513)

To graph a dilation in a coordinate plane, reduce or enlarge the figure by a scale factor and graph it according to the center of dilation.

Example   To graph a dilation of the figure below, use a scale factor of 2 and the origin as the center of dilation.

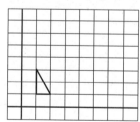 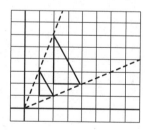

15

Glossary

A

absolute value

The absolute value of a number is the distance between zero and the point that represents the number on a real number line. The absolute value of a number is always greater than or equal to zero.

Examples The absolute value of –8, written as |–8|, is equal to 8.

The absolute value of 8, written as |8|, is equal to 8.

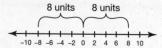

acute angle

An acute angle is an angle whose measure is greater than 0 degrees and less than 90 degrees.

Examples Angles A and B are acute angles.

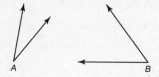

acute triangle

An acute triangle is a triangle with three acute interior angles.

Example Angles A, B, and C are acute angles, so triangle ABC is an acute triangle.

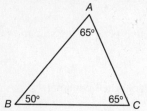

addend

An addend is one of the numbers being added in an addition problem.

Example In the addition problem 14 + 3 = 17, 14 and 3 are the addends.

additive inverse

The additive inverse of a number is the number such that the sum of the given number and its additive inverse is 0 (the additive identity).

Example The numbers –5 and 5 are additive inverses because –5 + 5 = 0.

adjacent angles

Adjacent angles are angles that share a common side and a common vertex and lie on opposite sides of their common side.

Examples Angle BAC and angle CAD are adjacent angles. Angle FEG and angle GEH are adjacent angles.

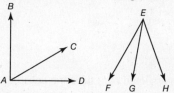

adjacent sides

Adjacent sides of a figure are sides that have a common endpoint called the vertex.

Examples In polygon ABCD:

Sides AB and BC are adjacent sides.

Sides BC and CD are adjacent sides.

Sides CD and DA are adjacent sides.

Sides DA and AB are adjacent sides.

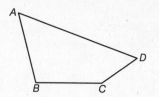

algebraic expression

An algebraic expression consists of numbers, variables, and operations to be performed.

Example If one pizza costs $7 and the pizza shop charges a $2.50 delivery charge, the cost of buying one or more pizzas can be represented by the algebraic expression 7p + 2.50, where p is the number of pizzas purchased.

alternate exterior angles

When two lines are intersected by a third line called the transversal, alternate exterior angles are angles that lie outside the lines and on opposite sides of the transversal. If the original lines are parallel then the alternate exterior angles are congruent.

Example Lines L_1 and L_2 are parallel lines intersected by transversal T. Angle 1 and angle 2 are alternate exterior angles that are congruent. This means that if $m\angle 1 = 103°$, then $m\angle 2 = 103°$.

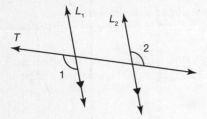

alternate interior angles

When two lines are intersected by a third line called the transversal, alternate interior angles are angles that lie inside the lines and on opposite sides of the transversal. If the original lines are parallel then the alternate interior angles are congruent.

Example Lines L_1 and L_2 are parallel lines intersected by transversal T. Angle 1 and angle 2 are alternate interior angles that are congruent. This means that if $m\angle 1 = 50°$, then $m\angle 2 = 50°$.

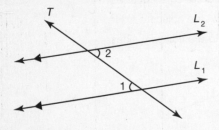

angle

An angle is a figure that is formed by two rays that extend from a common point called the vertex.

Examples Angles A, B, and C.

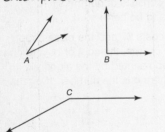

angle of rotation

The angle of rotation is the number of degrees through which a rotation occurs.

Example In the rotation shown, the angle of rotation is 90 degrees.

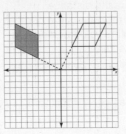

area

The area of a figure is the number of square units needed to cover the figure.

Examples The area of the rectangle is 18 square units.

The area of the triangle is 10 square units.

The area of circle is about 19.63 square units.

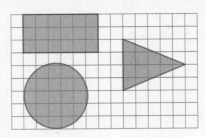

area of a circle

The area A of a circle is equal to pi times the square of the radius r of the circle.

$A = \pi r^2$.

Example In circle O, the radius is 6 centimeters. The area of the circle is
$A = \pi r^2 = \pi\left(6^2\right) \approx 113.1$ square centimeters.

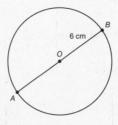

area of a parallelogram

The area A of a parallelogram is equal to the length of the base b multiplied by the height h.

$A = bh$

*CAUTION: The height is not necessarily equal to any of the sides!

Example In parallelogram $ABCD$, the length of base AB is 6 feet, the length of side AD is 4.24 feet, and the height (the length of segment BE) is 3 feet. So, the area of parallelogram $ABCD$ is

$A = bh = (6)(3) = 18$ square feet.

Sliding triangle BEC to the other side of the parallelogram forms a rectangle. So, the area of parallelogram $ABCD$ is the same as the area of the rectangle, which is $A = bh = (6)(3) = 18$ square feet.

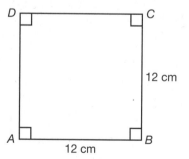

area of a square

The area A of a square is equal to the side length, s, multiplied by itself: $A = (s)(s) = s^2$

Example In square $ABCD$, the length of each side is 12 centimeters. So, the area of the square is $A = (12)(12) = 144$ square centimeters.

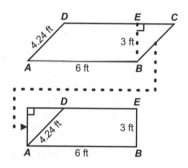

area of a trapezoid

The area A of a trapezoid is equal to one-half of the height, h, multiplied by the sum of the lengths of the bases, b_1 and b_2: $A = \frac{1}{2}h(b_1 + b_2)$.

Example In trapezoid $ABCD$, the base AD has a length of 14 millimeters, the base BC has a length of 8 millimeters, and the height BE is 7 millimeters. So, the area of trapezoid $ABCD$ is

$\frac{1}{2}(BE)(AD + BC) = \frac{1}{2}(7)(14 + 8) = 77$ square millimeters.

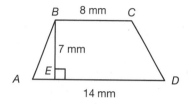

area of a triangle

The area A of a triangle is equal to one-half of the length of its base b multiplied by its height h:

$A = \frac{1}{2}bh.$

*CAUTION: The height is not necessarily equal to the length of any of the sides!

Example In triangle DEF, the length of base DF is 8 inches and the height EG is 3 inches. So, the area of triangle $DEF = A = \frac{1}{2}bh = \frac{1}{2}(8)(3) = 12$ square inches.

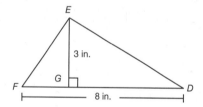

arithmetic

Arithmetic is the study of the positive integers 1, 2, 3, 4, 5, ... under the operations of addition, subtraction, multiplication, and division.

Examples $5 + 4$ $\qquad$ $7(8) - 2$

associative property of addition

The associative property of addition states that the way in which the terms of a sum are grouped does not change the sum. $(a + b) + c = a + (b + c)$:

Example Both $(3 + 4) + 5$ and $3 + (4 + 5)$ are equal to 12.

average

The average of a data set is the sum of all of the values of the data set divided by the number of values in the data set. The average is also called the mean.

Example The mean of the numbers 3, 7, 17, and 33 is found by adding the values and dividing by the number of values, 4.

$$\frac{3+7+17+33}{4} = \frac{60}{4} = 15$$

axis

An axis is one of two number lines that intersect to form the Cartesian coordinate plane. The horizontal axis, or x-axis, represents the line $y = 0$. The vertical axis, or y-axis, represents the line $x = 0$.

Example

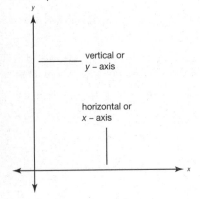

vertical or
y – axis

horizontal or
x – axis

B

bar graph

A bar graph is a graph that uses parallel bars to represent data. The heights of the bars represent quantities from the data set.

Example The bar graph shows John's earnings over a four-week period.

bar notation

Bar notation is used to write a decimal with repeating digits by placing a bar over the set of digits that repeat.

Example The fraction $\frac{1}{3}$ can be written as a decimal using bar notation: $\frac{1}{3} = 0.\overline{3}$.

base of a geometric figure

The base of a geometric figure is the side or face to which an altitude is drawn, or is considered to be drawn.

Example Altitude BD is drawn to side AC, so side AC is the base of triangle ABC.

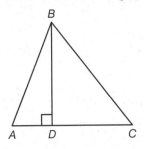

base of a power

The base of a power is the number or variable that is repeatedly multiplied.

Example In the expression 3^5, the number 3 is the base.

$$3^5 = (3)(3)(3)(3)(3) = 243$$

base ten pieces

Base-ten pieces are square blocks used to represent decimals.

1 one-piece

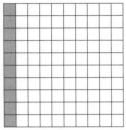

1 tenth-piece

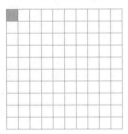

1 hundredth-piece

Example The base-ten pieces represent the decimal 1.23

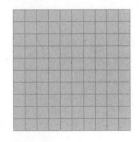

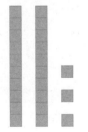

benchmark percent

A benchmark percent is a common percent that you can use to find the percent of any number.

Example To find 21% of 200, use the benchmark percent of 1%.

$$1\% \text{ of } 200 = \frac{1}{100} \times 200 = 2$$

21% of 200 = (1% of 200) × 21 = 2 × 21 = 42

box-and-whisker plot

A box-and-whisker plot is a visual display of data that organizes the data values into four groups using the upper and lower bounds, the median, and the upper and lower quartiles.

Example The box-and-whisker plot compares the test scores from two algebra classes.

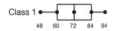

break-even point

The break-even point is the point at which expenses are equal to earnings. No profit or loss is made.

Example Suppose that the revenue R is given by $R = 0.75x$ and the cost C is given by $C = 0.25x + 30$. To calculate the break-even point, set the expression for revenue equal to the expression for cost.

0.75x = 0.25x + 30
0.50x = 30
   x = 60

So, in order to break even, 60 items must be sold. The break-even point is (60, 45).

C

center of a circle

The center of a circle is a fixed point in the plane that is at an equal distance from every point on the circle.

Example Point *H* is the center of the circle.

center of a regular polygon

The center of a regular polygon is the fixed point in the plane that is at an equal distance from each vertex of the polygon.

Example Point *S* is the center of regular polygon *POLYGN*.

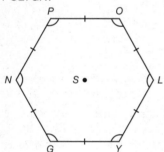

center of a sphere

The center of a sphere is a fixed point in space that is at an equal distance from every point on the sphere.

Example Point *A* is the center of the sphere.

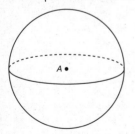

center of rotation

The center of rotation is the fixed point about which a figure is rotated.

Example In the rotation shown, the center of rotation is the point (0, 0).

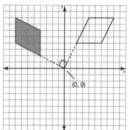

circle graph

A circle graph is a visual representation of data that compares parts of a whole to a whole. The area of the circle represents the whole, and sectors of the circle represent parts of the whole.

Example The circle graph shows how Kelly spends her weekly allowance. The area of the whole circle represents Kelly's whole allowance, and the sectors of the circle represent the different ways that she spent her allowance.

How Kelly Spends Her Allowance

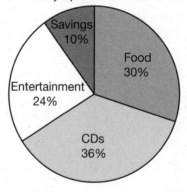

circumference

The circumference C of a circle is equal to π multiplied by the diameter d, or π multiplied by twice the radius r.

$C = \pi d = 2\pi r$

Example In circle O, the radius OA is 5 centimeters. The circumference of circle O is

$2\pi r = 2(\pi)(5) = 10\pi \approx 31.4$ centimeters.

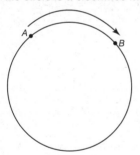

clockwise motion

A clockwise motion is a movement in the same direction of rotation as that in which the hands of a clock move around the clock face.

Example The movement from point A to point B on the circle is a clockwise motion.

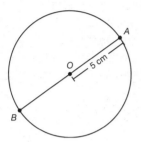

coefficient

In a term containing a number multiplied by one or more variables, the number is the coefficient of the term.

Example In the expression $24x^2$, the number 24 is the coefficient.

collinear points

Collinear points are points that lie on the same line.

Examples Points A, B, and C are collinear points. Points D, E, and F are not collinear points.

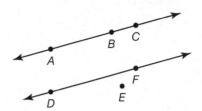

column

A column in a spreadsheet is a vertical section of the spreadsheet.

Example Column 1 is highlighted in the table below.

	1	2	3	4	5	6
A	A1					
B	B1					
C	C1					
D	D1					
E	E1					

commission

A commission is a fee or a percent of earnings that are paid to a sales representative or an agent for services rendered.

Example A salesperson is to receive a 5% commission on her sales. Suppose that she sells $500 worth of merchandise. Her commission will be $25: 5% of 500 = (0.05)(500) = 25.

common denominator

Two or more fractions have a common denominator if their denominators are the same.

Examples The fractions $\dfrac{3}{5}$ and $\dfrac{4}{5}$ have a common denominator of 5. The fractions $\dfrac{1}{5x}$ and $\dfrac{2}{5x}$ have a common denominator of $5x$.

common factor

A common factor is a whole number that is a factor of two or more integers or expressions.

Examples Because $12 = (4)(3)$ and $24 = (8)(3)$, 3 is a common factor of 12 and 24. Because $35xy = 35(x)(y)$ and $16x = 16(x)$, x is a common factor of $35xy$ and $16x$.

Glossary

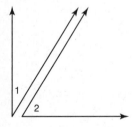 below is the left sidebar tab:

Glossary

common multiple

A common multiple is a multiple that is shared by two or more integers or expressions.

Examples A common multiple of 8 and 12 is 24 because (8)(3) = 24 and (12)(2) = 24. A common multiple of 6x and 4x is 36x because (6x)(6) = 36x and (4x)(9) = 36x.

commutative property of addition

The commutative property of addition states that the order in which the terms of a sum are added does not change the sum.

$a + b = b + a$

Example Both 35 + 43 and 43 + 35 are equal to 78.

commutative property of multiplication

The commutative property of multiplication states that the order in which two factors in a product are multiplied does not change the product.

$ab = ba$

Example Both 6 • 24 and 24 • 6 are equal to 144.

complementary events

Two events are complementary if one event or the other event can occur, but not both.

Example A jar contains red, blue, and green marbles. Choosing a red marble and not choosing a red marble are complementary events.

complementary angles

Complementary angles are two angles whose sum is 90 degrees.

Example Angle 1 and angle 2 are complementary angles. If $m \angle 1 = 32°$, then $m \angle 2 = 90° – 32° = 58°$.

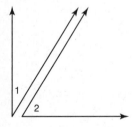

complex fraction

A complex fraction is a fraction that has a fraction in the numerator or the denominator or both.

Example The fraction $\dfrac{\frac{1}{2}}{\frac{7}{8}}$ is a complex fraction.

composite figures

A composite figure is a figure that can be divided into several common figures.

Example The figure is a composite figure because it can be separated into a rectangle and two half-circles.

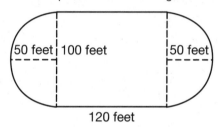

120 feet

composite number

A composite number is a whole number that is divisible by 1, itself, and at least one other positive number.

Example Because 35 is divisible by 1, 5, 7, and 35, it is a composite number.

compound event

A compound event is an event made up of two or more simple events.

Example A person has 3 pairs of slacks, 6 shirts, and 2 pairs of shoes. Choosing an outfit by choosing slacks, a shirt, and a pair of shoes is a compound event.

concentration

The concentration of a solution is the strength of the solution measured as a percent.

Example The concentration of lemon juice in a pitcher of lemonade is 40%.

© 2008 Carnegie Learning, Inc.

cone

A cone is a solid with a circular base and a vertex that is not in the same plane as the base. The lateral surface, the surface not including the base, is made up of all segments that connect the vertex with points on the edge of the base. The height is the perpendicular distance between the vertex and the plane that contains the base.

Example The radius of the base of the cone is 4 inches and the height is 8 inches.

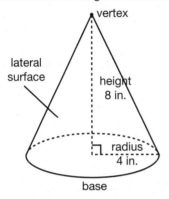

congruent

Two figures are congruent if they have the same size and the same shape.

Example Triangle *ABC* and triangle *DEF* are congruent triangles.

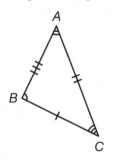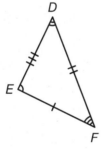

converse

The converse of an if-then statement is the statement that results from interchanging the hypothesis (the "if" part) and the conclusion (the "then" part) of the original statement.

Example The converse of the statement "If *a* = 0 or *b* = 0, then *ab* = 0" is "If *ab* = 0, then *a* = 0 or *b* = 0."

coordinate plane

A coordinate plane is a plane formed by the intersection of a vertical real number line and a horizontal real number line. The vertical number line is the *y*-axis and the horizontal number line is the *x*-axis. The number lines intersect at right angles and the point of intersection is the origin.

Example The origin is labeled on the coordinate plane below.

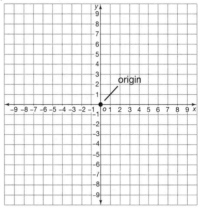

coordinate system

A Cartesian coordinate system is a method of representing the location of a point using an ordered pair of real numbers of the form (*x*, *y*).

Example Point *J* is represented by the ordered pair (5, 4).

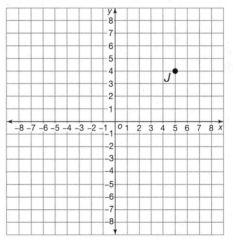

Glossary

coordinates

The coordinates of a point are an ordered pair of real numbers of the form (x, y) that are used to specify the location of a point in a coordinate plane. The first number in an ordered pair is the x-coordinate, and the second number is the y-coordinate.

Example The coordinates of point J are (5, 4).

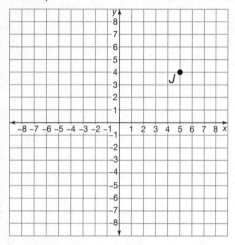

counterclockwise motion

A counterclockwise motion is a movement in the opposite direction of rotation as that in which the hands of a clock move around the clock face.

Example The movement from point A to point B on the circle is a counterclockwise motion.

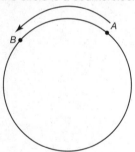

cube

A cube is a polyhedron with six square faces.

Example The polyhedron below is a cube.

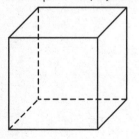

cube of a number

The cube of a number is the product that results when the number is used three times as a factor.

Example The cube of 4 is 64 because 4^3 is equal to (4)(4)(4), or 64.

cube root

The cube root of a given number is a number that, when cubed, equals the given number.

Example The cube root of 27 is 3 because 3^3 is equal to 27.

customary system of measurement

The customary system of measurement is the system commonly used in the United States to measure length, weight, and capacity.

Examples Common units of length in the customary system are inches, feet, and miles.

Common units of weight in the customary system are ounces and pounds.

Common units of capacity in the customary system are cups, pints, and gallons.

cylinder

A cylinder is a solid with two parallel bases that are congruent circles. The height of the cylinder is the perpendicular distance between its bases. The radius of the cylinder is the radius of the base.

Example The cylinder has a height of 7 feet and a radius of 3 feet.

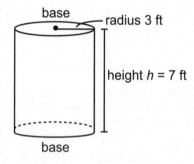

base

radius 3 ft

height h = 7 ft

base

decimal

A decimal is a number that is written in the base-ten place value system. A decimal can be used to represent a fraction or mixed number.

Example The mixed number $18\frac{6}{10}$ can be represented by the decimal 18.6.

decimal point

A decimal point is a period that separates the whole number part and the fractional part of a decimal. When reading a decimal, the decimal point is read as "and."

Example In the decimal 25.63, the period between 25 and 63 separates the whole number part 25 and the fractional part $\frac{63}{100}$. The decimal is read as "twenty-five and sixty-three hundredths."

degree of an angle

A degree is a unit of measure of an angle.

Examples Angle *H* has a measure of 90 degrees. Angle *B* has a measure of 12 degrees.

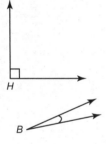

denominator

The denominator is the bottom number in a fraction.

Examples In the fraction $\frac{3}{4}$, the denominator is 4. In the fraction $\frac{1}{2}$, the denominator is 2.

dependent event

Dependent events are events in which the outcome of one event affects the outcome of the other event.

Example Choosing a card from a standard deck and, without replacing it, choosing another card are dependent events.

dependent variable

A dependent variable, or output value of a function, is a variable whose value is determined by an independent variable, or input value of a function.

Example In the relationship between driving time and distance traveled, distance is represented by the dependent variable *d* because the value of *d* depends on the value of the driving time *t*.

diagonal

A diagonal is a line segment that connects any two non-adjacent vertices.

Example Segment *FH* is a diagonal of quadrilateral *FGHI*.

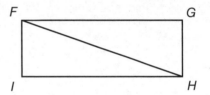

diameter

The diameter of a circle is the distance across the circle through the center. The diameter is equal to twice the radius of the circle.

Example In the circle, *O* is the center of the circle, segment *AB* is a diameter, segment *AO* is a radius and segment *OB* is a radius. The diameter *AB* is equal to twice the radius *OA*. The radius *OA* is 6 centimeters, so the diameter *AB* is 12 centimeters.

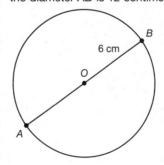

difference

A difference is the result of subtracting one quantity from another.

Example The difference of 85 and 12, 85 − 12, is 73.

dilation

A dilation is a transformation of a figure in which the figure stretches or shrinks with respect to a fixed point. The scale factor of a dilation is the ratio of a side length of the dilated figure to the original figure. An enlargement or reduction of a photo is an example of a dilation.

Example The original dark hexagon is dilated to produce the light hexagon by a scale factor of $\frac{1}{2}$ because $\frac{BC}{AC} = \frac{2}{4} = \frac{1}{2}$.

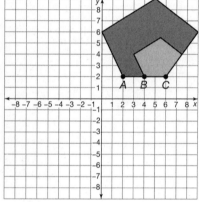

dimension

A dimension is a measure of the length, width, or height of an object.

Examples The dimensions of a carpet are 5 feet by 4 feet. This means that the length of the carpet is 5 feet and the width of the carpet is 4 feet.

The dimensions of a box are 5 inches by 4 inches by 6 inches. This means that the length of the box is 5 inches, the width of the box is 4 inches, and the height of the box is 6 inches.

discount

A discount is a decrease in the price of an item.

Example A music store may offer a 10% discount on new CDs.

distributive property

The distributive property states that for any numbers a, b, and c it is true that $a(b + c) = ab + ac$.

Example Both 2(3 + 4) and 2 • 3 + 2 • 4 are equal to 14.

dividend

In a division problem, the dividend is the number that is being divided.

Example In the division problem 135 ÷ 9 = 15 , 135 is the dividend.

divisible

A number p is divisible by another number q if the number q divides the number p evenly with no remainder.

Example The number 72 is divisible by 8 because 8 divides 72 evenly with no remainder.

divisor

In a division problem, the divisor is the number by which another number is being divided.

Example In the division problem 135 ÷ 9 = 15, the number 9 is the divisor.

Glossary

domain of a function

The domain of a function is the set of all possible input values for the function.

Example For the function $y = x^2$, the domain is the set of all real numbers.

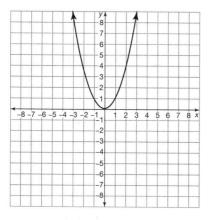

E

earnings

Earnings are the amount of pay received in exchange for work performed.

Example Juan worked 6 hours today. His rate of pay is $8.00 per hour, so his earnings are $48.00.

edge

An edge is a line segment common to two sides of a three-dimensional figure.

Example In the right prism, segment *ED* and segment *DG* are edges.

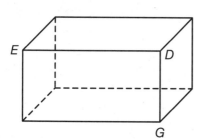

endpoint

An endpoint is a point at which a segment begins or ends, or the point at which a ray begins.

Examples Points *A* and *B* are endpoints of segment *AB*. Point *C* is the endpoint of ray *CD*.

equation

An equation is a statement that is formed by placing an equals sign between two expressions.

Example The statement $10 = 2x + 3$ is an equation.

equilateral triangle

An equilateral triangle is a triangle that has all three sides equal. The measure of each interior angle of an equilateral triangle is 60 degrees.

Example Triangle *ABC* is an equilateral triangle, so the measure of angle 1 is 60 degrees, the measure of angle 2 is 60 degrees, and the measure of angle 3 is 60 degrees.

$m \angle 1 = 60°$, $m \angle 2 = 60°$, and $m \angle 3 = 60°$

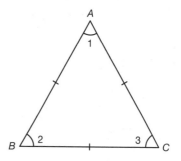

equivalent fractions

Equivalent fractions are fractions that represent the same part-to-whole relationship.

Example The fractions $\frac{1}{2}$ and $\frac{2}{4}$ are equivalent fractions.

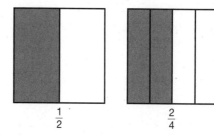

equivalent ratios

Equivalent ratios are ratios that have the same value.

Example The ratio of 3 boys to 5 girls and the ratio of 6 boys to 10 girls are equivalent ratios.

estimate

To estimate is to use rounding to find an answer that is close to the exact answer.

Example To estimate 697 + 309, round 697 to 700 and round 309 to 300. Then you can estimate that 697 + 309 is approximately 700 + 300, or 1000.

evaluate

To evaluate an expression is to find the value of an expression by replacing each variable with a given value, and simplifying the result.

Example To evaluate $3x + 6$ when $x = 5$, replace the x by 5, and then simplify.

$(3)(5) + 6 = 15 + 6$
$\qquad\qquad = 21$

even number

An even number is any integer that is divisible by 2.

Example The numbers –4, –2, 0, 2, and 4 are even numbers.

event

A simple event is a collection of outcomes of an experiment. An outcome is one possible result of an experiment.

Example Rolling a number cube and getting a 1, 2, 3, 4, 5, or 6 is an event. An outcome is rolling a number cube and getting a 2.

expanded form of a number

The expanded form of a number is the number written as a sum of each digit multiplied by the place value of the digit.

Example The number 13,297 can be written in expanded form as shown below.

$13,297 =$
$(1 \times 10,000) + (3 \times 1,000) + (2 \times 100) + (9 \times 10) + (7 \times 1)$

experimental probability

Experimental probability is probability based on repeated trials of an experiment.

Example If a number cube was rolled 12 times and the number 5 appeared 3 times, the experimental probability is $\frac{3}{12}$ or $\frac{1}{4}$.

exponent

An exponent indicates the number of times an expression is multiplied by itself; that is, the number of times the base is used as a factor.

Example In the expression 10^3, the number 3 is the exponent. This indicates that the base 10 is used as a factor 3 times: $10^3 = (10)(10)(10) = 1000$.

expression

An expression is any symbolic mathematical form that may include constants, variables, and operators.

Examples Three expressions are shown below.

$\quad 5y$

$4x - 2$

$6^3 + 8$

extremes

The extremes of a proportion are the two outside quantities of a proportion.

Example In the proportion
3 dimes: 5 quarters:: 15 dimes: 25 quarters,
the extremes are the outside quantities, 3 dimes and 25 quarters.

Glossary

F

face

A face is a side of a three-dimensional figure.

Example The rectangle *FACE* and the rectangle *FARM* are faces of the right prism. A right prism has a total of six faces.

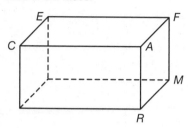

factor of a number

A factor of a number is a number that evenly divides the given number with no remainder.

Example The numbers 1, 2, 4, 5, 8, 10, 20, and 40 are positive factors of 40, because each number evenly divides 40.

factor pair

A factor pair is two natural numbers other than zero that are multiplied together to produce another number.

Example One factor pair for the number 16 is 2 and 8.

factor tree

A factor tree is a diagram that shows the prime factorization of a number.

Example The factor tree shows the prime factorization of 300: 300 = (2)(2)(3)(5)(5).

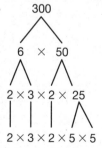

favorable outcome

A favorable outcome is a specific outcome chosen for a particular event.

Example When finding the probability of rolling an even number on a number cube numbered from 1 to 6, the favorable outcomes are 2, 4, and 6.

fixed cost

Fixed costs are expenses that remain the same, regardless of the quantity of a product that is produced or sold.

Example A company makes and sells computers. The company must pay wages, insurance, utilities, and telephone expenses each month. These expenses are fixed costs because they remain the same regardless of the number of computers that the company makes.

formula

A formula is an equation that states a general rule.

Example In the formula $d = rt$, d is the distance, r is the rate of speed, and t is the time.

fraction

A fraction is a number in the form $\frac{a}{b}$ where a and b are integers and b cannot equal zero.

Example The number $\frac{5}{12}$ is a fraction.

fraction in lowest terms

A fraction in lowest terms is a fraction whose numerator and denominator have no common factors.

Examples The fraction $\frac{2}{5}$ is in lowest terms because the numerator and denominator have no common factors. The fraction $\frac{4}{10}$ is not in lowest terms because the numerator and denominator have a common factor of 2.

Glossary

frequency

The frequency of a data set is the number of times that an item is repeated in the data set. The frequency can also be the number of items in a given category of a data set.

Example In the data set of test scores below, 95 occurs 3 times, so 95 has a frequency of 3.

95, 94, 78, 85, 94, 95, 83, 95

frequency table

A frequency table is a table that organizes data values into intervals.

Example

Data Intervals	0 - 0.9	1 - 1.9	2 - 2.9	3 - 3.9
Tally	II	I	III	I
Frequency	2	1	3	1

function

A function is a relation for which every input value has one and only one output value.

Example The relation $y = 2x + 1$ is a function because every value of x will have one and only one output value y.

function notation

Function notation is a notation used to write functions such that the dependent variable is replaced with the name of the function such as $f(x)$.

Example The equation $y = 4 + x$ written in function notation is $f(x) = 4 + x$.

G

graph

A graph is a visual representation of the relationship between two sets of values as points in a coordinate plane.

Example

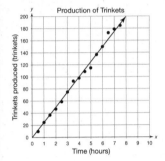

greatest common factor

The greatest common factor of two whole numbers is the largest whole number that is a factor of both numbers. The greatest common factor is abbreviated as GCF.

Example To find the greatest common factor of 24 and 60, list all of the factors of each number.
Factors of 24: 1, 2, 3, 4, 6, 8, 12, and 24
Factors of 60: 1, 2, 3, 4, 5, 6, 10, 12, 15, 20, 30 and 60
The largest factor common to both lists is 12, so 12 is the greatest common factor of 24 and 60.

gross pay

Gross pay is the total amount of money an employee earns before any taxes or deductions are subtracted.

Example Nadia's gross pay was $2400 per month.

H

height of a parallelogram

In a parallelogram, the height is the perpendicular distance between the two bases.

Example In parallelogram *PRLM*, the height is the length of segment *AG*.

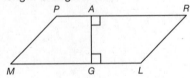

height of a trapezoid

In a trapezoid, the height is the perpendicular distance between the two bases.

Example In trapezoid *TRAP*, the height is the length of segment *HG*.

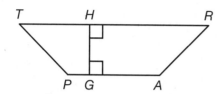

height of a triangle

In a triangle, the height is the perpendicular distance from a vertex to the side opposite the vertex.

Example In triangle *MAH*, the height is the length of segment *AT*.

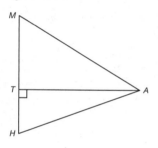

hemisphere

A hemisphere is a half of a sphere.

Example The figure below is a hemisphere.

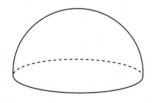

hexagon

A hexagon is a polygon with six sides.

Examples The polygon POINTS and the polygon BISECT are both hexagons.

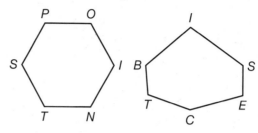

histogram

A histogram is a visual representation of a data set that uses bars to show the frequency of the items in the data set.

Example You can use a histogram to display the average number of text messages sent per day by participants in a survey.

horizontal axis

The horizontal axis is the *x*-axis in a coordinate plane.

Example

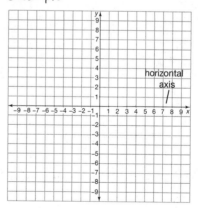

Glossary

hypotenuse of a right triangle

In a right triangle, the hypotenuse is the side of the triangle that is opposite the right angle.

Examples In triangle ABC, angle A is the right angle, so side BC is the hypotenuse. In triangle DEF, angle F is the right angle, so side DE is the hypotenuse.

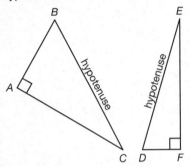

I

image

An image is a new figure formed by a transformation.

Example The figure below on the right is the image that has been translated +3 units horizontally.

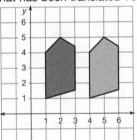

improper fraction

An improper fraction is a fraction whose numerator is greater than its denominator.

Examples The fractions $\frac{6}{5}$ and $\frac{11}{5}$ are improper fractions.

independent events

Independent events are two events in which the outcome of the first event does not affect the probability of the second event.

Example Flipping a coin and getting heads and rolling a number cube and rolling 5 are independent events because the outcome of "heads" doesn't affect the probability of "rolling a 5."

independent variable

An independent variable, or input value, is a variable whose value is not determined by another variable.

Example In the relationship between driving time and distance traveled, time is represented by the independent variable t because the value of t does not depend on any variable.

indirect measurement

Indirect measurement uses similar triangles and a proportion to measure an object that is not easily measured directly.

Example The height of the flagpole can be measured using similar triangles.

$$\frac{4 \text{ meters}}{3 \text{ meters}} = \frac{x \text{ meters}}{12 \text{ meters}}$$

The height of the flagpole is 16 meters.

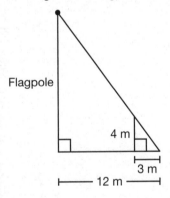

input

An input value of a function f is the x-value, or independent variable, of the function.

Example For the function $f(x) = x + 2$, the input values are all of the x-values.

Glossary

input-output table

An input-output table shows the relationship between the input values and the output values of a function.

Example The input-output table shows the relationship between the time traveled and the distance traveled for the function $d = 55t$.

Time Traveled (hours)	Distance Traveled (miles)
1	55
2	110
3	165
4	220

integer

An integer is any of the numbers . . .
−4, −3, −2, −1, 0, 1, 2, 3, 4, ...
Integers include all of the whole numbers and their additive inverses.

Examples The numbers −12, 0, and 30 are integers.

intercept

An intercept is the x- or y- coordinate of the point where a graph crosses the x- or y-axis.

Examples In the graph below, the x-intercept is 1 and the y-intercept is −3.

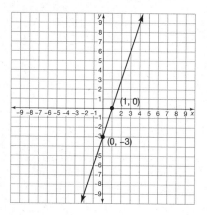

interest

Interest is the amount that is charged for borrowing money or the amount that is earned from saving money. Interest is usually given as a percent.

Example A bank may offer a savings account with 3% interest. This means that the bank will pay 3% of the amount in the savings account in a certain period of time.

intersect

Two lines or line segments intersect if they cross each other.

Example Line segment AB intersects line segment CD at point E.

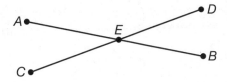

interval of a graph

An interval of a graph is the distance between two consecutive horizontal or two consecutive vertical grid lines on the graph.

Example In the graph, the x-interval is 2 and the y-interval is 20.

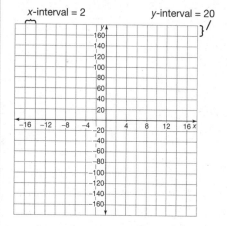

irrational number

An irrational number is a number that cannot be written as $\frac{a}{b}$, where a and b are integers.

Examples The numbers $\sqrt{2}$, 0.313113111..., and π are irrational numbers.

Glossary

irregular polygon

An irregular polygon is a polygon whose sides are not the same length and whose angles are not the same measure.

Example The sides of this polygon are not the same length, and the angles of this polygon are not the same measure.

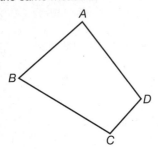

isosceles triangle

An isosceles triangle is a triangle with at least two congruent sides.

Example Triangle *ABC* is an isosceles triangle.

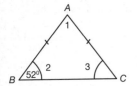

L

label

A label is a written description that identifies an object.

Example In the graph, the label on the *x*-axis is "Time (hours)" and the label on the *y*-axis is "Earnings (dollars)."

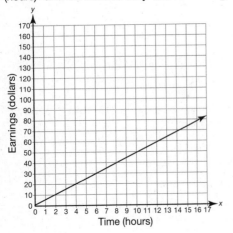

least common denominator

The least common denominator of two or more fractions is the least common multiple of their denominators.

Example The least common denominator of the fractions $\frac{3}{8}$, $\frac{2}{3}$, and $\frac{1}{6}$ is 24.

least common multiple

The least common multiple of two whole numbers is the smallest whole number that is a multiple of both numbers. The least common multiple is abbreviated as LCM.

Example To find the least common multiple of 4 and 6, list some of the multiples of each number.

Multiples of 4: 4, 8, 12, 16, 20, 24, 28, 32, 36

Multiples of 6: 6, 12, 18, 24, 30, 36

The smallest multiple common to both lists is 12, so the least common multiple of 4 and 6 is 12.

legs of a right triangle

In a right triangle, the legs are the two sides of the triangle that form the right angle.

Example In triangle *ABC*, angle *A* is the right angle, so sides *AB* and *AC* are the legs of the triangle.

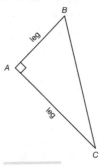

length

The length of a segment is the distance from one endpoint to the other. Length is often measured in centimeters, inches, meters, feet, kilometers, or miles.

Example In trapezoid *TRAP*, the length of base *TR* is 3 inches and the length of base *PA* is 1.5 inches.

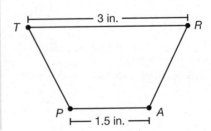

Glossary

like terms

Like terms are terms that have identical variables and exponents. Two or more constant terms are considered to be like terms.

Example In the expression $3c + 2c^2 + 5c^2 + 4c$, $3c$ and $4c$ are like terms, and $2c^2$ and $5c^2$ are like terms.

line

A line is made up of points that extend infinitely in two opposite directions. A line is straight and has only one dimension.

Example The line below can be called line k or line AB.

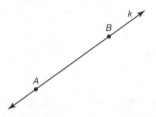

line graph

A line graph is a graph that has consecutive data points connected by a straight line.

Example The graph below is a line graph of John's scores on 9 math tests.

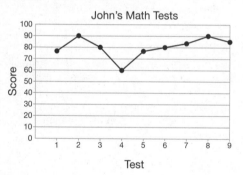

line of best fit

A line of best fit is a straight line that best represents the data on a scatter plot.

Example The line $y = \dfrac{7}{10}x + \dfrac{9}{10}$ is a line of best fit for the points (1, 1), (1, 2), (2, 2), (2, 3), (3, 3), (4, 3), (4, 4), (5, 4), (5, 5).

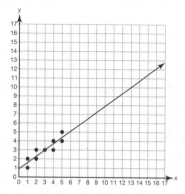

line of reflection

A line of reflection is a line in which a figure is reflected.

Example The triangle is reflected in line k, so line k is a line of reflection.

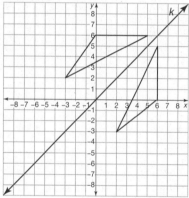

line segment

A line segment is a portion of a line between two points, called the endpoints.

Example The line segment below is named segment AB or segment BA.

A B

linear equation

A linear equation is an equation that can be written in the form $Ax + By = C$ where A and B are not both zero.

Example The equation $-4x + 6y = 3$ is a linear equation. The equation $y = -3x + 7$ is also a linear equation because it can be written in the form $Ax + By = C$.

Glossary

linear function

A linear function is a function that can be written in the form $f(x) = mx + b$, where m and b are both real numbers.

Example The function $f(x) = -3x + 7$ is a linear function.

line of symmetry

A line of symmetry is an imaginary line that divides a figure into two parts that are mirror images of each other. A figure can have one, many, or no lines of symmetry.

Examples The isosceles triangle below has one line of symmetry. The rectangle below has four lines of symmetry. The trapezoid below has no lines of symmetry.

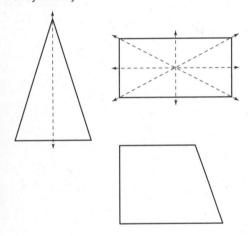

loss

A loss is the amount of money by which the expenses of a company are greater than the income of the company.

Example The income of a company is $20,000 and the expenses of the company are $23,500. The company had a loss of $23,500 - $20,000 = $3500.

lower quartile

The lower quartile is the median of the lower half of a data set.

Example For the data set

5, 5, 5, 8, 10, 13, 13, 16, 17, 18

the lower quartile is the median of the lower half of the data set, or 5.

M

markup

A markup is the increase in the price of an item.

Example The price of an item is $25. The price of the item increases to $30. Because $30 - $25 = $5, the markup on the item is $5.

means

The means of a proportion are the two inside quantities of a proportion.

Example In the proportion
4 girls: 7 boys:: 8 girls: 14 boys,
the means are the inside quantities, 7 boys and 8 girls.

mean

The mean of a data set is the sum of all of the values of the data set divided by the number of values in the data set. The mean is also called the average.

Example The mean of the numbers 3, 7, 17, and 33 is found by first adding the values and then dividing by the number of values, 4.

median

The median of a data set that is arranged in numerical order is either the middle value (when the number of data values is odd), or the average of the two middle values (when the number of data values is even).

Example When a data set has an odd number of values, arrange the values in order. The median is the middle value. In the data set {2, 7, 15, 56, 89}, the median is 15. When a data set has an even number of values, arrange the values in order. The median is the average of the two middle values. In the data set {3, 5, 10, 12, 20, 25}, the median is

$$\frac{(10+12)}{2} = 11.$$

metric system of measurement

The metric system of measurement is the decimal system that is used in countries outside of the United States to measure length, weight, and capacity.

Examples Common units of length in the metric system are meters, centimeters, and kilometers.

Common units of weight in the metric system are grams and kilograms.

Common units of capacity in the metric system are liters and milliliters.

mixed number

A mixed number is a number with a whole number part and a fractional part.

Example The numbers $2\frac{3}{4}$ and $5\frac{1}{2}$ are mixed numbers.

mode

The mode is the number (or numbers) that occurs most often in a data set. If there is no number that occurs most often, the data set has no mode.

Examples In the data set {45, 56, 75, 75, 80}, the number 75 occurs most often, so the mode is 75.

In the data set {25, 45, 25, 65, 45, 75}, the numbers 25 and 45 occur most often, so the modes are 25 and 45.

In the data set {45, 56, 64, 85}, there is no number that occurs most often, so the data set has no mode.

multiplicative identity

The number 1 is the multiplicative identity because when 1 is multiplied by any number, the product is that number.

Examples $1 \times 35 = 35$

$a \cdot 1 = a$

multiplicative inverse

The multiplicative inverse of a number $\frac{a}{b}$ is the number $\frac{b}{a}$. The product of any nonzero number and its multiplicative inverse is 1. The multiplicative inverse of a number is also called its reciprocal.

Example The multiplicative inverse of $\frac{3}{5}$ is $\frac{5}{3}$ because $\frac{3}{5} \times \frac{5}{3} = 1$.

multiple of a number

A multiple of a number is the product of the given number and a positive integer.

Example Multiples of 6 are 6, 12, 18, 24, 30, 36, 42, 48, 54, 60, and so on.

multiple representations

Multiple representations are different ways of visualizing a problem, including picture algebra, expressions, equations, tables, and graphs.

Example The relationship between the two sets of values can be represented as a table or as a graph.

Independent Variable	Dependent Variable
1	55
2	110
3	165
4	220

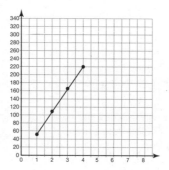

natural number

The set of natural numbers, or counting numbers, consists of all positive whole numbers beginning with 1.

Example The natural numbers are 1, 2, 3, 4, …

negative exponent

A power with a negative exponent is the reciprocal of the power with the opposite positive exponent.

$$x^{-a} = \frac{1}{x^a} \quad or \quad x^a = \frac{1}{x^{-a}}$$

Example

$$2^{-5} = \frac{1}{2^5} = 0.03125$$

negative number

A negative number is any number less than zero.

Examples The numbers -4, $-\frac{1}{5}$, and -3.81 are negative numbers.

net

A net is a two-dimensional model of a three-dimensional solid. When the net is folded, it forms the solid.

Example When the net below is folded, it forms the right prism shown.

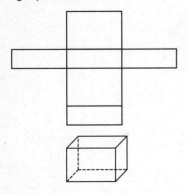

net pay

Net pay is the amount of money that an employee earns after deductions are subtracted from the employee's gross pay.

Example An employee earns $2400 per month of gross pay. Deductions of $432 in taxes and $164 in insurance are subtracted from this amount. So, the employee's net pay is

$2400 – $432 – $164 = $1804.

number line

A number line is a line on which a unique point is assigned to every real number.

Example The point on the number line below corresponds to the rational number 1.5.

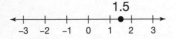

numerator

The numerator is the top number in a fraction.

Examples In the fraction $\frac{3}{4}$, the numerator is 3. In the fraction $\frac{1}{2}$, the numerator is 1.

obtuse angle

An obtuse angle is an angle whose measure is greater than 90 degrees and less than 180 degrees.

Examples Angle A and angle B are obtuse angles.

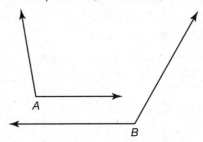

obtuse triangle

An obtuse triangle is a triangle with one obtuse angle.

Example Angle B is an obtuse angle, so triangle ABC is an obtuse triangle.

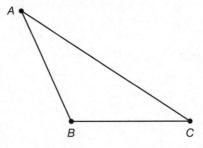

Glossary

octagon

An octagon is a polygon with eight sides.

Examples The polygon *ABCDEFGH* and the polygon *STUVWXYZ* are both octagons.

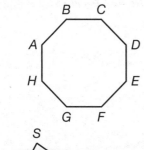

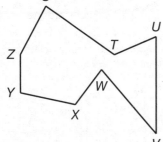

odd number

An odd number is any integer that is not divisible by two.

Examples The numbers –5, –3, –1, 1, 3, and 5 are odd numbers.

order of operations

The order of operations is a set of rules for evaluating an expression that states the order in which operations are to be done. The order of operations is:

1. Evaluate expressions inside grouping symbols such as parentheses.

2. Evaluate powers.

3. Multiply and divide from left to right.

4. Add and subtract from left to right.

Example To evaluate the expression $(3 + 4)^2 + 5 \bullet 2$, perform the operations in this order. Evaluate expressions inside parentheses first.

$$(3 + 4)^2 + 5 \bullet 2 = 7^2 + 5 \bullet 2$$
$$= 49 + 5 \bullet 2$$
$$= 49 + 10$$
$$= 59$$

ordered pair

An ordered pair is a pair of numbers of the form (x, y) that represents a unique position in the coordinate plane. The first number in the ordered pair is the *x*-coordinate and the second number is the *y*-coordinate.

Examples The ordered pairs (4, 2) and (–2, –3) are shown in the coordinate plane.

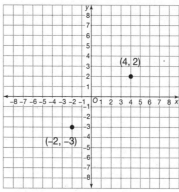

origin

The origin is the point where the *x*- and *y*-axes intersect in the coordinate plane. The ordered pair that represents the origin is (0, 0).

Example

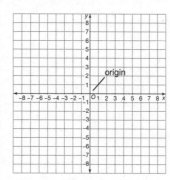

outcome

An outcome is a possible result of an event.

Example When flipping a coin, the coin landing heads up is an outcome.

Glossary

parallel lines

Parallel lines are lines that exist in the same plane and never intersect.

Example Lines *m* and *n* are parallel.

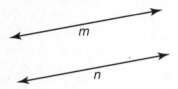

parallelogram

A parallelogram is a quadrilateral in which both pairs of opposite sides are parallel.

Examples In parallelogram *ABCD*, opposite sides *AB* and *CD* are parallel; opposite sides *AD* and *BC* are parallel.

In parallelogram *EFGH*, opposite sides *EF* and *GH* are parallel; opposite sides *FG* and *EH* are parallel.

In parallelogram *IJKL*, opposite sides *LK* and *IJ* are parallel; opposite sides *JK* and *IL* are parallel.

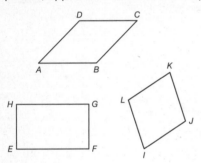

pattern

A pattern is an ordered sequence of numbers, shapes, or other objects that are arranged according to a rule.

Examples The pattern *a*, *b*, *a*, *b*, *a*, *b*, *a*, *b*, ... is the sequence of alternating letters *a* and *b*.

The pattern 0, 1, 4, 9, 16, 25, 36, 49, ... is the sequence of the squares of whole numbers.

percent

One percent of a quantity is $\frac{1}{100}$ of the quantity.

Example You buy a notebook for $4.00 and pay a sales tax of 7%. The sales tax is equal to $\frac{7}{100}$ of $4.00, or $.28.

percent decrease

A percent decrease in a value is the ratio of the amount of decrease in value to the original value, written as a percent.

Example The decrease in the price of an article from $20 to $15 is a percent decrease of 25%.

$$\frac{\text{Decrease in price}}{\text{Original price}} = \frac{20-15}{20} = \frac{5}{20} = \frac{1}{4} = 25\%$$

percent increase

A percent increase in a value is the ratio of the amount of increase in value to the original value, written as a percent.

Example The increase in the price of an article from $20 to $30 is a percent increase of 50%.

$$\frac{\text{Increase in price}}{\text{Original price}} = \frac{30-20}{20} = \frac{10}{20} = \frac{1}{2} = 50\%$$

perimeter

The perimeter of a polygon is the distance around the sides of the polygon.

Example The perimeter of the polygon is
4 + 3 + 2 + 3 + 1 + 4 + 2.5 = 19.5 units.

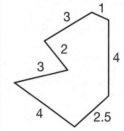

Glossary

perimeter of a rectangle

The perimeter of a rectangle is equal to the sum of twice the length L and twice the width W of the rectangle:

$P = 2L + 2W$

Example The perimeter of rectangle $ABCD$ is

$(2)(8) + (2)(3) = 22$ inches.

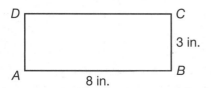

perimeter of a square

The perimeter of a square is equal to four times the length of a side s:

$P = 4s$

Example The perimeter of square $ABCD$ is

$(4)(5) = 20$ centimeters.

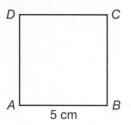

perpendicular lines

Perpendicular lines are two lines (or segments or rays) that intersect to form a right angle. The symbol for "is perpendicular to" is $\perp$.

Examples Lines m and k are perpendicular lines. Segment $AB \perp$ ray AC.

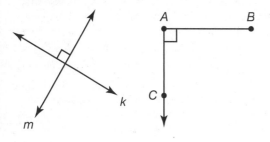

pi

Pi is the symbol that is used to represent the ratio of a circle's circumference to its diameter. Pi is an irrational number and its value is approximately 3.14.

$\pi \approx 3.14159265358979323846...$

Example The diameter of a circle is 2 inches and the circumference of the circle is approximately 6.28 inches. The ratio of the circumference to the diameter is $\dfrac{6.28}{2} = 3.14 \approx \pi$.

place-value chart

A place-value chart identifies the place value of each digit in a number.

Example Each digit of the number 725.421 is shown in the place-value chart.

Place-Value Chart						
hundreds	tens	ones	.	tenths	hundredths	thousandths
7	2	5	.	4	2	1

plane

A plane can be visualized as a surface with no thickness that extends without end in two dimensions.

Example A plane does not have sides but can be represented by drawing a four-sided figure, as shown in the representation below of plane M.

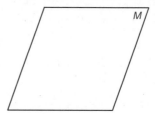

point

A point has no dimension, but can be visualized as a specific position in space, and is usually represented by a small dot.

Example The point below is point A.

•A

Glossary

polygon

A polygon is a two-dimensional figure that is formed by three or more segments called sides. Each side of a polygon must intersect exactly two other sides, one at each endpoint. No two sides intersect each other more than once.

Examples Figure *ABCDE*, figure *FGHI*, and figure *JKL* are polygons.

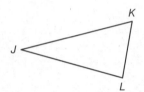

polyhedron

A polyhedron is a solid that is bounded by polygons, called faces, which enclose a single region of space.

Example A pyramid is an example of a polyhedron.

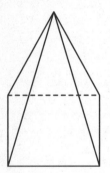

positive number

A positive number is a number greater than zero.

Examples The numbers 10, $\frac{2}{3}$, and 6.34 are positive numbers.

power

A power is an expression in which a number or variable is raised to an exponent. A power is a notation used to represent repeated multiplication.

Examples The expression 5^2 is a power. The expression x^3 is a power.

pre-image

A pre-image is the original figure in a transformation.

Example On the graph, the figure below on the left is the pre-image before a translation of +3 units horizontally.

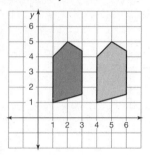

power of ten

A power of ten is any power whose base is 10.

Example The power 10^4 is a power of ten.

prime factorization

The prime factorization of a number is the representation of a number as a product of prime numbers.

Example The prime factorization of 84 is $2 \cdot 2 \cdot 3 \cdot 7 = 2^2 \cdot 3 \cdot 7$. The numbers 2, 3, and 7 are prime numbers.

prime factors

The prime factors of a number are the prime numbers that will exactly divide the number.

Example The factors of 45 are 1, 3, 5, 9, 15, and 45. The prime factors of 45 are 3 and 5.

prime number

A prime number is a whole number greater than 1 that has exactly two whole number factors, 1 and the number itself.

Examples The number 11 is a prime number because 1 and 11 are the only numbers that will evenly divide 11.

The number 12 is not a prime number because it can be divided by 1, 2, 3, 4, 6, and 12.

principal

The principal is an amount of money that is borrowed or invested.

Example If $18,000 is borrowed at a 6.9% interest rate for 60 months to buy a car, $18,000 is the principal.

prism

A prism is a polyhedron with two parallel faces, called bases, that are congruent polygons. The other faces, called lateral faces, are parallelograms that are formed by connecting the corresponding vertices of the bases.

Example A prism is named for the shape of its bases. The prism shown is a hexagonal prism.

lateral face

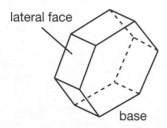

base

probability

A probability is a number between 0 and 1 that is a measure of the likelihood that a given event will occur. The probability of an event when all outcomes are equally likely is equal to the number of desired outcomes divided by the number of possible outcomes.

Example A bag contains 3 red marbles, 1 blue marble, and 4 green marbles. A marble is chosen at random from the bag. The probability of choosing a red marble is

$$\frac{\text{Number of red marbles}}{\text{Total number of marbles}} = \frac{3}{8}.$$

product

A product is the result of multiplying one quantity by another.

Example The product of 2 and 3, 2 • 3, is the number 6.

profit

The profit made by a company is the amount of income left over after expenses have been subtracted.

Example A company has a monthly income of $10,000 and monthly expenses of $8000. The company's profit is $10,000 – $8000, or $2000.

proper fraction

A proper fraction is a fraction whose numerator is less than its denominator.

Examples The fractions $\frac{5}{6}$ and $\frac{7}{22}$ are proper fractions.

proportion

A proportion is an equation that states that two ratios are equal.

Examples The equation $\frac{4}{8} = \frac{1}{2}$ is a proportion. The equation $\frac{x}{12} = \frac{5}{60}$ is a proportion.

protractor

A protractor is a tool that is used for measuring angles. The markings on a protractor are usually in degrees.

Example The measure of the angle is 45 degrees.

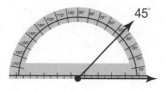

Glossary

pyramid

A pyramid is a polyhedron that has one base that is a polygon. The lateral faces of the pyramid are triangles that meet at a common vertex.

Example A pyramid is named according to the shape of its base. The pyramid below is a triangular pyramid.

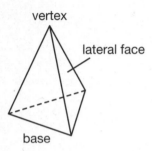

Pythagorean theorem

If a and b are the legs of a right triangle, and c is the hypotenuse, then the sum of the squares of the lengths of the legs equals the square of the length of the hypotenuse:

$a^2 + b^2 = c^2$.

Example In triangle ABC, angle C is the right angle, so side BC is a leg, side AC is a leg, and side AB is the hypotenuse.

$a^2 + b^2 = c^2$

$3^2 + b^2 = 8^2$

$9 + b^2 = 64$

$b^2 = 64 - 9$

$b^2 = 55$

$b = \sqrt{55}$

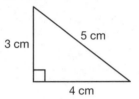

So, the length of side AC is $\sqrt{55} \approx 7.42$ centimeters.

Pythagorean triple

A Pythagorean triple is a set of three positive integers a, b, and c that represent the lengths of the sides of a right triangle that satisfy the equation $a^2 + b^2 = c^2$.

Example The numbers 3, 4, and 5 are a Pythagorean triple.

$a^2 + b^2 = c^2$

$3^2 + 4^2 = 5^2$

$9 + 16 = 25$

$25 = 25$

Q

quadrant

A quadrant is one of the four regions created in a Cartesian coordinate plane by the intersection of the x-axis and the y-axis.

Example The point (2, –3) lies in the fourth quadrant.

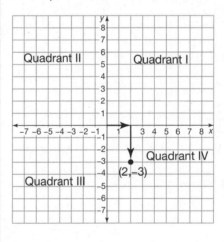

Glossary

quadrilateral

A quadrilateral is a polygon that has four sides.

Examples Figure *ABCD*, figure *FGHI*, and figure *JKLM* are quadrilaterals.

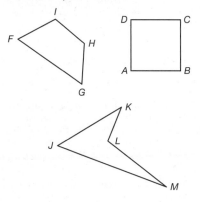

quantity

A quantity is a value that can be increased, decreased, measured, or counted.

Examples Miles driven and gallons of gasoline used are both quantities because each can be measured.

quartile

A quartile is one of three values which divide a data set into four equal parts. The middle quartile is the median. The other two values are the upper quartile and the lower quartile.

Example In the data set

13, 17, 23, 24, 25, 29, 31, 45, 46, 53, 60

the median, 29, divides the data into two halves. The lower quartile, 23, is the median of the lower half of the data. The upper quartile, 46, is the median of the upper half of the data.

13 17 **23** 24 25 **29** 31 45 **46** 53 60

      ↑   ↑   ↑

   lower   median   upper
  quartile   quartile

quotient

A quotient is the number that results from the division of one number by another. The quotient is the answer of a division problem.

Example The quotient of the division problem $96 \div 12 = 8$ is the number 8.

R

radical

A radical is an expression that represents the root of a number. This root is indicated by the index, a number written above and to the left of the radical sign, $\sqrt{}$. In the case of a square root, the index is omitted.

Examples The expressions $\sqrt{25}$ and $\sqrt[3]{27}$ are radicals.

radicand

A radicand is the quantity under a radical sign in an expression.

Example In the expression $\sqrt[4]{25}$, the number 25 is the radicand.

radius

The radius is the distance from the center of a circle to a point on the circle.

Example In the circle, *O* is the center and the length of segment *OA* is the radius.

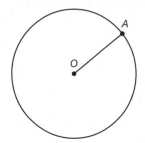

random

A random outcome is an outcome that occurs by chance.

Example In a coin toss, the coin landing tails up is a random event.

range

The range of a data set is the difference between the greatest number and the least number in the data set.

Example In a data set whose greatest number is 90 and whose least number is 16, the range is $90 - 16 = 74$.

Glossary

range of a function

The range of a function is the set of all output values for the function.

Example For the function $y = x^2$, the range is all values greater than or equal to zero.

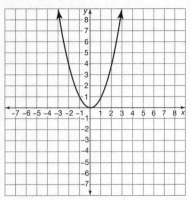

rate

A rate is a ratio in which the two quantities that are being compared are measured in different units.

Example A car uses 20 gallons of gasoline to drive 600 miles. The car's fuel consumption rate is

$$\frac{600\,\text{miles}}{20\,\text{gallons}} = \frac{30\,\text{miles}}{1\,\text{gallon}}$$

or 30 miles per gallon.

rate of change

A rate of change is a comparison of two quantities with different units that are changing.

Example A person on a train travels 120 miles in 4 hours. The rate of change of the train is 120 miles per 4 hours, or 30 miles per hour.

ratio

A ratio is a comparison of two numbers that uses division. The ratio of two numbers a and b, with the restriction that b cannot equal zero, can be written in three ways.

a to b

$a : b$

$\frac{a}{b}$

Example Three ways to write the ratio of 4 to 5 are shown below.

4 to 5

4 : 5

$\frac{4}{5}$

rational number

A **rational number** is a number that can be written in the form $\frac{a}{b}$, where a and b are both integers and b is not equal to 0.

Example The number –0.5 is a rational number because –0.5 can be written as $-\frac{1}{2} = \frac{-1}{2}$.

ray

A ray consists of a point P on a straight line and all points on the line on one side of P.

Example The ray below is ray AB.

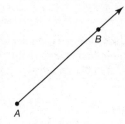

real numbers

The real numbers consist of all rational numbers and irrational numbers. Real numbers can be represented on the real number line.

Examples The numbers –3, 1.25, $\frac{11}{4}$, and $\sqrt{13}$ shown below are real numbers.

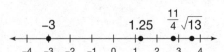

reciprocal

Two nonzero numbers are reciprocals if their product is 1. The reciprocal of a number is also known as the multiplicative inverse of the number.

Examples The numbers $\frac{1}{2}$ and 2 are reciprocals because $\left(\frac{1}{2}\right)(2) = 1$. The numbers $\frac{3}{4}$ and $\frac{4}{3}$ are reciprocals because $\left(\frac{3}{4}\right)\left(\frac{4}{3}\right) = 1$.

rectangle

A rectangle is a parallelogram with four right angles.

Examples Figure *ABCD*, figure *FGHI*, and figure *JKML* are rectangles.

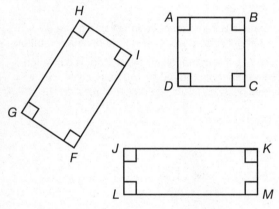

regular polygon

A regular polygon is a polygon whose sides all have the same length and whose angles all have the same measure.

Examples Figure *ABCD* and figure *EFG* are regular polygons.

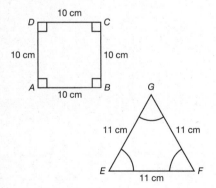

reflection

A reflection is a transformation in which a figure is reflected, or flipped, in a given line called the line of reflection.

Example The triangle on the right is a reflection of the triangle on the left.

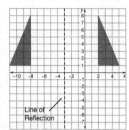

relation

A relation is any set of ordered pairs.

Example The group of ordered pairs (2, 4), (3, 7), (4, 10), and (5, 13) represents a relation.

remainder

The remainder is the whole number left over in a division problem if the divisor does not divide the dividend evenly.

Example When 17 is divided by 3, the remainder is 2.

$$
\begin{array}{r}
5 \\
3\overline{)17} \\
\underline{15} \\
2
\end{array}
$$

repeating decimal

A repeating decimal is a decimal with one or more digits that repeat infinitely. A repeating decimal can be represented by placing a bar over the repeating digits.

Example The decimal 0.14141414... is a repeating decimal that can be written as $0.\overline{14}$. In the decimal, the digits 1 and 4 repeat in a pattern infinitely.

Glossary

rhombus

A rhombus is a parallelogram whose four sides have the same length. The plural form of "rhombus" is "rhombi."

Examples Figure *JKLM* is a rhombus. Figure *ABCD* is a rhombus.

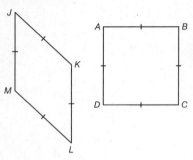

right angle

A right angle is an angle with a measure of 90 degrees.

Example Angle 1 is a right angle, so its measure is 90°.

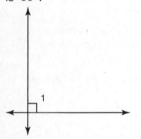

right prism

A right prism is a prism whose lateral edges are perpendicular to both bases. All of the lateral faces of a right prism are rectangles.

Examples The prisms below are right prisms.

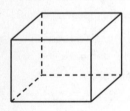
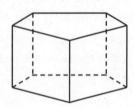

rise

The rise is the vertical change between any two points on a line.

Example The rise of the points (1, 4) and (3, 8) is $8 - 4 = 4$.

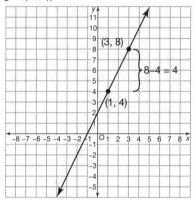

rotation

A rotation is a transformation in which a figure is turned about a fixed point called the center of rotation.

Example The rectangle at the bottom is a rotation of the rectangle at the top of 150 degrees counterclockwise about the center of rotation *P*.

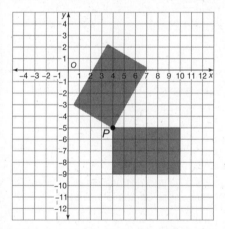

Glossary

rounding a number

Rounding a number is approximating the number to a given place value. To round a number to a given place value, look at the digit to the right of the place where you want to round the number. If the digit is less than 5, round down. If the digit is 5 or greater, round up.

Examples To round 1237 to the nearest hundred, look at the digit to the right of the hundreds place, 3. Because 3 is less than 5, round down. So, 1237 rounded to the nearest hundred is 1200.

To round 658 to the nearest ten, look at the digit to the right of the tens place, 8. Because 8 is greater than 5, round up. So, 658 rounded to the nearest ten is 660.

row

A row in a spreadsheet is a horizontal section of the spreadsheet.

Example Row B is highlighted in the table below.

	1	2	3	4	5	6
A						
B	B1	B2	B3	B4	B5	B6
C						
D						
E						

run

The run is the horizontal change between any two points on a line.

Example The run of the points (1, 4) and (3, 8) is 3 – 1 = 2.

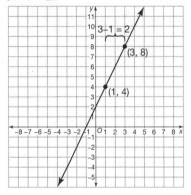

s

sample

A sample is a group of items that are selected at random from a larger group of items called the population.

Example If the population of a study concerning health care is everyone born in the United States from 1995 to 2005, then everyone born on May 22 of each year from 1995 to 2005 is a sample.

sample space

A sample space of a random experiment is the set of all possible outcomes of the experiment.

Example For the random experiment of rolling a number cube numbered 1 through 6, the sample space is the set of numbers 1, 2, 3, 4, 5, and 6.

scale

A scale is a ratio that represents the relationship between the measurements of a scale drawing or scale model and the actual measurements of an object.

Example In the map of the lake below, the scale 1 inch : 5 miles means that 1 inch on the map is equal to 5 miles of actual distance.

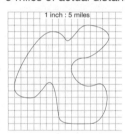

1 inch : 5 miles

Glossary

scale drawing

A scale drawing is a two-dimensional drawing that is similar to the actual object that it represents. It is drawn using measurements that are proportional to the measurements of the actual object.

Example The diagram below is a scale drawing of a water tank. One inch on the drawing is equal to 3 feet on the actual water tank. The height of the actual water tank is

$$(2\text{ inches})\left(\frac{3\text{ feet}}{1\text{ inch}}\right) = 6\text{ feet}.$$

The diameter of the actual water tank is

$$(1.5\text{ inches})\left(\frac{3\text{ feet}}{1\text{ inch}}\right) = 4.5\text{ feet}.$$

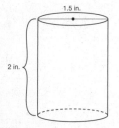

1.5 in.

2 in.

scale factor

A scale factor is a ratio that compares a measurement of a scale model or drawing to the corresponding measurement of an original object. A scale factor is also called a dilation factor.

Example A photograph has a width of 4 inches and a length of 5.5 inches, as shown below. An enlargement of the photograph has a width of 8 inches and a length of 11 inches. The scale factor of the enlargement to the original photograph is

$$\frac{EH}{AD} = \frac{8}{4} = 2.$$

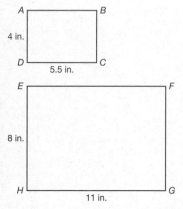

A   B

4 in.

D   C
   5.5 in.

E   F

8 in.

H   G
     11 in.

scale model

A scale model is a three-dimensional drawing that is similar to the actual object that it represents. It is drawn using measurements that are proportional to the measurements of the actual object.

Example The model below is a scale drawing of an office building. One inch on the drawing is equal to 15 feet on the actual office building. The height of the actual office building is

$$(17.5\text{ inches})\left(\frac{15\text{ feet}}{1\text{ inch}}\right) = 262.5\text{ feet}.$$

The depth of the actual office building is

$$(4\text{ inches})\left(\frac{15\text{ feet}}{1\text{ inch}}\right) = 60\text{ feet}.$$

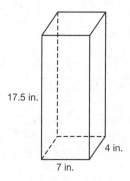

17.5 in.

4 in.

7 in.

scalene triangle

A scalene triangle is a triangle with no sides of equal length.

Examples None of the side lengths of triangle *ABC* are the same. So, triangle *ABC* is a scalene triangle. None of the side lengths of triangle *DEF* are the same. So, triangle *DEF* is a scalene triangle.

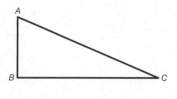

A

B   C

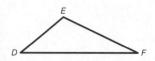

E

D   F

Glossary

scatter plot

A scatter plot is a graph in the coordinate plane in which values of x and y are plotted as points (x, y).

Example The table shows the number of calories that a 125-pound person burns for different amounts of time spent exercising. A scatter plot of the data shows that as the amount of time increases, the number of calories burned increases.

x	y
5	23
18	80
35	158
44	198
58	266
72	324
78	350
85	383

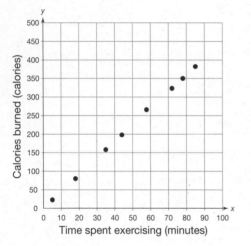

scientific notation

Scientific notation is a way of writing very large or very small numbers. A number written in scientific notation has the form $c \times 10^n$, where c is greater than or equal to 1 and less than 10 and n is an integer.

Examples The number 4050 written in scientific notation is 4.050×10^3.

The number 0.004050 written in scientific notation is 4.050×10^{-3}.

side

A side of a polygon is one of any of the line segments that form the polygon.

Example Line segments AB, BC, and AC are the sides of triangle ABC.

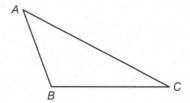

signed number

A signed number is a positive number or a negative number. Zero is not a signed number.

Examples The numbers -3, $\frac{1}{2}$, and -1.5 are signed numbers.

simple interest

Simple interest is when interest is paid only as a percent of the principal. To find simple interest, multiply the principal P by the annual interest rate r written as a decimal and the time t in years: $I = Prt$.

Example The simple interest on a $300 principal at an annual interest rate of 4% over 10 years is

$I = 300 \times 0.04 \times 10 = \$120$.

simplest form of a fraction

The simplest form of a fraction is a fraction that has no common factors in the numerator and denominator other than 1.

Example The fraction $\frac{2}{4}$ can be written in simplest form as the fraction $\frac{1}{2}$. The numerator and denominator of $\frac{1}{2}$ have no common factors other than 1.

Glossary

slope

The slope of a nonvertical line is the ratio of the vertical change to the horizontal change from point *A* to point *B* on a line. Graphically, the slope is a measure of the steepness of a line.

$$slope = \frac{\text{vertical change from point } A \text{ to point } B}{\text{horizontal change from point } A \text{ to point } B}$$

Example The slope of the line that passes through the points (2, –4) and (3, –6) is –2 because the vertical change is –2 units and the horizontal change is 1 unit.

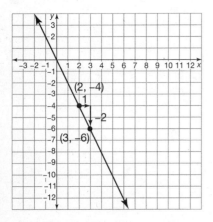

slope-intercept form

The slope-intercept form of a linear equation is $y = mx + b$, where *m* is the slope of the line and *b* is the *y*-intercept of the line.

Example The equation $y = 3x + 4$ is written in slope-intercept form. The slope of the line is 3 and the *y*-intercept of the line is 4.

solution of an equation

The solution of an equation is a number that, when substituted for a variable, makes the equation true.

Example The solution of the equation $3x + 4 = 25$ is 7 because 7 makes the equation true:

$3(7) + 4 = 25$, or $25 = 25$.

solid

A solid is a three-dimensional figure that encloses a part of space.

Example The cube shown below is a solid.

sphere

A sphere is the set of all points in space that are a given distance from a fixed point called the center of the sphere.

Example Point *C* is the center of the sphere, and *r* is the radius of the sphere.

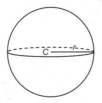

square

A square is a parallelogram with congruent sides and four right angles.

Examples Figure *FGHI* and figure *ABCD* are squares.

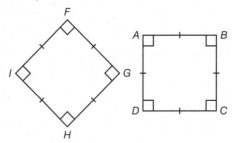

square of a number

The square of a number is equal to the number multiplied by itself.

Example The square of the number 5 is equal to $(5)(5) = 5^2 = 25$. You can also say that 5 squared is equal to 25.

Glossary

square pyramid

A square pyramid is a pyramid whose base is a square.

Example The pyramid below is a square pyramid.

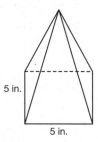

5 in.

5 in.

square root

The square root of a number n is a number r such that when you square r, it is equal to n. A nonnegative square root is represented by a radical sign $\sqrt{\ }$.

Examples $\sqrt{9} = 3$

The square root of 9 is 3 because $3^2 = 9$.

$\sqrt{64} = 8$

The square root of 64 is 8 because $8^2 = 64$.

square unit

A square unit is a unit of measure for the area of a figure. A unit (not squared) is a unit of measure for the length of a figure.

Example In the figure, assume that each square is one square inch. The area of the entire figure is one square foot. The area of the entire figure is also 144 square inches:

1 square foot = (12)(12) square inches

= 144 square inches

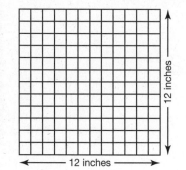

12 inches

12 inches

standard form

A number in standard form is the way that numbers are usually written. In standard form, the position of the digit represents the place value of the digit.

Example The number 349.57 is written in standard form.

stem-and-leaf plot

A stem-and-leaf plot is a visual display of data organized by digits. Each data value is separated into a stem and a leaf. The leading digits of the data value are represented by the stem and the last digit is represented by the leaf.

Example A stem-and-leaf plot can be drawn to represent test scores.

55, 62, 73, 75, 76, 79, 80, 83, 86, 87, 87, 88, 88, 89, 89, 89

The tens place represents the stem and the ones place represents the leaves.

Stem-and-Leaf Plot of Test Scores

Stems	Leaves
1	
2	
3	
4	
5	5
6	2
7	3 5 6 9
8	0 3 6 7 7 8 8 9 9 9

Key: 7 | 3 = 73

straight angle

A straight angle is an angle whose measure is 180 degrees.

Example The measure of angle *ABC* is 180 degrees, so angle *ABC* is a straight angle.

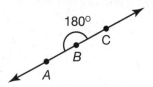

180°

C

B

A

sum

A sum is the result of adding one quantity to another.

Example The sum of 26 and 13, 26 + 13, is the number 39.

supplementary angles

Supplementary angles are two angles whose measures have the sum of 180 degrees.

Example Angle 1 and angle 2 are supplementary angles. If $m \angle 1 = 75°$, then $m \angle 2 = 180° - 75° = 105°$.

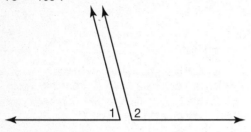

surface area

The surface area of a polyhedron is the sum of the areas of its faces.

Example The surface area of the prism is the sum of the areas of each of its six rectangular faces:

$S = 2(10)(6) + 2(5)(6) + 2(10)(5) = 280$ square feet

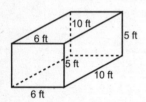

surface area of a cylinder

The surface area of a cylinder is the sum of the areas of the bases and the area of the lateral surfaces (the surface not including the bases):

$S = 2\pi r^2 + 2\pi rh$

where r is the radius and h is the height.

Example The radius of the base of the cylinder is 3 feet and the height of the cylinder is 7 feet. So, the surface area of the cylinder is

$2\pi r^2 + 2\pi rh = 2\pi 3^2 + 2\pi(3)(7) \approx 188.40$ square feet.

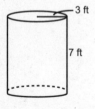

surface area of a prism

The surface area of a prism is the sum of the areas of the bases and the areas of the lateral faces:

$S = 2(\text{area of base}) + \text{lateral areas}$

Example The surface area of the triangular prism is the sum of the areas of the triangular bases and the areas of the lateral faces:

$2\left(\dfrac{1}{2}\right)(4)(3.46) + 3(4)(9) = 121.84$ square millimeters

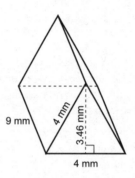

surface area of a sphere

The surface area of a sphere is a measure of the area of the outside surface of a sphere. The surface area of a sphere is four times the area of a circle that has the center of the sphere as its center, called a great circle. In other words, four great circles will completely cover the sphere. So, the surface area of a sphere is equal to $4\pi r^2$, where r is the radius.

Example The surface area of the sphere with a radius of 3 inches is:

$4\pi r^2 = 4\pi(3)^2 = 36\pi \approx 113.1$ square inches.

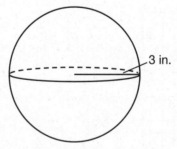

Glossary

symmetry

Symmetry is a property of an object such that the object remains unchanged under certain transformations such as reflections and rotations.

Examples A figure has line symmetry if a line can divide the figure into two parts that are reflections of each other in the line. A figure has rotational symmetry if a rotation of 180 degrees or less (clockwise or counterclockwise) about the figure's center produces an image that fits exactly on the original figure. If you rotate the hexagon below 60 degrees about point A, it will exactly fit on the original hexagon.

 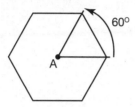

table of values

A table of values is a list of some of the input values and output values for a given function.

Example The table below is a table of values for the function $y = 6x + 3$. In the table, the x-values are the input values and the y-values are the output values.

x	y
2	15
5	33
7	45
9	57

term

The terms of an expression are the parts that are added together. A term may be a number, a variable, or a product of a number and a variable or variables.

Example The terms 2x and 3 are terms of the expression $2x + 3$. Other examples of terms are z, c^3, xy, and $\frac{1}{2}a^4$.

terminating decimal

A terminating decimal is a decimal with a finite number of digits.

Example The decimal 0.625 is a terminating decimal.

theorem

A theorem is a statement that has been proven to be true.

Example The Pythagorean theorem states that if a right triangle has legs of lengths a and b and hypotenuse of length c, then $a^2 + b^2 = c^2$.

theoretical probability

Theoretical probability is probability based on knowing all of the possible outcomes that are equally likely to occur.

Example The theoretical probability of rolling a 2 on a number cube numbered from 1 to 6 is $\frac{1}{6}$.

transformation

A transformation is an operation that maps, or moves a figure, called the pre-image, onto a new figure, called the image. Three types of transformations are reflections, rotations, and translations.

Examples

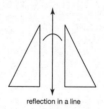

reflection in a line

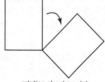

rotation about a point

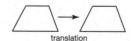

translation

Glossary

translation

A translation is a transformation in which a figure is shifted or slid, so that each point of the figure moves the same distance in the same direction. The shift can be in a horizontal direction, a vertical direction, or both.

Example The top trapezoid is a vertical translation of the bottom trapezoid by 5 units upward.

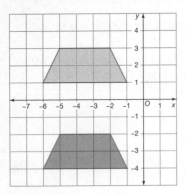

transversal

A transversal is a line that intersects two or more lines in the same plane at different points.

Example Line *t* is a transversal that intersects line *m* and line *n*.

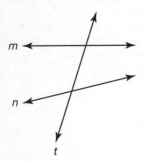

trapezoid

A trapezoid is a quadrilateral with exactly one pair of parallel sides. The parallel sides are called bases and the nonparallel sides are called legs. The perpendicular distance between the bases is the height of the trapezoid.

Example Quadrilateral *ABCD* is a trapezoid. The height is 4 meters, the length of base *AD* is 12 meters, and the length of base *BC* is 6 meters.

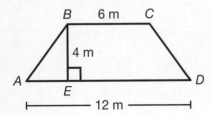

triangle

A triangle is a three-sided polygon that is formed by joining three points called vertices with line segments.

Example In triangle *ABC* below, vertices *A*, *B*, and *C* are joined by segments *BA*, *AC*, and *CB*.

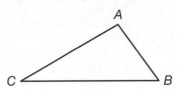

unit

A unit is a standard measurement of one, such as one inch, one pound, or one second.

Examples A unit of money is one dollar. A unit of distance is one foot.

unit rate

A unit rate is a rate that has a denominator of 1 unit.

Example The rate $\dfrac{150 \text{ miles}}{3 \text{ hours}}$ can be written as the unit rate of 50 miles per hour:

$$\frac{(150 \div 3) \text{ miles}}{(3 \div 3) \text{ hours}} = \frac{50 \text{ miles}}{1 \text{ hour}}$$

upper quartile

The upper quartile is the median of the upper half of a data set.

Example For the data set 2, 4, 4, 5, 7, 8, 8, 9, 11, 13 the upper quartile is the median of the upper half of the data set, or 9.

variable

A variable is a letter used to represent one or more numbers.

Example In the expression 2*x* + 3, the letter "*x*" is a variable.

variable expression

A variable expression is an expression that consists of numbers, variables, and operations to be performed.

Example The expression $3x + 4$ is a variable expression.

Venn diagram

A Venn diagram uses circles to show how elements among sets of numbers or objects are related.

Example

Whole numbers 1-10

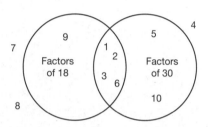

vertex of an angle

The vertex of an angle is the point where the two rays forming the angle intersect.

Example Point G is the vertex of the angle below.

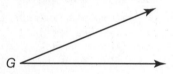

vertex (of a solid)

The vertex of a solid is the point where the edges meet.

Example

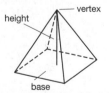

vertex of a polygon

A vertex of a polygon is a point where two sides of the polygon intersect. The plural of vertex is vertices.

Examples In quadrilateral *JKLM*, *J* is a vertex, *K* is a vertex, *L* is a vertex, and *M* is a vertex. In quadrilateral *ABCD*, *A* is a vertex, *B* is a vertex, *C* is a vertex, and *D* is a vertex.

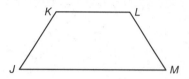

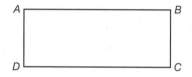

vertical angles

Two angles are vertical angles if their sides form two pairs of opposite rays.

Examples Angles 1 and 3 are vertical angles. Angles 2 and 4 are vertical angles.

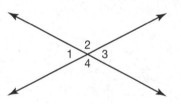

vertical axis

The vertical axis is the y-axis in a coordinate plane.

Example

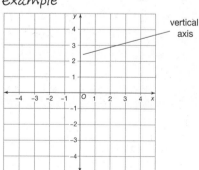

© 2008 Carnegie Learning, Inc.

Glossary

volume

The volume of a solid is the number of cubic units that will completely fill the interior of the solid.

Example The volume of the right prism is 24 cubic units.

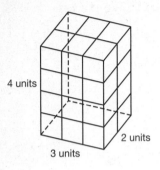

4 units

2 units

3 units

volume of a cone

The volume of a cone is the number of cubic units contained in the interior of the cone. The volume of a cone is one third of the product of the area of the base and the height:

$$V = \frac{1}{3}\pi r^2 h,$$

where r is the radius of the base and h is the height.

Example The radius of the cone is 1.5 meters and the height is 4 meters. So, the volume of the cone is

$$\frac{1}{3}\pi(1.5)^2(4) \approx 9.42 \text{ cubic meters.}$$

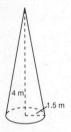

4 m

1.5 m

volume of a cylinder

The volume of a cylinder is the number of cubic units contained in the interior of the cylinder. The volume of a cylinder is the product of the areas of the circular bases and the height of the cylinder:

$$V = \pi r^2 h$$

where r is the radius of the base and h is the height.

Example The radius of the circular base is 5 millimeters, and the height is 9 millimeters. So, the volume of the cylinder is

$\pi(5)^2(9) \approx 706.5$ cubic millimeters.

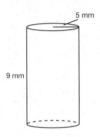

5 mm

9 mm

volume of a prism

The volume of a prism is the number of cubic units contained in the interior of the prism. The volume of a prism is equal to the product of the area of the base and the height:

$$V = Bh$$

where B is the area of the base and h is the height.

Example The base of the prism is a rectangle with an area of (4)(10) = 40 square inches. The height of the prism is 7 inches. So, the volume of the prism is

(40)(7) = 280 cubic inches.

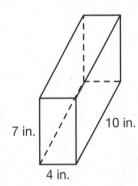

7 in.

10 in.

4 in.

Glossary

volume of a pyramid

The volume of a pyramid is the number of cubic units contained in the interior of the pyramid. The volume of a pyramid is equal to one third of the product of the area of the base and the height:

$$V = \frac{1}{3}Bh.$$

Example The base of the pyramid is a square with an area of $6^2 = 36$ centimeters. The height of the pyramid is 4 centimeters. So, the volume of the pyramid is

$\frac{1}{3}(36)(4) = 48$ cubic centimeters.

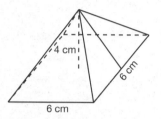

volume of a sphere

The volume of a sphere is the number of cubic units contained in the interior of the sphere. The volume of a sphere of radius r is

$$V = \frac{4}{3}\pi r^3.$$

Example The radius of the sphere is 5 centimeters. So, the volume of the sphere is

$\frac{4}{3}\pi (5)^3 \approx 523.60$ cubic centimeters.

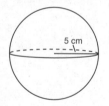

W

whole number

A whole number is any counting number or zero.

Examples The numbers 0, 1, 2, 3, 4, 5, 6, 7, 8, 9, 10... are whole numbers.

width

The width of an object is the distance across the object.

Example The width of the picture frame is 11 inches.

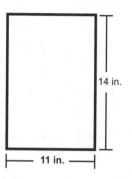

X

x-axis

The x-axis is the horizontal axis in a coordinate plane.

Example

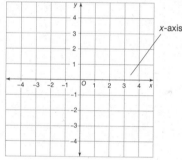

x-coordinate

The x-coordinate of a point is the first number in an ordered pair. It indicates the distance of the point from the y-axis.

Example In the ordered pair (2, 5), the number 2 is the x-coordinate.

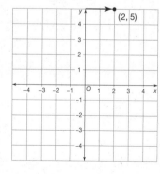

The point (2, 5) is 2 units from the y-axis.

Glossary

x-intercept

The x-intercept is the x-coordinate of a point where a graph crosses the x-axis.

Example The x-intercept of the graph below is 4.

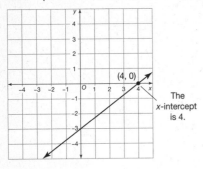

The x-intercept is 4.

y-intercept

The y-intercept is the y-coordinate of a point where a graph crosses the y-axis.

Example The y-intercept of the graph below is –3.

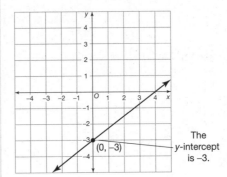

The y-intercept is –3.

y-axis

The y-axis is the vertical axis in a coordinate plane.

Example

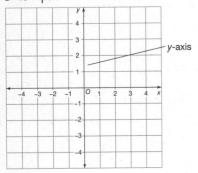

y-axis

y-coordinate

The y-coordinate of a point is the second number in an ordered pair. It indicates the distance of the point from the x-axis.

Example In the ordered pair (2, 5), the number 5 is the y-coordinate.

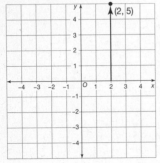

The point (2, 5) is 5 units from the x-axis.

Glossary

Index

© 2008 Carnegie Learning, Inc.

Index

Expanded form
  decimal, 117
  power, 219
Experimental probability, 343
Exponent
  definition of, 28
  negative, 224
  positive, 28, 219
Expression(s)
  algebraic, 238
  definition of, 9
  variable, 10
Extremes, 151

F

Face, 381
Factor(s)
  common, 30
  definition of, 11
  greatest common, 30
  prime factorization, 24
Factor pair, 11
Factor tree, 24
Favorable outcome, 341
Fluid ounce, 101
Foot, 101
Fraction(s)
  definition of, 40
  denominator, 40
  equivalent, 54
  improper, 82
  like, 75
  numerator, 40
  reciprocal, 91, 93
  unlike, 75
Frequency table, 358
Function(s)
  definition of, 419
  domain, 422
  linear, 423
  range, 422
  relations and, 419
Function notation, 422

G

Gallon, 101
Geometry
  cone, 383
  cube, 385
  cylinder, 382
  polyhedron, 382
  prism, 381
  pyramid, 382
  Pythagorean theorem, 325
  solid, 382
  sphere, 383, 401
Gram, 134

Graph(s),
  circle, 372
  definition of, 256
  histogram, 357
  scatter plot, 450
Greater than, 66
Greatest common factor, 30

H

Height, 381
Hemisphere, 403
Histogram, 357
Hypotenuse, 325

I

Identity property of
  multiplication, 22, 89, 477
Image, 505
Improper fractions
  definition of, 82
  mixed numbers and, 82, 91
Inch, 101
Independent event, 346
Independent variable, 421
Indirect measurement, 291
Input, 419
Input-output table, 420
Integer
  addition, 206
  definition of, 199, 463
  division, 213
  multiplication, 211
  negative, 199
  positive, 199
  subtraction, 210
Integer addition, 206
Integer subtraction, 210
Intercept(s)
  x-intercept, 438
  y-intercept, 438
Inverse
  additive, 217, 478
  multiplicative, 91, 478
Inverse operations, 248
Irrational number, 474
Irregular polygon, 286
Isosceles triangle, 280

L

Least common denominator,
  66, 78
Least common multiple, 17
Leg, 325
Length, 101
Less than, 66

Like fractions, 75
Line of best fit, 450
Line of reflection, 509
Linear equation, 444
Linear function, 423
Liter, 134
Loss, 201
Lower quartile, 367

M

Markup, 182
Mean, 351
Means, 151
Measurement
  capacity, 101
  customary system, 85
  indirect, 291
  metric system, 85, 133, 134
  perimeter, 305
  pi, 312
  weight, 101
Median, 352
Meter, 134
Metric system
  definition of, 85, 133, 134
  gram, 134
  liter, 134
  meter, 134
Mile, 101
Mixed number
  definition of, 82, 91
  improper fractions and, 82
Mode, 352
Multiple, 14
Multiple representations, 261
Multiple transformation, 515
Multiplication
  product
    of decimals, 127
    of integers, 211
  properties
    associative, 25
    commutative, 12
  identity, 22, 91
  inverse, 91, 478
Multiplicative identity, 22, 91, 478
Multiplicative inverse, 91, 478

N

Natural number, 462
Negative exponent, 224
Negative integer, 199
Net, 405
Notation(s)
  bar, 472
  function, 422
  scientific, 223

Index

Number(s)
composite, 21
integer, 199, 463
irrational, 474
natural, 462
prime, 21
rational, 465
real, 475
whole, 462
Number line
adding integers on, 206
definition of, 199
subtracting integers
on, 210
Numerator, 40

O

Obtuse angle, 274
Obtuse triangle, 280
One-step equation, 243
Operations
order of, 9
Opposites, 217
Order of operations, 9, 238
Ordered pair
definition of, 253, 491
input, 419
output, 419
x-coordinate, 253, 491
y-coordinate, 253, 491
Origin, 252
Ounce, 101
Outcome, 341
Output, 419

P

Parallelogram, 283
Percent
benchmark, 174
commission, 177
decrease, 189
definition of, 169
discount, 182
increase, 189
markup, 182
simple interest, 186
Percent decrease, 189
Percent increase, 189
Perfect square, 321
Perimeter, 305
Pi, 312
Pint, 101
Place-value chart, 116
Polygon
congruent, 295
definition of, 285

diagonal, 285
irregular, 286
regular, 286
similar, 287
Polyhedron, 382
Positive integer, 199
Pound, 101
Power(s)
base, 28
definition of, 28, 219, 467
expanded form, 219
exponent, 28, 219
negative, 224
power of ten, 219
scientific notation, 223
Power of ten, 219
Pre-image, 505
Prime factorization, 24
Prime number, 21
Principal, 186
Prism
base, 381
cube, 385
definition of, 381
edge, 381
face, 381
height, 381
vertex, 381
Probability
of an event, 341
event, 341
complementary, 344
compound, 345
dependent, 346
independent, 346
experimental, 343
outcome, 341
favorable outcome, 341
random, 342
sample space, 342
theoretical, 343
Product, 127, 211
Profit, 201
Properties
Associative Property of
Addition, 478
Associative Property of
Multiplication, 25, 478
Commutative Property of
Addition, 478
Commutative Property of
Multiplication, 12, 478
distributive, 481
Distributive Property, 481, 482
Reflexive Property of Equality, 478
Symmetric Property of
Equality, 479
Transitive Property of
Equality, 479

Proportion
definition of, 150, 499
extremes, 151
means, 151
Protractor, 274
Pyramid, 382
Pythagorean Theorem
converse of, 329
definition of, 325
Pythagorean triple, 332

Q

Quadrant, 492
Quadrilateral
definition of, 283
parallelogram, 283
rectangle, 283
rhombus, 283
square, 283
trapezoid, 283
Quart, 101
Quotient, 131, 213

R

Radical sign, 321
Radicand, 321
Radius, 311
Random, 342
Range, 352, 422
Rate
definition of, 150
unit, 156
Rate of change, 430
Ratio, 145
Rational number, 465
Real number, 475
Reasonable solution, 48
Reciprocal, 91, 99
Rectangle, 283
Reflection
definition of, 509
line of, 509
Reflexive Property of Equality, 479
Regular polygon, 286
Relation, 419
Remainder, 89
Repeating decimal, 472
Rhombus, 283
Right angle, 273
Right triangle, 280
Rise, slope and, 427
Rotation
angle of, 506
center of, 506
definition of, 506

Index

Round a decimal, 122
Run, slope and, 427

S

Sample space, 342
Scale, 499
Scale drawing, 497
Scale factor, 288, 409, 513
Scale model, 501
Scalene triangle, 280
Scatter plot, 450
Scientific notation, 223
Sides
  congruent, 280
  corresponding, 288
Similar polygons, 287
Similar solids, 409
Simple interest, 186
Simplest form, 58
Simplest terms, 58
Slope
  definition of, 427
  rate of change, 430
Slope-intercept form, 445
Solid(s)
  cone, 383
  cube, 385
  cylinder, 382
  definition of, 382
  polyhedron, 382
  prism, 381
  pyramid, 382
  similar, 409
  sphere, 383, 401
Solve, 243
Sphere, 383, 401
Square
  definition of, 283
  number, 321
    perfect square, 321
Square root
  definition of, 321
  radical sign, 321
  radicand, 321
Standard form, 116
Statistics
  mean, 351
  median, 352
  mode, 352

quartile
  lower, 367
  upper, 367
range, 352
Stem-and-leaf plot, 363
Straight angle, 273
Supplementary angles, 275
Surface area
  definition of, 387
  of a cylinder, 393
  of a prism, 387
  of a sphere, 404
Symmetric Property of Equality, 479

T

Table
  definition of, 256
  frequency, 358
  input-output, 420
  of values, 256
Terminating decimal, 472
Theoretical probability, 343
Ton, 101
Transformation(s)
  definition of, 503
  dilation, 513
  image, 505
  multiple, 515
  pre-image, 505
  reflection, 509
  rotation, 506
  translation, 503
Transitive Property of Equality, 479
Translation, 503
Transversal, 275
Trapezoid, 283
Triangle(s)
  acute, 280
  definition of, 279
  equilateral, 280
  isosceles, 280
  obtuse, 280
  right, 280
    hypotenuse, 325
    leg, 325
  scalene, 280
Two-step equation, 245

U

Unit rate, 156
Unlike fractions, 75
Upper quartile, 367

V

Variable
  definition of, 10, 160, 231
  dependent, 421
  independent, 421
Variable expression, 10
Venn diagram, 475
Vertex
  angle, 273
  prism, 381
Vertical angles, 277
Volume, 23
  of a cone, 398
  of a cylinder, 391
  definition of, 386
  of a prism, 386
  of a pyramid, 397
  of a sphere, 402

W

Weight, 101
Whole number, 462

X

x-axis, 252
x-coordinate, 253, 491
x-intercept, 438

Y

Yard, 101
y-axis, 252
y-coordinate, 253, 491
y-intercept, 438